THE WAR COUNCIL

Andrew Preston

The War Council

McGeorge Bundy, the NSC,
and Vietnam

HARVARD UNIVERSITY PRESS

Cambridge, Massachusetts, and London, England

First Harvard University Press paperback edition, 2010

Library of Congress Cataloging-in-Publication Data

Preston, Andrew 1973–
  The war council : McGeorge Bundy, the NSC, and Vietnam / Andrew Preston.
    p. cm
  Includes bibliographical references and index.
  ISBN 978-0-674-02198-3 (cloth : alk. paper)
  ISBN 978-0-674-04632-0 (pbk.)
  1. Vietnamese Conflict, 1961–1975—United States. 2. Bundy, McGeorge. 3. United
States—Politics and government—1961–1963. 4. United States—Politics and government—
1963–1969. 5. National Security Council (U.S.) I. Title.

DS558.P745 2006
959.704'3373—dc22   2005056389

To Fran, for everything

Contents

Acknowledgments

I have accumulated numerous debts in the course of writing this book; it is my pleasure to be able to acknowledge them properly.

First and foremost, at the University of Cambridge John Thompson carefully read numerous drafts of the manuscript. His continuing advice and constructive criticism have been invaluable, and it is no exaggeration to say that I would not have been able to write this book without him. I also benefited tremendously from Tony Badger's support, and I am immensely grateful for all of his efforts, intellectual and otherwise, on my behalf. David Reynolds invited me to participate in his Christ's College international history seminar and in the process provided the imaginative spark for the third chapter. Jonathan Haslam and Brendan Simms very kindly hired me to teach part of the Cold War seminar at the Centre of International Studies, an experience from which I benefited enormously. I would also like to acknowledge the friendship and support of Simon Hall, Nathaniel Millet, David Milne, Matthew Mayer, Andrew Webster, Meghan Nealis, Adam Smith, and especially Dominic Sandbrook.

The people at Yale University's International Security Studies, where I spent two years as a John M. Olin Postdoctoral Fellow, were personally and professionally supportive: in addition to Professors Paul Kennedy and John Gaddis, I would like to single out Ted Bromund, Ann Carter-Drier, Charles Hill, Minh Luong, and Monica Ward for all their help. I was immensely fortunate to share an ISS office with Jeffrey A. Engel—traveling companion, sounding board, constructive critic, and friend.

Many people have helped in specific ways. Tony Badger, John Gaddis, Lloyd Gardner, Gary Hess, Fred Logevall, and Odd Arne Westad read the entire manuscript and provided encouragement and unsparing but always helpful criticism. Jeff Engel, Paul Kennedy, Mark Lawrence, Lorenz Lüthi, David Milne, Lien-Hang Nguyen, Dom Sandbrook, Mark Sheetz, Jeremi Suri, and Marilyn Young read various chapters and made invaluable suggestions. Fred Logevall deserves additional mention for all his advice at various stages. It is fitting indeed that the title of the book was his idea. Jon Persoff's hospitality, boundless enthusiasm, and willingness to share information and documents have always been much appreciated. Kai Bird, Bundy's biographer, very unselfishly allowed me to copy as many documents from his private collection as I could manage and gave me some quiet space in his study. I would also like to acknowledge the informal but vital contributions of Bob Bothwell, Kate Carté Engel, Ilya Gaiduk, Jussi Hanhimäki, Matthew Jones, Scott Kleeb, Anne Nguyen, Gagan Sood, Ray Takeyh, and Ted Wooley. Ceara Donnelley and John Gow were excellent research assistants. My thanks to colleagues at the University of Victoria are simply too numerous to list individually. For providing me with company and accommodation during long research trips, I would like to thank Sarah Cashore, Chris and Laurie Garrison, Matt and Isabelle Garrison, Michael Guest, C. K. Lee, Nicola Mansworth, Yvonne Murray, Ed and Su Patrick, Dickon Reid, Marc Shewchun, and the late Sue Garrison, whose curiosity, kindness, generosity, and intelligence will be sorely missed. In addition, I am lucky to have had Kathleen McDermott, whose advice and faith in the project were critical, as my editor at Harvard. Finally, I am also grateful to Sharon Grant, who copyedited the manuscript with rare insight and improved the quality of my writing.

An earlier version of Chapter 2 was published in the December 2001 issue of *Presidential Studies Quarterly,* published by Blackwell Publishing, Ltd. An earlier version of Chapter 5 was published in the March 2003 issue of *The International History Review.* I am grateful for permission to reprint portions of these articles in revised form.

I would like to thank the following for financial and fellowship assistance: International Security Studies, Yale; the Fox International Fellowship, Yale; Sidney Sussex College, Cambridge; the Sara Norton Fund and Parry-Dutton Scholarship, Cambridge University; the Cambridge Commonwealth Fellowship; the George C. Marshall Foundation; and the Lyndon Baines Johnson Foundation.

My deepest gratitude goes to my family. Peter and Teresa Patrick have been more supportive than a son-in-law has any right to expect. I have enjoyed the most stimulating and challenging debates over U.S. foreign policy, along with every other topic imaginable, with my brother, Kevin. Words cannot express how much I appreciate my parents, Mary and Harry, and everything they have done for me. My daughters, Rosie and Lizzie, have been welcome distractions from their Daddy's obsession with a stranger named Mac Bundy. And last but certainly not least, my wife, Fran, has stoically persevered while her husband brought Bundy into the family and moved us all to a different city and university every year or two. She has never flagged in her belief in me and for that I am overwhelmingly grateful. For me, nothing could exist without her love and support.

I know you all, and will awhile uphold
The unyok'd humour of your idleness:
Yet herein will I imitate the sun,
Who doth permit the base contagious clouds
To smother up his beauty from the world,
That, when he please again to be himself,
Being wanted he may be more wonder'd at,
By breaking through the foul and ugly mists
Of vapours that did seem to strangle him.

Prince Henry, *Henry IV, Part 1*, act 1, scene 2

Now, lords, if God doth give successful end
To this debate that bleedeth at our doors,
We will our youth lead on to higher fields
And draw no swords but what are sanctified.
Our navy is address'd, our power collected,
Our substitutes in absence well invested,
And everything lies level to our wish:
Only, we want a little personal strength;
And pause us, till these rebels, now afoot,
Come underneath the yoke of government.

King Henry, *Henry IV, Part 2*, act 4, scene 4

Introduction

While he was dean of Harvard College from 1953 to 1960, McGeorge Bundy taught two courses on the theory and practice of American foreign relations. Bundy, who was renowned for his intellect even at Harvard and who had been the intimate of secretaries of war and state, admirals, and generals from boyhood, was able to teach from both learning and experience. America's role in the world, and the dilemma of how the United States should wield its awesome power, represented his life's work, and it remained the target of his ambition. Government 185, his survey lecture class on U.S. foreign policy, was consistently one of the more popular courses at Harvard. He also taught a more specialized undergraduate seminar on the subject. "You can't possibly understand American foreign policy," he once remarked to this smaller group, "without having read *Henry IV*."[1]

It is an intriguing comment. Could Bundy have been referring to the progress of Prince Henry, otherwise known as Hal, Henry IV's son and heir to the throne? Shakespeare's play (written in two parts) is as much a tale of a prodigal son beginning to realize his potential and fulfill his duty to his father and country as it is about the reign of King Henry IV. Hal, of course, eventually became Henry V, whose victory over the French at Agincourt earned him his reputation as one of England's most glorious rulers. Perhaps Bundy, who feared the isolationist and unilateralist tendencies in U.S. foreign policy above all else, was thus comparing the rebellious Hotspur, Northumberland, and Bardolph to the stubborn anti-imperialists and isolationists who had stood between America and its rightful role as world leader. Bundy may also have been comparing the complacent and self-satisfied indolence of Falstaff, who had deflected Hal from his duties, with the lethargy of U.S. foreign policy in the interwar period. A progressive conservative who valued gradual

1

change as a means to achieve and ensure international stability (much like his mentor Henry L. Stimson), Bundy may also have been thinking of Shakespeare's twin messages that chaos threatens everything and that nothing can be secure without order. Or perhaps it was simply the central theme of attaining national greatness through foreign affairs—which Henry IV suggests and Hal, as Henry V, later achieves—that most strongly resonated with Bundy. Whichever interpretation it was, the consolidation of Henry IV's power and the dramatic rise of Henry V's is, in this sense, a symbolically powerful tale. For Bundy—whose formative experiences as a young man coincided with the emergence of "the American Century" and were shaped by the grand struggles at home and abroad against isolationism, fascism, and communism— *Henry IV* would have provided a powerful allegory indeed.

Bundy's enigmatic praise of *Henry IV* is fitting. Even after decades of study of the Vietnam War, Bundy and his role remain poorly understood. Was he the warmongering action-oriented intellectual who, while an undergraduate, called himself "Odin" after the Norse god of wisdom, poetry, war, and the dead?[2] Was he the architect of war whom Gore Vidal later dubbed "McGenghis" Bundy?[3] Or was he the closet dove who faithfully served Presidents John F. Kennedy and Lyndon B. Johnson even when he disagreed with their aggressive, militaristic policies? Neither of these portrayals is particularly accurate; Bundy's role in the escalation of the Vietnam War was not so straightforward. The truth, as always, lies somewhere in between.

As National Security Adviser to Kennedy and Johnson from January 1961 to February 1966, Bundy played a significant part in shaping America's policy toward Vietnam. He seemed to represent the inherent irony of those whom David Halberstam has called "the best and brightest": just as Bundy embodied the Kennedy and Johnson administrations' intelligence, drive, and sophistication, he also epitomized their hubris, blind ambition, and overconfidence. How could Bundy, with his tremendous talent, energy, and ability, have made such a colossal error by helping to steer America toward war in Vietnam? This is, intrinsically, a general question that is not necessarily unique to Bundy. Indeed, explaining the origins of the American war in Vietnam has perplexed historians for decades, whether they have examined the question in the context of a single individual, a presidential administration or two, or an entire nation. Nonetheless, more than almost any other person, Bundy and his role lie at the heart of this question. It seems, then, that using Bundy to answer this central, elusive question will also yield more general conclusions about American policy toward Vietnam.

And yet much of the secondary literature has given Bundy a rather constricted role. Although most accounts feature him prominently, very few portray his contribution as decisive.[4] Robert S. McNamara, Dean Rusk, Maxwell D. Taylor, and even George Ball have all been subject to more intensive historical scrutiny than the relatively neglected Bundy. Instead, Bundy's part is usually limited to that of a convenient and largely superficial narrative device: in much of the scholarship, he surfaces at key points in the story to write a vital memo or impart critical advice, only to disappear and reemerge, ten pages or so later, when a crux in the narrative requires him to circulate yet another extremely important document. As a screenwriter would put it, his character has not been fully developed. Bundy, in other words, has been portrayed neither as a person in his own right nor as a powerful official with great control over the pace of American decision making. In fact he was both, and without his participation the Vietnam War would not have unfolded as it did. Aside from Presidents Kennedy and Johnson, only Secretary of Defense McNamara had as much influence over America's decision to go to war in Vietnam. Both as an individual and as a policymaker, the figure of McGeorge Bundy lies at the center of this story.

If Bundy's importance has been somewhat marginalized, the part played by his staff on the National Security Council (NSC) has been almost completely ignored. Among them, only Walt W. Rostow, Bundy's deputy in 1961, has received even scant attention from historians. Others on the NSC staff, such as Michael V. Forrestal, Carl Kaysen, Robert H. Johnson, Robert W. Komer, Chester L. Cooper, and James C. Thomson, Jr., have rarely been the subject of intensive academic study. Without their efforts, Bundy's would have been far less influential. The NSC staff even produced several important Vietnam policymakers in their own right, including Rostow, Forrestal, and Cooper.

Probing the origins of the Vietnam War through an intensive study of the 1960s raises the question of whether these beginnings were not the consequence of earlier events. Given the long period of initial U.S. involvement in Indochina—roughly from the closing stages of World War II to the inauguration of John F. Kennedy, with each year deepening the ties between Washington and Saigon—and given the communists' relentless drive to reunify all of Vietnam under their rule, to what extent were other options realistically available to policymakers in the Kennedy and Johnson administrations? In other words, did the Cold War make an American war in Vietnam inevitable? These may be seen as examples of a more general question. Historians have long differed over whether events are best explained by long-term "structural"

factors or by more "contingent" ones, particularly the role of individual decisions and actions. Like many historians before me, I can hardly do better than
approvingly quote Karl Marx's famous dictum that people "make their own
history, but they do not make it just as they please; they do not make it under
circumstances chosen by themselves, but under circumstances directly found,
given and transmitted from the past."[5] It is the historian's task to determine in
which instances structure trumps contingency or vice versa, or to explain how
the relationship between the two caused a particular historical outcome.

As this book seeks to illustrate, it was a blend of structural pressures and,
more important, human choices that eventually led, in the mid-1960s, to a
major American war in Vietnam. The structure, in this case, would be found
in the Cold War context of the 1960s and the bipolar (United States vs. USSR)
international system of the time. In one sense, structural pressures were predominant. By the time McGeorge Bundy and the members of the NSC staff
first grappled with the Vietnam problem, the United States had already deeply
involved itself in the politics of decolonization in Indochina, investing
resources and prestige to prevent it from being dominated by communist
movements, particularly the Viet Minh. Successive governments in Washington, with broad support from the press and the electorate, had since 1946 conducted a vigorous, global, anticommunist foreign policy. Given the existing
American presence in Vietnam, this Cold War consensus, underpinned by a
cohesive ideology and an expansive conception of national security, made it
difficult to avoid direct military intervention as the situation in Vietnam
worsened.

Bundy and the members of the NSC staff very much shared these deeply
held ideological preconceptions. Rarely, if ever, did they even reflect upon
their inherited worldview, let alone question or scrutinize it. Indeed, by the
1960s, American politicians, diplomats, and bureaucrats prosecuted an anticommunist campaign in Southeast Asia largely because they could conceive
of no other alternative. Thus the struggle to prevent the collapse of noncommunist South Vietnam was accepted reflexively as integral to U.S. national
security. As Frank Ninkovich points out, "human understanding is perme-
ated by irrational and particularistic preconceptions that, because of their pre-
reflective role in shaping perceptions and values, enjoy privileged or axiomatic
status."[6] This dynamic is also found to be at work in other major episodes in
international history. In a different but analogous context, James Joll has identified the influence of deeply held preconceptions as the phenomenon of
"unspoken assumptions," which, using his example, led inexorably to the

outbreak of war in August 1914.[7] Similarly, in explaining why the United States intervened in the Korean War despite consistent public declarations and private inclinations to the contrary, Ernest R. May has argued that the members of the Truman administration believed, axiomatically, that the advance of communism on the Korean peninsula represented a grave threat to U.S. national security. There was little discussion of why the United States should respond to the North Korean attack, or of whether it would be wise to do so. They simply believed, and acted promptly on this belief.[8] Following this pattern, American officials in the Kennedy administration gave little thought to whether the commitment to the defense of noncommunist South Vietnam was wise or even necessary. They simply believed that it was and set about making the commitment successful.

The foundations of this policy were not new. The Vietnam policymakers on the NSC staff had inherited from their predecessors a functional, relatively successful, and ideologically cohesive foreign policy. Many members of the Kennedy administration had been, to use Dean Acheson's famous phrase, "present at the creation" of the American-dominated postwar world. They were drawn from, and representative of, a cohesive elite, often called "the Establishment," that guided America's foreign relations after World War II. The historian Alan Brinkley notes that "social cohesion . . . lay at the heart of the idea of the establishment"; this social cohesion among the nation's key foreign policymakers, in turn, fostered an "ideological affinity." It also fostered ideological rigidity. The result, Brinkley argues, was a firm belief "that there was a seamless connection between American national interests and the interests of the world."[9] The Vietnam debacle, which was a direct product of this elite's stewardship of foreign policy, proved to be both the Establishment's zenith (in terms of influence) and its nadir (in terms of performance). But unlike Acheson, Bundy and the NSC staff had mostly been spectators rather than participants, and had learned the lessons of the early Cold War all too easily and thus superficially. By the 1960s, moreover, they had become policy experts over regions in which they had no genuine expertise. In confronting Vietnamese communism, they applied their European Cold War lessons axiomatically, only to produce disastrous results. All this created an environment that made intervention in Vietnam a logical outcome of U.S. foreign policy.

But did it make war inevitable? Although the structural pressures outlined above appear in retrospect to have been dominant, they were hardly overwhelming. As recent scholarship has demonstrated, the Cold War consensus was not so consensual once it was forced to consider what the American response should be toward the deteriorating situation in Vietnam.[10] To America's closest allies, such as Britain, France, and Canada, a war in Vietnam seemed to be as unwise as it was unnecessary. Key insiders who stood officially outside Washington's governing circle but nonetheless enjoyed a considerable measure of influence or prestige, such as the columnist Walter Lippmann or the renowned diplomat George F. Kennan, also objected. Support for intervention among members of Congress was anything but unanimous, especially in the Senate. Even within the Kennedy and Johnson administrations, highly placed officials, particularly in the State Department, dissented from a full-scale commitment of U.S. political prestige and military resources to South Vietnam. In an atmosphere charged with such intense opposition, interventionist figures such as Bundy had to cajole, convince, prod, outmaneuver, and occasionally threaten their opponents. To an extent that remains relatively unrecognized, the escalation of the war was dependent upon the actions of a few of the president's most influential advisers. It is therefore essential to understand what motivated these individual decision makers, such as McGeorge Bundy.

Basic human choices always determine the contours of history, and individual decisions are those that ultimately determine how events unfold. This dynamic, of course, was not unique to the outbreak of war in Vietnam. As Janice Knight has shown, but for a few key human decisions, the success of John Winthrop's vision for Puritan Massachusetts—the vision that would shape the development of American society, politics, and culture for centuries afterward—was in serious danger of losing out to a rival, and quite different, Puritan vision.[11] Political stability and success in America's first decades as a nation, James Roger Sharp argues, were largely contingent upon the outcome of personal rivalries, conflicts, and alliances among the young Republic's leaders.[12] "Armies, navies, railways, economies, ideologies, history," Margaret MacMillan observes, are all vital to our understanding of the end of World War I and the 1919 Paris Peace Conference. "But so too are individuals because, in the end, people draw up reports, make decisions and order armies to move."[13] And in the field of Vietnam War studies, Fredrik Logevall has exploded the myth that an American war in Vietnam was inevitable, or "overdetermined," due to the prevailing political climate and pressures of the Cold War.[14] As we shall see, at key moments between the spring of 1961 and the summer of 1965, Bundy and the NSC staff moved quickly and effectively to squash dissent and limit the presidents' choice of action to a very narrow one of how and when, rather than whether, the United States should wage war in Vietnam. The war itself, then, was largely contingent upon their actions.

But what makes Bundy and the NSC staff themselves so essential to the history of American decision making on Vietnam? Their importance stems primarily from the institutional changes Bundy initiated and the effect they had on the balance of foreign policymaking in the Kennedy and Johnson administrations. Bundy completely transformed the duties and prerogatives of the Special Assistant for National Security Affairs, elevating it to a status virtually, if unofficially, equivalent to that of a cabinet secretary. Although this key development has not gone unnoticed by scholars of the period, the change and its impact upon America's Vietnam policy have yet to be explored in any great detail. Along with the institutions of the Joint Chiefs of Staff, the Office of the Secretary of Defense, and the Central Intelligence Agency, the National Security Council was established in the 1947 National Security Act. Between 1947 and 1961, the NSC was an advisory body comprising the president and certain members of the cabinet, with occasional outside participation. As the secretary of the NSC, the Special Assistant was almost exclusively an administrative position under Truman and Eisenhower. At no time in these years did the Special Assistant actually contribute substantively to the decision-making process. Both Truman and Eisenhower saw their Special Assistant as a facilitator, rather than a formulator, of foreign policy.

Bundy, with considerable assistance from Rostow, significantly changed this arrangement. In its place, they re-created the NSC staff as a small, cohesive group of area and policy experts who would analyze, devise, and propose policy options of their own. Sometimes they would do so through Bundy, but several NSC staffers had direct access to the president and would often discuss their views and proposals directly with Kennedy. Bundy, in other words, had created a "Little State Department."[15] Kennedy convened meetings of the full NSC much less frequently than Truman or Eisenhower and did not use it much as a decision-making body. Instead, Kennedy informalized the policy process, relying more on personal interaction and crisis management techniques and less on the traditional bureaucratic structure. This meant that the Special Assistant and the NSC staff—which numbered about half a dozen experts, was located inside the White House, and managed the Situation Room—could outmaneuver the large, more unwieldy State Department. Bundy and his subordinates were aided by the fact that Rusk largely abdicated his authority as secretary of state during the Kennedy years. Moreover, as

Special Assistant, Bundy controlled the flow of information to and from the president. Bundy, then, was the first powerful, autonomous "National Security Adviser," as the position has come more grandly to be known. As such, he was the progenitor of, among others, Henry Kissinger, Zbigniew Brzezinski, Brent Scowcroft, and Condoleezza Rice.

It would be difficult, if not impossible, to overstate the impact this concentration of power had on U.S. foreign policy. But for Vietnam in particular, this was an absolutely crucial transformation. Although Rusk was certainly a hawk, the State Department itself was a haven for doves. At various stages, Chester Bowles, George Ball, Averell Harriman, Adlai Stevenson, John Kenneth Galbraith, Paul Kattenburg, and Thomas Hughes all subscribed to the view that Indochina was not the place to draw the line against communism, that a political solution through negotiations was preferable, and that South Vietnam was neither a place nor an ally worthy of a war. Bundy and the NSC staff, on the other hand, believed very much the opposite. Although Southeast Asia did not receive much of Bundy's attention during the Kennedy presidency—he was concerned more with Cuba, Berlin, and nuclear strategy, and with how the crises in Indochina affected these issues—he believed firmly that containment should be applied in that region also. Those on the NSC staff who did immerse themselves in Vietnam policy—Rostow, Komer, and Forrestal—were even more emphatic in this belief. With their smaller numbers, physical and bureaucratic proximity to the president (their offices were in the White House basement), cogent, forceful reasoning, and, most important, support from the powerful Special Assistant, the NSC staff was able to outflank the dovish policy emanating from the State Department and steer decision making toward military escalation.

Deeper intervention was a legacy that the new president, Lyndon Johnson, inherited after Kennedy's assassination in November 1963. The escalatory trend was exacerbated under Johnson, partly due to the deteriorating situation on the ground in South Vietnam, but largely because Johnson tended to concentrate foreign policy deliberations at the highest levels. In response to both the growing crisis in South Vietnam and his own enlarged role within the administration, Bundy focused almost obsessively on Vietnam after the Diem coup in November 1963. As the hawks on the NSC staff departed and were replaced by the more cautious Cooper and Thomson, it is no small paradox that the NSC staff's influence with the president waned as Bundy's simultaneously increased. These, then, were the means by which Bundy, aided by the

NSC staff, was able to guide American policy in Vietnam along a path of escalation, direct military intervention, and eventually war.

Was Bundy therefore a warmonger, the "McGenghis" of Gore Vidal's satire? The record is complex. It is often said that biographers fall in love with their subjects. Although what follows is not exactly a biography, in the course of research and writing about Bundy I have come to develop a respect, admiration, and even fondness for him. Yet he did play a large part in initiating a course of action that resulted in the unnecessary deaths of thousands of Americans and millions of Vietnamese. And contrary to the "Cold War context" myth—that, as Ernest R. May puts it, given the ideologically overheated milieu of the early 1960s, "it seems probable that any collection of men or women would have decided as did members of the Kennedy and Johnson administrations"—he did so in the face of tremendous internal opposition, external pressures, and a continually failing strategy.[16] It has become common to describe the Vietnam War as a tragedy;[17] if by this one means that the war was miserable and violent, the term is fitting. But in one key sense it is quite inappropriate. Tragedy, whether ancient Greek or Shakespearean, has an element of inevitability to it. Be it the tale of Oedipus Rex, or the tragic flaws of Hamlet (indecision), Othello (pride), or Macbeth (ambition), tragic characters are never able to escape the fate that destiny or the gods have assigned them. Tragedy is unavoidable; the Vietnam War was not. Bundy was not a warmonger, but neither was he a tragic hero, unable to escape the curse of his tragic flaw. He should have known better, and often he did.

Of course, this book's concentrated focus on Bundy and the NSC staff should not be taken to imply that Presidents Kennedy and Johnson were simply pliant recipients of their advisers' recommendations or that they were passive foreign policy decision makers.[18] War in Vietnam could not have happened if either president had truly opposed it. Nonetheless, although much of the literature on the escalation of the war does pay attention to other major figures, including Bundy, it has dealt too narrowly with the president as the primary agent for policymaking. Constitutionally this may be so, but the record on the Vietnam War is not so clear. Although both Kennedy and Johnson were strong presidents, neither was particularly passionate about Vietnam, and neither of them was ever certain about the best course of action. They were not enthusiastic about waging a difficult war in pursuit of murky aims, but they also did not want to risk the domestic and international consequences that seemed likely to follow disengagement. At this point Bundy and the NSC staff enter the story, and it is the president's uncertainty that makes them so important. Unlike their chief executive, they were rarely unsure. Their strong advice, their skill in promoting it, their bureaucratic dexterity, and their professional intimacy with the president enabled them to skew the internal debate over Vietnam in their favor. This book, then, is both a bureaucratic history of the changes in presidential decision making and a diplomatic history of the origins of the Vietnam War. It is a story with two inseparable themes: the acquisition and consolidation of power, and how that power was then used.

CHAPTER 1

The Mentor:
Stimson's Influence
on Bundy

The Tet Offensive of January and February 1968 dealt the decisive blow to the American commitment to Vietnam. Despite the fact that it would take the United States another five years to withdraw completely, the decision to seek a negotiated settlement and eventually withdraw from Vietnam was made irrevocably, if not explicitly, during Tet. President Lyndon B. Johnson, his chief advisers, and the U.S. military had spent much of the previous year proclaiming slow progress, but the Tet Offensive belied this cautious optimism and proved that there would be no early solution to the problem of Vietnam. Johnson was unsure of what to do—some advisers favored withdrawal, some urged a continuation of the same strategy, while the military pleaded for more troops. In March he convened a meeting of the "Wise Men," a group of esteemed and experienced former officials who had served as foreign policy advisers to presidents at one time or another during the Cold War. The group included former cabinet secretaries, both Democratic and Republican, dating back to the presidency of Harry Truman. By 1967 this group also included McGeorge Bundy, who had been Special Assistant for National Security Affairs to John F. Kennedy and Johnson, and was thus one of the principal architects of the Vietnam War. Although the membership of the Wise Men often changed, their advice on Vietnam did not: on every occasion to date they had firmly supported the Johnson administration's decisions to preserve a noncommunist South Vietnam by escalating America's military role. Johnson's reason for calling the Wise Men together in the wake of Tet was simple. He was looking to them to provide confirmation of his policies. He was seeking reassurance.

What Johnson received instead was a rejection, an alarmed call to begin the process of disengagement. At the meeting, Bundy expressed the new prevailing opinion. "There is a very significant shift in our position," he stated bluntly. "When we last met [in late 1967] we saw reasons for hope. We hoped then there would be slow but steady progress. Last night and today the picture is not so hopeful particularly in the countryside . . . We can no longer do the job we set out to do in the time we have left and we must begin to take steps to disengage." Also present was Walt Rostow, Bundy's successor as Special Assistant. Still an optimist and unrepentant hawk, a dismayed Rostow now realized that the war in Vietnam, built on the Cold War strategy of containment and a thirty-year tradition of political bipartisanship in foreign policy, had lost its most vital support. "I thought to myself," he recalled of the meeting, "that what began in the spring of 1940 when Henry Stimson came to Washington ended tonight. The American Establishment is dead."[1]

Rostow's remarks could not have been more appropriate. Although Stimson had died nearly two decades before, he remained the very embodiment of America's eagerness to reform the international system, and therefore the world, according to its own ideals. Stimson was also the epitome of a willingness to use military force to achieve this goal. (Rostow's comment was true in another sense, one which he could not have foreseen in March 1968: the next president and Special Assistant, Richard Nixon and Henry Kissinger, discarded the progressive instincts of the Stimson tradition in favor of a more European style of foreign policy, *realpolitik*.) Both tendencies—the reformist impulse and the use of military power—were fixtures of postwar U.S. foreign policy, and both had provided the intellectual foundation on which American involvement in Vietnam had been built. Bundy, for whom Stimson had been not only a mentor but also an inspiration, was as much a part of this tradition as anybody.

The Stimsonian Legacy

Several works on the Vietnam War have noted the connection between Henry L. Stimson and McGeorge Bundy.[2] Bundy's policies have even been labeled "Stimsonian." Indeed, Stimson's impact on Bundy, among others, lasted long after the elder statesman's death in 1950. During the initial days of the Cuban missile crisis in October 1962, when the Kennedy administration was unsure of an appropriate course of action, former Secretary of Defense Robert A. Lovett spotted a framed photo of Stimson on Bundy's desk and said, "Mac, I think the best service we can perform for the President is to try to approach this as Colonel Stimson would."[3] But what do the connection and the label mean? Although such descriptions of Bundy as Stimsonian are to some degree accurate, they do not adequately explain the bond between Stimson and Bundy or just how directly the intellectual current in American foreign relations ran from the former to the latter.

McGeorge Bundy's father, Harvey Hollister Bundy, was the original conduit between Stimson and the younger Bundy. Stimson was a mentor to the father long before he played the role for the son. Harvey Bundy, a successful Boston lawyer and a prominent member of the East Coast Establishment, had been recruited into government service by Stimson when he was President Herbert Hoover's secretary of state. Bundy became the assistant secretary, serving from 1931 to the end of Hoover's term in 1933. Stimson soon became a role model for the assistant secretary, and the two formed a close bond. As one historian has noted, "Harvey's loyalty to Stimson [was] legendary."[4] Both men were staunch Republicans and returned to their respective private law practices after Hoover's defeat to Franklin D. Roosevelt. However, although neither Stimson nor Bundy could stomach the New Deal, both were strongly opposed to the isolationist foreign policy espoused by their fellow Republicans. The Japanese and German efforts to revise the post–World War I peace settlements by force greatly alarmed the Roosevelt administration, and by 1940 the Democratic President was reaching out to Republicans of Stimson's caliber and mindset to create a bipartisan cabinet. In June 1940, Stimson was named secretary of war; by April 1941, he had managed to convince Bundy to return to Washington, once again as assistant secretary. In his memoirs, Stimson recalled that Harvey Bundy became " 'my closest personal assistant.' A man of unusual tact and discretion, Bundy handled many of [the] troubling problems of administration and correspondence and served as [a] filter for all sorts of men and problems."[5] This was, interestingly enough, essentially McGeorge Bundy's job description as the president's Special Assistant in 1961, although the younger Bundy would also assume a principal role in actively shaping U.S. foreign policy. Most important, Harvey Bundy bequeathed to his son McGeorge the opportunity to learn from Henry Stimson.

Stimson's foreign policy was grounded in what George F. Kennan would later call "the legalistic-moralistic approach" to international relations. Kennan, a preeminent realist and the Truman administration's chief foreign policy theorist in the late 1940s, decried the legalistic-moralistic approach's "idealistic" or liberal view that American diplomacy should bring about positive, progressive change in the international system according to America's own values and interests. Kennan did not deplore the intent of the legalistic-moralistic policy; what he feared was the messianic impulse behind it, one which made widespread American political, cultural, economic, and military intervention in the affairs of other nations inevitable. Kennan and other realists feared that the United States lacked the resources to assume such a burden of perpetual global leadership. Stimson, had he lived to read Kennan's realist critique, would have disagreed strongly. For him moral and legal considerations, backed by military power, were the very fundamentals by which the United States should conduct its foreign relations. They were certainly the considerations by which Stimson himself guided his own conduct in making American foreign policy.[6]

A certain moralistic tone came to define Stimson and the Stimsonian approach to American foreign policy. Hoover wrote in his memoirs that "instinctively, Mr. Stimson's first love was the law; and his second, the military field. Mentally, he was a mixture of a soldier and an advocate."[7] Stimson's authorized biographer reached the same conclusion, using these traits to describe him: "Trust, truth, justice, virtue, the reign of law, the call of duty, the shining example, the active service."[8] Offsetting this moralism was a good deal of caution. In both foreign and domestic affairs, Stimson's era was one of revolutionary change and sudden bursts of growth. Above all, he feared the instability and loss of control caused by such rapid change. Following an intellectual trail already blazed by his own mentors, Theodore Roosevelt and Elihu Root, Stimson believed that a modest amount of progress was necessary to stave off instability.[9] He was, to use an oxymoron first coined by Canadian politicians, a "progressive conservative." And like Roosevelt and Root, Stimson had in him an imperialist streak, intensified by his higher sense of moralistic altruism. Finally, he was a qualitative exceptionalist—that is, he considered America not only different from other countries but also better—who believed that American values offered the best inspiration for international change and development.

If Stimson's moralism was expressed in his belief that American-inspired progress was the essential goal of international relations, his legalism was expressed in the conviction that the pursuit of such goals should be codified as international law in the form of treaties, agreements, and multinational organizations. Thus he was a devout internationalist who believed that the United States should lead not only by example but also by active, involved participation. After World War I Stimson was, along with Root, one of the few members of the Republican Party to support Woodrow Wilson's concept of a League of Nations, although both objected to the stringent conditions for mutual defense outlined in Article X of the League Covenant. Even after the

Senate voted to reject the League—which he thought was a grave error—Stimson lauded its "community spirit" in Europe, "which was steadily working against war."[10] Much later when he discussed an eventual postwar settlement with Winston Churchill at the height of World War II, Stimson argued that "it was wrong to say that the League had failed. It was rather the member States who had failed the League." What was important to Stimson was that a principle had been established and a precedent set by the existence of an international organization that sought stability through progress. Stimson was an emphatic supporter of the United Nations as a worthy successor to the League of Nations. He also enthusiastically endorsed the war crimes trials at Nuremberg and the relatively new legal precept of crimes against humanity. "Our anger, as righteous anger," he reminded the readers of *Foreign Affairs*, "must be subject to the law."[11]

As Hoover's secretary of state, Stimson pursued similar policies. The Kellogg-Briand Pact of 1928 (also known as the Pact of Paris) resolved to prohibit armed force as a tool for conflict resolution. The Pact's utopian aim was, simply put, to end war. Stimson was an ardent supporter, and the pact secured Senate ratification in 1929 during his tenure as Secretary. Stimson's response to the Manchurian Crisis of 1931–1933 was similarly legalistic. By its aggression in Manchuria, Japan violated a number of obligations established by the League of Nations Covenant, the principle and practice of the Open Door (formalized in the Nine-Power Treaty of 1922), and the Kellogg-Briand Pact, all of which Japan had signed. Stimson cited the same violations in an open letter to Senator William E. Borah, chairman of the Senate Foreign Relations Committee and a leading isolationist, to convince skeptics at home. "What was left," Stimson rhetorically asked the Japanese Ambassador to Washington, "on which we could rest for the stability of the world when treaty obligations began to be broken[?]"

In what came to be known as "the Stimson Doctrine," the secretary of state refused to recognize Japan's gains in Manchuria or its newly created client state of Manchukuo. Stimson at first wanted to work with the League, whose members quickly proved to be unwilling and ineffectual. Punitive economic sanctions against Japan were the next rung on Stimson's ladder of escalation, but Hoover, who was much more cautious, firmly decided against it. Hoover's refusal to use economic sanctions left the administration with only the Stimson Doctrine, but nonrecognition would not, as Stimson himself realized, compel the Japanese to withdraw. The Manchurian Crisis thus confirmed for Stimson the principle that no foreign policy, no matter how well intentioned or formulated, could succeed if not backed by the threat of effective military force.[12]

Along with a sense of moralistic purpose in foreign relations, Stimson also shared the imperial instincts of Roosevelt and Root. If other nations would not follow America's example on their own, Americans themselves would have to lead. Stimson's successful 1927 mission to impose a ceasefire agreement in Nicaragua, on behalf of President Calvin Coolidge and with the backing of the U.S. Marines, is a case in point. Against charges that America was behaving like a selfish bully, Stimson justified his mission by arguing that it "follows well-known principles of law and amity recognized among nations, and not only will not impair the independence of Nicaragua but will conduce toward placing it upon an assured foundation." Stimson's premise ultimately rested on an interpretation of the Monroe Doctrine that was a paternalistic variant of altruistic imperialism, sensitive to American, rather than Latin American, needs. It was "only proper that our Latin-American neighbors . . . should keep in mind our long and honorable fulfillment of this obligation [the Monroe Doctrine]. For a century we have been the scrupulous protector of their independence, not only against Europe but sometimes even against themselves."[13] As governor-general of the Philippines in 1928, Stimson adopted a similar policy. The United States, he believed, should prepare its colony for local democratic self-government rather than full independence. The imperial mission would last, Stimson promised, until the United States was satisfied that it had been accomplished.[14]

Most important, Stimson believed fervently that the use of force was always necessary to pursue and secure objectives when diplomacy could not. Indeed, the main purpose of military strength was to augment diplomacy. The pitiful state of America's armed forces in 1911 was obviously inadequate to serve this function, and so as President William Howard Taft's secretary of war, Stimson strove to heighten the level of preparedness and improve the quality and standards of the Army. In his memoirs, Stimson recorded that Roosevelt "took stands that Stimson considered wholly right: he was in favor of action against Germany [before 1917], placing righteousness ahead of peace." The most convincing argument Stimson carried with him to Nicaragua in 1927 was the threat to use the U.S. Marines to coerce an agreement, a tactic that had not been approved ahead of time by the State Department. During the Manchurian Crisis, Stimson could not even get Hoover to apply economic sanctions against Japan, so the use of force was out of the question. However, if that opton had been open to him, he surely would have used it. Years later, Harvey Bundy remembered their frustration with Hoover's timidity. Stimson,

Bundy said, was "prepared to go a long way" to confront the Japanese. He "believed in the exercise of power" and in "taking the bit by his teeth and going forward." Indeed, Stimson's staunch opposition to any form of conciliation or compromise with Japan helped to make war virtually inevitable, as did his unfailing support for Britain's efforts to hold out against Germany from 1939 to December 1941. Thus, he recalled that "the coming of war in 1939, not for the first or last time in [my] life, was a relief."[15]

The use of force was not an end in itself; rather, force was an integral means to establish an international system based on order through gradual progress. Stimson believed very much that the United States had the leading role to play in maintaining this system. As we have seen, he had been a firm supporter of U.S. membership in the League of Nations and saw its repudiation by his Republican colleagues as a mistake, "the greatest error made by the United States in the twentieth century," because it deprived the world of American guidance of its affairs. The United States, Stimson believed, had an obligation. Due to the inherent primacy of America's political, economic, and cultural values, the world needed America as much as America needed the world, and so the burden of leadership was the only way to maintain global peace and stability. By rejecting the league, the Senate "deprived the world's peace efforts of the cooperation of the United States, with the potential strength of its enlightened moral influence." Moreover, Stimson recognized that "members of the League were constantly under a feeling of apprehension lest the efforts which they made through the machinery of the League might meet with frustration by reason of some different policy on our part." Disheartened, Stimson saw the entrenchment into further isolationism in the 1930s as a refusal of the duty Americans owed the world. In a speech at Princeton University in 1934 he observed that, since the United States was the world's most powerful and enlightened nation, Americans "are the people . . . who can most easily and safely give sympathy, encouragement and help to the world in its vital struggle to protect our common civilization against war." Stimson returned to this message after World War II when he sensed that Americans might be tempted to repeat the mistakes of the interwar period by retreating from world affairs once again. In a 1947 article for the journal *Foreign Affairs* that was actually drafted by McGeorge Bundy, Stimson warned that Americans "face a challenging opportunity, perhaps the greatest ever offered to a single nation. It is nothing less than a chance to use our full strength for the peace and freedom of the world." The American people, therefore, "must now understand that the United States has become, for better or worse, a wholly committed member of the world community. This has not happened by conscious choice; but it is a plain fact, and our only choice is whether or not to face it."[16]

The antithesis to this view was of course isolationism, and for virtually all of Stimson's long career isolationists were his chief adversaries and the main target of his rhetorical fire. A retreat from the leading role on the world stage was not simply undesirable; it was dangerous, because it would lead directly to another world war. This view was the paramount lesson learned from the interwar period. America's refusal to ensure European political stability by joining the league in 1919, its refusal to face down Japan during the Manchurian Crisis and after 1937, and the appeasement of the European dictators all provided powerful evidence of the folly of isolationism. The "great lesson" of World War I, Stimson felt, "was that the United States could not remain aloof from world affairs and still keep the world 'safe for democracy'." In the mid-1930s, with one eye on Imperial Japan and the other on Nazi Germany, he warned: "Should we insist upon our government retiring into isolation and turning its back upon all efforts for peace in other portions of the world, we must face the fact that the peace machinery will be infinitely weakened and that mankind will be periodically faced with wars which may be as disastrous to us and our own civilization as to that of the rest of the world." Stimson strengthened this view as the decade wore on and the imminent threat from Japan and Germany became clearer. He served as honorary chairman of the American Committee for Non-Participation in Japanese Aggression, a group that pushed for a tougher American stance in the Far East, and he continued to argue vehemently against American neutrality legislation.[17]

The possible resurrection of isolationism after 1945 troubled Stimson greatly. He informed the readers of *Foreign Affairs* that he found it "not surprising . . . that some are tempted to seek refuge from their confusion either in retreat to isolationism or in suggested solutions whose simplicity is only matched by their folly. In the main, our difficulties arise from unwillingness to face reality." Taking aim squarely at prominent isolationists, Stimson continued in similarly unambiguous language that it "would be shriveling timidity for America to refuse to play to the full her present necessary part in the world. And the certain penalty for such timidity would be failure. The troubles of Europe and Asia are not 'other people's troubles;' they are ours . . . Foreign affairs are now our most intimate domestic concern. All men, good or bad, are now our neighbors. All ideas dwell among us." In 1949, Stimson again used Bundy to compose his thoughts when he wrote a letter to Senate Republicans urging them to ratify the North Atlantic Treaty. Stimson stated that if the Senate defeated the treaty, "we shall not soon be able to repair the damage."[18] For Stimson, only the circumstances surrounding the Cold War differed from those that had surrounded the interwar period; the principles remained the same.

Despite, or perhaps because of, these enduring principles, race and ideology were also tremendous but inadvertent influences on Stimson's thought. His sense of threat within the international system was exacerbated when confronted with a seemingly implacable enemy of a completely foreign race or ideology. His Eurocentric view and habit of racial stereotyping were, to be sure, products of their time; but even given this context, Stimson's views on foreign lands, people, cultures, and problems were unusually unimaginative and inflexible. When he felt it was required, he was not at all wary of using American military might, and at times his perception of the nature of the adversary could exaggerate the urgency of this requirement. The Manchurian crisis, for example, left him with the conclusion that it was "almost impossible . . . [that] two such different civilizations" as Japan and the United States could avoid war. As secretary of war in 1940, Stimson borrowed from Abraham Lincoln's famous Civil War "House Divided" speech, extended the metaphor from a divided nation to a divided world and from the Confederacy to Nazi Germany, and declared that humanity could not survive "half slave and half free." Stimson's response to the Soviets after World War II was identical: "I have often said that the surest way to make a man trustworthy is to trust him. But I must add that this does not always apply to a man who is determined to make you his dupe . . . Americans who think they can make common cause with present-day Communism are living in a world that does not exist." Undoubtedly, Stimson based his opinion on the growing tension between the United States and the Soviet Union, but he also saw it as an inevitable conflict between ideologically incompatible systems. "The Nazi leaders," he wrote elsewhere in reference to the Soviets, "are not the only ones who have renounced and denied the principles of western civilization." The inescapable conclusion of this outlook was that foreign ideologies—"civilizations" to Stimson—were bound to clash if the rival chose to challenge or compete with American leadership in the world.[19]

All of these beliefs expressed by Stimson left a deep imprint on the intellectual development of McGeorge Bundy. Born in Boston in 1919, Bundy came of age among a generation whose formative experiences were molded by the twin failures of isolationism and appeasement, and by participation in world

war. As an undergraduate at Yale University in the late 1930s, Bundy perceived this well before his contemporaries. As one of his classmates at Yale
recalled, Bundy "was carrying the war on his shoulders long before we were
in." His column in the *Yale Daily News* provides good evidence of his thinking.
After the British and French appeasement of Hitler at Munich in 1938, Bundy
sensed a growing disaffection with Germany. Some of his fellow students, he
wrote in October 1938, "wished the English and French and Russians would
smash Hitler now. I have said it myself. And while we who said it were
painfully surprised by our own belligerence, our sentiments were quite sober
and sincere." A preventive war "to smash Hitler seems in times of crisis to
be a desirable purgative . . . we are prepared to face the horror of battle and
bombs because we almost subconsciously envision a new era when the war
is done." As Bundy identified it, the problem was that preventive war was
anathema to democracies. "Barring a revolution, the government of a democracy will generally be in the hands of the cautious," and although democracies could issue ultimatums and threats, "nothing is more futile than a stick
languidly brandished at a foe standing complacently behind a *fait accompli.*"
Instead, Bundy felt that the nations aligning themselves against Nazi Germany
(and he saw the United States as one of them) should issue the threat and
mean it: "Least of all should we hesitate merely because we may make Hitler
angry."[20]

The eagerness to do battle and, most important, the refusal to distinguish
conceptually between what *should* be done and what *could* be done in foreign
policy, were geopolitical views Bundy had already inherited from Stimson.
Bundy's personal experience reinforced these views. While traveling in Germany in 1938, he met the mother of a Jewish friend from Yale; the diamonds
which he agreed to smuggle on her behalf back to New York eventually
funded her efforts to flee the country. This brief encounter with the terror
engendered by Nazi Germany bolstered his sense of moral outrage and provided ammunition for his attacks against isolationists. However, the majority of students at Yale, not unlike those at most other universities and colleges
in the United States, were not keen on American entry into the war. Esteemed
faculty members, such as historian Samuel Flagg Bemis, supported the isolationist cause, and the organization America First had a chapter at Yale with
Richard Bissell and Kingman Brewster as its spokesmen. It was their opinion
that prevailed on campus. It was this attitude that Bundy swore to reverse.[21]

He intensified his efforts as the situation in Europe deteriorated from crisis
to catastrophe. In an essay written just after the fall of France in June 1940,

Bundy called on his fellow young Americans to resist the German drive for hegemony. Although he invoked the long-term threat to American "national security," Bundy's call to arms was based primarily on moral and ideological grounds:

> I believe in the dignity of the individual, in government by law, in respect for the truth, and in a good God; these beliefs are worth my life, and more; they are not shared by Adolf Hitler, and he will not permit them to me unless he has to; I therefore believe that my efforts, and those of the countrymen with whom I share my beliefs, must be energetically given to their defense; I do not think Hitler a weak or negligible antagonist, and I believe that if we are to have our way and not his, we must act swiftly and vigorously; such a course involves sacrifice and evil, but to a smaller degree than the alternative of surrender.

"War is evil," he continued in words with which Stimson doubtless agreed. "This much is clearly true, and it is idiotic to think otherwise. What does not follow is the conclusion that war is at all costs to be avoided. For though war is evil, it is occasionally the lesser of two evils." Diplomacy and restraint had failed; now only war could settle the situation. "The aim of men like Hitler is to destroy men's freedom," and so Americans would have to fight in order to ensure the survival of "the ideals of America."[22] Moreover, Bundy did not hesitate to take action on his ideas. "We are going [traveling in South America] as Americans and as Hitler-haters," he wrote to poet and family friend Archibald MacLeish a few months later. "[W]e want to be as useful as possible in both categories."[23]

When the call to arms finally came after the Axis powers' declarations of war in December 1941, Bundy wasted no time living up to his own standards by joining the military. He wrote reports for a wartime bureau, the Office of Facts and Figures, after being rejected for combat duty because of poor eyesight. Determined to see active service and abetted by a sympathetic sergeant, he memorized the eye chart, passed the test, and was accepted into the Signal Corps. By 1943 the well-connected Bundy was an aide to Rear Admiral Alan G. Kirk, an appointment that Kirk himself arranged. The position afforded Bundy a role in the Allied invasions of Sicily and Normandy, although he did not see combat in either campaign. After victory in Europe he requested a transfer to the infantry, even if it required a demotion in rank, so that he could fight in the final stages of the war against Japan. The transfer was arranged personally by an extremely proud Secretary of War Stimson, who confided to his diary that he would "feel very keenly the responsibility if anything happens to such a promising boy." The Japanese surrendered before Bundy saw any action, but he remained in uniform until 1946 as a member of the occupation forces in Japan and Korea. Although World War II had a tremendous impact on the young Bundy, its lessons may have come too easily and too superficially. Bundy was never a front-line soldier, and he did not participate in any of the actual fighting. His duties were those of a well-placed assistant to members at the highest echelon of power; he was even privy to the Ultra secret, an advantage most Allied field commanders lacked. Although meritorious—he received a Bronze Star for his role in the Normandy invasion—Bundy's World War II service impressed upon him the uses and benefits of military power without imposing the harsh lessons of combat.[24]

Toward the end of the war, Bundy publicly advocated continued military vigilance. Even before the outbreak of war in Europe, he declared to the foes of rearmament: "It is folly to argue . . . that a big navy is an inducement to wars of aggression." Echoing Stimson's belief in military preparedness, Bundy declared that "force . . . is still the final arbiter among nations. It is time the anti-preparedness forces began to look realistically at this overwhelmingly evident fact and begin to come to grips with the military problem." He returned to the theme of military preparedness in 1945, writing of his belief "that universal military training after victory is an urgent national necessity . . . It is the focal point of any solid United States policy for post-war peace." The best way to preserve peace was the preparation for war, he believed. Retention of the draft, Bundy argued, would prevent future wars from happening: "Peaceful peoples like ourselves get into wars for *want* of a military and national policy, not for too much of it. We get into wars because we let situations govern us when we should be governing the situations."[25]

Prior to the war, Bundy had accepted a position at Harvard University's Society of Fellows as a junior fellow. Election to the prestigious society was (and remains) an achievement of outstanding academic distinction. But although he had attended Groton, an elite private school, and graduated with high marks from Yale—historian Arthur M. Schlesinger, Jr., recalled that Bundy arrived at Harvard "billed as the brightest man to graduate from Yale since Jonathan Edwards (class of 1720)"—family connections had as much to do with his selection to Harvard as scholarship. Bundy's great-uncle, A. Lawrence Lowell, founded the Society of Fellows in 1933 with funds from his own estate, and MacLeish assiduously promoted Bundy's candidacy. This occasion would not be the last when Bundy's connections, in addition to his record, would advance his career. With the war at an end, Bundy returned to Harvard to complete his fellowship studies. His project was unusual in that it was not his own: he became the editor and coauthor of Stimson's memoirs, *On Active Service in Peace and War*, published in 1948. Bundy also ghost-wrote shorter pieces for the elderly, ailing Stimson, including a magazine article for the February 1947 issue of *Harper's* magazine on the increasingly controversial decision to bomb Japan with nuclear weapons; the article in the October 1947 issue of *Foreign Affairs*, which called for America to embrace the role of world leadership; and the 1949 letter urging Senate Republicans to accept and ratify the North Atlantic Treaty.[26]

It is clear that Bundy already looked up to, and was influenced by, Henry Stimson. Their postwar collaboration firmly cemented the relationship. Stimson was, more than any other person, the figure to whom Bundy looked for inspiration and instruction. The feeling was reciprocal; the older man saw in the younger an able and willing protégé, one who possessed enormous talents and potential. Stimson praised him as being "remarkably mature" and "one of the most charming young men that I know." Others also noted the closeness between Stimson and the young Bundy. Allen Klots, who had been Stimson's close friend and legal colleague for nearly half a century, felt stumped when asked a question about the Stimson Doctrine. "Ordinarily I would turn to Mac Bundy for help, but I understand that he is on his way to Boston," Klots replied, and he could not think of anyone else competent enough to answer.[27]

It was Bundy, though, who most valued the relationship. As he confided to Supreme Court Justice Felix Frankfurter, when considering "the problems of policy in Nicaragua, the Philippines, the State Department, and War," Stimson "brought [a] relentless instinct for the real issue." In his collaborations with Stimson, he felt comfortable and confident enough to change drafts that Stimson had already approved. After informing Stimson of one such change, he wrote: "I think you will find it is your sort of thinking, even if it is not yet sufficiently your sort of writing. If the thinking is wrong, I have been badly trained in this last year."[28] More directly, Bundy articulated his feelings in a letter to Stimson:

Meanwhile I am settling into a beginning on work for my lectures in March [a series of lectures on foreign affairs Bundy gave in Boston]. So much of these lectures will be based on what I learned with you that I feel in a way that I am still working with you. You . . . must know that after

a year and a half of steady work and play and life together, I cannot
believe that the end of the book means anything but the end of an
episode in a connection which means more to me than any outside my
immediate family. Your patience and kindness and your wonderful
insight into men and events, coupled with your almost unique honesty in
assessing your own magnificent record, make a combination that so far as
I know no other student in the country is likely to find for a match in his
teacher.[29]

When confronting his own foreign policy crises, Bundy would always look
for guidance to Stimson's example.

From Assisting Stimson to Running Harvard

After completing *On Active Service* with Stimson, and with a number of articles
to his credit, Bundy had established a reputation as an articulate and incisive
writer. He was now in high demand. In late 1947 Bundy began and then
abandoned an effort to revise Walter Lippmann's landmark book, *The Good
Society*, which had been published a decade earlier. In a series of prestigious
odd jobs, Bundy turned his attention to the theory and practice of U.S. foreign policy. He served as an analyst and speechwriter for Republican candidate Thomas Dewey in the 1948 presidential election. For most of 1949, he
worked as a research fellow at the Council on Foreign Relations in New York.
Under the chairmanship of Dwight D. Eisenhower, then president of Columbia University, the group to which Bundy was attached analyzed the impact,
implications, and future of the Marshall Plan. Toward the end of the year he
accepted an offer to be a lecturer in the Government Department at Harvard;
in 1951 he was promoted to assistant professor. In 1950 he joined a New York
think tank, the Woodrow Wilson Foundation, to examine the interrelationship between America's domestic and foreign policies. He edited and added
commentary to a collection of Secretary of State Dean Acheson's speeches,
published in 1951 under the title *The Pattern of Responsibility*. A year later
Acheson named Bundy executive secretary of a State Department advisory
panel under the chairmanship of J. Robert Oppenheimer to study nuclear
disarmament and negotiations. This opportunity exposed Bundy to the intri-
cacies of nuclear strategy and the prospects for disarmament, and he drafted
the Oppenheimer Panel's final report.[30] This eclectic string of apprenticeships
finally culminated in his appointment, at the extremely young age of thirty-
four, as dean of the Faculty of Arts and Sciences at Harvard in 1953. Bundy,

whose reign at Harvard was enormously popular among faculty and students alike, served as dean until he agreed to join the Kennedy administration in December 1960. "It won't be easy to imagine Harvard without Mac," one senior professor remarked wistfully upon Bundy's departure.[31]

This period as a young academic and budding public intellectual provided Bundy invaluable experience in policymaking, but it also illuminated other, less auspicious trends. As with his election to Harvard's Society of Fellows, Bundy's career advanced very quickly without his having to produce much original work. In the Stimson, Lippmann, and Acheson book projects, and in drafting the Oppenheimer Panel's report, for example, he edited and synthesized views that were not his own. The majority of his articles, in such influential periodicals as *The Atlantic Monthly* and *The Reporter*, were book reviews in which he analyzed and responded to the views of others rather than producing opinions of his own.[32] Taken as a whole, the book collaborations, Oppenheimer Panel report, and book reviews are indicative of a pattern of unoriginal and acquired thinking. Bundy was enormously intelligent, but his intelligence was facile rather than imaginative. Throughout his life most people compared him to a computer. As his friend and newspaper columnist Joseph Kraft wrote, "one reason Bundy is so swift is that his mental apparatus is unclogged by general ideas." Kraft observed that Bundy preferred to "concentrate on process." A Harvard colleague less charitably characterized Bundy's brain as "more rapid than accurate." His eminent and powerful sponsors—Stimson, Acheson, MacLeish, Lippmann, and Frankfurter—usually provided him with more support than did his own accomplishments, which were surprisingly few by 1953. The ease with which he was awarded tenure at Harvard typified his early career. When it was decided in the Government Department that Bundy should be tenured, Harvard President James Bryant Conant, a renowned professor of chemistry, was puzzled when asked for his approval. Bundy, Conant discovered, had never taken a course in government at either the undergraduate or graduate level. "Are you sure that's right?" Conant asked the Department's representative. "I'm sure," was the reply. "Well," Conant sighed in acquiescence, "all I can say is that it couldn't have happened in Chemistry."[33]

The World According to Bundy

During this time Bundy's own opinions on foreign relations coalesced into a firmly held personal worldview, comprised of three primary, consistent themes, all of which were mutually dependent: the indispensability of military

power to diplomacy; the futility of appeasement; and a fervent, but sometimes pragmatic, anticommunist outlook. The target at which Bundy's worldview aimed was the same for him as it had been for Stimson—isolationism.
At the dawn of the Cold War, there emerged in America what Norman
Graebner called the "New Isolationism."[34] The New Isolationists, led by Stimson's nemesis, Republican Senator Robert A. Taft, believed mainly that American air power could enable the country to disengage from international
affairs and retreat into a "Fortress America" impregnable to foreign enemies.
Taft's arguments had lost some force and resonance by the mid-1950s, but
Bundy's hostility to isolationism was deep enough to guide his worldview
long after isolationists themselves had ceased to be powerful in American
politics. In the 1960s Bundy would hurl the epithet of isolationism at those
who disagreed with him over Vietnam. Thus even a friend and fellow internationalist like Walter Lippmann could earn Bundy's ire for opposing the Vietnam War with "isolationist attitudes."[35]

Bundy also targeted the realists of international relations theory. Led by
Kennan and Hans Morgenthau, a political scientist at the University of
Chicago, the realists were, like Bundy, internationalists and believers in the
application of military power. Unlike Bundy, their belief in foreign intervention was tempered by a cautious assessment of potential threats and American
capabilities to respond to those threats. If Bundy rejected the retrenchment
of the New Isolationists, he also rejected the balance of the realists, particularly
when it came to that vast part of the globe known as the Third World. He was,
like Stimson but to a lesser degree, a moralist who also deeply believed in the
capability of military power to act as a salve for America's foreign policy troubles. "God knows, Bundy was aware of power," recalled Harvard historian
Stanley Hoffman, a colleague of Bundy's. "But he talked about blending
power with idealism."[36] The three themes, plus the specter of isolationism
and the emergence of the realist school, would tremendously influence how
Bundy approached the problems of foreign policy while he was Special Assistant to Presidents Kennedy and Johnson.

The Importance of Military Power

First, and perhaps most significant, Bundy believed in the primacy of power.
"Very near the heart of all foreign affairs," he wrote in 1951, "is the relationship between policy and military power." For Bundy, "military power is not
something separate from foreign policy, nor even something that waits upon

and follows it; the two are one." The lesson of World War II was "to assure that right has might," so that the United States could never again be confronted militarily with such powerful foes. He viewed power as acutely important, not because of an American imperial disposition or as an end in itself, but because it was a means, sometimes unsavory but nonetheless necessary, to a just end. As Bundy wrote to Lippmann, the "concept of the balance of power [is] denounced rightly as a wrong ideal, but wrongly denounced because it is a necessary fact." He believed that the Soviets could not be trusted, as they had made perfectly clear since the end of World War II; they would seek their own security by whatever means necessary, regardless of what the rest of the world thought or did. Because of this, American leaders would have to embrace military power as an essential component of diplomacy.[37]

But Bundy's view could be pragmatic, even prudent. He did not foresee the necessity of preventive warfare to attain American objectives or maintain the fragile peace. The United States and its allies would have to exercise caution in the face of Soviet provocation; the best way to do this, Bundy reasoned, was by emphasizing political and economic methods in addition to those that were purely military. He argued in 1949 that the dominant objective of the North Atlantic Treaty "is rather to ensure that we do *not* have war with Russia . . . We are dealing not with a genuine *threat* of aggression, but with a prevalent *fear* of aggression, a very different thing." Thus the principal goal of American policy "is to put an end to the cold war without a hot war, and the basic position of the United States is so strong that we can afford a calm and unmenacing policy . . . The [North Atlantic] Pact . . . need not be a merely anti-Russian device." Nonetheless, this prudent approach did not obviate the basic requirements of security as the ultimate underpinning of American foreign policy: "We cannot omit necessary measures of true *defense* because they irritate the Russians." After all, Bundy reminded his colleagues at the Council on Foreign Relations, "today's villain is the Soviet Communist."[38]

Nor did Bundy rule out the prospect of tactical negotiations with the Soviet Union, even under Josef Stalin, whom he held personally responsible for the advent of the Cold War. In Bundy's view, negotiations could only be successful if they did not in any way compromise American interests. Instead, he hoped to gain concessions from the Soviets without relinquishing concessions by the United States. "I don't see why," Bundy once commented to Secretary of State Acheson, "we shouldn't negotiate with the Russkis, and perhaps outsmart 'em." But Bundy was not so determined or ideological to preclude the prospect of American-Soviet negotiations indefinitely. For one thing, the Cold

War world was far too unstable and some of its key issues—such as nuclear weapons—far too dangerous for the United States to be unremittingly hostile to the Soviet Union. After analyzing nuclear disarmament together, Bundy confided to Oppenheimer that "no real negotiation in this area would at present be fruitful or even desirable." However, he continued, "this may not always be the case, and it is important that no real opportunity be missed as a result of the behavior of the Government of the United States." Over time, his view of negotiations mellowed so that by 1969 he was admonishing the readers of *Foreign Affairs* that tough Soviet bargaining tactics provided "no reason for resentment; in another context similar behavior is praised as Yankee shrewdness."[39] Nonetheless, with the notable exception of treaties to limit nuclear weapons, during the 1960s Bundy took a dim view of productive, substantive negotiations with communists and instead saw talks as another means to achieve American ends. It was this approach that helped doom several U.S. bombing pauses and third-party peace initiatives during the Vietnam War.

Long before he arrived in Washington, Bundy also espoused a form of the politico-military strategy that the Kennedy administration would later call "flexible response." Proponents of this strategy argued that the Eisenhower administration's reliance on overwhelming nuclear superiority was unsuitable against low-intensity, anticolonial wars of national liberation in distant, developing lands. Even in April 1950, before Eisenhower's presidency, Bundy joined prominent liberals and fellow Harvard professors John Kenneth Galbraith and Arthur M. Schlesinger, Jr., in a letter to the *New York Times* to call for more flexibility in U.S. foreign policy. There were, the professors wrote, "degrees of Soviet pressure short of open military aggression; and to this form of limited aggression—such as sponsorship of 'revolution' or of guerrilla operations in independent countries—the United States may have no effective response except an atomic war." American policy would therefore have to "move beyond its present central reliance on atomic warfare and must accept the costs in money and inconvenience involved in such a shift in policy." This was precisely the strategy the Truman administration adopted after the outbreak of the Korean War. Bundy elaborated on this position two years later: "The United States is required by its own principles and purposes to act in opposition to and restraint of the aggressive and hostile pressures of the Soviet Union." But American leaders could not safely use just any strategy. There were limits to the potential for U.S. nuclear superiority, "for the Kremlin knows as well as we do how little we are eager for atomic war. But since we will not use the bomb for every crisis, we are required to act and react at lower levels of force, in ways that are as far from peace as Korea." A lack of flexibility, Bundy warned, would only lead to either "peace by submission or peace by all-out war."[40]

Throughout the decade Bundy became severely disenchanted with the Eisenhower administration's reliance on nuclear weapons, a strategy dubbed "the New Look." Although nominally a Republican, he thought his party's oscillation between the isolationism of Taft and the realism of Eisenhower to be unhealthy, unimaginative, and even dangerous. The main pillars of the New Look strategy—an emphasis on nuclear weapons, multilateral security treaties, and covert operations—were designed to achieve America's foreign policy goals without an increase in expenditures or commitment of conventional forces. It was this prudential sense of limits that offended Bundy's progressive, Stimsonian sensibilities. Partly for this reason, Bundy publicly endorsed Kennedy in the 1960 presidential campaign.[41]

The liberal belief in progress was also evident in Bundy's tendency to couple political and economic aspects of foreign policy with military strategy. In this regard, his thoughts paralleled the theory—if not the practice—of Truman's Point Four Program. He was therefore also an early, if unwitting, advocate of what would come to be called "modernization theory." This school of thought claimed that if the Western model of free-market capitalism were fostered within the newly decolonizing societies of Asia and Africa, communists would not be able to co-opt fledgling nationalist movements. The United States would then be able to create new allies while simultaneously denying them to the Soviet Union and the People's Republic of China. Bundy wrote to Lippmann as early as 1949 that the

problem of East and West—massive and intractable as it is—must be attacked in any contemporary analysis . . . We must not even discard that part of the eighteenth-century creed which boldly reasserted the possibility of human progress. The problem is one of revision, not rejection of the image held in earlier generations, and I am tempted to believe that the analysis of the Western tradition is the necessary underpinning for a contemporary cut into the problem . . . The Western image and the Western community may be confused in their thinking and mired in their economics, but they are worth preserving. Although we are tempted to think of Communism as the dynamic religion of the age, I think it is more accurate to assess Communism as a currently virulent heresy operating in a turmoil generated by the impact of the West as a whole on itself and the rest of the world.[42]

Ironically, Bundy also predicted how difficult it would be to infuse Eastern societies with Western values, particularly within a short span of time. Concerning liberal democracy, he warned Lippmann about "the assumption that this quality can be readily exported. If we have shown anything we have shown how hard and slow the growth of the liberal idea must be. [The] consequence of this illusion is disillusion." This is the problem that American policymakers such as Bundy would face in the 1960s with "nation-building" in South Vietnam and with the Alliance for Progress in Latin America. But by that time Bundy's belief in the American example had shed its early doubt and ambivalence, and in 1965 he professed adherence to what he had learned from Acheson. "In the final analysis," Bundy told a visitor to the White House, "the United States was the locomotive at the head of mankind, and the rest of the world the caboose."[43]

Bundy was certainly not alone in believing that a successful foreign policy required the support of military might and the willingness to use it. Frederick the Great of Prussia once observed that "diplomacy without armaments is like music without instruments."[44] What was true for Prussia in the eighteenth century was true for America in the twentieth. George Kennan, not usually known for his bellicosity, agreed. "You have no idea," he remarked in 1946, "how much it contributes to the general politeness and pleasantness of diplomacy when you have a little quiet armed force in the background." America's military "is probably the most important single instrumentality in the conduct of U.S. foreign policy."[45] The caveats and qualifications that Bundy attached to the use of force attest to the fact that he was no warmonger. But, ultimately, he did believe in the primacy of military power to solve international problems in which America's national security, very broadly defined, was at stake. While Kennan also felt that force was an essential component of diplomacy, he was much more circumspect than Bundy at finding situations in which American security was threatened enough to warrant its use. By the 1960s, against the cautionary advice of people like Kennan, Bundy would identify the defense of noncommunist South Vietnam as one of those vital interests.

Contempt for Appeasement

The second tenet of Bundy's foreign policy outlook was the futility of appeasement. This belief was a vindication of his interventionist stance prior to World War II and, for others who were not as prescient, a lesson to be learned from the failure of British and French diplomacy in the 1930s. A corollary to this tenet was that the United States must have a vigorously interventionist foreign policy to prevent the mistakes of the interwar period from reccurring. British and French acquiescence in Nazi Germany's aggressive expansion had a profound impact on Bundy, and he was certain that American officials should never repeat these mistakes in dealing with the Soviets. The United States had its own version of the debacle at Munich in the 1945 Yalta Conference, at which Bundy believed that Stalin had hoodwinked the guileless Americans. "It seems to me," he complained to Frankfurter in 1953, "that the atmosphere of naked joy which emerges in the party returning from Yalta is a pretty low point. I just don't think the evidence justified the rejoicing." Appeasement, defined very loosely as mutual compromise with the Soviets, was out of the question. Americans would simply have to project resolve rather than be willing to barter their security. "The stronger the United States can make her basic political commitment to defend Europe against aggression, the less likely we are to have a war with Russia," Bundy wrote while at the Council on Foreign Relations. "The more we are believed when we pledge ourselves to resist aggression, the less we shall have to spend on proving by military aid that we mean what we say." Resisting appeasement, then, rested on the credibility of American commitments; but, as Bundy was to discover with Vietnam a decade later, war was usually the only resort available when America's credibility was challenged directly.[46]

In *On Active Service* Bundy wrote of Stimson's belief that the causes of World War II could be traced directly to the Manchurian Crisis and the West's failure to check Japan's advance. And so, characteristically, he later took his cue from Stimson. Americans, he wrote elsewhere, found themselves at war in 1941 "because we had not the will, or the policy, or the force, to stop it. If we wait and see, we shall see my sons and grandsons in this same old horror." He dubbed Western statesmen of the interwar era "the self-deluded" and insisted that the use of force early in the European and East Asian crises would have prevented a world war. As a lecturer at Harvard, Bundy gave his famed international relations class to a rapt, standing-room-only crowd when the topic was appeasement. He imparted Munich's dangerous lesson, of allowing the bully free reign, with great drama and intensity. Referring to the decline of isolationism after the outbreak of the Korean War in June 1950, Bundy wrote that "with the end of American adolescence, many things become possible." Although isolationism in the United States had long been dead and discredited, its equivalent, neutralism in Europe, presented the gravest challenge to American foreign policy in the Cold War. The "most important similarity between neutralists and isolationists," Bundy wrote in 1952, "lies in the manner in which their very great qualities are stultified by a refusal to face reality, and that this act of voluntary withdrawal tends to aid the very forces they most energetically and properly hate." For Bundy, as it had been for Stimson, the willingness to stand fast in the face of grave challenges, with force if necessary, was a pillar of peace.[47]

Anticommunism

The belief in the interrelationship between diplomacy and power, and the disdain for appeasement, affirmed Bundy's view that military intervention would often best protect American interests and security. It also buttressed the third aspect of his worldview, a deep distrust of communism. Bundy perceived international communism as an avaricious menace; his view of communists at home was equally hostile. As early as 1940, he declared:

> I myself do not include members of the Communist Party . . . in the category of ordinary Americans; it seems to me perfectly evident that [this] group [is] essentially owned and controlled by unscrupulous foreign governments; this is a vexed issue, largely because so many people cannot see the difference between a Communist and other types of Leftist, but the facts of Communist action and thought speak clearly for themselves . . . The Constitution contains no justification of treachery.[48]

This view did not soften over time and instead hardened with the resurgence of Soviet-American antagonism after the war. To Bundy it was clear who was at fault for the deterioration: "The conduct of the Soviet Union, notably in its unrelenting hostility to the European Recovery Program and its success in dragging Czechoslovakia behind the Iron Curtain," was the predominant impetus for Soviet-American hostility. It was "the Russians who ended the wartime friendship," Bundy wrote testily to British socialist Harold Laski in 1949. "We can, of course, play hen-and-egg with Russian and American provocations, but I must say for myself that the weight of the evidence seems to me to indicate that the U.S.S.R. never intended to construct the postwar world on terms that would be acceptable to you and me." "The reality of the Soviet menace seems beyond reasonable doubt," he wrote on another occasion. "Soviet Communism has shown itself a system which is wholly hostile to the pursuit of liberty; wherever Communists have power, freedom dies. Nor is Soviet Communism an article for internal consumption only." He also equated the methods and aims of Soviet communism with German National Socialism, and fundamentally he trusted neither.[49]

It was natural for Dean Bundy later to see American universities as partners of the federal government in the effort to resist the advance of communism. He lauded and encouraged government funding in many academic departments—most notably in area studies programs that came into existence after World War II and that continued to receive funding from the CIA. More explicitly, Bundy told the Harvard ROTC in 1955 that "we are committed in a larger sense to developing the connection between our University and the Armed Services in a wide variety of ways . . . A university which does not try to develop to a maximal degree the interest, cooperation, and understanding between its staff members and those of the National Defense forces is not doing its full job." Area studies fulfilled this role perfectly. Faculty members of area studies programs, whose academic expertise was narrowly confined to the politics, history, language, and culture of one particular region or country, would tailor their research to suit the government's needs. The programs were also ideal breeding grounds for CIA recruitment.[50]

The university and the government could work together in other ways, such as ferreting out domestic communists and "fellow travelers" from the academic ranks. Normally Bundy would have objected to such an intrusion into people's private lives and academic freedom, but national emergencies, such as the Cold War, called for extraordinary methods. This was a dilemma that had vexed him for some time. In 1951 he bluntly asked the readers of the *American Political Science Review:* "Can we meet the challenge of Soviet imperialism without a major surrender of individual freedoms?" He did not believe that the United States could, and proceeded to explain why. He derided the then-fashionable analogy between domestic anticommunism and the seventeenth-century Salem witch trials as "uncommonly ill-advised" since "Stalinists, unlike witches, are real, and can be dangerous." Freedom, he argued, was neither unlimited nor absolute. Certain individual liberties would sometimes need to be curtailed for the greater good. In terms that would become familiar to Bundy during his stewardship of Harvard, he also suggested that it was "even conceivable that the constraints of a loyalty program are in some measure essential to freedom." In his view the communist threat was severe enough to warrant such unusual measures.[51]

A good example of this philosophy in action is Bundy's treatment of former Communist Party (CP) members at Harvard. Unsurprisingly, Dean Bundy did not think that CP members or fellow travelers made good teachers. Well after the high-water mark of McCarthyism, he offered this testimony to a Senate subcommittee in 1955: "And so in our search for [academic] excellence, once we are satisfied that a man is not a rascal (a standard which in Harvard's view excludes Americans who still surrender to Communist discipline), we do not worry much about his politics, or his manners, or his team spirit." He did not always regard communists as rational people and even advised one past communist, who was under consideration for a faculty appointment at Harvard, to undergo psychiatric evaluation. With this in mind, Bundy was extremely cooperative with federal investigators when their search for communists and fellow travelers brought them to Harvard Yard. Bundy proclaimed to the faculty that pledging the Fifth Amendment in testimony was unsuitable behavior (but on its own not grounds for dismissal). Those who did not cooperate were not tolerated and, whenever possible, divorced from the Harvard community. For example, a joint administrative-academic post was offered to Sigmund Diamond in 1955; upon discovering Diamond's past affiliation with the Communist Party (probably on information supplied by the FBI), Bundy demanded that Diamond cooperate with federal authorities. When Diamond agreed to answer questions about himself but not others, Bundy rescinded the offer and Diamond left Harvard, eventually finding a tenure-track position at Columbia University. The fear of a pervasive, insidious communist presence on campus was something in which Bundy sincerely believed. More than a decade later he not only argued that the student demonstrations against the Vietnam War were giving comfort to the enemy, he also insinuated that the antiwar movement itself was being manipulated by communists. "Now, look," he once said testily of the student demonstrators, "there is a reality to the notion that the communists, the Soviets, do what they can to louse up American policy whenever they get a chance."[52]

However, Bundy was no zealot. His anticommunism reflected the common political view of the time, which was mainly hostile to communism without necessarily being sympathetic to demagogues such as Senator Joseph McCarthy. Moreover, as an administrator with a commitment to running a major university as smoothly as possible, he could be pragmatic in the application of his anticommunism. As dean, Bundy maintained the ban at Harvard on government-sponsored classified research, established in 1946 by university President Conant, because he viewed such research as imminently threatening to the pursuit of open and unencumbered academic research. He believed "that in the service of [academic freedom and the advancement of knowledge], Harvard must, except in time of all-out war, avoid the hampering and restrictive impact of immersion in secret work." Far from being dogmatic, Bundy expressed great uncertainty about the policy of loyalty requirements. He recommended against dismissing a colleague from the physics department who had been subjected to accusations similar to those that would plague Diamond. Bundy testified in 1955 that the federal government's loyalty program "creates needless confusion and fear, spreads suspicion far beyond the range of reason," and generally poisons the relationship between academia and public service. At the end of the decade, after the intensity of domestic anticommunism had eased somewhat, Bundy revealed his uneasiness in a letter to Frankfurter: "Did you ever come closely to grips with the problem of loyalty oaths and affirmations for students while you were teaching? . . . I myself have never been able to get as much excitement over oaths and affirmations of an essentially irrelevant character as some of my perhaps more conscientious colleagues."[53]

Although Bundy did not possess a blind anticommunist faith, it was nonetheless sincere. When faced with a new situation that was tinged with communism, his first reaction was reflexively distrustful and combative. It was this attitude, combined with a belief in the uses of military force and a fear of appeasement, that shaped Bundy's worldview before he joined the Kennedy administration in January 1961. Stimson, had he lived to witness Bundy's appointment to the Kennedy White House, would have been proud. His protégé was continuing the Stimsonian tradition of basing U.S. foreign policy on internationalism, interventionism, military might, and political resolve. Although Bundy's moralism was not as fervent as Stimson's, his early embrace of modernization theory and anticommunism in the developing world reflected his belief that progress should be the main pillar of America's foreign policy. These were the concepts that would guide his thinking on Vietnam.

CHAPTER **2**

A Foreign Office in Microcosm: Creating the National Security Adviser and Re-creating the NSC Staff

In 1961 President Kennedy and McGeorge Bundy, the newly appointed Special Assistant for National Security Affairs, initiated sweeping changes to the National Security Council system and the role of the Special Assistant. A decade later, amid the resultant turmoil of the Richard Nixon–Henry Kissinger White House operation, Dean Acheson reflected on the change: "The new organization, with staffs of size and competence, has now survived a decade of political life and constant criticism. At its head Messrs. McGeorge Bundy, Walt Rostow and Henry Kissinger, all men of outstanding ability, have served successively to the announced satisfaction of their presidential chiefs. What emotions they stirred in the breasts of their colleagues at the State Department we must wait on future memoirs to learn. Meanwhile," Acheson continued portentously, "we can imagine that there has been strain." Acheson's presumption was more accurate than he realized.[1]

Under Presidents Truman and Eisenhower, the position of Special Assistant for National Security Affairs had been largely administrative and Special Assistants rarely if ever participated in actually shaping foreign policy. Under Kennedy, who wanted to act as his own Secretary of State and concentrate policymaking in the White House, Bundy fundamentally transformed the post by augmenting the Special Assistant's power and prerogatives. Whereas Kennedy's predecessors saw their Special Assistants as facilitators of national security policy, Kennedy wanted a contributor; whereas Truman and Eisenhower wanted their Assistants to be subordinate to the cabinet, Kennedy wanted his to be its equal. With his own staff of experts who became policymakers in their own right and inclusion in the administration's highest foreign policy decision-making councils, Bundy performed more like a cabinet official than a presidential aide.

The changes instituted during the Kennedy presidency were accentuated during Lyndon Johnson's, who relied on Bundy to formulate and coordinate foreign policy to an even greater extent than Kennedy had. This change was in large part due to the informality and personalization of decision making under Johnson. Paradoxically, as Bundy's authority increased, the scope of his staff's power decreased. Fewer people actually conducted U.S. foreign policy after November 1963, and those who did were concentrated at the highest levels. Under Johnson, only Secretary of State Dean Rusk and Secretary of Defense Robert S. McNamara could rival Bundy's influence. In 1964 and 1965, when the administration made its major decisions on Vietnam, there were very few internal obstacles to block the path that Bundy wanted the United States to take.

Why Kennedy Chose Bundy

Without actively seeking it, by the election of 1960 Bundy was ideally positioned for an important foreign policy job in a prospective Kennedy administration. Perhaps most important was his obvious affinity with the policies and positions advocated by Kennedy. Throughout the 1950s Bundy had made clear his preference for flexible response over the New Look and for modernization theory and nation-building over neglect of the Third World; but along with his anticommunism and internationalism, he had also managed to project an aura of toughness, blended with intelligence, that epitomized the Kennedy ethos. And in a remarkable and fortuitous coincidence, immediately after the 1960 presidential election a television documentary aired, written and narrated by Bundy and entitled "He Shall Have Power," on the value of strong presidential authority and leadership in American politics.[2] No better cause could be espoused by a hopeful presidential appointee. In short Bundy was intellectually and temperamentally the ideal Kennedy man—tough, pragmatic but with liberal instincts, and highly intelligent.

Campaigning for Kennedy against Richard Nixon in 1960 did not hurt Bundy's chances either, which revealed another of his assets: his belief in political bipartisanship, particularly over foreign policy. Bundy's true loyalty was to the nation and to the presidency, although he had always been an active, if moderate, Republican. In 1941 he ran as a Republican for a seat on the Boston City Council and lost badly. He also worked as an adviser on foreign policy for Republican candidate Thomas Dewey in the 1948 presidential election, during which he stressed Dewey's bipartisanship in international affairs as a main strength, and he publicly endorsed Eisenhower in the 1952 presidential election. Later, as a public intellectual in the late 1940s and throughout the 1950s, Bundy had been more circumspect than many of his Republican colleagues in criticizing the Democrats. He refused to blame Franklin Roosevelt for capitulating to the USSR at the 1945 Yalta Conference, and instead accused the Soviets of reneging on their commitments. He also lamented "the destructive debate over the fall of China"—primarily a Republican-led attack against the Democrats—even though he felt that the Truman administration had underestimated the consequences of Mao Zedong's communist victory. Above all Bundy believed in putting the interests of the nation ahead of the interests of the Republican Party. He thus represented the latest scion of a prestigious lineage of bipartisan statesmen, Republicans who had served Democratic Presidents; his predecessors included his mentor, Henry Stimson, and his father, Harvey Bundy. Because Kennedy sought to include moderate Republicans in his administration after winning one of the closest elections in modern American history, Bundy's political affiliation, however nominal, was also an important asset. Rather than hurting his chances, Bundy's status as a registered Republican was an asset to a young president who sought to emulate the bipartisan golden years of World War II and the early Cold War.[3]

The president-elect and the Harvard dean had also known each other personally for years and, as fellow aristocratic Bostonians, shared many mutual friends and acquaintances. Kennedy and Bundy had even attended the same school as children. Although they were not especially close, the two young men resumed their friendship when they returned to Boston after serving in World War II, and in the following decade they shared innumerable connections at Harvard. After the 1960 election, for example, Harvard professors and Kennedy advisers John Kenneth Galbraith and Arthur M. Schlesinger, Jr., strongly recommended Bundy for the position of under secretary of state. Walter Lippmann, another Harvard alumnus who knew both men very well, even suggested to Kennedy that Bundy would make a good secretary of state. Kennedy greatly admired Bundy's intellect—"You can't beat brains," the president once remarked of his Special Assistant—and wanted him for an important post, but he felt that the Harvard dean might be too young for secretary or under secretary of state. Perhaps more important, relations between Dean

Rusk, whom Kennedy had appointed secretary of state in December, and Bundy "had not been especially friendly," which effectively eliminated Bundy from consideration for a State Department position. Besides, the president-elect had in mind great changes for the post of Special Assistant for National Security Affairs and thought Bundy the right man for the job.[4]

The Transformation of the NSC System

As a means to help America wage the emerging Cold War more effectively, the National Security Council was created by the National Security Act of 1947 [the act's broad scope also included the founding of the Central Intelligence Agency (CIA), the Office of the Secretary of Defense, and the Joint Chiefs of Staff (JCS)]. The act established the NSC as a cabinet-level advisory body that coordinated for the president the advice of all relevant executive departments and agencies. The position of executive secretary, as it was initially known, was created to serve as the NSC's administrative head. As a top-level body that integrated various federal departments and agencies, the NSC's duty, when convened, was to advise the president on matters of national security. As was Truman's intention, the original role of the executive secretary was modest and essentially administrative: he and his support staff operated very much as bureaucratic presidential aides, ensuring that NSC meetings functioned smoothly and offering policy advice sparingly and infrequently, if at all. Truman also wanted the Executive Secretary and NSC staff to be nonpartisan, with functions and duties more akin to policy implementation rather than to planning and formulation.[5]

Eisenhower expanded, but did not significantly strengthen, the duties of the NSC and its staff. Given Eisenhower's military background, unsurprisingly the principal change was to add more formal structure: the executive secretary remained but was superseded by the newly created Special Assistant for National Security Affairs; the Planning Board was created to serve a long-range policy-planning function; and the Operations Coordinating Board (OCB) was established to ensure that the policy decided upon was being implemented. Robert Cutler, Eisenhower's longest-serving Special Assistant, liked to think of the NSC as "at the top of Policy Hill." The president and the cabinet secretaries—the statutory members of the NSC who made the actual policy decisions—were at the top. On one side, leading to the top, was the Planning Board; on the other side, leading down from the top, was the OCB. The task of the Special Assistant was to facilitate smooth progress up and down Policy Hill. NSC staff members were essentially anonymous bureau-cratic clerks rather than powerful, independent policymakers.[6]

The system as it had evolved under Truman and Eisenhower was not, how-ever, without its critics. Toward the end of the 1950s a consensus had devel-oped that the NSC was too large, too cumbersome, and much too slow to respond to the increasingly complex challenges of the Cold War. A Senate subcommittee, chaired by Democrat Henry "Scoop" Jackson, devoted much of its energy to criticizing the Eisenhower system and devising an alternative.[7] By the beginning of 1961, in contrast to the dynamism of Mao, Khrushchev, Castro, de Gaulle, and Kennedy, Eisenhower and his disciplined, highly reg-imented foreign policy structure seemed quite stale. And so, on December 31, 1960, while announcing Bundy's appointment at a press conference, Kennedy told reporters that he intended to use the NSC "and its machinery more flex-ibly than in the past" and that, to bring this about, he had asked Bundy to "simplify" the NSC system so "that we may have a single, small, but strongly organized staff unit to assist me in obtaining advice from, and coordinating operations of, the government agencies concerned with national security affairs."[8]

The first step Bundy took was to abolish not only the OCB, but the Plan-ning Board as well. Under instructions from the new Special Assistant, Robert H. Johnson, a member of the NSC staff since 1958 and the Executive Assistant of the OCB in 1960, seemingly committed professional suicide when he rec-ommended that Kennedy and Bundy "abolish the Planning Board, Planning Board Assistants, the Operations Coordinating Board and the OCB Assistants," and "assign, by Presidential order, all functions of the Planning Board and Operations Coordinating Board to the Special Assistant to the President (Mr. Bundy)." Bundy was also advised by another NSC consultant to replace the OCB with an "Executive Secretariat" within the NSC that would have "liaison responsibilities with all interagency groups concerned with national security matters" and could thus "persuade and cajole" State and Defense officials "to take a broad national approach to problems rather than a parochial, depart-mental view."[9]

Bundy agreed with this approach but did not form an Executive Secretariat; instead, he decided its proposed duties would be invested in the regular members of the NSC staff under the auspices of the Special Assistant. True to Johnson's recommendations, the myriad duties of the OCB were now invested in one individual—the Special Assistant. In place of the cumbersome OCB, Bundy initiated the National Security Action Memorandum (NSAM) series. An NSAM was a document, drawn up and circulated by Bundy, that informed each recipient of new policy directives. This solved, at one stroke, the "inherent limitations" of interdepartmental committees and their concomitant lack of authority. Each NSAM would explicitly outline approved national security policy; swift adoption was assumed because officials would otherwise violate presidential authority, as expressed and exercised through Bundy. As he put it artfully to Director of Central Intelligence Allen Dulles in March 1961, "I have the strong impression, from my brief experience, that departments and agencies will always be acting just as fast as they can to respond to the President's directives."[10]

The launch of the NSAM series, however, was not the primary source of the Special Assistant's new power. The NSAM reflected Bundy's authority as an administrator, rather than a maker, of foreign policy. The chief source of the Special Assistant's increased authority was in how he eliminated and replaced the Planning Board. A week after the inauguration a member of the NSC staff suggested to Bundy that the officials who previously wrote Planning Board papers could now be split into geographic specialties and work to create and shape new policy—in other words, a mirror image of the State Department, only much smaller. Thus the Special Assistant would not only have power due to presidential proximity; he would also be endowed with institutional authority and bureaucratic leverage. As Richard Neustadt, a Columbia political scientist whom Kennedy had hired to advise on the transition, argued, such a change would elevate the prestige and authority of the Special Assistant to "something more than just another 'palace guardsman' whose status depended wholly on the intimacy of his relationship with you." The NSC staff would have area experts who traveled abroad to deliberate with allies, visit crisis zones, and write policy memoranda. Bundy approved the concept, and the Planning Board died when he declined to convene it after the new administration commenced its duties. The NSC was now beginning to usurp much of the State Department's influence.[11]

Bundy justified the creation of a new level of policymaking bureaucrats by telling Kennedy that although the Departments of State and Defense did a good job formulating and advising on policy, "the matter is of literally life-and-death importance, and it also has plenty of political dynamite in it, so that the more advice you get, the better off you will be." In a modern presidency, Bundy later argued, there were tasks that "only the White House staff can do. We're just going to know better than the guys in the [State] Department . . . what's on the President's mind, what kind of stuff he will like and what he doesn't like. That is what we do for a living, and they do a lot of other things for a living." Crucially, the new, smaller NSC system would receive the same amount of funding as the old system had under Eisenhower. This too resulted in a more influential role for the Special Assistant and his staff. Rostow, who also had a large role in the planning of the new NSC, commented that while Kennedy liked the changes, he "noted that we were somewhat odd bureaucrats: here we were, handed a substantial empire—slots, budgets, and all—and our first recommendation was to liquidate a good part of it." Of course, Rostow was not being entirely candid. Rather than a liquidation, the move was a concentration of power in the hands of far fewer individuals— Bundy and his staff.[12]

Bundy's duties as Special Assistant for National Security Affairs were twofold. First, as before, the Special Assistant continued to be the coordinator of other people's policy. Because of his collaborative projects with Stimson, Acheson, Lippmann, and Oppenheimer, and his experience as Harvard's top administrator, Bundy was exceptionally good at this task. But unlike previous Special Assistants, Bundy was not limited to coordinating policy for a specific function, such as the presentation of policy options to an NSC meeting. Instead, he functioned as a conduit to the president. For example, Bundy would clear highly sensitive cables from the State Department to American diplomatic posts abroad. Drafts of cables would go from Benjamin Read, the State Department's executive secretary, to Bundy for approval. This was known as "the Read-Bundy channel." NSC staff member Michael V. Forrestal recalled: "We drafted in most cases every Presidential communication with a Head of State or a foreign Head of Government in our area [of expertise]. We also initiated a great many telegrams from the Department of State and the Department of Defense, not necessarily Presidential ones; and in fact . . . if one of us didn't actually write the telegram the department sent out, we were certainly there when it was born." To maximize White House control over the foreign policy process, Kennedy also ensured that Bundy and the NSC staff received every important incoming State or Defense Department cable. Bundy's job, then, was to serve as the President's foreign policy filter; the only limitations imposed on this function were from his own discretion. Moreover, the increase in his authority reflected a concomitant increase in stature and prominence. In his five years as Special Assistant, for example, Bundy appeared in the pages of the *New York Times* as often as his five predecessors combined.[13]

Second, Bundy was in charge of the NSC staff. Free from the requirements and constraints of Planning Board and OCB duties, those who remained on the NSC staff now focused on matters of policy, both short- and long-term. Bundy retained few members from the Eisenhower staff, which was a departure from the "nonpartisan" staff envisioned by Truman.[14] As in the State Department, members of the NSC staff divided their work into geographic and thematic sections so that only one or two staff members devoted their energies, for example, to the Middle East, or Southeast Asia, or international trade. At the top of the hierarchy in 1961 were Bundy and Rostow.

Although Bundy was, according to Rostow, "clearly in charge of the shop," another source of the NSC staff's influence was the fact that all of its senior members could report directly to the President. This was a privilege not enjoyed in the Kennedy administration by midechelon officials from the Departments of State or Defense unless they had explicit presidential favor. NSC staff members who had direct access to Kennedy were Rostow; Carl Kaysen, who was Bundy's expert on matters of European policy and nuclear strategy, and Rostow's successor as deputy Special Assistant; Robert W. Komer, who handled policy for the Middle East, Africa, South Asia, Indonesia, and occasionally Indochina; and Michael V. Forrestal, who from January 1962 dealt with East, and especially Southeast, Asia. Kaysen recalled that "there wasn't a strict line organization" in the NSC staff. "People dealt with each other as they thought the business at hand required . . . It was relatively easy to talk to the President. It was perfectly easy to give him pieces of paper which he . . . would look at if he were interested and . . . throw away if he weren't." Bundy and the NSC staff also acted as a final editorial clearing house for presidential speeches on foreign policy. Unlike State or Defense Department officials, who usually operated within a sharply defined hierarchy, the only people to whom NSC staff members were responsible were the president and the Special Assistant, in that order.[15]

Bundy and the NSC staff quickly became a separate center for the making of American foreign policy. Their colleagues in the Kennedy administration certainly noticed. Under Secretary of State George Ball recalled that Bundy and his staff "amounted to a foreign office in microcosm." White House aides Ted Sorensen and Arthur Schlesinger, and State Department official Roger Hilsman, concurred.[16] And due to the fact that the structure and functions of the NSC staff evolved by custom and Executive Order, rather than by statute—and the fact that the original National Security Act did not provide for the advice and consent of the Senate in choosing the Special Assistant—NSC staff members retained more flexibility and autonomy than their counterparts in the State Department. As Komer later observed, the result was "a fascinating exercise in a presidential staff technique, which insofar as I know, has been unique in the history of the presidency."[17]

In addition, because President Kennedy intended very much to act as his own Secretary of State, he needed to fill the actual post with a rather weak figure. Rusk, who had been recommended to Kennedy as the perfect lieutenant by both Dean Acheson and Robert Lovett, seemed to be the perfect candidate. Temperamentally Rusk was a manager rather than a leader and was probably better suited to be under secretary of state. His natural reticence made it easier for Bundy and his staff to flex their newly developed bureaucratic muscle. Prior to taking office, Rusk had expressed his view that the secretary of state was an agent of the president, that only the president should establish policy, that the secretary's job was simply to act on the president's will, and that the president should "not delegate excessively to the secretary of state." This was the main reason why Kennedy picked Rusk to be his secretary of state. As a result Rusk could not mobilize the State Department like Bundy could the NSC staff—the former was simply too large and too cumbersome, whereas the latter was small and flexible.[18]

Bundy and the NSC staff also benefited from the view, held particularly strongly by the White House, that the State Department was weak and ineffectual. While the NSC had not created this perception, they certainly cultivated and took advantage of it. Troubled by the State Department's ineffectiveness, in May 1961 Rostow encouraged Kennedy to initiate "a systematic review of the situation in the Department of State, which would increase its capacity to lead and to drive forward ahead of events rather than behind events." The State Department, Bundy reminded Kennedy in 1962, "has not proved to be as effective an agency of executive management as we had hoped." Kennedy evidently agreed. "Damn it," he remarked angrily later that year, "Bundy and I get more done in one day than they do in six months in the State Department." Or, as he bluntly complained to Ball after a series of leaks by the department to the *New York Times*, the "State Department isn't that powerful, and they just can't stand it."[19]

Finally, more often than not Rusk kept his own counsel and rarely attempted to express, much less impose, his own views on the president or the State Department. Nicholas Katzenbach, assistant attorney general under Kennedy and later an under secretary to Rusk in the Johnson administration,

recalled that Rusk "did not like to take positions. That made it awfully difficult for him to advise the President, [because] he had to know what the President thought before he advised him."[20] Bundy himself agreed, writing of
Rusk in early 1965:

> He is not a manager. He has never been a good judge of men. His instincts
> are cautious and negative, and he has only a limited ability to draw the
> best out of those who work with him. His very discretion seems like secre-
> tiveness in his dealings with subordinates; it is a constant complaint in
> the bureaus that even quite high officials cannot find out what the Sec-
> retary himself thinks and wants . . .
>
> Moreover, the Secretary has little sense of effective operation. He
> does not move matters toward decision with promptness. He does not
> stimulate aggressive staff work. He does not coordinate conflicting forces
> within his own department.[21]

Two decades later, Bundy admitted, "I did have the feeling that Dean Rusk
is a very careful fellow; he doesn't let his guard down." He felt that Rusk was
adept at summarizing the views of others, "but if you want to be sure what
he thinks, that's going to be a little harder, and that's not going to be the first
card he plays." Ironically, during the Kennedy era Rusk performed more like
an Eisenhower-era Special Assistant and Bundy more like the secretary of
state.[22]

Consequences from the Bay of Pigs

The increasing concentration of power within the NSC staff was given a
boost from an unlikely source—the botched Bay of Pigs invasion. On April
17, 1961, a secretly American-equipped and trained force of Cuban exiles
launched what was supposed to be a liberation of Cuba from the communist
regime of Fidel Castro. The Bay of Pigs invasion itself, poorly conceived from
the start, was an unmitigated disaster for the United States and an enormous
propaganda victory for Castro and the Soviet Union. The immediate result
was the solidification of communist rule in Cuba, but it also had significant
repercussions for the formulation and coordination of national security policy in Washington. Although publicly Kennedy accepted responsibility for the
disaster, privately he placed much of the culpability for failure on the CIA—
which organized and helped operate the invasion—and the JCS—whom,
Kennedy felt, had not provided honest and accurate advice. Bundy, who had

set aside initial skepticism about the plan and supported the invasion, likewise blamed the CIA and JCS for the failure. Kennedy responded to the Bay of Pigs by removing the CIA and JCS from the center of the decision-making process. "Never thereafter," Assistant Secretary of Defense William P. Bundy later wrote, "would civilian leaders and advisors accept military and professional judgments without exploring them so fully as to make them, in effect, their own." If the authority of these departments, including the already emasculated State Department, was curtailed, another must have benefited. In this case the main beneficiary was the NSC staff.[23]

Kennedy's first decision was to move the Special Assistant and his subordinates physically closer to himself, and so the NSC staff moved its headquarters across the street from the Old Executive Office Building to the White House basement. The Situation Room was established beside the NSC offices and run by the NSC staff, according to NSC staffer Bromley K. Smith, "to serve as a funnel for all classified information coming from all national security agencies." After the Bay of Pigs incident, all information essential to the conduct of foreign policy would pass through Bundy and the NSC staff via the Situation Room; conversely, most vital communications originating from Washington to American officials abroad would need to be cleared by Bundy or a member of his staff. Included were State Department cables to American embassies and some, but not all, military communications traffic from the Pentagon. Other changes signaled the growing institutional strength of the NSC staff, such as the privilege of dining at the White House mess (which signified their access to, and direct affiliation with, the president). Finally, in a move that weakened the role of the JCS, Kennedy appointed General Maxwell D. Taylor, former Army chief of staff, as his presidential military adviser. The military policy of the Kennedy administration would now be coordinated primarily by Secretary of Defense Robert McNamara, who already had a strained and uncomfortable relationship with the JCS, and by Taylor. The appointment of Taylor benefited Bundy and the NSC staff by shifting much of the balance of power in the military bureaucracy from the Pentagon to the White House, where the Special Assistant and his subordinates would have more input into, and influence over, the administration's military policy.[24]

These personnel and procedural changes, and the apparent amorphousness of the duties of the Special Assistant and the NSC staff, reflected a certain disorganization within the Kennedy presidency. Bundy later confessed that "untidiness in management was in some measure intrinsic to the President's way of work." Or, as William Bundy wrote of the Kennedy administration, "the excessive generalization of the Eisenhower era gave way to excessive individuality of policy."[25] Raymond Garthoff, a diplomat who worked for nearly every Cold War president, recalled that Kennedy and Bundy shocked the national security bureaucracy by deciding that they did not want drafted a standard but "unduly constraining" Basic National Security Policy—an overall consensus document that provides a platform for U.S. foreign policy goals. After the Bay of Pigs fiasco, many others believed that the Kennedy NSC system operated solely on the basis of improvization and poorly executed crisis management, and they did not like what they saw.[26]

However, such criticism did not take into account the extent to which Bundy and the NSC staff had in fact developed their own apparatus for the operation and coordination of national security policy. Nor was the ability of Bundy and his staff to thrive in the absence of a strictly regimented chain of bureaucratic command taken into account. Thus in introducing Taylor to the Kennedy White House, Kaysen emphasized "the informal and somewhat fluid nature of the [NSC] assignments" and that it was "the purpose of the operation to get as much done on the informal level as possible." Kennedy's Special Assistant and NSC staff did not suffer from a lack of organization or coherence. Quite the opposite was true, and this fact was their strength. Moreover, the disorganization and administrative informality that did exist in the Kennedy administration was a tremendous boon to the NSC staff, for with their small numbers and cohesiveness they could easily outmaneuver the larger, more unwieldy bureaucracies of the traditional departments. The direct access to the president enjoyed by Rostow, Kaysen, Komer, and Forrestal, not to mention their close relationship with Bundy or Bundy's with Kennedy, are good examples, particularly when contrasted with the relationship between most State Department officials and the president. As we shall see, the ability of the Special Assistant and the NSC staff to marginalize the State Department during the Kennedy administration would play a major role in determining the course of America's policy towards Vietnam.[27]

The Transition to Lyndon Johnson

The assassination of Kennedy on November 22, 1963, triggered a dramatic change in presidents, but it did not necessarily require a drastic change in Bundy's role. If anything, Lyndon Johnson initially leaned on Bundy much more than Kennedy ever had. "My own work load," Bundy reported to

Johnson shortly after the 1964 election, "has increased in your administration." Although Johnson's reputation, then and since, for inexperience in foreign affairs has been somewhat exaggerated, the new president was indeed much more comfortable and adept with domestic policy and, unlike Kennedy, did not intend to act as his own Secretary of State. Johnson quickly came to value Bundy's foreign policy acumen and administrative abilities. Francis M. Bator, who served as the international trade and economics expert on the NSC staff, recalled that Johnson "relied more heavily on Bundy" than Kennedy had.[28] In the summer of 1964, Johnson told Senator Richard B. Russell that he could not send Bundy to Saigon as the new U.S. ambassador because he was too valuable in Washington as Special Assistant. Legend has it that that in the chaotic wake of the assassination, Bundy alone kept his cool and virtually ran the government single-handedly, and that when Bundy left for a Caribbean holiday afterward, the Johnson administration's foreign policy process began to come apart. Aside from Washington lore it was clear to Johnson that Bundy was an integral component of the presidency, administratively and substantively, and that he should continue to serve as Special Assistant. Johnson was so intent on retaining Bundy's services that he even invited Katherine Bundy, the Special Assistant's mother, to the White House in the hope that Mrs. Bundy would convince her son to stay.[29]

Johnson need not have worried, for Bundy never intended to leave. He thanked the president for the "warm expression of confidence" and considered it "a duty as well as an honor to serve you as you have asked." In a display of loyalty that showed there was no question who was in charge, Bundy tendered Johnson an undated letter of resignation "to take effect at your pleasure and convenience." Unlike many of Kennedy's personal aides, such as Sorensen and Schlesinger, and much to the chagrin of Kennedy's brother and attorney general, Robert F. Kennedy, Bundy felt he owed allegiance to the presidency as an institution rather than to any one individual. Of Bundy's renowned sense of institutional loyalty, one politician commented suspiciously, "I know he did worlds for Kennedy. I know he does worlds for Johnson. But he would have done the same for Joe Stalin too." And at least initially Bundy and Johnson developed a friendly working relationship.[30] To avoid any ambiguity, and to reassure Johnson, Bundy proclaimed his loyalty to the presidency in a widely read article in *Foreign Affairs*. Although he was not a personal assistant, and thus did not rely solely on his relationship to the president for authority, this fact does not in itself explain Bundy's sense of higher responsibility; rather, in the fashion Stimson had taught him, Bundy believed deeply in the institutional obligations and sense of duty that underpinned the concept of public service. McGeorge Bundy was not engaged in politics.[31]

Along with Bundy the NSC staff remained with its members, duties, and functions largely intact. The day following the assassination, Bundy described the NSC operation to Johnson as nothing less than the coordination of the administration's foreign policy. "The most valuable asset of my office," he wrote, "is a staff of half a dozen first-rate men . . . who have learned to combine mastery of specific area problems with a sense of what it is about them that matters to the President." This was a system the Special Assistant valued highly. "Man for man," Bundy wrote to Johnson in another evaluation of the NSC staff, "I would not trade this staff for any other in Washington."[32] However, although the Johnson NSC operation continued to function essentially under the same premise as it had under Kennedy, there was one significant alteration: Johnson vested more trust and authority at the top of the decision-making structure and less responsibility in the lower levels. This shift enhanced Bundy's influence and simultaneously diminished that of the NSC staff. The change would have tremendous implications for America's Vietnam policy, as it neatly coincided with two other changes in the NSC system: the replacement of departing staff members who advocated intervention with those who were more cautious, and Bundy's own increased level of interest and direct involvement in devising Vietnam policy.

NSC veteran Robert H. Johnson attributed the change in policymaking to a difference in personality and style between Kennedy and Johnson. "President Johnson's approach . . . was more personal and informal than President Kennedy's," he recalled. Since Kennedy had already considerably informalized the NSC system, the difference between the Eisenhower and Johnson administrations, and the roles of their respective Special Assistants, was very great indeed. Deliberative meetings of the full NSC, which Kennedy had considered to be "a waste of time," met rarely during the Kennedy administration. Johnson went even further; he called the full NSC together even more infrequently, preferring to deliberate and decide policy in front of, and with the participation of, as few people as possible. There was little resistance to this change, as Johnson's principal foreign policy advisers also felt uncomfortable discussing policy in front of large gatherings. As one journalist reported, Johnson believed that full NSC meetings increased the chances of leaked information to the media: "Irritated over a steady stream of news leaks from NSC meetings, the President asked an aide, 'Do we have to have all these people?' He began scratching names off the list, [and] finally winnowed it down to Bundy, McNamara and Rusk. He still meets with the NSC, but when he really wants to speak his mind—or hear others speak theirs—he summons the Big Three."[33]

What came to replace meetings of the full NSC was the "Tuesday Lunch," an informal but regular meeting of Johnson, Bundy, Rusk, and McNamara to discuss the overall direction of America's foreign policy. Others, such as the director of the CIA or the chairman of the JCS, were occasionally included when the president felt it necessary, but during the Bundy era the Tuesday Lunch usually meant a meeting of the Big Three. Added to the Special Assistant's duties was the task of preparing the agenda for each meeting. The Tuesday Lunches began in February 1964 but did not come into their own until the Tonkin Gulf crisis the following August. Rostow later described the lunches as "a kind of regular NSC meeting," the difference being that only four members participated regularly.[34]

In terms of influence with the President, Bundy's rise paralleled the NSC staff's decline, although its ability to inform and shape the opinions not only of the Special Assistant, but members of other departments as well, remained important. Except during the Tonkin Gulf crisis, Johnson did not have much contact with Bundy's staff until after the 1964 presidential election. Even after Johnson's landslide victory, NSC staff members—other than the deputy Special Assistant—found they did not have direct access to Johnson as they had had with Kennedy. This was partly because some NSC staff members in the Kennedy presidency, such as Rostow and Forrestal, had been personally selected by the president, which was not the case under Johnson. But the best explanation lies in the fact that Johnson relied almost exclusively upon his most senior-ranking officials. With the freewheeling days of the Kennedy era over, the NSC staff felt confined under the new arrangement. Referring to a series of large meetings on Vietnam in the crucial month of January 1965—and of the propensity to save actual policy decisions for the Tuesday Lunches—Chester L. Cooper of the NSC staff complained to Bundy, "I know all the reasons why these meetings tend to be hurried and harassed, but some fairly important decisions are being made without time for thoughtful discussion . . . Perhaps," Cooper added wryly, "the meetings you and the Secretaries have had with the President take care of this problem."[35]

Roles and Relationships at the Top

Two notable traits, both potential sources of trouble, characterized Bundy's personality. According to Schlesinger, these traits were a "dazzling clarity and speed of mind" and a "great distinction of manner and unlimited self-confidence." Schlesinger's polite descriptions translate, respectively, into "brilliance" and "arrogance." The combination of these characteristics, and his infamous intolerance of those less clever and confident than he, often made Bundy seem abrasive and intimidating. One national magazine euphemistically referred to him as "briskly articulate," while the editors of *Time* were less charitable—Bundy, they claimed, "can chill a polar bear with his codfish-cold scorn." Even a good friend such as the Oxford political philosopher Isaiah Berlin could be shocked by Bundy's steely temperament. Bundy, Berlin confided metaphorically to a friend in 1963, "clearly does not mind walking over corpses."[36]

But most of those who worked closely with Bundy were more impressed than intimidated. Canadian Ambassador Charles A. Ritchie, who became good friends with Bundy, recalled that it "was a delight to encounter that steely intelligence, that far-ranging competence, and that sharp wit." Ritchie acknowledged that "Mac's intellectual cocksureness might be putting-off," but Bundy was by no means unique—"they are all cocksure here." Among his colleagues, Bundy was well liked and admired. One Harvard professor noted that "Mac Bundy positively scintillates. He goes off like a fireworks factory, bing, bing, bing, and thinks so fast that he often outruns his troops." George Ball was amazed by Bundy's "extraordinary facility to grasp an idea, summarize or analyze it, and produce an orderly response as fast as a computer." But Ball did not find the Special Assistant arrogant. On the contrary, Bundy was mostly "extremely helpful" and so secure in his own abilities that he did not find it necessary to wage endless bureaucratic and political battles. Other colleagues from the Kennedy and Johnson administrations agreed with Ball's assessment. Lady Bird Johnson confided to her diary that Bundy was "one of the brightest men I've ever met." The First Lady even hoped that her daughter Lynda would someday marry "a twenty-five-year-old McGeorge Bundy."[37]

Bundy had created a powerful new institution within the foreign policy-making process. With his strong personality and incisive mind, the risk of tension with his colleagues was very high. But remarkably, despite the many obvious opportunities to abuse his power, he managed his responsibilities with little friction between his office and the Departments of State and Defense. He preferred to work with, instead of against, his colleagues. Against the backdrop of severe infighting within the Nixon administration between Henry Kissinger and Secretary of State William Rogers, Rusk wrote another former secretary of state, Dean Acheson, that he had "never felt that [Bundy] was causing problems for the intimate triangle made up of the president, the

Secretary of State and the Secretary of Defense." Glenn Seaborg, the chairman of the Atomic Energy Commission in the 1960s, recalled that unlike Kissinger, Bundy "provided for me a most trustworthy pipeline to the president's desk and mind." McNamara's personal and professional opinion was similarly high: Bundy "had an extraordinary intellect and a deep understanding of [his] role as National Security Adviser." Ball admired Bundy's ability to play "a strong hand in formulating our foreign policy with only a minimum of friction with the State Department." Garthoff thought of Bundy as the most able National Security Adviser he had ever worked with. Unlike the internecine bureaucratic warfare characteristic of the Nixon, Carter, Reagan, and George W. Bush administrations, Bundy for the most part respected the prerogatives of his colleagues and recognized the limits of his own power.[38]

Although Bundy may have, according to Rostow, "executed his mission with extraordinary sensitivity to the prerogatives of the Secretaries of State and Defense," his ability to do so stemmed partly from a convergence of interests with his colleagues. McNamara and Bundy not only liked one another personally, they also usually agreed on policy matters, so there was no need for the Special Assistant to outmaneuver the Secretary of Defense. Rusk also agreed with Bundy most of the time; when he did not, any differences were smoothed over due to Rusk's reticence and reluctance to raise such matters.[39] However, others in the State Department, with whom he did not agree on policy, did not lack a sense of grievance. Chester Bowles, the under secretary until November 1961 and a staunch opponent of intervention in Vietnam, recalled that "inevitably the White House staff under McGeorge Bundy assumed more and more responsibility for questions which should have been handled by the State Department." By fall 1961, Bowles already felt that he had been "poked around" and his role marginalized by Bundy. Bundy later admitted as much to Johnson in 1964: "You'll see that we tried pointedly to sidetrack Bowles," who was by then ambassador to India and still critical of American policy toward Vietnam. One way Bundy sidetracked Bowles was by soliciting Deputy Under Secretary of State U. Alexis Johnson's assistance in establishing an alternate channel of communication, bypassing Bowles, between the White House and State Department. Bundy would sometimes even go around Rusk and Ball to deal directly with midechelon State Department officials. As Bundy later admitted of the relationship between the NSC staff and the State Department, "there was institutional difficulty."[40]

Congressional leaders also came to view Bundy's NSC operation with skepticism. The position of Special Assistant was not subject to the advice and consent of the Senate, and so opponents of the Vietnam War, such as chairman of the Foreign Relations Committee J. William Fulbright, could not compel Bundy, a major architect of American policy, to testify before Congress. They were similarly unable to meet informally with Bundy as often as they wished, as they could with Rusk or McNamara. "I don't want the President's employees to be subject to [congressional] committees," Johnson explained to aide Bill Moyers as escalation mounted in Vietnam in the spring of 1965. "Just like Roosevelt had to keep Harry Hopkins from going down [to Capitol Hill], I've got to keep Bundy from going down." But Hopkins, for the most part, was powerful only because of his personal relationship with FDR. Bundy functioned more like an official bureaucratic and policy heavyweight, and thus he had broader institutional influence than a presidential aide like Hopkins. Frank Valeo, assistant to Senate Majority Leader Mike Mansfield, recalled that the administration arrogantly thought that Bundy was a foreign affairs specialist, particularly on Vietnam, whereas "Congress is supposed to know about other things."[41] The 9/11 Commission found itself in an identical standoff with George W. Bush's National Security Adviser, Condoleezza Rice, although in 2004 public opinion eventually forced Rice to testify.

As much as anything else, it was this concentration of power in the hands of Bundy and the NSC staff that would largely determine American policy in Southeast Asia. During the Kennedy era several officials, particularly from the State Department, argued against a military commitment to South Vietnam. The period between the inauguration of Kennedy in January 1961 and the initiation of the Rolling Thunder bombing campaign in March 1965 was a highly fluid one in which decisions on Vietnam could have favored withdrawal as easily as they did intervention. Holding the balance of decision-making power in the Kennedy and Johnson administrations, Special Assistant Bundy and the NSC staff were largely responsible for the ultimate decision to wage war instead of peace.

CHAPTER 3

Learning to Fear the Bomb: Kennedy's Crises and the Origins of Détente

From the beginning Bundy and Rostow decided not to concentrate their focus on the same issues. Their division of responsibilities was geographical: Bundy turned his attention to events and problems in Europe and the Western Hemisphere; Rostow took the rest. Except during especially acute crises, from 1961 to the first half of 1963 Bundy did not play a great role in formulating U.S. policy toward Vietnam. According to Carl Kaysen, "Bundy did not pay much attention to Vietnam in the early Kennedy years."[1] While Rostow focused exclusively, almost obsessively, on forestalling the communist advance in Southeast Asia, Bundy dealt with the two other perennial crises of the Kennedy presidency, Cuba and Berlin, in addition to policy on nuclear weapons, strategy, and proliferation.

However, Vietnam was never very far from Bundy's mind, and by the first year of the Johnson administration it had come to represent perhaps the single most important part of his worldview. In fact, Bundy was now leading the administration's charge on its two most significant foreign policy challenges—the Vietnam conflict and détente with the Soviet Union—and in his mind the two were inextricably linked. Historians have long argued that drawing the line against communism in Vietnam was a test case for containment.[2] More recently, several historians have identified the year 1963, when the superpowers began their search for détente, as a turning point in the Cold War. The Limited Test Ban Treaty and Kennedy's American University speech marked the initial steps of this new peace process, upon which Lyndon Johnson, Richard Nixon, Gerald Ford, and Jimmy Carter would continue to build. According to this view it is possible to divide the postwar era into the First Cold War (roughly 1946–1963) and the Second Cold War (1979–1989), with a period of relatively peaceful coexistence in between.[3] Curiously, the period of the Vietnam War fits exactly into this interval of détente. Why is it that the era of superpower peace coincided precisely with America's longest war? What can explain this paradox?

While the existing literature does not shed much light on this question, a close examination of Bundy's thinking does. The Cuban and Berlin crises taught him that nuclear weapons had made the Soviet-American rivalry far too dangerous to continue. And yet, if Moscow were to take Washington seriously and not take advantage of détente, the United States had to prove that its patience was not inexhaustible. Thus Vietnam, where nuclear weapons were never a major part of military planning, ironically became a test case for superpower cooperation. Détente, in other words, was predicated upon confrontation. As Bundy later put it, this strategy relied on "a careful balance between our necessary role as the decisive opponent of Soviet expansionism and an equally essential role as the partner of the USSR in the cause of survival without nuclear war."[4] Agreement with communists in Europe and over the danger of nuclear weapons did not necessarily mean agreement with communists in Asia. It was this asymmetrical conception of détente that would help drive America to war in Vietnam.[5]

Nuclear Danger and Survival

Bundy's belief in the use of military power, fear of appeasement, and fervent anticommunist outlook, which shaped his worldview before 1961, continued to influence his thinking on foreign policy during the Kennedy administration. This is not to say that Bundy's behavior predictably followed an established pattern; although the parameters of his worldview were rigidly defined, they were not always rigidly applied in practice. As a pragmatic centrist, Bundy was adept at shifting his stance—often from resolve to reconciliation— to suit, if necessary, newly arisen circumstances. Usually these shifts stemmed from the fear that any conflict between the United States and the Soviet Union would lead to the use of nuclear weapons. Throughout his life, Bundy sustained an aversion to the prospective use of nuclear weapons, and his central beliefs could all be tempered by that fear.

Through a process that historian Wesley T. Wooley has called "learning to fear the bomb," Bundy was echoing, and in large part resurrecting, a sense of insecurity that prevailed for a brief period after World War II.[6] This stance was yet another part of his intellectual inheritance from Henry Stimson, who had advocated the international control of atomic energy shortly after he sanctioned its use in the final days of the war against Japan.[7] Even before the advent of the New Look—fears of which Eisenhower's Secretary of State John Foster Dulles exacerbated with imprudent talk of nuclear brinkmanship—Bundy deplored America's strategic reliance on its nuclear arsenal; only the frequency of his criticisms increased after January 1953. As a member of the Oppenheimer Panel, the rather junior Bundy made an extraordinary appeal to Vannevar Bush, the renowned scientist who had helped organize the Manhattan Project, to push Truman and Acheson to delay testing the hydrogen bomb.[8]

Bundy maintained this position after he became one of the President's top foreign policy advisers. Much of his position was a reaction to the cruel logic of the particular strain of deterrence theory, massive retaliation, upon which the Eisenhower administration had relied. Should even limited fighting break out between the United States or its allies and the Soviet Union, the Pentagon had devised a nuclear response, known as the Single Integrated Operations Plan, or SIOP, that would require total nuclear annihilation. Because the Red Army dwarfed its American and Western European counterparts, the United States would have little choice but to resort to nuclear war by implementing the Pentagon's drastic contingency plan.[9] This was the sort of dire scenario that troubled Bundy most. To him, disproportionate massive retaliation—deploying America's nuclear might in a crisis short of total war with the Soviet Union—was anathema. Shortly after assuming his duties as Special Assistant, Bundy warned Kennedy that the "only plan the United States had for the use of strategic weapons was a massive, total, comprehensive, obliterating attack upon the Soviet Union." The President could only authorize an "attack on everything Red." What worried Bundy just as much were the Eisenhower administration's relaxed and highly devolved procedures for launching nuclear weapons. A "subordinate commander . . . could start the thermonuclear holocaust on his own initiative" if communications broke down, a startled Bundy reported to Kennedy.[10] The Cuban missile crisis in October 1962 merely confirmed Bundy's fear. During an NSC staff meeting the following winter, a colleague noted that "Bundy said in the most serious way that he felt there was really no logic whatever to 'nuclear policy.' What he meant by this was that the military planners who calculate that we will win if only we can kill 100 million Russians while they are killing 30 million Americans are living in total dreamland."[11] Similarly, Bundy was vehemently opposed to the planned civil defense programs in the early 1960s, which were designed to minimize U.S. civilian casualties in the event of nuclear war. Aside from the fact that such programs were costly, fearmongering, and probably ineffective, he worried that they could give an impression that the United States was preparing to withstand a nuclear war, a stance that the Soviet Union could easily mistake for offensive preparation and intention.[12]

Bundy also worried about the effects of nuclear testing on the atmosphere. Working against the Pentagon, he consistently lent his support both to opponents of a missile buildup and to proponents of a ban on atmospheric testing. Bundy's reasons were based upon both reason and emotion: logically, he felt that the United States had a clear advantage in the quality and size of its nuclear arsenal, making a buildup and further testing unnecessary; emotionally, he expressed revulsion at the polluting effects of atmospheric testing.[13] He suggested, for example, that Kennedy's response to the resumption of Soviet nuclear testing in August 1961 should include this uncharacteristically emotional statement: "We share in the worldwide disgust at the irresponsible, militarily senseless, and poisonous Soviet tests." And to Dean Rusk, he described atmospheric testing as "unpalatable." Of course, Moscow's decision to resume its own testing program made Bundy's twin struggles to hold the line on both nuclear testing and a weapons buildup much more difficult, but he carried on. In October 1961, with Kennedy still undecided on whether to resume testing, Bundy implored the president and McNamara not to test unless "required by military necessity to do so."[14] Kaysen supported him in both causes, arguing forcefully throughout 1962 that a new round of tests and an increase in missile production would be unnecessary, and therefore redundant and needlessly provocative; both Bundy and Kaysen, moreover, successfully convinced Kennedy to contradict the national security bureaucracy and propose to the Soviets a mutual pledge not to deploy nuclear weapons in space. Finally, Bundy was also one of the few people in Washington to support British Prime Minister Harold Macmillan's push to maintain a voluntary Anglo-American moratorium on testing. This was, however, one of the few battles within the administration that Bundy and the NSC staff were destined to lose, and on April 25, 1962, the United States resumed atmospheric nuclear testing.[15]

Still, to Bundy nuclear weapons were simply too terrible to use or even contemplate using except as a theoretical abstraction for the most extreme scenarios. Although the resumption of Soviet and American testing had severely undermined the momentum for disarmament, the 1963 Limited Test Ban Treaty, which emerged as one of the few tangible benefits of the Cuban missile crisis, infused the cause with new life. Yet, driven by the Soviets' ambition to match the American arsenal, the unique danger nuclear weapons posed only grew throughout the decade. If left unchecked, it would spiral out of control. In the race for nuclear superiority, Bundy believed that the superpowers were only heading for catastrophe. It is thus unsurprising that Bundy continued to push for disarmament in the Johnson administration. Presiding over his first NSC meeting as president, Johnson read a short, powerful statement drafted by Bundy: "The greatest single requirement is that we find a way to ensure the survival of civilization in the nuclear age. A nuclear war would be the death of all our hopes and it is our task to see that it does not happen."[16] That Bundy wanted the President to read such a vague and seemingly naive policy statement is testament to his sincerity and conviction. Indeed, nuclear disarmament was a banner he would carry for the rest of his life. Long after he had left government service, Bundy's opposition to nuclear weapons expanded to include a call for the massive reduction, if not virtual elimination, of nuclear arms, and an American pledge to a policy of "no first-use." Nuclear arms, he wrote in his 1987 survey of the atomic age, "should be designed for survivable sufficiency, since nothing more can be achieved, and since the attempt to get more will only arouse political fear and disturbing reply; that is the lesson of American overarmament in the fifties and sixties . . . and Soviet overarmament thereafter."[17] Not long before he died, Bundy expressed inchoate doubts about the decision to use the atomic bomb against Japan in 1945, a decision on which he had spent much time and energy defending as Stimson's protégé and ghostwriter.[18] Throughout his life, nuclear arms control was probably the issue Bundy felt most passionately about.

Nonetheless, nuclear danger did not cancel out the basic tenets of Bundy's worldview; it simply softened their application. In foreign policy he still strove for stability through strength. With his appreciation of the hard realities of world politics, Bundy believed that nuclear weapons had helped to keep the peace during the Cold War. Rather than superiority, he advocated sufficiency and welcomed parity with the Soviet Union. Each side had guaranteed that nuclear war would be equally damaging on a previously unimaginable scale and thus futile. This was the premise behind the doctrine of mutual assured destruction, to which Bundy fully subscribed: neither side would wage war for fear of provoking a catastrophic reprisal; and because both sides realized this fact, and realized that nuclear weapons maintained a balance of terror, neither would ever completely relinquish its nuclear arsenal. In the words of one scholar, Bundy belonged to the "punitive retaliation school," although Bundy fervently hoped such measures would never be necessary.[19] To prevent war he thought it wise to maintain some semblance of a nuclear option. Thus he was not inconsistent when he recommended in 1962 that the United States maintain its top secret laboratory testing even as he advocated an atmospheric test ban. The "steps toward peace rest upon adequate readiness for defense, at every level of force," he told an audience at the 1963 World Affairs Conference in Albany. "The indispensable connection between military strength and the maintenance of peace is obvious—and frequently forgotten." In 1964, drawing upon one of the central lessons of the Cuban missile crisis, Bundy told a visiting delegation of generals from Latin America that the "first requirement for the defense of the non-communist world is and has been throughout the nuclear age that there should be adequate strategic forces at the disposal of the United States and its friends." Peace through strength was a theme which could be expanded even to include nuclear weapons. "It seems to me wholly plain," he wrote in 1969, "that a credible strategic nuclear deterrent is indispensable to the peace, and for that reason no task is more clearly indispensable than that of maintaining and protecting such a force."[20] For Bundy a sensible nuclear policy, based upon deterrence rather than the hysteria of an unlimited arms race, was an essential component of foreign policy. The tough part was maintaining the balance between deterrence and prudence.

The Chinese Conundrum

What Bundy feared most, aside from the actual outbreak of war, was the proliferation of nuclear arms, particularly to those countries that behaved threateningly and erratically. In this regard it was the People's Republic of China that posed the most serious challenge to the stability of the Cold War and the gravest threat to American interests in Asia. Despite Bundy's subsequent claims to the contrary, the Kennedy administration seriously contemplated the use of preventive air strikes to knock out the Chinese nuclear project.[21] In fact, it was Bundy who most fervently promoted this option and coordinated its planning. As he weighed the conundrum, the risk of losing control of the Soviet-American nuclear balance far outweighed the risks of military action against China. Losing control would lead to Bundy's worst nightmare: nuclear anarchy.

Initially the Kennedy administration hoped that a multilateral treaty banning the atmospheric testing of nuclear weapons, which Bundy enthusiastically supported, would restrict or perhaps even destroy China's efforts to become a nuclear power. This is how the Chinese themselves perceived the initiative, and as a result they refused to participate. Although a test ban treaty would be politically important and symbolically powerful, there would be no way to force reluctant countries to sign or prevent nonsignatories from testing. In this sense the obstinacy of France, which also refused to participate, posed as much of a problem as China. Thus the Limited Test Ban Treaty, signed in July 1963 by Britain, the United States, and the Soviet Union, could not deflect China from its drive to acquire its own independent nuclear capability.[22]

While the Kennedy administration found it useful to work with the Kremlin toward a more stable Cold War order, it did not see China in quite the same light. The Chinese, after all, were believed to be ultimately behind the Vietnamese communist insurgency. More ominously, Beijing had rejected the diplomacy of the treaty and seemed intent on procuring its own nuclear weapons. Among Kennedy's foreign policy advisers, Bundy sensed the Chinese threat—particularly one armed with nuclear weapons—perhaps more acutely than anyone else. "A Red China nuclear presence," he warned Kennedy in November 1962, "is the greatest single threat to the status quo over the next few years." Shortly after the new year, he impressed upon Director of Central Intelligence McCone that a successful Chinese nuclear test "was probably the most serious problem facing that world today." Nuclear weapons "in the hands of the Chinese Communists," he declared, "would so upset the world political scene it would be intolerable to the United States and to the West." Especially after the Chinese had successfully tested a nuclear device in October 1964, China seemed to pose the most dangerous threat to American security. Although Moscow was interested in establishing peaceful relations with the West, Beijing was not; its support of the communist insurgency in Vietnam provided proof of its hostile ambition. "Communist China is quite a different problem" than the Soviet Union, he told Lyndon Johnson, "and both her nuclear explosion and her aggressive attitudes toward her neighbors make her a problem for all peaceful people."[23]

The prospect of a nuclear-armed China combined Bundy's two worst fears of expansionist communism and nuclear proliferation. That Beijing seemed to represent an even more radical strain of communism made the threat even greater. Drastic situations required drastic measures, and at the time such measures seemed as feasible as they were desirable. The Chinese had shown that they could not be constrained diplomatically and thus peacefully, and until the summer of 1964 it was not clear that a successful Chinese test was imminent. Given these circumstances, and given the apparently dire nature of the threat, it is not surprising that Bundy should countenance the use of armed force to prevent, or at the very least delay, the Chinese nuclear threat from materializing. Bundy's belief in the uses of military might, his unwillingness to compromise under pressure, and his anticommunism were not yet restrained by the prospect of Chinese nuclear retaliation. In other words his instincts, if left unchecked by the threat of nuclear war, almost always initially favored a military response. It was a pattern of advice that emerged during the crises in Cuba and Berlin, but China's nuclear ambitions troubled him the most; in Bundy's eyes they presented a threat that warranted a military response. As one authoritative study has noted, "Bundy was in fact the point man in countering the Chinese nuclear effort."[24]

Over a period of eighteen months, from the spring of 1963 to the fall of 1964, Bundy coordinated and managed a contingency plan to attack China's nuclear facilities. As his warning about China to Johnson demonstrates, Bundy's view of the Cold War had begun to shift as evidence of the Sino-Soviet split unfolded before Western eyes: no longer was the Soviet Union an implacable enemy determined to bury capitalism; and in its place stood the People's Republic of China. While it seemed possible to work with the Soviets, thanks to the moment of clarity provided by the Cuban missile crisis and the awkward efforts at cooperation that followed, the same could not be said of the Chinese. In a meeting with the British Foreign Minister at the end of 1962, Bundy called China's nuclear ambitions "the most dangerous element" and, given the incipient détente and Sino-Soviet split, it was "increasingly clear" that the Americans and Soviets "had a common interest in this field."[25] But even considering this new framework, Bundy's efforts to enlist the Soviets in a preventive strike against China's nuclear project are startling. On May 17, 1963, over the course of lunch with the Soviet Ambassador to Washington, Anatoly Dobrynin, Bundy hinted that the United States and the Soviet Union shared the Chinese threat. The "nuclear posture of Communist China must be a matter of real common interest to us," he told Dobrynin. In case Dobrynin missed the point, Bundy also stressed that President Kennedy believed "that this problem was one on which it would be useful to have a quite private and serious exchange of views." Dobrynin ignored the subject altogether and preferred to discuss the more immediate problem of nuclear weapons in Europe. Four months later Bundy found a more receptive audience when he told Chiang Ching-kuo, a Taiwanese Army general who also happened to be Chiang Kai-shek's son, that the "United States is very interested in whether something could be planned" militarily to damage China's nuclear installations.[26]

However, not everyone in Washington shared Bundy's alarm. Simultaneously to Bundy's efforts to push for a military operation, the Policy Planning Council of the State Department deliberated the Chinese problem and decided that it was not much of a problem at all. In two important papers written in the fall of 1962 Robert H. Johnson, formerly under Bundy's supervision on the NSC staff, concluded that even if China acquired a nuclear weapons capability it would not affect Asian security for many years; in the meantime nuclear arms would actually make the Chinese more cautious. Underpinning Johnson's analysis was the preponderance of American military strength in the region, particularly when compared directly to China's glaring weakness and insufficiency. Moreover, the likelihood of a complete military success was slim and the risk of provoking considerable international outrage, and thus incurring significant geopolitical damage, was high. Rostow, who had left the NSC staff as deputy Special Assistant to head the Policy Planning Council, and Dean Rusk both agreed with Johnson. More surprisingly, so did Robert W. Komer, a mainstay of the NSC staff during Bundy's tenure. Despite finding himself in the minority (which, as we shall see regarding Cuba and Berlin, was not uncommon), Bundy continued to argue the case for a preventive strike against China. Significantly, aside from the president himself, Bundy's main ally was the NSC staffer for Vietnam policy, Michael V. Forrestal. Bundy and Forrestal believed China to be the driving force behind the Vietnamese communists' war with Saigon.[27]

Unable to convince his colleagues in the Kennedy administration, in the summer of 1964 Bundy was forced to abandon the idea of a preventive strike after Lyndon Johnson showed no great interest in it and a Chinese test appeared to be increasingly imminent. After sounding out a noncommittal Dobrynin one last time in September, Bundy resigned himself to the fact that China was about to join the most exclusive club in world politics.[28] Although his efforts were unsuccessful, they are enormously instructive: Bundy's first inclination was to resort to military force, even in a situation which posed great military and political risk; his view of Asian communism, which he considered much more foreign than the Soviets' brand, was decidedly alarmist; and, finally, the fear that drove this alarmist view was the threat posed by nuclear weapons.

The Cuban Crises

Although Bundy's caution regarding nuclear weapons was not initially evident in his approach to communist Cuba, his alarm and aggressiveness regarding China were. Like China, Cuba appeared to pose a serious threat to American security. Since overthrowing the corrupt and repressive Fulgencio Batista in January 1959, the communist-dominated regime of Fidel Castro had been, in Senator J. William Fulbright's vivid phrase, "a thorn in the flesh" of the United States. But while Fulbright was cautious about how to deal with Castro, Bundy was not. Even before joining the Kennedy administration, Bundy told students at Harvard that communist Cuba posed a challenge not only to American interests and security, but also to the political independence of the whole of Latin America. Kennedy agreed and, within three months of becoming president, acted. The Eisenhower administration had handed down a scheme to invade Cuba by proxy—using over a thousand disgruntled Cuban exiles backed by American support, training, and materiel—with the ultimate goal of removing Castro from power. The result was the failed Bay of Pigs invasion, an embarrassment for Kennedy personally and the United States geopolitically.[29]

Bundy had supported the invasion in the belief that the United States must deal Castro a decisive blow. The previous February, Bundy's initial reluctance to endorse the plan stemmed not from qualms about its wisdom, necessity, or morality, but from an apprehension that in its present conception the invasion would probably not succeed. He nonetheless ensured that Kennedy read the details for the operation, which had been drawn up by Bundy's old economics instructor at Yale, CIA Deputy Director of Plans Richard M. Bissell. In March, after Bissell and the CIA had tinkered with the original plan, Bundy became a keen supporter. Bissell, he told Kennedy, had "done a remarkable job of reframing the landing plan so as to make it unspectacular and quiet, and plausibly Cuban in its essentials . . . My own belief is that this air battle has to come sooner or later, and that the longer we put it off, the harder it will be. Castro's Air Force is currently his Achilles' heel, but he is making drastic efforts to strengthen it with Russian planes and Russian-trained pilots." He concluded that "I have been a skeptic about Bissell's operation, but now I think we are on the edge of a good answer." According to journalist Stewart Alsop, Bundy met with Bissell and approved the plan the day before the invasion. Clearly, Bundy had come to feel strongly about removing Castro and would not tolerate internal dissent. He went so far as to banish Richard Good-win, the pugnacious Kennedy aide and speechwriter who opposed the invasion, from White House meetings on Cuba.[30]

As Kennedy, Bundy, and the rest of the world discovered on April 17, Bissell and the CIA did not in fact have a "good answer" to the Castro regime. The poorly trained, ill-equipped invasion force of exiles was no match for the Cuban army. The landings were no secret, and Castro was able to respond quickly and effectively. The Cuban police had also preemptively killed any chance of a popular uprising, crucial to the CIA plan, by imprisoning potential dissenters. The invasion had no chance of succeeding when Kennedy decided not to authorize a second air strike that would destroy what remained of the Cuban Air Force. At the moment of decision, Bundy urged the president to reconsider. "In my own judgment," he wrote, "the right course now is to eliminate the Castro air force, by neutrally-painted U.S. planes if necessary, and then let the battle go its way."[31]

Kennedy did not heed the advice and instead braced his administration to weather a torrent of international criticism. But within the White House, Bundy remained unmoved and unrepentant. The Bay of Pigs incident, he remarked to his staff, was merely "a brick through the window" that only proved that the Cubans had learned more from the 1954 CIA-orchestrated overthrow of Guatemalan President Jacobo Arbenz than the Americans had. The goal of removing Castro was still imperative. A month after the invasion and shortly after an interagency task force on Cuba had reached its findings, Bundy presented Kennedy with a comprehensive plan to apply various forms of political, economic, and military pressure to the Castro regime. The United States should invade Cuba if at all provoked, he advised, or if the Soviets established a military installation on the island. Prophetically, he also recommended that "emergency and long-range plans should be developed promptly for anti-Communist intervention in the event of crises in Haiti or the Dominican Republic." Bundy's recommendations to Kennedy did not include covert operations against Cuba itself, but after the creation of Operation Mongoose—the top-secret campaign of sabotage and subversion in Cuba, including the possibility of assassinating Castro—he joined its supervisory committee, the cryptically named "Special Group, Augmented," and offered to serve as its chairman. As long as the "noise level" was low enough that the United States would not be implicated and the USSR would not retaliate against West Berlin, Bundy supported covert operations against Cuba.[32]

The Bay of Pigs incident and Operation Mongoose campaign, combined with the USSR's strategic inferiority to the United States, led Soviet leader Nikita Khrushchev secretly to place nuclear missiles on the island of Cuba in the summer and fall of 1962. Once the missiles were operational, Khrushchev believed, the Soviet nuclear deterrent would be twofold: it would help alleviate the nuclear imbalance, numerically and psychologically, between the superpowers and thus constrain the American strategic advantage; and, just as important, it would prevent the United States from invading Cuba or seeking to depose Castro. In October the Kennedy administration's discovery of the Soviet missile deployment and its decision to implement a naval quarantine around Cuba brought the Americans and the Soviets to the edge of nuclear war. Kennedy's eventual choice of a quarantine—a diplomatic euphemism for a blockade—was not an easy one. Many of his advisers, most notably the Joint Chiefs of Staff and their chairman, General Maxwell Taylor, Secretary of the Treasury C. Douglas Dillon, and Dean Acheson called on the President to launch a quick and decisive air strike against the Soviet missile installations in Cuba.[33]

Bundy also favored an air strike.[34] On October 16, the same day he notified Kennedy of the missiles' existence, Bundy spoke to the newly established Executive Committee of the NSC (ExComm) to support a military solution. The "political advantages are very strong, it seems to me, of the small strike" rather than a full-scale invasion, he told the President. He also suggested, in addition to an air strike, that the U.S. Navy mine Cuban harbors and that the military and the CIA continue various other forms of sabotage against the Castro regime. Later, with the crisis nearing its climax, Bundy tossed and turned over the crisis in the course of a sleepless night. "A blockade would not remove the missiles," he told the ExComm the following morning. "Something more would be needed to get the missiles out of Cuba . . . An air strike would be quick and would take out the bases in a clean surgical operation." Fearful of getting lured into inconclusive negotiations while the Soviets and Cubans worked to make the missiles operational, he "favored decisive action with its advantages of surprise and confronting the world with a fait accompli." When Attorney General Robert Kennedy remarked that what Bundy was recommending amounted to a Pearl Harbor in reverse, Bundy retorted that "this was very well but a blockade would not eliminate the bases; an air strike would." After this exchange, the ExComm divided roughly in half between those who favored the blockade and those who favored a military solution; those who recommended the latter coalesced around Bundy in a group that bore his name. Kennedy rejected Bundy's advice and instead opted to impose the quarantine. Shortly before the president arrived at this decision, Bundy changed his position and recommended against the air strike. He did, however, also continue to recommend against negotiations and maintain that an air strike was the only possible solution if the Kremlin did not accede quickly to the American ultimatum.[35]

The United States and the Soviet Union settled the Cuban missile crisis peacefully. In return for withdrawing the offending missiles, Khrushchev received a public American declaration not to invade Cuba and a private assurance that U.S. nuclear-tipped Jupiter missiles in Turkey would be removed. Additionally, Kennedy terminated Operation Mongoose in December, a decision with which Bundy concurred. But with Soviet nuclear weapons gone from Cuba, Bundy nonetheless wanted to maintain pressure on Castro's regime, which was, if anything, more of a threat than before the crisis. Nuclear danger made cooperation with the USSR necessary, but the new détente did not necessarily include Cuba. "We have to live on the same world with the Soviet Union," he stressed, "but we do not have to accept Communist subversion in this hemisphere." This meant advocating a series of measures designed to apply "gradual pressure . . . so that Castro could be made to confront a decisive choice between his overthrow and an accommodation on terms acceptable to us."[36] And yet, chastened by the crisis, his tone also changed. The pressure he sought to apply to Castro was more gradual and relatively noninvasive than Mongoose had been. Eventually, he abandoned the goal of overthrowing Castro altogether.

Berlin

Cuba was not the only crisis that faced the Kennedy administration in its first year in office, nor did it present the only potential nuclear confrontation between the United States and the Soviet Union. The conflict over the city of Berlin was as heated and intractable as that over Cuba, but more complicated. The partition of Berlin into a zone of Western influence (itself divided among the United States, Britain, and France) and a zone of Soviet influence was intended to be temporary when it came into existence in 1945. Cold War tensions forestalled a permanent, official settlement, preventing the unification of the German capital and its absorption into East Germany. West Berlin thus became a potent symbol of American and West European resolve, a process that had been facilitated by the unsuccessful Soviet blockade of the city in 1948–1949. Khrushchev began threatening to act against West Berlin in 1958;

he repeated those threats with renewed urgency in 1961. By signing a bilateral peace agreement with East Germany, as Khrushchev warned he would do, the Soviet Union would transfer responsibility for access to West Berlin to the more irascible and unpredictable leadership of East Germany. Khrushchev had not done so by 1961 because such a move was understood by both sides to be a possible prelude to war.[37]

Initially, as with Cuba, Bundy recommended a tough, unyielding stance on Berlin. In April 1961 Kennedy asked Acheson, who had presided over the original division of Berlin as Truman's under secretary and then secretary of state, for his views. Acheson responded with a memo that, with characteristic alacrity, called for a firm, militant posture. Bundy passed the memo on to the president, describing it as "first-rate." Attempts "to negotiate this problem out of existence have failed in the past," he added forcefully. "Berlin is no place for compromise, and our general friendliness and eagerness for improvement on many other points really requires strength here in order to be rightly understood." Spurred by Acheson, Bundy pressed the Pentagon to devise scenarios for U.S. military action to relieve Berlin, including a naval blockade of Eastern Europe, "air harassment," and the use of ground troops. Acheson prepared another, lengthier report on the growing crisis. Aside from the increased word count, he also bolstered the toughness of his rhetoric and stated that Berlin was worth defending to the point of war. Bundy again endorsed Acheson's recommendations, although this time with less enthusiasm. At this point in the crisis, Bundy was certain that if the crisis deteriorated the Kennedy administration would have to defend the U.S. position with force. In June, he advised Kennedy to make "serious military preparations" in tandem with current diplomatic initiatives; he repeated the advice a month later, and repeated it again in December during a meeting with wary Canadian diplomats. And although his attention was not focused on events in Europe, Rostow supported Bundy's efforts to promote vigilance over Berlin. Rostow's strategy to seize the initiative was typically audacious. His goal was to "make Mr. Khrushchev share the burden of making sacrifices to avoid nuclear war." According to Rostow, this meant sending a "divisional probe . . . to take and hold a piece of territory in East Germany that Khrushchev may not want to lose" and placing tactical nuclear weapons in Berlin "at an appropriate tense moment."[38]

The Soviets decided in August to alleviate the pressure by blocking—literally, first with a barbed-wire fence and then a concrete wall—East Berliners from fleeing westward, which was the East Germans' immediate source of concern. Privately, Bundy accepted the building of the Berlin Wall as a step toward defusing tensions. But publicly, and in discussions with American allies, his view remained firm. Shortly after the construction of the wall, Canadian Ambassador to Washington Arnold Heeney joined Bundy and Rusk for dinner and was branded an "appeaser" for articulating his view (and that of the Canadian government) that quadripartite negotiations among the United States, Britain, France, and the Soviet Union would best settle the crisis. Almost exactly a year later, with still no treaty between the Soviets and the Western powers, Bundy told Ted Sorensen, Kennedy's main speechwriter, to tell Dobrynin that "it would be a most dangerous business to confuse our calmness and good manners with any weakening of determination whatsoever. Any move against our vital interests in Berlin will be met by appropriate, prompt, and energetic responses, and no one can doubt the dangers which such activity would imply for all concerned." For Bundy it was essential that that United States avoid appearing weak or irresolute in the face of communist pressure and provocation.[39]

There was more to Bundy's position, however, than his uncompromising language suggests. Unlike many of his cold warrior contemporaries, he certainly did not see the crisis as an opportunity to roll back the Iron Curtain, starting with East Germany. Rather than an American capitulation to Soviet aggression, he viewed the wall itself as an unsightly, but much needed, panacea. The Berlin Wall, he wrote to Kennedy as it was being built, was something the Soviets "have had the power to do," it was something "they were bound to do sooner or later," and, since it was "bound to happen, it is as well to have it happen early, as *their* doing and *their* responsibility." The key issue, Bundy thought, was not whether Berlin should be reunited under noncommunist rule, but whether West Berlin would remain accessible to the West. It is thus unsurprising that it was Bundy who was the *New York Times*'s "highly qualified" anonymous source who argued that only "extreme counter-measures" would bring down the wall. "These would probably lead to war," Bundy told *Times* journalist Max Frankel, "and are not justified so long as the West is assured access to West Berlin."[40]

Despite his admonition that Berlin was "no place for compromise," Bundy did not unequivocally preclude any negotiations with the Soviets. Although he believed that "firmness on allied access to Berlin is indeed fundamental," he also conceded that "a willingness to hear the Soviet argument on other problems will not be harmful" as long as the Soviets and East Germans realized that the United States was not "feeble on Berlin itself." Above all, it was vital to appear strong without appearing reckless. Arguing against the prevailing wisdom among America's allies and within the administration itself, he proposed that the United States enter directly into bilateral talks with the USSR over Berlin. The Canadian Embassy in Washington, which in 1961 had carefully made note of Bundy's confrontational stance, reported back to Ottawa in February 1963 that the Special Assistant was in the mood for détente. H. Basil Robinson, the chargé d'affaires at the embassy, observed that Bundy "thought it unwise to say categorically that the West must for all time be intractably and resolutely against any roll back of Soviet and Western forces from central Europe. The general import of his remarks was that in the context of a broad East-West settlement a certain amount of thinning out of forces, possibly as part of a disarmament agreement, might be desirable."[41] This was a view of the Cold War that was the polar opposite of what Bundy had espoused a year earlier. This new, conciliatory tone also ran counter to the basic premises of flexible response. What could inspire such a conversion?

Détente through Confrontation

From his reaction to the crises over Berlin and Cuba, it is clear that a fear of nuclear war triggered Bundy's oscillation between détente and confrontation. In each case, Bundy's initial aggressiveness gave way to caution once the risk of nuclear war appeared. During the Berlin crisis, for example, Acheson's June 1961 report, which Bundy had found somewhat troubling, contained a provocative section entitled: "The Decision to Resort to Nuclear War, if Necessary." Conversely, Acheson's earlier April report, which Bundy had praised so highly, did not even address the nuclear question. The June memo seems to have been something of a turning point for Bundy, and he subsequently expressed his disagreement with Acheson's brinkmanship in a meeting with Kennedy and Rusk.[42] Critically, although Rostow was not afraid to play nuclear chicken, others on the NSC staff were. Kaysen provided Bundy with U.S. casualty estimates after a Soviet nuclear strike that ranged alarmingly from 10 million to 100 million. Consultant Henry Kissinger, who split his time between the White House and Harvard during the 1961 crisis, alerted Bundy to the fact that Kennedy had to make decisions about nuclear weapons "in the abstract." Kissinger's main worry was that the Pentagon had not revised the SIOP to avoid an automatic nuclear exchange. "As things stand now," he warned Bundy, "I fear that the military will try to force the President's hand during a crisis." Bundy promptly relayed these concerns. The "current strategic war plan is dangerously rigid," he wrote Kennedy after reading his staff's memoranda, "and, if continued without amendment, may leave you very little choice as to how you face the moment of thermonuclear truth." A week later, both Kissinger and Arthur Schlesinger urged Bundy to recommend that Kennedy leave Khrushchev an "escape hatch" that would lead to diplomatic negotiations over Berlin. When the Berlin crisis intensified again in 1962, Bundy reacted swiftly to block JCS contingency planning that would, if implemented, lead inexorably to a nuclear exchange with the USSR. In addition to his desire to prevent nuclear war, Bundy realized that within the decade the Soviet Union would be able to match the U.S. nuclear arsenal, and he believed that it was better to negotiate from strength in 1961 than from parity at the end of the decade.[43]

This pattern repeated itself in the aftermath of the Cuban missile crisis, which brought the world to the edge of a nuclear abyss. This was precisely the type of situation that Bundy wanted to avoid in the future at almost any cost. By the fall of 1963, after the futility of sabotage operations and the inevitability of Castro's continued rule became obvious, Bundy helped to spearhead efforts to arrive at a rapprochement between Castro and the Kennedy administration. The initiative, led by William Attwood of the State Department, was put "on ice" by a cautious President Johnson after the Kennedy assassination. With Castro increasingly secure, the United States would have to use military force openly to bring about change in Cuba. By 1963 this would virtually guarantee a conflict between the United States and the Soviet Union. Bundy realized that continued pressure on Castro was as dangerous as it was futile.[44]

These were the circumstances in which Bundy underwent the unlikely conversion from arch cold warrior to advocate for peaceful coexistence. But in regions of the world that were still being contested by the superpowers, and where the threat of nuclear danger did not really exist, such as Southeast Asia, Bundy maintained a position of unmovable determination as expressed through confrontation. Interestingly, Bundy's view of easing tensions with the Soviet Union in the early 1960s resembled the Soviets' own conception of détente in the 1970s—peaceful competition rather than peaceful coopera-tion. Bundy sought, in other words, a *détente* (easing of tensions) rather than an *entente* (positive, close, and cooperative relations).[45] This was a two-tiered approach to détente, with limited cooperation on one level and unfettered competition on another. Marcus Raskin, a specialist in nuclear deterrence theory on the NSC staff whom Bundy considered the "Oppenheimer of the administration," identified the crux of the problem as early as April 1961.

"The policy of military deterrence has caused us to lose the initiative in foreign policy," Raskin wrote to Bundy. "We are chained because of the sheer power which we possess, and yet we appear muscle bound before the rest of the world." The answer was not to strengthen America's nuclear capability but to promote détente through "unilateral acts of a *tension reducing nature.*" Raskin realized that in doing so, the United States would place itself "on the horns of a serious dilemma," one that would trouble Bundy into the era of the Johnson presidency. Unchecked competition with the Soviet Union would only risk the outbreak of nuclear war. "On the other hand," Raskin noted, "we cannot appear as the 'paper tiger' without power, prestige, and purpose in world politics."[46] Although Bundy could not approve of unilateral initiatives that could leave the United States dangerously exposed, he did recognize that the nuclear-tipped Cold War could not continue unmitigated at the superpower level. The trick was to remove the United States from the horns of Raskin's serious dilemma, and from 1963 to 1965 doing so became Bundy's main priority. The key was to ease tensions with Moscow while not appearing weak to communists around the world.

After the Cuban missile crisis, Bundy became one of the Kennedy administration's most ardent proponents of détente. Aside from his support for a test ban treaty, he also played a large role in drafting President Kennedy's famous "peace speech" at American University in June 1963. Later he compared Kennedy's speech at American with another of his mentors who had been shaken by his glimpse into the nuclear abyss and who had responded with a call for Soviet-American cooperation and control to reduce nuclear tension. "There is indeed a close and direct connection," Bundy reflected, "between the thinking of Henry Stimson in September 1945 and that of John F. Kennedy in the spring of 1963, and it was the thinking of true statesmanship in both cases."[47]

But where foreign policy matters did not turn on the threat of nuclear annihilation, as was the case in Southeast Asia, Bundy thought it essential that the United States stand fast. Embracing negotiations with the Soviet Union while simultaneously refusing equivocation elsewhere could, Bundy hoped, preserve American credibility. In this fashion he was able to overcome Raskin's dilemma by reconciling the need to preserve peace with the equally pressing need to ensure American security. This was precisely the advice he gave Johnson in January 1964, as the new administration began to think about its relations with Moscow. Bundy warned that although progress toward peace had begun under Kennedy, the toughest challenges lay in the immediate future. The "next steps toward peace," he believed, would require bold multilateral initiatives, especially in Europe, in addition to the existing unilateral and bilateral projects with the USSR. But other areas, such as Vietnam, still needed "constant attention . . . where we continue to oppose Communist subversion." For Bundy, détente with the Soviet Union did not include vital, contested, nonnuclear terrain such as South Vietnam. As he wrote in a passage for a suggested 1965 presidential address, the United States "continues to believe that it is both possible and necessary for all the great powers of the world to live in peace, in this age of weapons of extraordinary danger and power . . . But anyone who asks us to accept aggression as the price of lowered tension is wasting his time."[48]

Robert Komer agreed and, toward the end of 1964, came independently to the same conclusion. Komer was the NSC staff's jack-of-all-trades: his regional responsibilities included policy toward the Near and Middle East, Africa, Central and South Asia, Southeast Asia (especially Indonesia), and China. These myriad geopolitical specialties often centered on the People's Republic of China, and it was toward this country that he saw the advantages to a two-tiered system of détente. His principal aim was to use U.S. policy in Vietnam as a means to include China in the Soviet-American club of peaceful coexistence. "If we take a tougher stance in VN [Vietnam]," Komer wrote Bundy, "it can hardly be taken as a sign of undue weakness to be flexible" on China. Such an approach "would demonstrate that while we were determined to resist Communist aggression, we were simultaneously prepared to deal with the ChiComs [Chinese Communists] whenever there was some peaceful purpose to be served." Komer was essentially urging the United States to use its Vietnam policy as a means to bring about a rapprochement with the entire Sino-Soviet bloc. "In effect," he explained to Bundy, "I see increased pressure in Vietnam as permitting greater flexibility" toward China.[49]

It was an audacious strategy, one that Richard Nixon and Henry Kissinger would deploy seven years later with great fanfare and some success, but also one that was too ambitious and risky at the time. However, conceptually it was very much consistent with Bundy's own visions of relations with the communist world, although Bundy had not yet thought to extend his basically Soviet-American approach to include the Chinese. The impetus for Komer's gambit toward China, moreover, was doubtless the same as Bundy's toward the Soviet Union: nuclear weapons and the prospect of nuclear war. As a result of its first successful nuclear test in October 1964, China's stature as a great power underwent a fundamental transformation. To Komer the People's Republic of China could no longer be treated as before; the United States would have to respect its new power and assume that a future crisis would have the potential to become a nuclear standoff. Nuclear weapons changed the rules in Komer's mind just as they had done for Bundy's.

But China, for various reasons, would have to wait. Bundy's asymmetrical view of the Cold War, of détente with the Soviets on one level and escalated tension with Asian communists on another, hinged on the struggle in South Vietnam. It was by the mid-1960s the only region of the world where an American-sponsored state was in grave and constant danger of being politically subsumed, even obliterated, by a communist rival. It was also the one area of the world where the United States had explicitly and repeatedly staked its prestige on the fortunes of a beleaguered ally whose interest to America was somewhat peripheral and thus largely symbolic. And, perhaps most important to Bundy, it was a rare Cold War battleground where nuclear weapons were still largely irrelevant. The conflict in Vietnam never really threatened to explode into a nuclear exchange. To be sure, this program required a delicate balancing act. As they prepared for the 1965 State of the Union address, Bundy informed Richard Goodwin that a

> second double threat relates to the Communists. I think we should be strategically peace loving, and tactically pretty sharp. We must not give the Communists the idea that by calling off their direct threat to us they can get a free license everywhere else, nor conversely should we allow our necessary toughness against subversion to turn us away from bridge-building and cultural relations and efforts for arms control and all the rest. This is subtle but it is a part of the Kennedy-Johnson policy which very much needs reaffirmation.[50]

The obvious pivot upon which Bundy's strategy would turn was South Vietnam. If noncommunist rule in Saigon collapsed, a main pillar of American determination would follow. Failure in Indochina would thus remove the new foundations of détente. South Vietnam did indeed represent the ultimate domino.

Bundy's structure of asymmetrical détente formed the basis of the Johnson administration's grand strategy, although it was never articulated as such. This two-tiered approach, however, did not function as Bundy thought it would. It simply did not work. A relaxation of tensions with Moscow was actually incompatible with an escalation of hostilities with Hanoi; instead of the latter reinforcing the former, as Bundy hoped, they were mutually exclusive. In fact waging war in Vietnam ruined any real chance of détente with the Soviet Union. Because of the Sino-Soviet split, even had the Soviets wanted to they could never completely separate their relations with the United States from their obligations to the Vietnamese communists. What the Vietnam War did was apply pressure to the Soviet-American relationship at the very moment both parties sought to reduce such pressures. As Dobrynin recalled years later, by 1966 "it became difficult to prevent Vietnam from impairing Soviet-American relations."[51]

Even more worrying for the United States was that when détente did become official policy in both Washington and Moscow in the early 1970s, it had the opposite effect that Bundy had intended: rather than discouraging communist expansion in the developing world by defeating communist guerrillas and deterring the Soviets, détente may have stimulated, even encouraged, Soviet support for their allies in the developing world. As early as 1965 Yuri Andropov predicted that "the future competition with the United States will take place not in Europe, and not in the Atlantic Ocean. It will take place in Africa, and in Latin America. We will compete for every piece of land, for every country."[52] A decade later, Soviet Politburo member Andrei P. Kirilenko boasted that "détente, warding off the threat of nuclear war for mankind and responsive to the most profound aspirations of all peoples, is also creating favorable conditions for the struggle for national liberation and social progress."[53] Moreover, when Soviet-American competition emerged in peripheral countries, such as Vietnam and Angola, détente was ill-suited to remedy the superpowers' concerns or alleviate their tension. During the October 1973 Arab-Israeli war Kissinger himself conceded privately to Dobrynin that "détente had its limits" when addressing regional issues.[54] But all these events were to come. In 1963 and 1964, before the Vietnamese civil conflict had degenerated into America's war, Bundy believed that the best way to achieve and maintain peace between the superpowers was to hold the line in Vietnam.

CHAPTER 4

The Hawk: Rostow
and the First Attempt
at Americanization

Before becoming Deputy Special Assistant for National Security Affairs in January 1961, Walt Whitman Rostow had been a successful academic in economic history at the Massachusetts Institute of Technology. With a sterling curriculum vitae and esteemed reputation, Rostow was one of the Kennedy administration's brightest intellectual stars. He was a product of Yale at the undergraduate and doctoral levels and a Rhodes Scholar to Oxford; prior to settling at MIT in the 1950s, he had taught at Cambridge, Oxford, and Columbia universities. A prolific writer, he had authored several influential books, particularly on the economic development of modern Britain, his initial area of specialization. Like his fellow New Frontiersmen McGeorge Bundy, John Kenneth Galbraith, Carl Kaysen, Jerome Wiesner, Lucian W. Pye, Lincoln Gordon, and Arthur Schlesinger (all from either Harvard or MIT), Rostow made a smooth transition from the academy to the administration. And like Bundy and Schlesinger, Rostow brought to the White House much experience in advising previous administrations, most notably his work on Eisenhower's 1955 Open Skies proposal.

By the time he succeeded Bundy as Special Assistant in 1966, Rostow had earned notoriety as a hard-line anticommunist (although, as his fervent support for massive amounts of foreign assistance showed, he was neither a political nor an economic conservative). His belief that "the Soviet government is committed to strive in the direction of world hegemony for Communism," and that communist movements throughout the world were generally subservient to Moscow, consistently shaped his worldview and guided his policy recommendations.[1] As Deputy Special Assistant in 1961, Rostow quickly became known as one of the administration's most ardent cold warriors. To Chester Bowles, Rostow was "a classic example of the militarized liberal."[2]

Townsend Hoopes, who served as assistant secretary of defense and under secretary of the Air Force in the Johnson administration, recalled that Rostow "proved to be the closest thing we had near the top of the U.S. government to a genuine, all-wool, anti-Communist ideologue and true believer." Rostow could be an imaginative and incisive theorist, "but once the pattern of his belief was established," Hoopes wrote, "some automatic mental filter thereafter accepted only reinforcing data, while systematically and totally rejecting all contrary evidence no matter how compelling."[3] Robert McNamara, Rostow's colleague for seven years, wrote in his memoirs that Rostow was "optimistic by nature" and that "he tended to be skeptical of any report that failed to indicate we were making progress."[4] These traits—zealous anticommunism and unfettered, often unrealistic, optimism—characterized Rostow's views throughout 1961, particularly regarding American policy toward Vietnam.

Modernization and War

When he joined the Kennedy administration in 1961, Rostow was best known and most influential for his theories on the political economy of the Third World. His formulations of modernization theory—which drew on his study of British economic history and culminated in the extremely influential 1960 book, *The Stages of Economic Growth*—provided a conceptual framework by which the United States could encourage and manipulate Third World economic development within a capitalist system. In this way it was hoped the United States and its allies could stake a claim to the ideological allegiance of decolonizing nations in the developing world, an area in which the Soviet Union—with its avowed support for "wars of national liberation" and longstanding antipathy to European imperialism—was enjoying some success. With a characteristic touch of hubris, the book's subtitle, *A Non-Communist Manifesto*, represented the political side of the modernization theory coin. By following the prescribed "stages of economic growth," developing states would not only enjoy rapidly rising living standards, they would also be embraced both economically and politically—that is to say, ideologically—by the United States as they were simultaneously denied to the Soviet bloc. As Rostow wrote in 1956 for a lecture at the Naval War College, "in Africa powerful forces are boiling up, and we have no policy capable of either controlling them or aligning them with our abiding interests." The United States, therefore, needed a "foreign economic policy capable of harnessing their acute, rampant nationalist feelings and ambitions into constructive domestic channels."[5]

In his position as Bundy's deputy, and as one of the Kennedy administration's foremost intellectuals, Rostow sought to reconstruct American foreign policy toward the developing world according to modernization theory. In a 1961 policy paper, which Rostow redrafted after an attempt by the State Department he deemed weak, he wrote that as new, "truly independent" nations emerged, "each nation will be permitted to fashion, out of its own culture and its own ambitions, the kind of modern society it wants." The United States was "prepared to gamble" that "if the independence of this process can be maintained over the coming years and decades, these societies will choose their own version of what we would recognize as a democratic, open society."[6] Two ironies from this paper stand out; both would echo violently in Vietnam over the next decade. First, considering that the United States was never entirely comfortable with even neutralist states, except possibly Yugoslavia, it is highly doubtful that Rostow did indeed have in mind "truly independent" nations. Second, although the Soviet Union was certainly guilty of violating "the independence of this process," so too was the United States. This was not a process the United States was about to relinquish control over, particularly if it meant losing control to communists. But as Rostow would find out shortly, maintaining control over the modernization process would mean fighting a protracted, unwinnable war in the jungles of Vietnam.

Rostow assumed that the modernizing efforts of developing nations were susceptible to communist influence. Often the clash between the Western powers and local communist movements resulted in the outbreak of guerrilla warfare, and it was America's job to oppose communist guerrillas wherever they threatened American interests and allies. In a widely noted speech at Fort Bragg in June 1961, which Kennedy had approved as an expression of official policy, Rostow declared that guerrilla warfare was "a product of that revolutionary [modernizing] process and the Communist effort and intent to exploit it." He warned that it "is on the weakest nations," such as South Vietnam, "that the Communists concentrate their attention. They are the scavengers of the modernization process." It was, Rostow reminded his audience, an American responsibility to check the advance of communist guerrillas in the Cold War, especially "those hard-pressed states on the periphery of the Communist bloc, which are under acute military or quasi-military pressure which they cannot bear from their own resources."[7] As Rostow once wrote in a letter to Dean Acheson, the combination of military intervention and modernization theory would enable Washington to prevent "Moscow continuing the game of stick and carrot in Asia, the Middle East, and Africa."

Counterguerrilla war, Rostow wrote Rusk early in 1961, "depended for [its] success on a mixture of attractive political and economic programs in the underdeveloped areas and a ruthless projection to the peasantry that the central government intends to be the wave of the future."[8]

In the most volatile regions where the communist adversary used guerrilla tactics—such as Vietnam—the United States would need to adopt the strategic military companion to modernization theory, which at the time also happened to be the most popular doctrine of limited war: counterinsurgency. Proponents of counterinsurgency argued that the U.S. military would not have much success if it tried to fight innovative guerrillas with conventional means. To beat the insurgents, the Americans and the South Vietnamese would have to learn how to fight like insurgents. Rather than employing tactics designed for the cities, plains, and forests of Europe, Rostow advocated the adoption of tactics more suited to the villages, rice paddies, and jungles of Indochina. The problem, Rostow soon discovered, was that counterinsurgency, at least how the U.S. military practiced it in Vietnam, was no match for the Vietnamese communists. Beleaguered by a popular insurgency it could not contain, South Vietnam first needed stability before it could have prosperity; and without security, stability was unattainable. And so, even as early as the summer of 1961 Rostow increasingly abandoned both modernization theory and counterinsurgency in favor of more and more conventional firepower. The troops and bombing campaign of 1965 had their origins in Rostow's NSC planning four years earlier.

Alarm and Action in Washington

Rostow did not have to wait long to test his theories. The world seemed in turmoil, and Kennedy immediately faced serious crises in Cuba, Berlin, Laos, and the Congo. However, it was Vietnam that would emerge as the most insoluble problem facing the new administration. On January 27, 1961, a week after Kennedy had been inaugurated, Bundy wrote to Rusk, McNamara, and Allen Dulles to set the agenda for the administration's first cabinet-level meeting on Vietnam. The discussion, Bundy informed them, was to focus on a report by General Edward Lansdale, who had recently visited South Vietnam. Kennedy knew of Lansdale's report because of Rostow's insistence that he read it; after finishing the report the President looked up at Rostow and said, "this is the worst one we've got, isn't it?" Kennedy's "concern for Vietnam," Bundy wrote to the secretaries of state and defense, "is a result of his keen interest in General Lansdale's recent report and his awareness of the high importance of this country."[9] Rostow noted that during the ensuing discussion, Kennedy "asked whether guerrilla forces could be mounted in the Viet Minh area . . . The President asked how do we change morale; how do we get operations in the north; how do we get moving?" The meeting concluded with Kennedy's request, over Rusk's misgivings, that Bundy organize an interagency task force to examine the crisis in Vietnam and devise possible responses.[10]

Lansdale's admonition that "the Communists regard 1961 as their big year" cut close to Rostow's geopolitical bone.[11] Finding ways to stem the communist tide would occupy his thoughts and energies for the rest of the year. Supporting him in these efforts was Robert Komer, whose diverse topical and geographical responsibilities led him to fit Vietnam into a wider, globalized Cold War perspective. Komer, who in 1966 came to be known as "Blowtorch Bob" for his indefatigable optimism and relentless energy when he served as Johnson's civilian director for Vietnamese pacification, viewed Indochina from the same anticommunist and modernization perspectives as Rostow.[12] At the beginning of February he offered his first thoughts on the Vietnam problem as a member of the Bundy-Rostow team. Ngo Dinh Diem, the authoritarian leader of South Vietnam, had "proven to be a leader of courage and principle." Thinking of the failed November 1960 coup attempt, in which Diem suspected American involvement, Komer advised: *"We should move quickly to reestablish Diem's confidence in us."* Increased military aid, assistance, and training would help to achieve this end. "This will probably require circumvention of the [1954] Geneva Accords," he continued bluntly. "We should not let this stop us." The thrust of the memo, however, called for a "firm and public US commitment to defend South Vietnam against overt international Communist aggression." Because the Southeast Asian Treaty Organization (SEATO) was effectively useless, South Vietnam "should receive US guarantees against overt aggression," which would also spur the South Vietnamese themselves to greater efforts. Komer followed this memo with one that framed the Indochina conflict in stark, divisional Cold War terms. "In line with current Soviet strategy," he told Rostow, the most likely "threats will be the smallest and most ambiguous ones . . . on the order of Laos [and] Vietnam."[13] Four years later, Bundy would heed Komer's advice to fix South Vietnam's political problems with U.S. troops.

By March Rostow had comfortably established himself as perhaps the administration's most ardent hawk on Southeast Asia, and on Vietnam in particular. He was not wary of committing the American military to the conflict, but its level of participation should be, he told Kennedy, dependent on the severity of the crisis within South Vietnam itself. The first stage would be covert American military assistance; this would be followed by increased, partially overt, participation; then, if necessary, "overt limited war in which U.S. military forces are committed." With the establishment of the National Liberation Front (NLF), an organization that would provide overall leadership and manpower for the insurgency, in December 1960 the Vietnamese communists had decided to escalate their own side of the struggle. Correspondingly, the sense of crisis in Washington was more acute than ever, and Rostow began to prod Kennedy to deploy the initial-stage counterinsurgency measures against the NLF. After the first of several trips to inspect the Army's Special Forces Center at Fort Bragg, Rostow recommended the use of U.S. military helicopters and greater integration between the CIA and the Special Forces.[14] "It will be," Rostow wrote, "urgent business to get ourselves properly organized to launch an effective counter-offensive in Viet-Nam." In case Kennedy did not heed the warning, Rostow appealed to the president's renowned inclination for action, for doing something rather than waiting. "We must somehow bring to bear our unexploited counter-guerrilla assets on the Viet-Nam problem," he urged. "It is somehow wrong to be developing these capabilities but not applying them in a crucial active theater. In Knute Rockne's old phrase, we are not saving them for the Junior Prom." Less than a week later, Rostow recommended that Kennedy order an "urgently needed" high-level review of Vietnam.[15]

Kennedy must have liked the idea of a review, for on April 20 one was formed under the directorship of Roswell L. Gilpatric, the deputy secretary of defense. Rostow joined the eight-member Presidential Task Force on Vietnam as the White House/NSC representative. The task force's goal was simple: "To counter the Communist influence and pressure upon the development and maintenance of a strong, free South Vietnam." On April 26 the Task Force circulated within the administration two different, but essentially similar, drafts of its conclusions. The thrust of both versions was that the United States needed to commit itself much more substantially to the survival and strengthening of a noncommunist South Vietnam.[16]

Reaction to the draft report was mostly favorable, especially among the NSC staff. Unsurprisingly, Komer thought that it "looks like a sensible putting together of most of the ideas floating around." The crux of the matter was leadership in Saigon. "This is war for Diem too," he warned. Diem had better "understand that continued procrastination on his part will be fatal." But leadership in Saigon was bound to fail if unsupported by leadership in Washington. "How do we demonstrate our determination in unmistakable terms?" he asked plaintively. At the very least, the United States should "give Diem now a public commitment that if things get to the stage of overt fighting, we will come to his support."[17] Komer's answer was an archetypal application of flexible response. The American reaction to continued aggression would be carefully calibrated to alert the communists that U.S. policy was firmly supportive of a noncommunist South Vietnam, that the United States was willing and able to retaliate militarily to any increased communist pressure on South Vietnam, and that military reprisals would intensify if communist pressure persisted. Such indications of American firmness and readiness would, the thinking went, deter further North Vietnamese provocation and thus render actual American military intervention unnecessary.

While it was essential that the Kennedy administration begin to apply a combination of pressures and inducements to improve Diem's political and military performance, Komer also felt that if necessary the United States must not shrink from placing American combat troops in South Vietnam to back the Diem regime. On Vietnam the chief lesson learned from the communist Pathet Lao's recent successes in Laos was that "we must insulate such a crisis area from outside intervention *before the event rather than after.*" The United States should seek to "seal off" South Vietnam from North Vietnamese, Soviet, and Chinese interference. Moreover, the Geneva Accords should be unilaterally abrogated so that, for political and propaganda reasons rather than for military purposes, troops from other SEATO members could augment U.S. forces in South Vietnam.[18]

Rostow, naturally enough, was pleased with the task force report, which was partly his own creation. In some respects, however, he found that it had not sufficiently emphasized the scale of the problem facing Saigon and Washington. The domestic wage controls and productivity-increasing price cuts for which the task force called were certainly steps in the right direction, but they were not enough. The American people must be placed psychologically on a war footing. "In addition," Rostow wrote Kennedy in his best Churchillian prose, "our society must understand that it is in a protracted struggle which will require from time to time that we face with unity, poise, and determination very dangerous tests of will." "The American commitment to the independence of Viet-Nam is a most serious commitment," Rostow reminded Kennedy a few days later. "If the situation degenerates in Southeast

Asia, it will affect the whole cast of American policy."[19] According to Rostow's particular view of the world, Vietnam's national security was linked inexorably to America's. If the American people did not yet appreciate this, they must be made to.

In a significant change of heart, it was at this point, in the spring of 1961, when Rostow also began to move away from believing that modernization alone could protect South Vietnam. Rostow was no longer as concerned about South Vietnamese politics and society as he was about the eradication of the communists and the establishment of order. To be sure, political and socioeconomic conditions were immensely important to Rostow, but their existence depended entirely on internal stability. They were not to be sacrificed for stability, and so they became, for the time being, dependent variables. The fact that Rostow saw the Vietnamese communists' strength as based mostly upon Soviet and Chinese support simply reinforced his view that the United States had to respond in kind. "The situation on the ground was so bad," he recalled, "that I didn't see how diplomacy, by itself, was going to work."[20] With this in mind, he began once again to push for the introduction of American forces to South Vietnam, in an advisory capacity initially and then as regular forces if needed.[21]

But in the midst of Rostow and Komer, a skeptic emerged within the NSC staff. Robert Johnson, Rostow's principal assistant on Southeast Asian policy, immediately questioned the recommendations of the task force. "My general concern," he wrote to Rostow, "is that [the report] does not seem to me to contain a clear program of political action for South Vietnam." Unlike Rostow and Komer, Johnson felt that the findings were too elaborate on military solutions and too silent on the issue of fundamental political reform. "Are we clear as to our own longer-run as well as our short-run political objectives and will adequate account be taken of the former in seeking to achieve the latter?" Above all, Johnson was concerned with the absence of planning for "the strengthening of political organization at the village level" and the strengthening of political ties between the rural villages and the central government in Saigon. And although he stressed that he agreed with Komer about the desirability of applying pressure on Diem to shape up, Johnson also felt that such pressure might be taking on too military a character. The memo asked directly: "Should the [South] Vietnamese government be presented simply as one 'dedicated to resisting Communist aggression'?"[22]

Bundy also developed qualms about the report that were similar to Johnson's. After discussing the matter with Bundy and Bureau of the Budget Director David E. Bell, Ted Sorensen, one of the President's most trusted advisers, wrote Kennedy that "We need a more *realistic* look." On behalf of Bundy, Bell, and himself, Sorensen urged that the task force report be approved in only its most "basic concept" of maintaining a noncommunist South Vietnam, and that political and socioeconomic reforms become prerequisites to any possible improvement of South Vietnam's internal security and military situation. With characteristic eloquence, Sorensen concluded that there "is no clearer example of a country that cannot be saved unless it saves itself . . . We do not want Vietnam to fall—we do not want to add to Diem's burdens—and the chief purpose of insisting upon [political and socioeconomic reforms] should not be the saving of American dollars but the saving of Vietnam."[23]

Two premises that would come to characterize the NSC staff's deliberations during the Kennedy years are evident from these memoranda. The first is that despite the doubting tone adopted by Johnson and Bundy, neither memo could be construed as dissent from the overall objective. Political realities, they believed, were in danger of being eclipsed by military requirements; both felt instead that the two dimensions should be, at the very least, equal. Neither of them challenged, or even reexamined, the basic U.S. commitment to South Vietnam. The second premise was the desire to compel a change in Diem's political behavior. This was intervention of a different sort, with sociopolitical reform to be coupled with victory on the battlefield, but it was intervention nonetheless. Komer thought it essential to strengthen and widen Diem's political and economic base. Neither Bundy nor Johnson argued against the fundamental commitment to Diem; they merely placed a higher priority on political reform. Only Rostow—who feared that the state of military insecurity in South Vietnam was too advanced to allow for political and social experimentation—demurred. There existed, then, a consensus among the NSC staff that the American commitment to a noncommunist South Vietnam was an essential, irrevocable one. And with the exception of Rostow, all agreed that political concerns were as important as the military campaign. While they may have differed over the means, the NSC staff was unanimously supportive of the ultimate end.

Kennedy approved most of the task force's proposals at an NSC meeting in early May. Bundy subsequently enshrined them as policy on May 11 in NSAM 52, and the State Department sent them to the embassy in Saigon a week later. Coincidentally, but not unfittingly, on the same day that Bundy issued NSAM 52 Vice President Lyndon Johnson arrived in Saigon to, as Rusk put it to the embassy in Saigon, "signalize our strong support for President

Diem." Johnson also visited the Philippines, Taiwan, Hong Kong, Thailand, India, and Pakistan after leaving Saigon, but South Vietnam was his most important stop. Kennedy asked Johnson to convey the message that the United States was "ready to join with [South Vietnam] in an intensified endeavor to win the struggle against communism and to further the social and economic advancement of Vietnam."[24] And in terms of publicly solidifying the American commitment, Johnson's mission was indeed successful. The Vice President's visit had two purposes, Ambassador Frederick E. Nolting cabled Washington: to reassure Diem of American support and "to reassure the Vietnamese people that despite" American setbacks in Laos and Cuba the United States "will continue to stand firmly with them in [the] crisis with [the] Communist world." Nolting confirmed that both of these purposes "have been excellently served . . . We are convinced Diem's confidence in [the] US has been greatly increased by [the] visit." The popular reception in Saigon was even more enthusiastic. When he returned to Washington, Johnson duly sounded the alarm. "Among the countries which I visited," Johnson wrote in his official report, "the threat to peace and progress is most direct and immediate in Viet Nam."[25]

Like the task force report, the Johnson mission was largely a product of Rostow's efforts to heighten the administration's political and military commitment to South Vietnam. As early as March Rostow had suggested to Kennedy that at "some stage Diem himself might come to visit you; or, perhaps, the Vice President might go out to see him, if the situation is too tense for him to leave." In mid-April Rostow again told Kennedy that a good way "to gear . . . up the whole Viet-Nam operation" would be a "visit to Viet-Nam in the near future by the Vice President." As Rostow undoubtedly realized, both the report and the Johnson mission would be perceived as early benchmarks in the administration's Vietnam policy; both were intentionally designed to reaffirm the American commitment to South Vietnam. Bundy certainly thought so. He wrote to Johnson at the end of May to praise "the important effect of your mission in arresting the decline of the situation and setting the stage for action . . . especially in the most critical areas of South Vietnam and Thailand." Without Rostow's constant prodding, there may never have been a Johnson mission.[26]

Convinced of the essentially external nature of the insurgency—that the Democratic Republic of Vietnam (DRV) wholly supported, directed, and controlled a campaign in the South ostensibly run by the NLF—and hastened by the worsening situation in South Vietnam, in the summer of 1961 Rostow began to urge Kennedy to tackle the problem at its source. There were two measures upon which Rostow was particularly insistent: an international anti–North Vietnam propaganda offensive and direct American military action against both the insurgents in the South and the DRV itself. The former would, of course, pave way for the latter.

In launching a propaganda campaign Rostow hoped that the administration would expose Hanoi's deliberate subversion of South Vietnam. This should have been the job of the International Control Commission (ICC)—whose membership comprised neutralist India, communist Poland, noncommunist Canada—which had been created by the 1954 Geneva Accords to keep and monitor the peace in Indochina. The ICC, however, turned out to be inherently unstable and ineffectual, and unable to perform the tasks for which Washington hoped. By revealing the North Vietnamese as the effective leaders of the insurgency, Rostow believed that the United States could capture the political and diplomatic, and ultimately military, initiative. Simultaneously this tactic would also hinder the communists' military strategy by making it more difficult for them to justify intensifying the conflict. With this in mind, and over State Department objections, Bundy told the interagency group on counterinsurgency that "we are engaged in support of an all out civil war, and that consequently [CIA] overflights designed to drop agents for either intelligence or sabotage purposes" were necessary.[27]

Rostow first discussed the matter with Taylor and with State Department official U. Alexis Johnson in mid-July. He suggested that the initiative could be directed from either Washington or Saigon. Rostow also told the Indian and Canadian ambassadors to Washington of American willingness to expose, unilaterally if necessary, North Vietnam's role in the insurgency. He also asked Robert Johnson to press the issue with his contacts in the State Department. Critically, in underlining the importance of a diplomatic offensive, Johnson "suggested that any [propaganda] plan that was developed would have to envisage various sorts of possible military responses and suggest the different sorts of propaganda responses that might be required under various different situations."[28] Behind Johnson's rather contorted explanation lay the fact that the NSC staff, under Rostow's direction and with Bundy's concurrence, was counseling the adoption of an escalated American war effort in Vietnam. Bundy revealed the quandary during a meeting with Kennedy and Rusk at the end of July:

> Another related element is the problem of international opinion with respect to the situation in Viet-nam. It would greatly improve our position if the world could understand more clearly what in fact is happening

there. In particular, any landing operations in Northern Viet-nam would be much more likely to escape from international condemnation if world opinion understands the character of the attack which is now being mounted from the north against Diem. One grave question here is whether certain kinds of information available to the United States should on balance be brought to the surface and placed before the United Nations.[29]

Strategically the NSC staff's desire to launch a diplomatic campaign against the DRV was as much a military initiative as it was political. Instead of using the evidence of Northern subversion to force Hanoi and the NLF to the negotiating table as the United States would do with Laos, Bundy and Rostow wanted to use it to justify expanding the American role in the war. They were, then, using diplomatic means to achieve a military end. Already in June Rostow spoke of "the threat of action" against the North as a tool to discourage its support for the insurgency. Such threats were not idle contingency plans, as Rostow himself acknowledged, because if the threat were ignored—if the North Vietnamese called the American bluff—it would have to be carried out. Rostow also believed that military action against the DRV would benefit other aspects of U.S. foreign policy. He explained to a skeptical Rusk that the United States was "unlikely to be able to negotiate anything like a satisfactory Laos settlement unless the other side believes that we are prepared, as an alternative to a satisfactory settlement, to fight." He assured Rusk that "a posture aimed more directly against North Viet-Nam is more likely to be diplomatically persuasive." The Berlin crisis, which was unfolding around the same time, could also have a mutually beneficial effect on the conflict in Vietnam, Rostow argued to Kennedy, but only if the president were willing to "be prepared to increase the risk of war on [the Soviet] side of the line as well as facing it on ours." For a tough stance in Vietnam to augment a tough stance in Berlin, Rostow told Kennedy, the United States "may wish to put Moscow, Peking, Hanoi, and the World Community on notice that an expansion of the attack on Diem may lead to direct retaliation in Vietminh territory. This would require using the Geneva Conference on Laos, the UN, or both, to present and dramatize Vietminh aggression against Viet-Nam, and to present the case for moving against the source of aggression."[30]

In Rostow's view Kennedy could wait no longer to use U.S. military force against North Vietnam. Just as it would for Bundy, Vietnam had become for Rostow the hinge upon which the rest of America's foreign policy would turn.

Action there could stimulate results elsewhere, such as in Berlin or Cuba. In any event the matter was most urgent. The situation in South Vietnam "is extremely precarious," Rostow warned Kennedy in July. "I believe Viet-Nam requires from us a radical push in the right directions." Political pressure on the North, which would result from the propaganda campaign, was thus "the diplomatic foundation for a military contingency plan which would be aimed in part against North Viet-Nam." The mounting international opposition to an enlarged U.S. military presence in South Vietnam, to which Bundy referred in his meeting with Kennedy and Rusk, also necessitated the construction of a diplomatic foundation. The "USA would be prepared faithfully to observe the 1954 [Geneva] Agreements provided the Communists would do so too," Rostow told Canadian Ambassador Heeney. But based on Rostow's comments it seemed to Heeney that the Americans "consider themselves morally justified in failing to observe strictly the terms of the cease-fire agreement because it has so far proved impossible to get [the DRV] to stop its 'massive and widespread violation' of the agreement."[31]

With support from Bundy, Rostow argued emphatically for an intensified military commitment to South Vietnam. By late summer, he had completely eschewed any political or diplomatic methods of solving the Vietnamese dilemma. Withdrawal from Indochina was also absent from his thoughts. Negotiations between the superpowers and their allies in Geneva over the fate of Laos did not seem to be having much success, and Rostow feared that the communist Pathet Lao, supported by North Vietnam, would resume its drive for Vientiane, the capital. If so, Rostow asked Kennedy rhetorically, "what follows? We must produce quickly a course of action which convinces the other side we are dead serious." Of Diem and the other noncommunist leaders of Southeast Asia, he warned that it was "clear that only American leadership as well as American ultimate guarantees can pull these chaps together."[32] In early October Rostow increased the scale and pitch of his overtures to Kennedy. Cleverly, but also disingenuously, he implied that he spoke for a majority within the administration. Rostow presented a three-pronged strategy: first, direct messages to the Soviets that all communist subversion in South Vietnam must cease; second, the anti-DRV propaganda campaign; and third, the placement of American and allied troops along South Vietnam's vulnerable borders. Rostow concluded his memo with a thinly veiled reference to the dangers of appeasement. The issue was sure to resonate with Kennedy, who had literally written a book, *Why England Slept*, on the subject. "For us the gut issue as I see it is this," Rostow urged. "We are deeply committed in Viet-Nam; if the situation deteriorates, we will have to go in; the situation is, in fact, actively deteriorating; if we go in now, the costs—human and otherwise—are likely to be less than if we wait."[33]

The willingness of Bundy, Rostow, and Komer to resort to military action provoked the first of many squabbles between the NSC staff and the State Department, especially its more senior officials. This marked the beginning of a bureaucratic battle whose result would ultimately determine the course of American policy in Vietnam. Although they did not yet counsel a complete withdrawal from Vietnam, most State Department officials disapproved of using American troops to stave off a collapse of noncommunist Southeast Asian regimes (with the possible exception of Thailand). Reaction from the State Department to a hawkish paper written by Komer—entitled "A Doctrine of Deterrence for SEA," which during the summer Rostow had circulated throughout the administration without Komer's knowledge—was unanimously negative. Applying the main premises of flexible response, the paper predicted that communist aggression could be prevented through a series of steps that culminated in the deployment of U.S. troops. Their presence would provide a "plate glass window" defense, impressive enough to deter communist advances but minimal enough so as not to burden the host country. The last resort was to "have a credible response in case the 'plate glass window' is broken."[34] The State Department's response, which came from both its Policy Planning Staff (S/P) and Bureau of Intelligence and Research (INR), was caustic. Komer protested to Rostow that "they miss the point. Sure there are lots of difficulties but this is no reason for not trying to find the best ways to achieve an indispensable result. What appears to worry S/P most," Komer complained, "is the use of US troops." Undeterred by this initial resistance from the State Department, many of Komer's recommendations found their way into another, less influential, Vietnam Task Force Report, written mostly by Rostow in August. However, Rusk and Ambassador at Large Averell Harriman reacted strongly against the August report and effectively told the task force to redraft its conclusions to reflect a greater emphasis on diplomatic negotiations, such as the Geneva talks on Laos.[35]

The Taylor-Rostow Mission and Report

The long road from initial involvement under President Truman to the Americanization of the war in 1965 had many major turning points. The Taylor-Rostow mission and report were perhaps one of the most important. The high profile of the mission and its leaders ensured that it received wide attention and generated high expectations. By securing a massive infusion of military aid and assistance for South Vietnam without necessarily committing U.S. troops to the conflict, the report itself established the guidelines that would steer U.S. policy until the spring of 1965. "I'm often reminded," Taylor remarked a few years later, "how little change there is in our basic program since 1961."[36] The most significant and controversial aspect of the report— the recommendation to introduce 8,000 American troops to South Vietnam, disguised as a flood relief team—was not adopted. Rather, the report's enduring significance was to divide the administration roughly in three: "hard" hawks, those who favored sending U.S. troops; "soft" hawks, those who supported the American commitment but did not think it wise to send troops, at least for the moment; and doves, those who advocated for complete disengagement following a diplomatic settlement. The report spurred each of these groups to pursue its respective agenda with renewed energy. In the end it alienated the doves and gave greater momentum to the hard and soft hawks, both of whom believed in the basic American commitment to South Vietnam.[37]

The proximate reason for the Taylor-Rostow mission was a spate of NLF battle victories against the ARVN in September, which led Diem to ask the United States for a mutual defense treaty. However, the mission's longer-term origins can, as with the Vice President's trip in May, be traced directly to Rostow and his efforts to deepen the American commitment to South Vietnam. Rostow began to urge Kennedy to send Taylor on an inspection tour of Indochina shortly after Taylor joined the administration in the spring of 1961.[38] Throughout the summer, Rostow and Taylor joined forces to prod Kennedy to toughen American policy toward Southeast Asia. In a jointly authored memo to the President in July, Taylor and Rostow argued that the United States should seek "to build as much indigenous military, political and economic strength as we can in the area, in order to contain the thrust from Hanoi," while at the same time "preparing to intervene with U.S. military force" should the situation continue to deteriorate.[39]

One method of pledging the United States to the fate of South Vietnam was to send another high-level mission to Saigon. In this regard, the Johnson trip had clearly worked. Rostow believed that another mission would fasten the American–South Vietnamese relationship even tighter, particularly if it were led by a military official as esteemed as Taylor. By this time Rostow had already convinced his counterparts in the State Department of the need for a Taylor-led mission to South Vietnam. Kennedy agreed with Rostow, but Taylor did not want to go to Southeast Asia until he had attained a better a grasp of how policy was made in the Kennedy White House.[40]

The successful autumn NLF campaign meant that Rostow's advice to have Taylor "take a good, hard look at Viet-Nam on the ground, soon," could no longer be put off. The mission, led by Taylor and Rostow, was formed hastily on October 11 and arrived in Saigon a week later. The mission was overwhelmingly military (including Taylor, nearly two-thirds of the team were military officers). Of the fifteen mission members, only two midechelon officials from the State Department were included.[41] This composition was certainly what Taylor and Rostow preferred, but also in no small part resulted from Rusk's decision to defer to the White House and the Pentagon on Vietnam policy. As Director of INR Roger Hilsman recalled, Rusk "did not want the State Department to play a prominent role in the upcoming decisions on Vietnam. For he regarded Vietnam as essentially a military problem even though a number of his colleagues in the State Department disagreed." Similarly, Arthur Schlesinger observed that "Kennedy doubtless acquiesced because he had more confidence in McNamara and Taylor than in State." Kennedy certainly had more confidence in Bundy, Rostow, and the NSC staff than he did in the State Department.[42]

From his barrage of alarmist memos, it was obvious that Rostow intended to use the mission as a method to promote a greater American role in Vietnam. Several of his colleagues in the administration now reinforced his instincts by sending him troubling reports of the situation in South Vietnam. A week before the mission's departure, Sherman Kent of the CIA passed Rostow an intelligence summary that stated that the "Communist Bloc probably views the guerrilla and subversive campaigns in Laos and South Vietnam as two parts of a single broad political-military strategy, and of the two, considers South Vietnam as the more significant prize." An analysis provided to Rostow by the Rand Corporation, a prestigious think tank that did classified work for the Pentagon, concurred. A day later Lansdale sent him a gloomy first-hand assessment by a military friend of Lansdale's who had "a pretty bright pair of eyes" for communist tactics.[43] And, shortly before Rostow left, Robert Johnson gave his boss an unexpected and somewhat superfluous reminder about the importance of assisting Diem militarily despite the objections of various State Department officials: "At a time when we are considering intervention ourselves, it seems incongruous that we should be so reluctant to provide additional aid" to Saigon.[44] It is not surprising that Rostow exhorted Taylor to push the military to begin planning for air strikes against the DRV while the mission was still in Hawaii en route to Saigon.[45]

As Rostow anticipated, high expectations among the South Vietnamese greeted the American visitors. William Bundy, who was assistant secretary of defense at the time, recalled that the Taylor-Rostow mission "was of course extremely conspicuous, and its very presence increased speculation among both Americans and South Vietnamese that the US was preparing to take big new actions . . . To Diem and his close associates, the status of Taylor and Rostow as men close to JFK was apparent."[46] Ambassador Nolting cabled Washington to report that the "attention of both [the government of South Vietnam] and [the] Vietnamese people is now riveted on [the] Taylor Mission and expectations [are] high about [the] outcome." The Soviet Union and North Vietnam also signaled the importance of the mission by their official condemnation of the visit as an initial step in the road to a wider, Americanized war.[47]

Upon arrival Taylor and Rostow found the situation to be worse than they had expected. Recent communist successes, record flooding in the Mekong Delta, and the assassination of the very popular South Vietnamese liaison officer to the ICC, Colonel Hoang Thuy Nam, all combined to make it, according to Taylor, "a time when the situation was the darkest since the early days of 1954 . . . In the wake of this series of profoundly depressing events, it was no exaggeration to say that the entire country was suffering from a collapse of national morale—an obvious fact which made a strong impression on the members of our mission."[48] Meeting the enigmatic Diem also made a strong impression on Taylor and Rostow. In their first visit Taylor delicately raised the issue of introducing U.S. troops to South Vietnam, if only at first for logistical purposes. Diem replied, cautiously but positively, that the ARVN suffered chronically from a shortage of troops and that, because Diem viewed the "Communist attack on Viet-Nam as [an] international problem," the South Vietnamese people would welcome additional assistance from the U.S. military. A vital boost to South Vietnamese morale would result from a more explicit U.S. commitment, such as a bilateral defense treaty. For these reasons Diem stated that the Kennedy administration should be prepared to send "American forces" should the situation worsen. "In this connection," Nolting reported to Washington, "Diem seemed to be talking about combat forces."[49]

This was the heart of the matter. Diem had always been wary of hosting American soldiers: psychologically, foreign troops in Vietnam would, he feared, evoke the days of the hated French colonial regime; politically, he also worried that large numbers of U.S. troops would limit his country's sovereignty and his own ability to govern independently. The setbacks of 1961, however, tempered Diem's nationalism and softened his resistance to more direct forms of American assistance, including the deployment of troops. Rostow needed no further incentive. After hearing from American personnel in Saigon that South Vietnam's "border is like a sieve" and that the ICC could not guarantee its inviolability, he felt that the American military must do the job. Later, Taylor and Rostow toured South Vietnam together and met with South Vietnamese and American officials. Rather than reassure Taylor and Rostow, the tour merely added to their alarm. When they met with Diem again at the end of their visit, both recommended that South Vietnam accept a contingent of American troops. Taylor also told Diem that the ARVN had to improve its pitiful intelligence operations and its ability to staunch the flow of infiltration across the porous border with North Vietnam and Laos. With his facile view of the conflict and its solutions, Rostow bluntly told Diem that the "secret of [a] turning point is offensive action."[50]

After spending a week in South Vietnam, the Taylor-Rostow mission left Saigon on October 25. Following stops in Bangkok and the Philippines, the mission returned to Washington to present its report. All members of the mission were asked to present their conclusions as appendices. Although the main report was presented to Kennedy under Taylor's name alone, it accurately conveyed the majority sentiment on the mission. The cover letter, written mostly by Rostow, summarized the consensus in typically shrill Rostovian fashion:

> Can we admit the establishment of the common law that the party attacked and his friends are denied the right to strike the source of aggression, after the fact of external aggression is clearly established?
>
> We cannot refrain from expressing, having seen the situation on the ground, our common sense of outrage at the burden which this kind of aggression imposes on a new country, only seven years old, with a difficult historical heritage to overcome, confronting the inevitable problems of political, social, and economic transition to modernization. It is easy and cheap to destroy such a country whereas it is difficult undisturbed to build a nation coming out of a complex past without carrying the burden of a guerrilla war.

After framing the nature of the conflict in such stark terms, Taylor and Rostow argued that to combat "Khrushchev's 'wars of liberation,'" the United States could "declare our intention to attack the source of guerrilla aggression in North Vietnam and impose on the Hanoi Government a price for participating in the current war which is commensurate with the damage being inflicted on its neighbors to the south." The report presented Kennedy with a comprehensive plan to remedy South Vietnam's ills with its call to send American bureaucrats to assist Diem's government, improve South Vietnamese intelligence capabilities with American training and assistance, train and equip the ARVN with additional American advisers and materiel, provide Diem with American aerial reconnaissance of South Vietnam, bolster the official American military presence in Saigon, and send American troops ostensibly as a flood relief team but in reality to enter the war. It also unveiled the most detailed and sophisticated plan yet to Americanize the war.[51]

Reaction to the report naturally revolved around the proposal to introduce 8,000 U.S. combat soldiers to South Vietnam. Although other aspects of the report were debated, the troop recommendation received the most attention and caused the most controversy. Within the administration the State Department provided virtually all of the dissent, mainly from its most senior members. Even before the formation of the Taylor-Rostow mission, Chester Bowles had devised a detailed plan for the political nonalignment—that is, neutralization—of all of Southeast Asia, including Vietnam. "A direct military response to increased Communist pressure," he warned, "has the supreme disadvantage of involving our prestige and power in a remote area under the most adverse circumstances." Therefore Bowles concluded, "we need an alternative *political* approach which may save us from having to choose between diplomatic humiliation or a major military operation."[52] Of course, Bowles's political approach was much different from that of Komer and Bundy: whereas Bowles wanted to use diplomacy to maneuver America out of Vietnam, the NSC staffers wanted to use international politics to justify attacking the North and use improvements in domestic South Vietnamese politics to wage the war more effectively. Kennedy quietly ignored the Bowles memo. After reading the Taylor-Rostow report, a worried Bowles resubmitted his neutralization proposal. Kennedy responded this time, but told Bowles the "time was not yet ripe" for such a bold departure.[53]

Others in the State Department similarly recoiled from the report's conclusions, but without offering a concrete alternative as Bowles had. After reading the report, George Ball raised questions that marked the beginning of his long battle against American intervention in Vietnam. "The inclusion of Rostow worried me," recalled Ball, who thought of him as "an articulate amateur tactician . . . unduly fascinated by the then faddish theories about counter-insurgency and that intriguing new invention of the professors, 'nation building.'" Ball told an unresponsive McNamara and Gilpatric that he was "appalled at the report's recommendations." In a private meeting with Kennedy a few days later, Ball stated flatly: "Within five years we'll have three hundred thousand men in the paddies and jungles and never find them again. That was the French experience. Vietnam is the worst possible terrain both from a physical and political point of view."[54]

Averell Harriman, who headed the U.S. delegation to the Geneva talks on Laos, thought American escalation in Vietnam would cripple any efforts to settle the Laotian crisis politically and peacefully. "If you put in troops," the veteran diplomat warned Taylor and Rostow, "there is no real negotiation possible with the Russians." A few days later Harriman stressed to Kennedy that a diplomatic solution in Vietnam based on the 1954 Geneva Accords and maintained by a "strengthened and modernized" ICC was more likely to achieve American aims than a purely military solution. Harriman was so worried by "unwise advisers" who were "unduly" influencing Kennedy, he told British diplomats in Geneva, that he urged Indian Prime Minister Jawaharlal Nehru personally to pressure Kennedy not to escalate. "The proper solution," Harriman said, "is a peaceful negotiated one."[55]

While back in Washington for consultations, Ambassador to India John Kenneth Galbraith, a friend of Kennedy's and a former academic colleague of Rostow's, was characteristically acerbic in assessing the report. Taylor and Rostow "are advocating exceedingly half-baked intervention," Galbraith confided to his diary. He then met with Bundy at the White House to discuss the report. Galbraith's old Harvard dean chided him on his wariness of intervening in Vietnam: "Mac thinks there is no occasion when I would urge the use of force. I have to admit that my enthusiasm for it is always low." Their differences erupted during a "very frank and at times heated" dinner with Kennedy and the British Ambassador, David Ormsby Gore. Galbraith, Ormsby Gore reported, "took what one might call the Harriman line" and was "strongly against American military intervention." Bundy, on the other hand, "clearly did not accept this line and by implication neither did the President."[56] Nonetheless, Galbraith officially put his reservations in writing to Kennedy, to which the President asked Rostow to respond. "If Ken is advocating that we disengage promptly from Vietnam and let Southeast Asia go," Rostow replied, "I think he should say so. In my view South Vietnam is not yet lost and one of the crucial variables is that we go forward with a clear-eyed view of our assets as well as an equally tough-minded view of our liabilities and problems." The main problem was that the communists enjoyed both freedom to maneuver in South Vietnam and a safe haven in North Vietnam. Given these facts, Rostow angrily charged that Galbraith "grossly underestimated the military significance of the infiltration process." Undeterred, while returning to India Galbraith cabled Kennedy from Saigon with an extremely negative assessment. A week later, after he had returned to New Delhi, Galbraith reiterated the message with an equally pessimistic letter to Kennedy. Galbraith's opinions were again subjected to the scrutiny of the NSC staff, although this time it was Bundy, rather than Rostow, who deflected the Ambassador's protest.[57]

Along with the doves, there were also several influential soft hawks in the State Department. Unlike Galbraith, Alexis Johnson had no qualms about applying American military force to Southeast Asia, but he also thought that the actual deployment of U.S. soldiers was still unnecessary. "Can we save South Viet-Nam with steps short of putting in US forces?" Johnson asked at a meeting to discuss the report. In Saigon, Nolting adopted a similar position—agreement with virtually everything in the report except the troop proposal.[58] Moreover, the two officials who coordinated the State Department's intelligence and analysis units—in effect, the brain for the Department's massive body—also expressed serious reservations about putting U.S. troops into South Vietnam. After the debate over the Taylor-Rostow report had subsided, Hilsman informed Rusk that "the most effective way of meeting a guerrilla threat like that of the Viet Cong is not with regular troops, but rather by a sophisticated combination of civic action, intelligence, police work, and constabulary-like counter-guerrilla forces that use a tactical doctrine quite different from the traditional doctrine of regular forces." Shortly after Hilsman wrote to Rusk, Policy Planning Staff Director George C. McGhee recommended against using American combat soldiers in South Vietnam. These were the same two officials who had attacked Komer's paper, "A Doctrine of Deterrence," in August.[59]

But the key figure in beating back the rush to send ground troops was, surprisingly enough, Dean Rusk. Rusk remained secretary of state until 1969, by which time he had become indelibly labeled one of the administration's most strident, unyielding supporters of the war. Like Rostow, he had become an ideologue. In 1961, however, Rusk sought to preserve the American commitment to South Vietnam without sending combat soldiers or otherwise heavily committing American military power and prestige. The increasing ineptitude of the Diem regime and the ARVN, the delicate diplomacy required of the Laos talks in Geneva, and the enormity of sending U.S. soldiers to fight another Asian land war—he had been assistant secretary of state during the Korean War—led Rusk to recommend against the Taylor-Rostow troop proposal. His position was strikingly similar to many of his subordinates in the State Department, such as Alexis Johnson and Nolting. From Japan, Rusk sent his preliminary assessment back to Washington that "special attention should be given to [the] critical question whether Diem is prepared [to] take necessary measures to give us something worth supporting." If not, Rusk continued, it would be "difficult to see how [a] handful of American troops can have [a] decisive influence." Rather than regular soldiers, Rusk leaned "strongly toward introducing administrators, MAAG [the Military Assistance Advisory Group], etc.—it does not commit [the] US as does combat forces."[60]

With this firmly in mind, Rusk moved to contain the rush to commit troops. First he needed to convince the most powerful hawk, the secretary of defense. As Ball had discovered from his meeting with McNamara and Gilpatric, the Pentagon favored the report in its entirety. On November 8 McNamara sent Kennedy a memo on behalf of himself, Gilpatric, and the JCS that not only endorsed the deployment of 8,000 troops but also estimated that up to six divisions (approximately 205,000 soldiers) could eventually be sent to South Vietnam. Rusk blanched at such sweeping measures, and he pressed McNamara to reconsider. In a compromise paper of November 11 drafted by Alexis Johnson, Rusk and McNamara each modified their positions. The secretary of state agreed that U.S. troops might be sent to South Vietnam, but only if it was absolutely necessary; likewise, the secretary of defense conceded that troops should only be sent as a last resort and that the administration should first try all other means of assisting Saigon. This was, with no major changes, the option Kennedy chose.[61]

The State Department's resistance and the Pentagon's vacillation frustrated the best escalatory efforts of the hawks on the NSC staff. It certainly came as a shock to Rostow. After careful inspection, he and Taylor had appreciated the severity of South Vietnam's plight and returned to Washington confident of their views and in their exhaustive report. "We agreed," Rostow later wrote, "that South Vietnam was caught up in a double crisis of confidence: doubt that the United States was determined to save Southeast Asia and doubt that Diem's methods could frustrate and defeat communist purposes and methods." Giving the U.S. military an active combat role would, he believed, ease both of these anxieties. But when the weight of decision began to swing against him, Rostow reverted to framing the issues in stark terms of moral principle. At a crucial meeting to discuss the report—which Ball, Alexis Johnson, Taylor, McNamara, Gilpatric, William Bundy, and Chairman of the JCS General Lyman Lemnitzer attended—Rostow pleaded that the real issue "is whether we will accept a guerrilla war supported externally as a legal international process . . . The Vice President's trip and the Taylor Mission lay on the need for action. There is no soft option." Even after the decision went against him, Rostow continued to ply Kennedy and Bundy with alarmist assessments.[62]

Rostow must have made quite an impression on Bundy. Since joining the administration at the beginning of the year, Bundy had deliberately decided not to wield much influence over policy toward Vietnam. In the wake of reaction to the Taylor-Rostow report, however, he began to take notice. In addition to the report and Rostow's constant prodding, Bundy received a strongly worded memo from Komer, who admitted that "over-reacting, if anything, is best at this point." The stakes in South Vietnam, especially after the "loss" of Laos to neutralism at Geneva, were just too high. Just as Rostow had done all year, Komer stressed that time was not on their side. He conceded that there might be alternatives to U.S. troops. "But I doubt it. And if the alternatives fail, we still face the question of sending troops—at a later and less satisfactory time." Deploying troops could lead to international resistance and even a wider war, but it was more likely that "*risks and recriminations would be much greater, say, a year from now* when the whole situation is a lot more heated up." Finally, Komer admitted that while greater intervention may not solve things in the short term, "at least it buys us time to do so."[63]

Bundy had also been influenced unexpectedly by Robert Johnson. The views of the lone soft hawk on the NSC staff had undergone a torturous evolution during the lengthy period of discussion over the Taylor-Rostow report. In the end he too adopted the posture of a hawk, although his perspective was different: he worried more about the adverse consequences of *dis*engagement from South Vietnam *after* American troops had been committed. There was no turning back once Kennedy deployed troops. The "longer the troops remain," Johnson warned Bundy shortly before the presentation of the report, "the more they are likely to become involved in combat operations." If U.S. soldiers did indeed find themselves in the thick of the fighting and were then hastily withdrawn "when the going got rough we will be finished in Viet Nam and probably in all of Southeast Asia."[64] Johnson was not opposed in principle to the commitment of U.S. soldiers; he merely wanted to clarify the political and military objectives for which Kennedy had the troops in mind and the extent to which the president was willing to go in pursuit of those objectives. Above all Johnson feared that Kennedy might stumble into a potentially humiliating war without fully realizing it. Johnson cautioned Bundy that while Kennedy probably should send troops, he must not do so "without deciding in principle whether we are prepared to go beyond such action by stepping up our military commitment in Viet Nam very considerably."[65]

Johnson thus did not oppose the use of American military might under any circumstances. He had in fact been leaning in favor of sending troops, and the intense debate over the Taylor-Rostow report convinced him by helping to clarify American objectives. Thus he told Rostow he feared "that we are losing a strategic moment for the introduction of U.S. troop units. The world has been made aware of the crisis in Viet Nam as a result of the Taylor Mission. Both the Bloc and the Free World are going to look upon the *actions* we take now as the key to our future actions no matter what we may *say*. A plate glass window on the 17th parallel or a flood relief task force could make a great political difference not only in Viet Nam, but in the whole area." It was imperative that Kennedy decide quickly, for the crisis would only worsen and "in the interim uncertainty as to our intentions will grow."[66] That this analysis came from Johnson, who had consistently been the most doubtful member of the NSC staff on sending American soldiers to South Vietnam, must have made a significant impression on Bundy. Moreover, the Johnson approach to the report, and to military escalation in general, is indicative of the primary difference between the collective attitude of the State Department and the NSC staff. Johnson's initial position on a troop deployment was strikingly similar to that of Alexis Johnson, Hilsman, Nolting, or for that matter Rusk. And yet while they were perceived to be the hawks of the State Department, Robert Johnson was seen to be the dove of the NSC staff. In the more subtle climate of the State Department it is difficult to imagine Alexis Johnson or Hilsman undergoing Johnson's transformation from soft hawk to hard hawk.

Bundy was naturally inclined to favor deploying troops. Aside from his own worldview, he had always taken a dim view of SEATO's effectiveness. "To be successful," Dean Bundy told an audience at the Council on Foreign Relations in 1956, a collective security pact "requires specific conditions, few, if any, of which are met by SEATO." According to Bundy, SEATO was "not worth the effort," did not reflect "a broad enough political effort," consisted of nations too "spread out," did not have "an agreed upon strategy," and prohibited military alliances between South Vietnam and member nations, including the United States. Little had happened since then to change his mind. The credibility and capabilities of SEATO, and the stability of South Vietnam, had deteriorated considerably since Bundy had delivered this address. Thus in 1961 it was even clearer to him that only the United States could bring about a positive change, forcefully if necessary, in Vietnam. The situation "is genuinely coming to a head," Bundy wrote Kennedy even before the departure of the Taylor-Rostow mission, "and I myself am now persuaded that we must promptly find a way of acting much more vigorously in South Vietnam."[67]

Bundy wove together the disparate threads from the report, his staff's advice, and his own inclinations to form a recommendation for Kennedy. Bundy presented his conclusions—those of a committed, but still somewhat cautious, hawk—after a chat with Kennedy while the two were paddling around in the White House swimming pool. "So many people have offered their opinions on South Vietnam that more may not be helpful," Bundy began modestly. He then followed with his most substantive Vietnam policy recommendation to date:

> I believe that we should commit *limited* U.S. combat units, if necessary for *military* purposes (not for morale), to help save South Vietnam. A victory here would produce great effects all over the world. A defeat would hurt, but not much more than a loss of South Vietnam with the levels of U.S. help now committed or planned.
>
> I believe our willingness to make this commitment, *if necessary*, should be clearly understood, by us and by Diem, before we begin the actions now planned. I think without that decision the whole program will be half-hearted. *With* this decision I believe the odds are almost even that the commitment will not have to be carried out . . . This has now become a sort of touchstone of our will.
>
> I believe the actions now planned, *plus* the basic decision to put in limited combat troops if necessary, are all that is currently wanted. I would not put in a division for morale purposes. I'd put it in later, to fight if need be.

With some hesitation, Bundy recommended the report's troop proposal. He agreed that U.S. troops should be sent to South Vietnam, but only if and when they were absolutely required to prevent a collapse of the Diem regime. Bundy did not seem to be as convinced as Rostow or Komer of the imminence of communist success or of Diem's collapse. He was concerned but saw no reason to panic. Like Rusk he blended elements of the soft and hard hawk positions: not necessarily troops, but troops if necessary.[68]

The only real point of contention between Bundy and Rostow was whether U.S. soldiers would best serve as morale boosters—and even this was a point on which Rostow had oscillated in the previous two weeks. The other primary reasons for sending troops—as a deterrent force (Komer's "plate glass window"), as a means to halt communist infiltration, and as a diplomatic wedge—were points of the hawks' strategy on which Bundy, Rostow, and the entire NSC staff agreed. As such, Bundy informed Kennedy that if he accepted the NSC staff's arguments, new policy guidelines for Nolting should state that "U.S. combat troops will be put into South Vietnam when and if the U.S. military recommend it on persuasive military grounds for internal action," and that "Diem must take U.S. military counsel on a wholly new basis."[69]

Despite the ambivalent tone of Bundy's recommendation, the President's Special Assistant for National Security Affairs had made it clear that a noncommunist South Vietnam was ultimately a cause worth fighting for. Although he would soon leave the NSC staff, Rostow had already determined the direction in which Bundy would steer American policy in South Vietnam.

CHAPTER 5

The Soft Hawk:
Forrestal and
Nonmilitary Escalation

Walt Rostow left the NSC staff in December 1961. His departure, if sudden, was neither unexpected nor acrimonious, and was only one facet of a major reorganization of the Kennedy administration's foreign policy team. The primary reason for the late-November shake-up, dubbed the "Thanksgiving Day Massacre," was to remove Chester Bowles from the highest echelon of the State Department. Bowles had become unpopular among his colleagues, particularly those, like Bundy, who considered his views on foreign affairs too soft. Bowles seemed to exemplify the malaise that was perceived to have gripped the State Department. As early as the spring of 1961, in a remark clearly directed at Bowles, Bundy told friends at a party that "something has to be changed at State and you can't fire the Secretary of State."[1] By July the dissatisfaction with Bowles had become obvious, and Bundy suggested to him, gently but unambiguously, that he was temperamentally and intellectually unsuited to the position of under secretary. By November, with Bowles's opposition to the administration's policy on Cuba and Vietnam on record, neither Kennedy nor Dean Rusk could tolerate Bowles as under secretary any longer. As part of a general shuffle, which Bundy designed and Kennedy approved, George Ball replaced Bowles, Rostow replaced George McGhee as the head of the Policy Planning Council, Averell Harriman became the assistant secretary of state for Far Eastern affairs, and Bowles was left with the meaningless post of ambassador at large. Michael Forrestal replaced Rostow on the NSC staff in February 1962. Shortly after leaving his post as under secretary, Bowles published an article calling for "better control and coordination of foreign policy in Washington. The logical focus for such coordination lies in the regional assistant secretaries of state." He did not need to write that it was Bundy who had largely shifted such focus away from the State Department.[2]

The adoption of most, but not all, of the Taylor-Rostow report as official policy meant that both the doves and the hawks had been defeated. The soft hawks, with their dedication to maintaining a viable noncommunist South Vietnam through measures short of sending U.S. troops, were the clear victors. Despite the doves' fears, American intervention in Vietnam continued but at a much slower pace than the hawks would have liked. Thus 1962 began as the year in which the soft hawks would be given a chance to make their policy succeed in South Vietnam.

Forrestal and the Cold War

In the vast literature on the American war in Vietnam, Michael Forrestal's role remains somewhat enigmatic. In most historical accounts he does not figure prominently. Historians originally portrayed him as a closet dove and skeptic. Much of this early portrayal stemmed from David Halberstam's influential 1972 bestseller *The Best and the Brightest,* in which Forrestal emerges as a prescient dove waging a furtive and largely futile battle against deeper intervention. Some historians and a few former colleagues subsequently adopted this view.[3] Bundy himself eulogized Forrestal at his funeral in 1989 by claiming that the "courses that he advocated would be ones to consider if one could replay the tragic history of our connection to Southeast Asia."[4] But although Forrestal was certainly skeptical about the Kennedy administration's relationship with the Diem regime, he was no closet dove. A firm adherent to America's anticommunist Cold War consensus, he believed fervently in the basic U.S. commitment to a noncommunist South Vietnam and the capability of American political and military power to preserve this commitment.

Forrestal's father, James V. Forrestal, was the first secretary of defense and a principal architect of the postwar strategy of containment. After his father committed suicide in 1949, young Michael was unofficially adopted by another foreign policy titan of the day, Averell Harriman. Although Harriman, first as U.S. ambassador to Moscow and later as the head of the Marshall Plan in Paris, had also advocated a tough policy toward the USSR, he would become well known in the following decades for developing an appreciation of the Soviet threat that had more nuance and balance. By the 1960s he was known more as an advocate of détente than of confrontation, although this did not mean that he had abandoned America's Cold War cause altogether.[5]

Michael Forrestal generally followed these often contradictory patterns established by his two illustrious father figures. After graduating from Princeton, but before going to Harvard Law School, he studied at the Navy's Russian Language School, was posted to Berlin and Moscow shortly after the war, and subsequently joined Harriman's staff in Paris. Like his father, the young Forrestal developed an acute sense of the communist threat—Secretary of the Navy Forrestal often circulated Michael's impressionistic letters from Moscow throughout the Truman administration—but, like Harriman, he also came to develop a sophisticated view of the USSR, and of Soviet-American relations. Close friend Arthur Schlesinger perhaps put it best in 1962 when recommending Forrestal for a position on the NSC staff: "He may not quite have his father's concentrated and ambitious drive, but he also does not have his father's somewhat narrow views." After leaving government service in 1965 to return to his law firm in New York, Forrestal worked to promote a better understanding between the United States and the Soviet Union. Ironically, his tenure as president of the U.S.-USSR Trade Council from 1978 to 1980 coincided with the collapse of genuine superpower détente.[6]

When Forrestal joined the NSC staff in February 1962, however, he was very much a firm believer in the concepts that underpinned American Cold War foreign policy. This view was not especially surprising given that his formative experiences had all been in Europe, where the course of U.S. foreign policy was relatively successful and straightforward. But, inauspiciously, he did not join Bundy's team as an expert on the Soviet Union or Europe. Instead he assumed responsibility for policy toward East and Southeast Asia, particularly Indochina, despite having almost no knowledge of those regions' geography, politics, history, or culture. As Forrestal confessed to Kennedy before joining the NSC staff: "Mac tells me that you want me to work in the Far East, but I want you to know one thing before taking this job. I don't know anything at all about the Far East. I've never studied it. I've never been there. I know a little bit about the Soviet Union and Eastern Europe from past government service, but nothing at all about the Far East." Kennedy replied flippantly: "That's fine. That's just what we want. Somebody without preconceptions and prejudices." In the spring of 1962 Forrestal made his first trip to Southeast Asia "to find out where all these countries were."[7]

While Forrestal was undoubtedly qualified for an important foreign policy position in the administration, he was grossly unprepared to manage American interests in Asia. Intellectually and physically far removed from the realities of Vietnam, he was hobbled by a fundamental misunderstanding of its politics, history, and culture. According to Alan Brinkley, members of the Establishment, to which Forrestal most certainly belonged, "displayed a limited ability to understand social or political systems different from their own."[8] True to form, Forrestal tried to apply the lessons of Europe to the problems of Southeast Asia. Faced with the postcolonial tumult and ideological ambivalence of civil war in Vietnam, Forrestal relied upon solutions designed to counter a very different kind of threat from the Soviet Union. Revealingly, in 1971 Forrestal confessed to CBS News that Asia had not been his "forte" and that, because Vietnam was a strange country and what he knew best had been Europe, "we tended to be somewhat blind, and perhaps somewhat overoptimistic about the role that the United States and its institutions, our military, our aid, and our intelligence and political people could play in a country like Vietnam. I think we did overestimate that."[9] Similarly, he approved of General Duong Van "Big" Minh, who overthrew Diem in November 1963, because Minh was "tall, a good tennis player, and spoke English."[10] Minh was, in short, a familiar type of figure to whom Forrestal could relate, unlike the inscrutable, "oriental" Diem. Forrestal instinctively sought to apply familiar solutions to unfamiliar problems. In doing so, he mistook a postcolonial civil war in Vietnam for a vital Cold War battleground.

The Inner Club

If Rostow epitomized the hawks' push to Americanize the war in South Vietnam, Forrestal represented the ascendance of the soft hawks. Even without the inclusion of the proposal to send 8,000 regular U.S. combat soldiers to South Vietnam, the approval of the Taylor-Rostow report crippled the doves' chances of reversing American intervention in Vietnam. And although the report signaled a greater political and military commitment to the Diem regime, Kennedy's decision not to send troops deflected momentum from the hawks. The President's middling policy fit very well into the soft hawks' agenda of promoting American involvement in South Vietnam without an explicit and open-ended obligation to commit troops. For now, Kennedy's steadfast commitment to South Vietnam, coupled with his aversion to sending regular combat forces to uphold that commitment, gave the administration's soft hawks the upper hand.

The Taylor-Rostow report was also a watershed for Bundy. After November 1961 he found himself contributing more and more to the administration's increasingly interventionist policy. With assistance from Komer and Harold Saunders, also an NSC staffer, Bundy issued NSAM 119 in December, which directed the Departments of State and Defense "to develop methods for supporting whatever contribution [U.S.] military forces can make to economic and social development in less-developed countries." By this, Bundy explained, "we mean using [U.S.] military forces on projects useful to the populace at all levels in such fields as training, public works, agriculture, transportation, communication, health, sanitation, and others helpful to economic development." American military advisers in South Vietnam, whose numbers had increased from less than a thousand to 3,205 during 1961, would be in an ideal position to enact this policy. In January 1962 Bundy circulated NSAM 124, which established the Special Group (Counter-Insurgency) to direct and monitor counterinsurgency operations in South Vietnam, Laos, and Thailand. By promoting counterinsurgency and nonmilitary forms of intervention, as outlined in NSAMs 119 and 124, Bundy was establishing his credentials as a soft hawk. And it was no coincidence that Bundy replaced Rostow, a renowned hard hawk, with Forrestal, a fledgling soft hawk.[11]

Bundy could look, with some assurance, upon Forrestal as a future soft hawk because of Forrestal's intimate ties to Harriman, who straddled the positions of both the doves and the soft hawks. But, like American policy itself, Harriman was coming increasingly to favor the latter. Although Harriman had opposed the deployment of American troops called for in the Taylor-Rostow report, he nonetheless viewed the main problem in South Vietnam as a case of communist aggression that the United States should defeat. In April 1962 Harriman told Kennedy that he was "not in favor [of] a neutral solution in Viet-Nam" even though he had negotiated one for Laos. He instead preferred an American diplomatic offensive and increased support for the Diem regime. And although Harriman had come to advocate détente with the USSR, like Bundy his view of Asian communism was less sanguine. "I don't know how you can distinguish between Chinese communism and Chinese imperialism," he remarked in 1963. During this period Harriman was no hawk, but neither was he in any sense a dove.[12]

Kennedy and Bundy also had ulterior motives in selecting Forrestal for a position on the NSC staff. The relationship between Kennedy and Rusk—and, for that matter, between Bundy and Rusk—had never been close or productive. The president and his Special Assistant felt they needed their own back channel to the State Department. Independent, powerful, and certain that he should have been secretary of state, Harriman was a natural fit. As Bundy described the job to Forrestal: "Well, you're supposed to be a kind of ambassador to that separate sovereignty known as Averell Harriman." Kennedy and Bundy doubtless anticipated that the relationship between Forrestal and Harriman would be symbiotic: Forrestal would apprise Harriman of White

House thinking and vice versa, and Forrestal would evolve, under Harriman's tutelage, into a soft hawk.[13]

Forrestal developed another intimate relationship that, as far as Vietnam policy was concerned, became as close as his bond with Harriman. Forrestal found that his views mirrored those of Roger Hilsman, who headed INR until April 1963 when he was promoted to succeed Harriman as assistant secretary of state for Far Eastern affairs. A West Point cadet and a graduate student in international relations at Yale, two other elements of Hilsman's background are particularly significant when considering his place in the Kennedy administration: during World War II Captain Hilsman of the OSS successfully commanded a guerrilla force behind Japanese lines in Burma; and during the 1960 presidential campaign Hilsman, now of the Library of Congress's Legislative Reference Service, provided candidate Kennedy with foreign policy analysis and speech drafts. Hilsman, in short, had ample reason to believe that he completely understood the subtleties of both guerrilla warfare (and thus its remedy, counterinsurgency) and President Kennedy. Abrasive, brilliant, and energetic, in the words of one British diplomat in Washington Hilsman sought "to present himself as a 'man of action' " who had taken "too much to heart Napoleon's aphorism about it being better to do the wrong thing quickly than the right thing hesitantly." With abundant confidence and energy, a shared outlook on the problems facing Southeast Asia, and relatively similar positions of influence with the president and, more generally, within the foreign policy bureaucracy, Forrestal and Hilsman quickly established themselves as a dynamic and effective team. Kennedy thought of the Bundy-Forrestal-Hilsman triumvirate as his "inner club" on Vietnam. Forrestal, with his proximity to Kennedy, often acted as Hilsman's channel to the president.[14]

Hilsman was, moreover, an ardent soft hawk who believed that fighting guerrillas could never be successful unless military and nonmilitary means were used in equal measure. With a peculiarly suitable metaphor he declared to the American Hospital Association that "President Roosevelt once said that 'Dr. New Deal' had been succeeded by 'Dr. Win the War,' but in guerrilla wars in underdeveloped nations both 'doctors' are needed. Military action and a social new deal have to proceed together."[15] After attending the Defense Department's Conference on Vietnam in Hawaii in January 1962 and subsequently touring South Vietnam, he returned to Washington to present his soft hawk conclusions on the conflict. According to Hilsman and contrary to American conventional wisdom, the communist insurgency was predominantly an indigenous phenomenon, and it was succeeding politically as well as militarily. The United States would thus need to respond in kind. "The people of South Vietnam," Hilsman wrote in his report, "want to fight and are basically anti-Communist." American officials "should turn our attention to providing help at the local level," primarily in alleviating the social, political, and economic plight of ordinary South Vietnamese. "Finally," he concluded, "there is an immediate need to develop a better understanding of the strategic concept for counterinsurgency war among working level Americans in all United States agencies in South Vietnam."[16] The blending of political and social reform with counterinsurgency was basically a reflection of the course Bundy had set forth in NSAMs 119 and 124. Thus Bundy, Forrestal, Hilsman, and Harriman were all thinking alike as they approached Vietnam in 1962.

Forrestal and the War in South Vietnam

The manner in which Washington and Saigon fought the war in South Vietnam mattered a great deal to Forrestal. It was essential for the United States to provide as much military, political, and economic assistance as it could, but it was also essential that such efforts did not overwhelm or replace those of the South Vietnamese. Because the conflict was by nature as much political as it was military, as Hilsman had outlined in February, Forrestal believed political considerations to be crucial in devising an American strategy.

Consider the issue of crop destruction and defoliation in South Vietnam. By dumping chemical herbicides from the air onto prime agricultural land suspected of being under communist control, the South Vietnamese could simultaneously starve communist guerillas while denying them cover for military operations. Forrestal, however, was not entirely convinced that the benefits of crop destruction and defoliation would outweigh the drawbacks from the anticipated adverse reaction, in Southeast Asia and throughout the world, to the resort to "chemical warfare." In May he warned Kennedy that because of a lack of conclusive testing the effectiveness of defoliation remained unproven. The Pentagon, Ambassador Nolting, and especially the South Vietnamese themselves enthusiastically approved of crop destruction and defoliation for military reasons, and throughout the summer they pressed their case with the president. Forrestal, backed by Bundy, Hilsman, and Harriman, tried to persuade Kennedy that the use of defoliants would do more political harm than military good. As Forrestal wrote to Bundy and Carl Kaysen, "in return for a military advantage in a very limited area . . . we would be paying a very high political cost throughout the entire country."[17] Harriman and Hilsman were "doubtful" about defoliation, he informed Kennedy at the end of September. "My own feeling continues to be that the program may be premature . . . It is almost certain we will pay dearly for it in terms of Asian opinion." Worried about adverse publicity, particularly in Asia and Africa, the United States Information Agency shared their concern.[18]

Despite these objections Kennedy approved defoliation in August and a crop destruction program in early October. At McNamara's request the crop destruction program was significantly expanded the following month. Although his fears of international outrage were not unfounded, Forrestal viewed the outcome pragmatically. "I believe [Kennedy's] main train of thinking was that you cannot say no to your military advisors all the time," he wrote to Bundy immediately after the approval of crop destruction in October, "and with this I agree." Forrestal was not in principle opposed to an increase in American military assistance to South Vietnam. His objections stemmed more from an adherence to a different strategy rather than to the objective itself. He simply wanted to ensure that the United States did not pay "a rather high political price for little practical return," and he often suggested that defoliants be extensively tested elsewhere before being used in South Vietnam. Moreover, thanks to a CIA analysis Forrestal realized that Saigon was incapable of conducting its own defoliation program. Large-scale defoliation and crop destruction therefore had the potential to act as a first step in the Americanization of the war. It was this creeping intervention that Forrestal sought to prevent.[19]

The Strategic Hamlet program, another initiative shared between Washington and Saigon, posed problems of a different sort. Strategic Hamlets were South Vietnamese villages fortified to defend themselves against communist encroachment and to promote internal social cohesion. Although the concept had been devised independently by the Diem regime, the Kennedy administration felt that it had played a key role in creating the program and thus acted in the belief that it was a cosponsor of Strategic Hamlets.[20] Hilsman in particular saw himself as one of the program's supervisors. "The objective," he explained, "is to cut the Viet Cong off from their sources of supplies and recruits. Since both supplies and recruits come from within South Vietnam, this means cutting off the Viet Cong's access to the villages and the people." The Strategic Hamlet program, inaugurated in the spring of 1962, seemed to provide an effective method of fighting the NLF without heavily committing American resources, prestige, and, most important, soldiers. For these reasons

Forrestal was very much in favor of it. In May he reported to Kennedy that the "programs for strengthening village defenses and pacifying" were "proceeding satisfactorily."[21] The CIA and State Department agreed, and both provided the NSC staff with reports that progress continued through the summer and fall. Forrestal's only complaint was that nonmilitary components of the anticommunist effort—for example, "medicines, seeds, pesticides, small tools, roofing materials, etc."—were still being neglected in favor of counterinsurgency and other military exigencies. Nonetheless the Strategic Hamlets seemed to provide a successful example of fighting the communists with nonmilitary means.[22]

However, lurking beneath this apparent success were fundamental weaknesses that proved crippling to the Strategic Hamlets. Unsurprisingly, Vietnamese peasants did not think that the fortification of their ancestral villages, enclosed behind gates and barbed wire, was a strategic necessity. Nor did they willingly move from their villages to specially constructed hamlets in areas free from communist control, as Saigon's Operation Sunrise attempted to do in the spring of 1962. "Is this normal?" a distressed Bundy asked Forrestal after learning of Operation Sunrise and the fierce local opposition to it. Forrestal shared Bundy's alarm. " 'Normal' is not quite the right word to describe the reported loss of male villagers in Operation Sunrise," he replied. The premise of the Strategic Hamlet program itself was sound; its faulty implementation in this instance was due to the incompetence of Ngo Dinh Nhu, Diem's brother and chief political adviser. "Against our advice and better judgment," Forrestal continued, "the Vietnamese authorities (principally Brother Nu [sic]) insisted that the village relocation program begin in the toughest area of Viet Cong infiltration, instead of areas where free forces at least had an equality of strength." Forrestal also entreated Bundy "to distinguish between Operation Sunrise in these tough areas and the milder relocation programs going on in the south under more favorable conditions."[23] Forrestal's disquiet over the execution rather than the substance of the program was, toward the end of the year, widely known within the Kennedy administration. By this time it was a conclusion with which Harriman, and even Hilsman, concurred.[24]

The difficulties the Americans and South Vietnamese had in successfully implementing defoliation and the Strategic Hamlet program indicated that the war was not going well. Forrestal now understood this better perhaps than anybody else in Washington. As the instigator of neither defoliation nor the Strategic Hamlets he was not personally tied to their success and was thus better prepared to identify their shortcomings. South Vietnam's economic deficiencies, based primarily on a shortage of local capital to finance the costs of waging war, also beset the war effort and greatly troubled Forrestal.[25] All of these problems were indicative of a much larger problem, one which Forrestal recognized before virtually any other Kennedy administration official: while progress in South Vietnam was understandably slow, the Diem regime was making it even slower. The South Vietnamese leader, authoritarian and increasingly out of touch, had never really been subjected to pressure from the Americans to reform. In 1961 the hawks on the NSC staff had marginalized the soft hawk notion, frequently advocated by Robert Johnson, that the United States should use its leverage with Diem to compel him to reform South Vietnam socially, politically, and economically. Now, in the summer of 1962 Forrestal resuscitated Johnson's idea and used it as the premise on which to base Vietnam policy. He then succeeded in making it the foundation for the administration's entire approach to Vietnam, particularly after the eruption of the Buddhist Crisis the following year. As Forrestal wrote Kaysen in August 1962, "I sense . . . that we have been pussy-footing with Diem for too long. It seems easier to talk about crop destruction than about means of pressuring Diem to do what we think must be done." Without providing a solution, Forrestal then broached the ultimate dilemma: "I don't think we have much time to decide whether to stay with SVN [South Vietnam] on our terms or get out."[26]

The Doves' Last Cry

The soft hawks' strategy emerged as the consensus view within the administration after November 1961, and Forrestal, from his position on the NSC staff and relationship with Kennedy, became one of its most influential architects. This did not mean, however, that the doves had completely abandoned their opposition to American intervention in South Vietnam. Of the four major doves who emerged from the debate over the Taylor-Rostow report, only two remained by the spring of 1962. George Ball, who as Bowles's successor as under secretary of state would become by 1964 the administration's most persistent dove, turned his attention away from Southeast Asia to Europe, in which he had a passionate interest. Averell Harriman had shifted his stance to become one of the administration's most preeminent soft hawks. Later, in the mid-1960s under Lyndon Johnson, Harriman worked to extricate the United States from Vietnam, but in 1962 he still believed quite firmly in the basic American commitment. It was thus left to Ambassador to India

John Kenneth Galbraith and Ambassador at Large Bowles to argue the doves' side of the dilemma Forrestal had posed to Kaysen: should the United States stay in Vietnam or go?

Whereas Forrestal favored continuing the U.S. presence and even increasing it, Galbraith unequivocally pressed for American withdrawal. Back in Washington to testify before a congressional committee on India in April 1962, Galbraith took the opportunity to write Kennedy a brief memo on South Vietnam. It referred ominously to America's "growing military commitment" and Diem's "weak" and "ineffectual government." "There is consequent danger," Galbraith stated bluntly, "we shall replace the French as the colonial force in the area and bleed as the French did." Galbraith's conclusion was as forceful as his language: Kennedy should seek a political solution, use diplomacy, terminate U.S. military assistance to Saigon, and forsake the Diem regime.[27] Forrestal sent Galbraith's memo to McNamara to elicit the Pentagon's views. Unsurprisingly, the Joint Chiefs responded negatively, which Forrestal doubtless anticipated before forwarding it. Hilsman and Harriman also "vigorously opposed" Galbraith's recommendations and as a result they faded from the debate.[28]

Bowles proved to be more resilient. Undeterred by his demotion in the Thanksgiving Day Massacre, on April 4 Bowles sent Kennedy an uncommonly lengthy memo outlining a political solution for Southeast Asia. As American policy toward Vietnam had changed only marginally from "the very sterile approach which we inherited" from the Eisenhower administration, as Bowles had put it to Bundy—if anything, the United States had become more entangled with the fate of noncommunist South Vietnam under Kennedy—his memo could be construed only as a thinly veiled criticism of current policy. And so it was. Bowles denigrated SEATO as a pact which did "more damage than good to the cause of regional unity and security." But he also took care to differentiate himself from hawks like Rostow and soft hawks like Bundy, who also despaired of SEATO but thought the best alternative would be unilateral U.S. intervention, military or otherwise, rather than withdrawal. A "conspicuous" U.S. military role "in an area bordering directly on Communist China" would likely act "more as a magnet for Communist pressures than as an effective defense." Bowles instead proposed a completely neutral, nonaligned Southeast Asia as the only choice the United States had to prevent both communist domination and endless American entanglement.[29]

Bowles anticipated that the memo would be controversial. "Because of this," he warned when he sent it to Komer, "I am strictly limiting the number of available copies." Bowles nonetheless recognized the importance of convincing the NSC staff if his proposals were ever to succeed. Despite "strictly limiting" the memo's circulation, he sent it directly to Bundy, Forrestal, Komer, and Kaysen. In doing so he undermined his own efforts. The NSC staff's reaction killed the Bowles proposal. Bundy did not forward the memo, either to the president or within the administration, while Forrestal rejected its conclusions.[30] With remarkable persistence, and a stoical willingness to withstand his colleagues' humiliating condescension, Bowles pressed on. In a June memo accompanied by a suggested presidential speech, Bowles reiterated his case for Southeast Asian neutralism. Again he undercut himself by trying to pass his ideas to Kennedy via the NSC staff.[31] This attempt was followed by an article in *Foreign Affairs* and yet another memo, this time to Rusk. To keep Bowles busy and get him out of Washington, Kennedy and Rusk asked him to tour Southeast Asia. Bowles accepted, on condition that he be permitted to test the concept of neutralism.[32]

Bundy and the NSC staff were not so indulgent, primarily because they thought Bowles's ideas were too dangerous to humor. Komer's sarcastic reaction was indicative of just how unpopular Bowles and his views were. "I'm through with being polite," he told the affable Kaysen, "and it's about time you quit being polite too. I'm telling you, and I want you to tell the President that he's got to tell the Nation—this afternoon—that we LOVE the neutrals, that *INDIA, YUGOSLAVIA, POLAND, INDONESIA,* and *THE UAR* are our ONLY true allies and that we can't conduct foreign policy if we won't help those who hate us." Bowles would "love to go [to Southeast Asia] *if* he can reassure them along lines he favors," Komer wrote to Bundy, but there "is a bit too much of his 'neutral Southeast Asia' concept." The danger lay in the deceptive allure of neutralism, which, as Laos was apparently illustrating, was merely a weak method of trading minor short-term benefits for catastrophic long-term costs. Communists could simply not be trusted to uphold Vietnam's neutralism any more than Laos's. "It seems clear that as soon as [the] Reds have 'neutral' Laos pinned down, *they will move to do the same with S. Vietnam,*" Komer warned Kaysen. "If I'm correct that US policy is to avoid this like the plague (at least until we have S. Vietnam on its feet), we should be working hard on spoiling action now."[33] As Komer knew, Bowles would not "tone down" his neutralist plan, and the trip was canceled.[34]

The dovish call for military withdrawal and a diplomatic solution had virtually no impact on American policy other than to discredit noninterventionist options. In ensuring that only the NSC staff had full access to his iconoclastic views, Bowles had identified the locus of decision making in the Kennedy administration. In doing so he ensured that his views would receive virtually no consideration. Even into 1963 Bowles continued to send Kennedy and Bundy his proposals for Indochina, but he received little response and even less encouragement.[35] Generally the NSC staff exhibited two reactions to the Galbraith and Bowles perspective: skepticism bordering on incredulity or malign neglect. Forrestal, who for much of 1962 had been wrestling with the challenge of Vietnam, put his ultimate dilemma to one side and turned his energies toward composing a new strategy to wage the war more effectively and thus more successfully.

The Diem Regime and the Forrestal–Hilsman Mission

When he joined the NSC staff Forrestal believed that the United States should assist Saigon in fighting the communist insurgency but that ultimately the war itself should not become an American affair. U.S. aid and expertise, subsequently employed by the South Vietnamese themselves, would win the war. Forrestal emphasized to Bundy in May 1962, "this is *their* war and not ours." Rather than Korea, where Americans did much of the actual fighting, Forrestal preferred the analogy of the Greek Civil War, during which the Truman administration sent material assistance rather than troops. The conflict in Vietnam, he reiterated, "is not a U.S. war—it will be won or lost by the Vietnamese." For the same reasons Forrestal dismissed the Galbraith-Bowles solution of negotiations leading to American withdrawal. It was simply not in the American interest to bargain away the future of South Vietnam. One State Department official who worked on Vietnam reported to Nolting that "Forrestal thinks our best argument is that this is a Vietnamese war and we cannot presume to drag them to the peace table when they are fighting for their independence." But Diem, as Forrestal was discovering, was an uncooperative and truculent ally who continually threatened to frustrate the soft hawks' strategy of sending only aid and expertise. "The least we can expect," an exasperated Forrestal complained to Kennedy about Saigon, "is for those Governments whom we help to take their fair share of the burden."[36]

By the summer of 1962 Forrestal had reached two conclusions that would guide his thinking on Vietnam into the crucial year of 1963. First, he believed that under no circumstances should the United States withdraw its commitment to a noncommunist South Vietnam. In wrestling with this problem he decided firmly that the stakes were too high and the geopolitical consequences too severe to disengage. For one thing, he commented in 1964, the Kennedy administration had inherited from its predecessor "a moral commitment to support Vietnam." Moreover, like all of his NSC staff colleagues Forrestal did not believe that the revolution in South Vietnam was indigenous; it was, rather, a clear case of foreign aggression by North Vietnam, supported by Moscow and Beijing. After visiting Harriman in Geneva, he came to the conclusion that "while the Soviets were happy with the agreement on Laos, they have little or no interest in being helpful in South Vietnam."[37] Toward the end of the year these impressions hardened into conviction. As he revealed to Bundy in December even Forrestal now entertained the previously taboo notion of American military action against the DRV itself. There was "no doubt that Hanoi controls and directs Viet Cong activities in the South," he argued. "So long as this continues, so will the war in South Vietnam. I therefore cannot help agreeing with Walt [Rostow] that we must include in our planning the possibility of bringing some kind of direct pressure to bear upon Hanoi."[38]

Second, after identifying Diem as the main obstacle to progress Forrestal decided that the South Vietnamese leader would have to be pushed and if necessary forced to reform. This decision was not an easy one, for many feared that the Diem regime would either collapse, come to an arrangement with Hanoi, or ask the Americans to leave if Washington pressured Saigon too strenuously. But Forrestal remained unconvinced that Diem would improve on his own. "Consequently," he explained to Bundy, "I would think that our job was to get on with the pacification of South Vietnam and be a little more vigorous with the Diem Government in insisting on political improvements." Like Rostow before him Forrestal sensed that the situation in South Vietnam was deteriorating and, as it did so, that the options open to Washington would narrow dramatically. Therefore he told Bundy in the summer of 1962 the administration needed to do more to improve the performance of its ineffectual partner: "I suspect that our pressures on Diem are a little too slow acting and need to be stepped up even at some risk."[39]

Depending on the source, reports from South Vietnam oscillated between pessimism and unrestrained optimism. Relying on information from the Diem regime, the U.S. Embassy, and the Pentagon, President Kennedy and most of his administration were fairly pleased with the effort in Vietnam. Forrestal, however, remained pessimistic unless Diem could be made to reform. "South Vietnam has by no means won its struggle," he chided Bundy. "The fight continues and much remains to be done, especially for the social and economic welfare of the vast majority of the Vietnamese people" who live in the countryside. "It is obviously not enough merely to assure the security of the countryside. Far greater efforts need to be made by the Government of South Vietnam to gain the enthusiastic support of all its people." Shortly afterward, he informed Bobby Kennedy that "the war is not going as well out there as one might be led to believe" and that the "major fault" for the decline rested with Diem.[40]

Spurred by wildly conflicting reports on the situation in Vietnam, Kennedy decided to send his two Vietnam lieutenants, Forrestal and Hilsman, to Southeast Asia for a reappraisal. The idea of a Forrestal-Hilsman mission had been originally suggested by Bundy and Forrestal as a way to get a first-hand look at what was turning out to be a very confusing war. Forrestal and Hilsman arrived in Saigon on December 31, 1962, and traveled throughout South Vietnam for the next ten days; shorter visits to Laos, Thailand, and Indonesia followed. Hilsman, who had placed great faith in the Strategic Hamlet program and counterinsurgency, was generally more sanguine about the war than Forrestal. As Nolting recalled, "Hilsman seemed quite optimistic during this visit, Forrestal less so. I was never quite sure where Mike Forrestal stood."[41] Nolting had difficulties comprehending Forrestal's views simply because they were so opposite to his own. The Ambassador was, much to Forrestal's chagrin, habitually optimistic and very close, politically and personally, to Diem. By January 1963 Forrestal had tentatively come to the opposite conclusion that Diem was the primary obstacle to winning the war, much to Nolting's great annoyance.

The mission's conclusions can be described best as cautiously optimistic—Forrestal provided the caution, Hilsman the optimism. It greatly concerned them both, however, that the highest ranking Americans in South Vietnam felt no such trepidation at all. "I have the impression that things are going much much better than they were a year ago," Hilsman observed shortly after arriving, "but that they are not going nearly as well as the people here in Saigon both military and civilian think they are." He described as "a fraud" and "a sham" Saigon's claims that the U.S. counterinsurgency program outlined in the Taylor-Rostow report had been implemented successfully. Forrestal worried mostly about Diem. If the enigmatic South Vietnamese leader refused to reform, much of the progress already achieved would disappear and any future progress would be impossible. "No matter how one twisted and turned the problem," Hilsman reflected in his memoirs, "it always came back to Ngo Dinh Diem." Despite the fact that Diem was "calmer, more self-possessed, and more statesmanlike" than they had anticipated, Forrestal doubted that he would be anything but a hindrance to the anticommunist effort. A conversation with Nhu merely reinforced his anxiety. Because of Nhu's ability to motivate and focus the energies of Diem, "he is at the moment probably necessary to our purposes in South Vietnam," Hilsman wrote of their talk. "But at the same time he is clearly not the man for the long pull . . . In the long run it seems doubtful that Nhu's influence is on the credit side. In the short run, it is apparently necessary."[42]

Called home early from Indonesia by Bundy, Forrestal and Hilsman presented Kennedy a report of their trip and resultant recommendations on January 25. The report generally reflected Hilsman's qualified optimism. "The war in South Vietnam," it began, "is clearly going better than it was a year ago." The South Vietnamese themselves, bolstered by American support, aid, and expertise, were now waging a remarkably successful campaign. This in turn was improving the morale of both the government and the people. The insurgency was almost completely indigenous, as Hilsman had already noted a year before; thus the conflict remained essentially as much political and socioeconomic as it was military. The ultimate strategic objective—eradicating the communist insurgency to provide stability for a noncommunist state—and many of the tactics used to achieve the objective—Strategic Hamlets, an augmented police program, improved civic programs—needed improvement but were basically sound. Nonetheless the NLF remained a powerful force. "Our overall judgment," they wrote, "is that we are probably winning, but certainly more slowly than we had hoped." Diem and Nhu, and an American tendency to respond militarily to what were essentially social and political problems, provided the only obstacles to further progress. To this end the report concluded that the administration should use its economic and military influence with Saigon to compel the Diem government to change. In an "Eyes Only" annex intended solely for the president, Forrestal's cynicism was given freer rein. Much of it was thinly disguised criticism of Nolting: "In general, we don't use all the leverage we have to persuade Diem to adopt policies which we espouse . . . We should push harder for a gradual liberalization of the authoritarian political structure" of Saigon. Forrestal also told Bundy that Washington had to "get our people [to] recognize that what we loosely call counter-insurgency is not primarily a military or even a police problem until [the] situation has deteriorated to [the] last stage before disaster; it is basically a social and economic problem requiring attack at the lowest levels."[43]

Kennedy thought very highly of the report. "Why the hell can't I get this kind of report from regular government people instead of from you two amateurs?" he complained to Forrestal after reading it. The Forrestal-Hilsman report mirrored Kennedy's own ambivalence about how to win the war in Vietnam. Less appreciative was General Paul Harkins, who, as head of the Military Assistance Command, Vietnam (MACV), was the commander of all U.S. armed forces in South Vietnam. Harkins rejected the report's skepticism and insisted that all of its military and counterinsurgency suggestions were already being implemented. Moreover he warned Admiral Harry Felt, the Commander-in-Chief of American military forces in the Pacific, that Forrestal and Hilsman had only acquired "patently a superficial impression" of the situation in South Vietnam. "The overall Report is reasonably fair," he concluded, "though somewhat less encouraging than we view affairs locally . . . My over-all comment is that improvement is a daily fact . . . and we are confident of the outcome."[44]

The administration held a series of high-level meetings at the beginning of February 1963 to reevaluate Vietnam policy based on the Forrestal-Hilsman report and the findings of Army Chief of Staff General Earle Wheeler, who had also just returned from a tour of South Vietnam. Forrestal agreed with Hilsman's conclusion that slow progress was being made in counterinsurgency and other military aspects of the conflict. But he also came to believe that the United States needed vigorously to push Diem to reform—and to this end he believed that Kennedy needed to replace Nolting at the earliest possible opportunity. These were conclusions Forrestal had drawn toward the end of 1962; after his trip to South Vietnam they became firm policy recommendations. To convince Kennedy, Forrestal posed a series of rhetorical questions shortly before a meeting to discuss General Wheeler's report: "In view of Ambassador Nolting's completion of his two-year extension in south Vietnam in mid-April, should we consider a new appointment? . . . Have we been as firm as we should with [Diem] in putting our views across on our military, domestic and foreign policy?"[45]

Forrestal's distrust of the U.S. Embassy in Saigon and the military's "rosy euphoria," as exemplified by Generals Harkins and Wheeler, was now complete. To counter the military he escalated his campaign to reevaluate support for Diem. As he wrote to Kennedy, the administration needed "to develop gradually a more independent posture for the U.S. in South Vietnam and very carefully to dissociate ourselves from those policies and practices of the GVN of which we disapprove with good reason."[46] One way of doing so was to foster links with opposition and other unofficial anti-Diem and anticommunist groups within South Vietnam. As Forrestal explained to Harriman, doing so would not only give American policy more independence, and with it greater flexibility, it would also "increase our alternatives in the event of an accident which results in a shift in the government." An "accident," of course, would probably come in the form of a coup, but Forrestal was unsympathetic and unsentimental despite Diem's longstanding, close relationship with the United States. Suddenly vulnerable, Diem "will become aware of [a] shift in our present policy of total public and private support of his person and family. We should face this likelihood squarely and without guilt feelings." Hilsman, who would also be instrumental in toppling Diem, enthusiastically agreed.[47] In broaching the idea so strongly, Forrestal set in motion the forces that would eventually lead to a coup against in November. This now became Forrestal's main goal. In Washington he met with representatives of the opposition Dai-Viet Nationalist Party, nurtured the anti-Diem views of South Vietnam's Ambassador, Tran Van Chuong, and suggested that the administration withdraw financial support for Nhu's Republican Youth organization.[48]

However, applying pressure to Diem by creating a politically symbolic and eventually punitive gap between Washington and Saigon would be nearly impossible with Nolting as U.S. Ambassador. Forrestal felt that Nolting, who had always strongly supported Diem, could not be expected to push for liberal reform in South Vietnam. "Start looking for a successor to Fritz Nolting," he urged Kennedy in January. "More vigor is needed in getting Diem to do what we want." Forrestal began attempting to convince others in the administration—beginning with Harriman, Hilsman, Kaysen, and Arthur Schlesinger, in addition to Bundy and Kennedy—of Nolting's failings. He doubled his efforts in the spring of 1963. "What is needed is fresh leadership in the field," he wrote Kennedy in May and suggested that the White House simply bypass the State Department in choosing Nolting's successor.[49]

Despite his growing skepticism about America's role in the conflict Forrestal maintained his belief in the fundamental American commitment to a noncommunist South Vietnam. He advocated neither a peaceful, diplomatic solution nor complete disengagement. The emphasis he placed on South Vietnamese political, social, and economic reform was designed to provide the best means to defeat the NLF and win the war; it was not designed to find a graceful way of avoiding the war. In so doing Forrestal may have passed up a rare opportunity to end the war before it had really begun. In February 1963 he was approached by an official from the Soviet Embassy, Alexander Zinchuk. Obviously acting upon instructions to develop the incipient thaw in the Cold War following the Cuban missile crisis, Zinchuk very delicately floated the idea of the United States and the USSR jointly sponsoring the neutralization of Vietnam. Unmoved by this extraordinary offer, Forrestal bluntly said that "the feeling of the U.S. Government remained unchanged, . . . i.e. that so long as there was militant subversion from the north it was very hard to think about any international action which could be helpful in South Vietnam." Forrestal brushed aside Zinchuk's suggestion by reciting the administration's official line that "the major problem in Southeast Asia was to bring an end to northern intervention in the south; and that once this was done, a wide range of possibilities would very likely open up." Despite the emerging détente in Europe and over nuclear weapons—or, as was the case with Bundy, perhaps because of it—Forrestal told Zinchuk that he

> was not aware of any shift in U.S. policy, and that on the contrary recent events in South and Southeast Asia made it all the more clear to us that it was essential that the countries of the areas be helped to maintain their independence from any foreign domination. Of course we look forward to the day when our involvement would not be so heavy; but we were determined to see stability restored.[50]

A few years later the United States would receive several unsolicited offers from communist states—most notably Poland and the Soviet Union—to help broker an end to the war. All of these initiatives, plus dozens of others launched by neutrals and U.S. allies, were futile and destined to fail because by mid-1965 there was little for the belligerents to discuss. Irreconcilable differences over the political future of South Vietnam—independent or reunified? capitalist or communist?—had, after all, brought the Americans and the Vietnamese communists to war in the first place. The two sides did not misunderstand each other; they understood one another's basic motives and objectives all too well. Rarely has Clausewitz's dictum that "war is merely the continuation of policy by other means" been so applicable as it is to the causes of the Vietnam War.[51] However, the war, at least the American phase of it, had not really started when Forrestal and Zinchuk spoke. The United States needed the Soviets' help in 1963 when it could have mattered, not in 1967 when it was much too late. But in 1963 Forrestal, although he was skeptical about U.S. tactics, believed in the overall strategy to keep South Vietnam free from communism. It was a sincere belief that Bundy, among others, shared. As he declared in a speech to the Harvard Club of Washington, the fate of South Vietnam "is probably more important than most of us in a group like this would think—and that it needs more of our attention. This is a major commitment which we have made, and it is unfinished business. And how it comes out is of the very greatest consequence to a very large part of the globe."[52] Much as they would later come to regret it, both Bundy and Forrestal believed it was vital to bear any burden for Vietnam.

The Buddhist Crisis and Overthrow of Diem

When its commandos fired into an unarmed crowd of Buddhist demonstrators on May 8, 1963, the Diem regime unwittingly began a process of internal turmoil and destabilization that would culminate, five months later, in its demise and the deaths of Diem and Nhu. The conflict between the largely Catholic political elite and the overwhelmingly Buddhist population also brought the rift between Washington and Saigon into the open. Forrestal had been one of the first in Washington to launch an anti-Diem campaign, and the outbreak of the Buddhist crisis enabled him to implement his views. Supporting Forrestal in these efforts were fellow members of the "inner club"—Hilsman and, at first more reluctantly, Bundy—in addition to Harriman. With the attacks on peaceful religious demonstrators in May and the sensational self-immolation by Buddhist monks in June, Diem and Nhu made Forrestal's efforts to replace them much easier. In an odd and eventually counterproductive way, Washington's ignorance of local culture and conditions in South Vietnam also simplified things. "How could this have happened?" Kennedy asked Forrestal about the Buddhists and their demands. "Who are these people? Why didn't we know about them before?" Forrestal could only answer that the Buddhists seemed to represent the people's aspirations better than the Ngos. His argument that Diem and his family represented the main obstacle to progress thus gained force with the onset of the Buddhist crisis.[53]

The replacement of Nolting with Henry Cabot Lodge dealt the Diem regime another blow. A moderate Massachusetts Republican whom Kennedy had twice defeated at the ballot box, Lodge had already concluded before setting foot in Vietnam that Diem represented the biggest obstacle to winning the war. This was good news to Forrestal, who had believed for quite some time that "one of our difficulties with Fritz Nolting was that he had gotten very wedded to the regime. He had become an apologist, really, for President Diem. A hell of a good Ambassador, but just stuck on President Diem and the more difficulties Diem raised, the more rigid Fritz Nolting became."[54] Forrestal, however, still had to move cautiously. Although he had converted to the view that Diem was now a liability, Bundy was not yet prepared to sanction a coup.

Nor, for that matter, was Kennedy. Forrestal's two main partners were also not as eager to force a change of government in Saigon. Hilsman recommended that U.S. policy "should continue to be neither to encourage nor to discourage coup attempts." Although Harriman had doubted Diem's abilities as an effective leader, he was also not ready to abandon him. "I get a little tired," he complained to Kennedy in 1962, "of people who expect the Vietnamese to have a Jeffersonian democracy." Before Lodge left for Saigon, Harriman advised him that for all the South Vietnamese leader's faults, "Diem is the best man. Who would succeed [him] if Diem dropped dead?" Forrestal thus had to settle with promoting an anti-Diem policy in the most cautious, and often ambivalent, fashion.[55]

On August 21 savage raids on Buddhist pagodas throughout South Vietnam by Nhu's American-trained Special Forces made such caution unnecessary. The devastation, carried out ruthlessly across South Vietnam, shocked American officials, and Forrestal and Harriman quickly drafted an angry official statement to be released by the State Department the following day. The "pagoda incident made [the] disappearance of [the] Diem regime a mere matter of time," Lodge felt. The "U.S. can get along with dictators but not this kind." The temerity of conducting the raids in the face of growing American pressure to reform and reconcile with the Buddhists elicited a similar reaction from virtually every member of the Kennedy administration. Forrestal needed no further encouragement when William C. Trueheart, the deputy chief of mission in Saigon, cabled Washington with the news that Diem's "decision to embark on this course" was made "with very little reference to his Cabinet or other civilian advisers with [the] exception [of] Ngo Dinh Nhu."[56] The Ngos, it seemed, were intent on defying and embarrassing the United States. A CIA intelligence summary, moreover, sent directly to Bundy and Forrestal by Director of Central Intelligence John A. McCone, confirmed that the Buddhist crisis was a genuine phenomenon, that it had not been created and was not being manipulated by the NLF, and that the Buddhists' "grievances would be removed only by a change in the government." Forrestal also received a State Department survey confirming the rapidly growing anti-Diem sentiment in South Vietnam. Pulling all this material together he reiterated the Diem regime's deficiencies to Kennedy and stressed that Hilsman and Harriman now agreed that "we must move before the situation in Saigon freezes."[57]

Confronted with a rapidly deteriorating position in South Vietnam, which now made it impossible for Kennedy to avoid making a decision, U.S. policy had reached a critical impasse. However, it was not clear to Forrestal that the president realized this or appreciated its significance. He believed that the United States could no longer support both the war against the communist insurgency and the Diem regime—the latter was impeding the former—and he was particularly concerned that Kennedy did not yet concur. Clearly, his entreaties to Kennedy had not yet swayed the president's mind. To settle the issue definitively, on terms of his own design, Forrestal moved to narrow Kennedy's options and irrevocably push American policy in a new direction. With breathtaking audacity—most comparable to the State Department's deliberate toughening of U.S. policy toward Japan against Franklin Roosevelt's wishes in the summer of 1941, and to the Iran-Contra scandal in 1986— Forrestal maneuvered behind the scenes to bring about a shift in America's Vietnam policy by sanctioning the removal of Diem and Nhu. As Kennedy would soon discover, a midechelon presidential aide could constrain the president's capacity to decide foreign policy. Nonetheless, although Forrestal's actions may have boxed Kennedy in, he had correctly anticipated the direction in which the president himself was headed.

Kennedy left Washington on August 24 for a weekend on Cape Cod with Forrestal's admonition to act "before the situation in Saigon freezes" fresh in his mind. But the president did not leave any firm instructions on exactly what should be done next. McNamara, Rusk, Bundy, and Chairman of the JCS Maxwell Taylor were also away that weekend, and like Kennedy, all to varying degrees continued to oppose a coup. Forrestal, abetted by Hilsman and Harriman, filled this propitious void by simply authorizing Lodge to seek the removal of Nhu and, if necessary, Diem. The "US Government cannot tolerate [a] situation in which power lies in Nhu's hands," the August 24 instructions to Lodge flatly stated. "Diem must be given [a] chance to rid himself of Nhu and his coterie and replace them with [the] best military and political personalities available. If, in spite of all of your efforts, Diem remains obdurate and refuses," the cable continued in the bluntest official language yet issued from Washington, "then we must face the possibility that Diem himself cannot be preserved."[58] With Forrestal's help, Hilsman drafted the text of the cable; Forrestal then secured its approval. He first sent a message and a draft of the cable to Kennedy and said that Under Secretary of State Ball would send it to Lodge after Forrestal secured Pentagon approval from Deputy Secretary of Defense Roswell L. Gilpatric. On the basis of presidential approval— which was based on implied approval from the appropriate officials in the State and Defense Departments—and without showing them the cable, Forrestal managed to get Gilpatric and Admiral Felt to endorse the instructions.

Forrestal, of course, had the authority to clear the cable on behalf of the NSC staff.[59]

When Kennedy, McNamara, and Taylor returned to Washington and discovered the extent of the policy shift, and the manner in which it had been effected, they were furious. In his memoirs Taylor memorably called Forrestal's tactic "an egregious end run." McNamara, whose reaction was likened to "an atomic blast," later reflected that while Diem was by no means perfect, "it shocks and saddens me today to realize that action which eventually led to the overthrow and murder of Diem began while U.S. officials in both Washington and Saigon remained deeply divided over the wisdom of his removal; no careful examination and evaluation of alternatives to Diem had been made by me or others; no high-level approach to Diem—with appropriate carrots and sticks—had been attempted to persuade him to mend his ways." Kennedy was livid. "This shit has got to stop!" he yelled at Forrestal the following Monday. A chastened Forrestal offered to resign, but Kennedy felt otherwise: "You're not worth firing. You owe me something, so you stick around." Even Lodge, who welcomed but was not expecting the August 24 cable, was "surprised . . . that no mention of it had been made" to him during meetings in Hawaii before he assumed his duties in Saigon.[60]

Although Hilsman later claimed, somewhat spuriously, that the cable had been cleared properly, and that Bundy himself saw and approved it, it is clear that Forrestal had overreached his authority and set the administration on a new course that would result in the overthrow of Diem and Nhu and the resultant Americanization of the war.[61] But despite Kennedy's anger, the ostracism of the Diem regime was not an entirely unwanted development. As a widely broadcast television interview with Walter Cronkite revealed on September 2, the president himself wanted to distance Washington from Saigon and urge Diem to reform. Forrestal was pushing Kennedy in this direction more vigorously than anybody else. Kennedy did not worry about implementing punitive measures against Diem; rather, his concerns stemmed more from anxiety about the intense feuding and bureaucratic politics over Vietnam within his own administration. "My God!" Kennedy exclaimed shortly after the cable had been sent. "My government is coming apart." Forrestal and the August 24 cable were simply slightly ahead of Kennedy's own desired pace.[62]

Despite efforts by McNamara, Taylor, and Rusk to halt the momentum created by the August 24 cable, Washington had indicated an official willingness to support anti-Diem forces. Intentionally or not, the overthrow of the Diem regime now became the primary U.S. policy option. For his part, Forrestal strove to maintain the anti-Diem drive by emphasizing Diem's political ties to the despised and distrusted Nhu. One method of doing so was to furnish Bundy and Kennedy with intelligence reports jointly condemning the Ngo brothers.[63] Another was direct persuasion. "The United States cannot support a government in South Vietnam which is dominated by Counselor Nhu," Forrestal wrote Kennedy, because Nhu had become a liability in fighting the communists. "The fundamental objective of the United States in South Vietnam has not changed: it will continue to give wholehearted support to the prosecution of the war against the Viet Cong terrorists, and will continue assistance to any government in South Vietnam which shows itself capable of sustaining this effort." Before a key meeting on August 28, at the crux of deliberations on whether to seek the overthrow of the Ngos, Forrestal urged the president "to make a firm statement at the meeting . . . in order to counter any sense of wobbling here and in the field." Kennedy's interview with Cronkite thus encouraged Forrestal. The interview, he felt, "has shown our own people that our determination to resist Communist incursion in Southeast Asia remains unchanged, but that this determination does not paralyze us politically in our relations with those countries in whose struggle we are participating."[64]

Bundy, who had never been as staunchly opposed to a coup as McNamara or Taylor, now began to alter his stance significantly. He agreed that it was vital to the war effort to get rid of Nhu, but he also realized that if Nhu were forced from power Diem might have to be ousted as well. In one of the many NSC meetings of August 1963 Bundy logically "pointed out the great difficulty of attempting a coup which resulted in Diem's remaining as head of the government." Above all he felt it was crucial that any attempted coup be completely successful. Should the ARVN generals' seizure of power fail, Bundy feared, the United States would attract much of the responsibility and repercussions, which would in turn deal the war effort a blow from which it might not recover. He had also come to favor an American-encouraged, but not directly supported, overthrow of Diem and Nhu. Speaking in support of a coup and against suggestions from McNamara and Nolting of new conciliatory approaches to Diem, Bundy argued "that the US posture would be better if the [South Vietnamese] Generals made this attempt."[65]

In doing so, Bundy committed himself, and by extension Kennedy, to a forced change of political leadership in Saigon. Mainly because of Nhu, Diem had become a domestic and international liability. Most important, like Forrestal before him, Bundy concluded that Diem could no longer lead the anti-communist fight. Although he wavered slightly after Rusk (with strong support from McNamara and Taylor) rescinded the August 24 instructions to Lodge, Bundy remained consistently supportive of the ouster of Diem.[66] "The important thing," he told Hilsman, "is to win the war," and if a coup could help, then so be it. In a tense exchange with Nolting at a September NSC meeting, Bundy flatly rejected the argument that Diem had faced similar obstacles in the past only to emerge unscathed. "In 1961 the hatred and fear was [sic] directed against the Viet Cong," he argued. "It is now directed against the Diem government." He recruited Forrestal and Hilsman, renowned for their anti-Diem tendencies—that fall, *Time* magazine dubbed them the "Gung Ho Boys" for their enthusiasm for a coup—to write policy guidelines for the coming months. Inevitably their efforts produced a set of staunchly anti-Diem papers. He also supported Lodge's efforts from Saigon. "Cabot is a lion, isn't he?" an impressed Bundy remarked to Rusk after reading an anti-Diem cable from Lodge. At a subsequent White House meeting Bundy described a cable from Lodge that was the Ambassador's most explicit recommendation yet for a coup as "one of his best." "Bundy was visibly disturbed by the way things are going in Vietnam," one aide recorded of the meeting, "and, in a revelation one seldom sees, seemed at a loss about what to do." Referring to the Ngos, "Bundy . . . said that this was the first time the world had been faced with collective madness in a ruling family since the days of the czars."[67]

By the beginning of September Bundy was one of a handful of officials to take charge of Vietnam policy.[68] As he had during the Cuban and Berlin crises, he used his dual role as policy formulator and administrator to shape Washington's relationship with Saigon to fit his own view, which advocated change but not at any price. Thus he orchestrated a course between the Pentagon's stance that Diem was the best available leader of a bad bunch and the Forrestal-Hilsman-Lodge belief that Diem and Nhu posed the greatest obstacle to winning the war and must be removed immediately. Fearing that a failed coup attempt would do more damage than no attempt at all, he proceeded cautiously between these two extremes. On one hand, as he complained to Rusk, "McNamara and Taylor just don't buy the assessment that this is going to get worse and something serious must be done." On the other, he wanted to ensure that U.S. officials did not act hastily, that "we do not reach a crisis within days, but rather within weeks." One method of doing so was to send public signals to Diem, such as the evacuation of American dependents.

Another was to encourage Senator Frank Church to sponsor a resolution calling for an end to American aid to the Diem regime if the repression of the Buddhists did not come to a halt. Bundy hoped that these largely symbolic measures would apply pressure to the Ngos without tying the administration's hands.[69]

Characteristically, Kennedy vacillated. Unsure about a coup but still determined to prevent a collapse of noncommunist South Vietnam, he hoped that neither outcome would happen. In response both to the chaos in South Vietnam and mounting pressure from within his administration to cast the Diem regime adrift, Kennedy decided to send a McNamara-Taylor mission to Saigon. Forrestal, who had exhorted Bundy and Kennedy instead "to grasp the nettle" and encourage the overthrow of Diem, was unsurprisingly disappointed. Bundy agreed, and to dilute the pro-Diem mission he secured a place on it for Forrestal. He also urged Rusk to make it "clear" that McNamara's instructions did "not give Diem any comfort." Lodge, for the same reasons as Forrestal, also strenuously objected to the visit. In a telegram with instructions for Lodge, which Bundy and Forrestal drafted, Kennedy promised Lodge that "this visit is not designed to bring comfort to Diem." Forrestal was able to use the trip to reinforce Lodge's anti-Diem stance. A conversation in Saigon with Alain Félix of the Banque Française de l'Asie confirmed Forrestal's hunch that as long as American military assistance continued undiminished, the suspension of economic assistance, such as the Commodity Import Program, for which Forrestal had been pressing, would hurt Diem politically without hindering the overall war effort.[70]

With ARVN generals and U.S. officials plotting the Ngos's demise, the situation remained unstable throughout October. The McNamara-Taylor report reflected the Pentagon and MACV's view that the war had progressed militarily in 1963. The report conceded that the Diem regime had room for political improvement, but it also rejected a coup or any other overtly anti-Diem maneuvers.[71] Despite the McNamara-Taylor mission, the drift towards an American-endorsed coup proceeded apace. Nothing, it seems, could check the momentum unleashed by the August 24 cable. While the Pentagon and, to a lesser extent, the CIA were opposed to a coup, the NSC staff, the State Department, and the U.S. Embassy in Saigon were resolutely in favor. But Kennedy remained uncertain and indecisive. In his role as Kennedy's foreign policy gatekeeper, Bundy held the bureaucratic balance of power within an evenly divided administration. Although cautious, he thought it best that Diem and Nhu be removed from power. On October 5 he cabled Lodge not to push too obviously for a coup. "There should, however," he continued, "be urgent covert effort with closest security under [the] broad guidance of [the] Ambassador to identify and build contacts with possible alternative leadership as and when it appears." Such contacts, which Forrestal had been cultivating for months, marked another step in Bundy's conversion to support a coup.[72]

Intrigue over Diem's overthrow continued to build in Saigon through October, and by the end of the month a move by the ARVN generals seemed inevitable. On October 24 Bundy warned Lodge not to become involved "in an operation which is difficult to deny," but he did not warn the embassy away from encouraging a coup altogether. "We are particularly concerned about [the] hazard that an unsuccessful coup, however carefully we avoid direct engagement, will be laid at our door by public opinion almost everywhere," Bundy cabled Lodge the following day. As he expressed more bluntly in a section of the cable he did not send, the "difficulty is of course that we want to be able to judge these plans without accepting responsibility for them; the impossible takes a little longer." In other words Bundy wanted the United States to engineer a coup against Diem without revealing its ultimate involvement and responsibility.[73]

The overthrow of the Ngos and the end of the Diem era now came to a swift and grisly conclusion. On October 29, after discussing it at an NSC meeting, Bundy cabled Lodge with instructions not to discourage the ARVN generals—which itself implied American support—unless it was clear that the coup would fail. He repeated these instructions a day later.[74] By this time Bundy was more optimistic about the prospects for a coup, and the caution with which he conveyed Lodge's instructions simply hedged the American bet. With the balance of forces and "tactical surprise" in their favor, Bundy now felt that the generals would likely prevail. His chief concern remained that Lodge retain an appearance of "plausible denial" and, above all, that "once a coup under responsible leadership has begun . . . it is in the interest of the U.S. Government that it should succeed."[75]

The anti-Diem conspirators overthrew Diem and Nhu on November 1. News of the their murder reached Washington a day later. While Bundy and Forrestal were, like Kennedy, appalled at the killing, they were extremely pleased with the overall result. Forrestal thought "it was a well executed coup, much better than anyone would have thought possible." Bundy agreed. Unlike the overthrowing of Latin American governments, he felt that what happened in Saigon "was an example of the acceptable type of military coup" and thought it was crucial "to get something out very quickly to Saigon stress-ing [the] point we are not worried."[76] He told his staff that he was "impressed with the fact that the Saigonese people threw garlands of roses on the tanks and seemed genuinely pleased with the revolt." But he also "deplored the slaying of the brothers" and did not believe that, with their hands bound securely behind their backs, Diem and Nhu could have shot themselves as the generals were claiming. It was, he noted dryly at a White House meeting, "not the preferred way to commit suicide," and "regretted that the coup leaders still insisted that it was." Nonetheless, the largest obstacle barring the path to an improved war effort had been removed. Most important, the war against the NLF could now proceed unimpeded by the misrule of Diem and Nhu. "We now have nothing to divide us," Bundy declared at an NSC meeting after the coup.[77] He was undoubtedly thinking of the division between pro- and anti-Diem factions within the administration as well as those between Wash-ington and Saigon. Either way the ouster of Diem ensured, for the time being, that Washington and Saigon could concentrate on fighting communists instead of each other. Although he would not have guessed it, this was also the task that would absorb Bundy's energies for the next two years.

CHAPTER 6

Bundy the Adviser:
The Drift to War

Three weeks after the murder of Diem and Nhu, President Kennedy himself was assassinated. Forrestal was in Saigon on another fact-finding mission at the time, where the violent demise of the two presidents within a month caused a great deal of confusion, if not panic. "Everyone here [is] shattered and judgments [are] difficult to make," he cabled Bundy the day Kennedy was shot. His first instinct was to return immediately to Washington. But although Bundy was similarly saddened and shocked—he choked back tears and lost his voice several times while presiding over his first staff meeting after the assassination—he characteristically immersed himself in work, namely, the transition to a new president and a new administration.[1] Above all he believed that his ultimate duty was to the office of the president rather than to a particular individual. "I know how you loved the President," he replied stoically to Forrestal, "but [I] believe that [the] best interests of the country and therefore his own desire would be for you to complete" the visit. "Carry the flag till then."[2] During this period, to ease the transition and ensure continuity in the basic direction of foreign policy, Bundy sought to facilitate and formulate policy in equal measures. Although he strongly favored escalated military intervention in Vietnam, he concentrated on acting as the president's gatekeeper on foreign policy, filtering important information to Lyndon Johnson and enacting presidential wishes. His influence over policymaking did not wane—precisely the opposite occurred—but on Vietnam policy he was still unwilling to take control and impose his own views. He was content for now to play the role of adviser.

Bundy, Forrestal, and the Kennedy Counterfactual

The sudden and nearly simultaneous deaths of Diem and Kennedy did not significantly alter American policy in Vietnam. One school of thought has emerged to argue that had he lived, Kennedy would not have gone to war in Vietnam as Johnson did in July 1965. Bundy's voice joined this chorus shortly before his own death in 1996; he had come belatedly to believe that Kennedy would have been more wary of committing troops than Johnson. Thus it is Johnson—and not Kennedy, McNamara, Rusk, or Bundy—with whom ultimate responsibility for the disastrous Vietnam War rests. With such enormously high stakes it is not difficult to understand why this battle for history and historical reputation has been waged on this singular issue.[3]

Bundy himself had previously rejected this very argument. In 1978 he revealed to an audience at the Massachusetts Historical Society:

> I have never thought it wise to speculate in public as to what John Kennedy would have done about Vietnam had he lived. The public record shows him constantly asserting two propositions that could not have coexisted easily in later years: that we must not quit there and that in the end the Vietnamese must do the job for themselves. I find this contemporary public record much more persuasive than later suggestions that he was already determined to leave Vietnam.[4]

At various times Rusk, William Bundy, Chester Cooper, and, ironically, Robert Kennedy all concurred with this interpretation.[5]

Moreover, McGeorge Bundy felt this way during the actual moments of decision. In March 1965 he urged Johnson to proclaim publicly the link between Kennedy's Vietnam policy and his own. Such a speech, Bundy emphasized, would "give us protection and encouragement with some of the 'liberals' who are falsely telling each other that your policy is different from his." Others on the NSC staff have also, at one time or another, discounted the theory that Kennedy planned to withdraw from Vietnam. Shortly before the assassination, for example, Kennedy apparently asked Forrestal "to organize an in-depth study of every possible option we've got in Vietnam, including how to get out of there. We have got to review this whole thing from the bottom to the top." But Forrestal, who would soon press more vigorously for direct military measures against the DRV, believed that this was simply "devil's advocate stuff," Kennedy's method of maximizing his options without necessarily making a firm decision.[6] The issue is not simply a trivial historical game of "what if?" It is highly relevant in determining the role and relative importance of Bundy and the NSC staff in the decision making on Vietnam. If these advisers, on whom Kennedy relied so heavily, had no influence with Johnson, or were merely fulfilling a domineering president's agenda, their role and views become much less significant when explaining the origins of the Vietnam War.

Bundy and Forrestal did not believe that Kennedy was planning to withdraw from South Vietnam. More important, neither ever believed that the United States should disengage. As we have seen, as early as November 1961 Bundy had recommended a limited deployment of American ground troops to South Vietnam to pressure the Vietnamese communists and send a signal that the United States would not be pushed out of Southeast Asia. By the summer of 1964 he would stress to an uncertain Johnson that "America keeps her word," that the "issue is the future of Southeast Asia as a whole," that the American "purpose is peace," and that the war "is not just a jungle war, but a struggle for freedom on every front of human activity."[7] These are not the words of a reluctant warrior. And whereas Forrestal had originally emphasized the political and economic aspects of waging the conflict, in late 1963 and early 1964 he would come to press for an intensified military effort against the communists in South Vietnam and the use of direct American military pressure against the DRV. Both Bundy and Forrestal believed firmly in the basic American commitment to a noncommunist South Vietnam, and as a corollary they consistently argued that Washington would have to increase its own effort to maintain this commitment.

Pressures to Escalate

In one of the earliest versions of what the Nixon administration would later call "Vietnamization," the October 1963 McNamara-Taylor mission stressed that the war effort in South Vietnam should be prosecuted more vigorously and, in the event of success, eventually turned over entirely to the South Vietnamese themselves. McNamara in particular believed that the United States could withdraw 1,000 military personnel by the end of 1963 and completely withdraw militarily by 1965, provided that the war effort showed steady signs of progress. Kennedy approved the McNamara-Taylor military recommendations, although he did not want the withdrawal contingency plan to be made public. To guarantee that these recommendations were implemented, Bundy directed Forrestal to "draw together the recent materials on Vietnam and issue an appropriate NSAM." Accordingly, on October 11 Bundy enshrined the president's decision, already made some days earlier and relayed to the U.S.

Embassy in Saigon, by sending NSAM 263 to the State and Defense Departments and the Joint Chiefs of Staff. As the historian William Conrad Gibbons has pointed out, as an "action memorandum" NSAM 263 was something of a misnomer. Rather than directing the State and Defense Departments to pursue a new course of action, the memo simply made official an already implemented presidential decision. The new directive concerning the withdrawal of troops was merely provisional, completely reliant upon the continuation of military progress. The plan to remove U.S. soldiers became meaningless when reports of progress were revealed to be fraudulent in the months following the Diem coup. NSAM 263 did not represent a fundamental shift in policy, and it certainly did not constitute a plan to pull out of Vietnam.[8]

The coup against Diem and the chaos that quickly followed led to a November 20 meeting in Honolulu among virtually all of the important American decision makers on Vietnam except the president. Based on these deliberations Bundy drafted another NSAM to reflect the importance of South Vietnam and the urgency with which the administration now felt it had to wage the conflict. Although the first version had been drafted before, NSAM 273 was actually signed and issued with slight revisions on November 26, four days after the Kennedy assassination. Regardless of these circumstances, Bundy's original purpose was to stress the importance of maintaining the commitment to South Vietnam. Continuity between presidents was a residual and fortuitous subtext. "It remains the central object of the United States in South Vietnam," he wrote in the NSAM, "to assist the people and Government of that country to win their contest against the externally directed and supported Communist conspiracy. The test of all U.S. decisions and actions in this area should be the effectiveness of their contribution to this purpose." NSAM 273 called for a comprehensive, rather than an exclusively military, effort. The memo also explicitly stipulated that planning for attack on the DRV should begin. As Johnson's first policy directive on Vietnam, NSAM 273 signaled that the United States would not quit Vietnam. As such, it marked another crucial step in the process of military escalation.[9]

Bundy was in the vanguard of ensuring that the Johnson administration did not waver in its commitment to South Vietnam. In December he reminded Johnson to discuss the importance of Southeast Asia to U.S. national security in one of his first meetings with the congressional leadership, and to reiterate in a news conference the president's "determination to carry on the effort" in Vietnam. During this transitional period, with uncertainty in Washington and turmoil in Saigon, Bundy and Forrestal thought it imperative to stress that there was no change in America's determination to maintain its commitment. The war in the Mekong Delta and much of the South Vietnamese countryside was, Forrestal revealed at a high-level meeting, deteriorating rapidly. Instead of diverting attention to "marginal problems," in which he included potential diplomatic solutions, he urged his colleagues to "concentrate on the war."[10]

With these remarks Forrestal touched briefly on a phenomenon that began to trouble the administration greatly. The replacement of Ambassador Frederick Nolting with Henry Cabot Lodge in August and, more important, the overthrow of the Diem regime in November belied indications that the war was progressing well. It was in fact not going at all well, which came as a shock to Bundy (but not to Forrestal, whose skepticism had inured him to the overoptimism of the Kennedy period). Post-Diem intelligence from the CIA, which demonstrated that the NLF was winning both the military and political struggles in South Vietnam, revealed to Bundy and the NSC staff the true state of affairs. One such memo explained that Saigon's new government had not yet been able to consolidate power, much less establish its authority over the NLF in the rest of South Vietnam, that security in some regions "has deteriorated to a disturbing extent," and that the Strategic Hamlets had been "particularly hard hit." In February 1964 Forrestal wrote to McNamara to inform him that in addition to the Strategic Hamlet program, the majority of American military and counterinsurgency projects in South Vietnam "have deteriorated badly." Forrestal's assessment was indeed pessimistic: "The next four or five months will be critical in the sense that if a favorable political and military trend does not develop in that period, we will slowly lose our position in Vietnam and the rest of Southeast Asia."[11]

Forrestal's warning reflected his sense, which Bundy shared, that the United States would have to undertake two major initiatives to improve conditions in South Vietnam. First, an entirely reformed, but not necessarily new, U.S. effort in South Vietnam was essential. As early as the Honolulu conference, Bundy had expressed his belief that the Strategic Hamlet program must continue to be a top priority.[12] As the previously accepted optimism gave way to the pessimism of December 1963, Forrestal wrote directly to President Johnson to convey the bad news that the "most urgent current problem" was the crumbling of the Strategic Hamlets. But he also expressed his hope that a new program would be created shortly, "something which should be rather easy for us to do, since it would draw heavily from the old Strategic Hamlet Program." On January 30 another coup in Saigon saw General Nguyen Khanh seize power from the military junta that had ousted the Ngos. Forrestal viewed this development with relief because the new government would be "more free to attend to the substantive problems of winning the war," something the junta, with its shared power under a somewhat anarchic organizational structure, was unable to do. He was also more willing to approve of defoliation than he had been in 1962. Before other measures could be adopted, such as attacking the North, Forrestal felt that the situation in the South would first have to be stabilized and improved. All these measures were designed to achieve this goal. And if Saigon could not defeat the insurgency, he was prepared to recommend a much larger U.S. role in running South Vietnamese political and military affairs.[13]

Second, to facilitate improvement in the South the Johnson administration would need to reorganize its own decision-making team, particularly within South Vietnam. The chief problem was the leadership of the American team in Saigon, especially the ambassador. Lodge was politically influential, temperamentally imperious, and often independent of Washington, traits that were ideal in handling the Diem regime but not at all conducive to helping a new government to establish its own political legitimacy. Instead of a "dominant personality" and a "strong-willed personal operator," what was needed now, Bundy thought, was "a good manager, who can develop a team to do a very complex job." Although Lodge had only served as ambassador for four months, by December both Bundy and Forrestal thought that he should be replaced as soon as possible.[14]

Although Lodge did not help the war effort, MACV Commander General Paul Harkins, who had been close to Diem and culpable for much of the misleading data and unwarranted optimism from South Vietnam, was seen as a positive liability. "I do not know anyone in the top circles of your government," Bundy informed Johnson in early January 1964, "who believes that General Harkins is the right man for the war in Vietnam now." Harkins "has been unimpressive in his reporting and analyzing, and has shown a lack of grip on the realities of the situation." The major difficulty in replacing Harkins, Bundy warned, was that he enjoyed complete backing from the Pentagon. Although McNamara recognized Harkins's weaknesses, he felt constrained in what he could do because of the firm support for Harkins from the military hierarchy. After an unsuccessful attempt to persuade McNamara to remove Harkins, Bundy turned to Johnson for help. "You, on the other hand, can give [McNamara] a direct order to do what in his heart he knows he should." The secretary of defense would welcome intervention from the president, Bundy insisted, for "he is a soldier."[15]

On top of all this was a large philosophical difference between civilians Bundy and Forrestal and the military. Bundy and Forrestal felt "that the military thought of the war in Vietnam too much in terms of regular conventional warfare" instead of in terms of counterinsurgency and political, social, and economic reform. "I don't think we do have enough [Americans] with a guerrilla and counterinsurgency mentality" in South Vietnam, Bundy argued on the telephone to Johnson. Forrestal did not think that the military, even the branches that concentrated on counterinsurgency such as Special Forces, properly understood what was required in fighting communist guerrillas. The Green Berets, he remarked, were merely "Boy Scouts with guns" matched against the hardened, ruthless NLF. He even strongly advised that a recent book on the failure of the French to adapt to guerrilla warfare in the 1950s be made required reading for civilian and military officials alike. Bundy and Forrestal were not conceptually opposed to a wider U.S. war against the North, but they thought the South must be stabilized first, whether through South Vietnamese sociopolitical reform or American counterinsurgency.[16]

The Specter of Neutralism

While Bundy and Forrestal worked to reorganize American policymaking and military tactics into a winning strategy, people beyond the administration began to question the commitment to South Vietnam itself. The overthrow of the Diem regime seemed to some contemporary observers to offer a way out of the deepening quagmire. On November 6 James Reston used his column in the *New York Times* to call for the United States to abandon hopes for a military victory and enter into negotiations to secure the neutralization of Indochina and American disengagement from South Vietnam. A few days later a lead editorial in the *Times* echoed Reston's message. Unsurprisingly, the NSC staff disagreed. Whatever the intellectual merits of the Reston-*Times* argument, Forrestal unequivocally dismissed the prospect of negotiations and neutralism. He derided the call for negotiations as an "old shibboleth" that "must be causing worries in Saigon." In response, he wanted Kennedy to reiterate forcefully the commitment to a noncommunist South Vietnam by stating that the United States would leave only when the North Vietnamese did so as well.[17]

Forrestal was concerned enough about the *Times* campaign, which marked a change of argumentative direction for America's most influential newspaper, to raise the matter with Bob Kleiman of the paper's editorial board. The *Times* editor "suggested rather strongly that we move as soon as possible toward a reconvening of the Geneva Conference and a negotiated settlement of the differences between North and South Vietnam." Kleiman argued that the administration should act now because the political strength and legitimacy of the governing junta in Saigon would only deteriorate. Just as he had with Zinchuk of the Soviet Embassy, Forrestal categorically rejected the diplomatic option:

> I told him that I had great difficulty with this suggestion and thought that it would be folly to pursue this line at the present time. South Vietnam was still not strong enough to approach the bargaining table with any hope of coming away whole. Furthermore, there was no indication that responsible Vietnamese *in Vietnam* would view the prospects of a new Geneva Conference as anything less than a complete sellout by the U.S. I emphasized that we definitely looked toward the time when South Vietnam would be strong enough to deal with the North on at least a basis of equality.[18]

Kleiman was doubtless more concerned with extracting the United States from a dangerous situation in Vietnam than he was with a "sellout" of the South Vietnamese. To Forrestal, however, ensuring the survival of a noncommunist South Vietnam was a much more important goal than the extrication of America from a difficult commitment. He repeated this position to the French ambassador to Washington, Hervé Alphand, who had asked why the United States continued to oppose the neutralization of Vietnam. "To be neutral, one had to be strong," Forrestal replied, "and it would take some time to build the necessary strength." It was a formula that Bundy and Forrestal would regularly employ to fend off the advocates of neutralism. Forrestal subsequently drafted a cable to Lodge, who was worried by the rumors floating around Saigon about a French-sponsored neutralist plan, to reassure the ambassador that "we are against neutralism and want to win the war."[19]

As Forrestal certainly realized, *New York Times* editorials were read closely around the world. Zinchuk confirmed as much when he told Forrestal "that a conference in Vietnam such as that proposed by the *New York Times* might be a good idea." In an astonishing admission Zinchuk observed, "rather philosophically," that Khrushchev had been disappointed with developments in the region. The Soviet Premier had instead hoped "that the entire Southeast Asian Peninsula, including Thailand, would eventually become non-aligned and independent of any great power influence," particularly the Chinese, who were now the Soviets' main adversary. Leadingly, Zinchuk then inquired about Vietnam. Forrestal ignored the overture and responded ritualistically that Americans were "firm in our determination" and that U.S. assistance to Saigon would continue indefinitely as required. Sooner or later the insurgency would be defeated and American assistance would no longer be necessary. "Once this has been achieved," Forrestal said in a recitation of the message he had given to Kleiman, "the matter of relations between the North and the South could be regulated in a normal manner." Yet again Forrestal had closed the United States off from the one diplomatic partner that might have been able to make a difference.[20]

Apart from the *Times* articles, the biggest threat to the administration's Vietnam policy was Senate Majority Leader Mike Mansfield, a powerful Democrat who also favored a neutralist solution for Indochina. Mansfield also happened to be an expert on Asia, a former history professor at the University of Montana who had made Indochina his specialty. As a Democratic Senator in the 1950s, he had vigorously supported the Eisenhower administration's decision to back Diem for the leadership of South Vietnam. However, the prospect of a long, inconclusive war of indefinite duration possibly escalating into another Asian land war between the United States and China greatly troubled him. On January 6 he wrote President Johnson, his old friend from the Senate, to oppose further U.S. military escalation and advocate a peaceful solution based on the neutralization of Indochina. Skillfully, Mansfield used domestic politics—at once Johnson's strongest and most vulnerable spot—to support his point. While Democrats certainly had to be wary of another domestic debate like the one following the "loss" of China in 1949, neither "do we want another Korea." After initial success and widespread public support, the Korean War degenerated into a bloody stalemate that crippled the Truman administration at home. Vietnam, Mansfield feared, had the potential to be another Korea. In each case American leaders had "tended to talk ourselves out on a limb with overstatements of our purpose and commitment only to discover in the end that there were not sufficient American interests to support with blood and treasure a desperate final plunge. Then, the questions followed invariably: 'Who got us into this mess?' " The United States was "close to the point of no return," Mansfield concluded prophetically. There should be "less official talk of our responsibility in Viet Nam and more emphasis on the responsibilities of the Vietnamese themselves and a great deal of thought on the possibilities for a peaceful solution through the efforts of other nations as well as our own."[21]

Not wanting to agree with Mansfield, but also not wanting to clash with him directly, Johnson did not reply to the memo himself but instead asked Rusk, McNamara, and Bundy each to draft a response. In a covering memo to all three replies, Bundy rejected Mansfield's warnings about the influence of domestic politics. He also repeated what Forrestal had said to Kleiman, Zinchuk, and Alphand in November—in its weakened condition, South Vietnam could not be abandoned to international diplomacy. "*When* we are stronger, *then* we can face negotiation," Bundy stressed to Johnson. He was even more explicit in his full response. Employing an extreme version of the domino theory, he warned that a neutral South Vietnam would mean the eventual neutralization of stalwart American allies Thailand, Japan, and the Philippines, and the loss of U.S. prestige in—and the possible neutralization of—South Korea and Taiwan. Bundy conceded that a political solution might become necessary, but in order to protect U.S. credibility it must come only after the United States had tried its best. "We may have to move in these painful directions, but we should do so only when there is a much stronger demonstration that our present course cannot work. If we neutralize, it should not be because *we* have quit but because *others* have." He also took the opportunity to castigate the French, whom Mansfield had obliquely referred to as "other nations" that supported a neutral solution for Indochina.[22]

Bundy's dismissal of Mansfield did not, however, diminish the specter of neutralism that loomed over the administration in early 1964. At the beginning of February Mansfield again tried to convince Johnson that a political settlement was the best possible solution to the Vietnam conflict. General Khanh's recent coup in Saigon, Mansfield wrote in yet another memo, and the deteriorating political and military situation in South Vietnam demonstrated that the conditions for victory did not exist and probably never would. The war was simply not winnable. Against such obstacles a diplomatic solution, led by the French, was the only option. "A deeper military plunge is not a real alterative," he argued. "Apart from the absence of sufficient national interest to justify it to our own people, there is no reason to assume that it will settle the question. More likely than not, it will simply enlarge the morass in which [we] are now already on the verge of indefinite entrapment."[23] For Bundy the chief difficulty with Mansfield's proposal for a neutral Vietnam was that it offered only a means by which the United States could disengage from the region; the plan offered nothing to ensure South Vietnam's survival. "You cannot neutralize the bottom half with the top half waiting to eat it up," he pointed out to Johnson. "And the north half is not about to be neutralized." Bundy suggested that "you should say to [Mansfield] that for the present any weakening of our support of anti-Communist forces in South Vietnam would give the signal for a wholesale collapse of anti-Communism all over Southeast Asia."[24]

France, which had begun to call for a diplomatic settlement during the Buddhist crisis, also continued to pose a problem. The extent to which the Mansfield memoranda openly endorsed French proposals worried Bundy as much as the senator's own position. Despite losing its colonies in Indochina, France retained an influential role in Southeast Asia. When President Charles de Gaulle called in August 1963 for the neutralization of Vietnam and the withdrawal of American forces, most concerned nations took notice. The following March Forrestal warned Bundy that French diplomacy—which Lodge suspected of attempting surreptitiously to influence Saigon—"needs watching," partly because Ambassador Charles Bohlen in Paris was not pressing the American case forcefully enough and partly because the French themselves could not be entirely trusted. Bundy responded by drafting a cable to Bohlen asking the ambassador to have a "frank discussion" on Vietnam with de Gaulle. The United States, Bohlen was instructed to point out, had carefully considered and rejected the French plan as untimely and unwise. Bundy wanted Bohlen to "stress our determination to assure that communist-directed aggression will not succeed in overthrowing independent states in Southeast Asia and our willingness [to] take necessary measures to implement that determination." Bundy also suggested that Lodge return to the United States via Paris to meet with de Gaulle and try to dissuade the French from promoting a neutralist solution.[25]

As Forrestal had discovered the previous November with the *New York Times,* many powerful voices in the American press expressed discomfort with the direction of U.S. policy in Vietnam. Walter Lippmann, the preeminent columnist and old friend of Bundy's, would become a persistent critic in 1965. In March 1964 Lippmann had already come to the same conclusion as Mansfield and de Gaulle: neutralism for Vietnam, if not all of Southeast Asia, was the only viable option. In response Bundy urged Johnson to ask the columnist: Why would neutralism not "be more than a way-station to [a] Communist take-over?" Forrestal meanwhile again sought to deflect the *Times.* Kleiman admitted to Forrestal that he "was in the process of writing an editorial attacking the concept of total victory in Vietnam" and advocating the search for a negotiated settlement. Forrestal responded by implying that the *Times* did not "comprehend the political facts of life in Southeast Asia. To talk irresponsibly of neutralization now is not only unrealistic, but positively dangerous." He urged Kleiman to "keep in mind what it would sound like to people fighting a life-and-death struggle in Vietnam." Resigned, Forrestal reported to Bundy, "I am somewhat afraid that the editorial . . . will not be helpful."[26]

Just as Bundy and Forrestal were attempting to orchestrate an improvement in America's position in South Vietnam, Mansfield, de Gaulle, Lippmann, and the *New York Times* seemed to conspire against their efforts. Whereas Bundy and Forrestal endeavored to deepen the U.S. commitment in order to save South Vietnam, this diverse bunch of critics strove to extract America from Vietnam by promoting neutralism. Tellingly, Bundy never substantively debated the various neutralist proposals and positions; he simply dismissed them, habitually and categorically, as easy but misguided attempts. The "*Times* editorial page is a soft page," he remarked flippantly to Johnson in February. "They're clever, but they don't have a whole lot of judgment." The disparate nature of his opponents, and the fact that these seemingly unconnected figures all foresaw the same dangers and prescribed the same solution, do not seem to have struck Bundy as portentous.[27]

Bundy believed very much that the opposite was true, and in response to the administration's critics just as much in reaction to the deterioration in Vietnam, he pushed Johnson to escalate American intervention. On March 14, two days before Johnson was to appear on television to discuss Vietnam, Bundy offered a few mock responses to anticipated questions on neutralism: "2. The right of people to choose their own course is exactly what we are supporting, and if foreign interference should end, the need for our help will end. 3. While the danger of the threat continues, American support will be firm and strong . . . 5. We are strong, calm and determined, in a situation which has danger but also hope." The administration's public reaction to the neutralization proposals was crucial, Bundy strongly believed. The following day he offered a more elaborate answer to the basic question, "Why is South Vietnam important to us?" With its strategic location and large population, Southeast Asia was vital to American interests, and Vietnam was "a key element in Southeast Asia." Just as important, America had "a commitment there in honor and national interest" that "speaks of our assistance against subversion and aggression." Bundy acknowledged the deterioration in South Vietnam but stressed that "this is no time to quit, and it is no time for discouragement." "I think the single most important problem we face now," Bundy wrote a week later, "is to stop the neutralist talk which is going on here in the Senate, in Paris and in Saigon."[28]

The real problem for Bundy, Forrestal, and the rest of the administration was the instability in South Vietnam, which continued to increase alarmingly. The Khanh government fared no better than its predecessors, while the NLF, supported by Hanoi, decided that 1964 was an opportune time to increase the intensity of the struggle in the South. McNamara toured South Vietnam in early March and did not find any signs of progress. "The situation has unquestionably been growing worse," he reported upon returning, and recommended several significant political, military, and economic initiatives designed to ensure improvement. On March 17 Bundy issued NSAM 288, a brief directive directing all of the primary federal agencies and departments concerned—including the State, Defense, Justice, and Treasury Departments, the CIA, the JCS, and the United States Information Agency—to implement immediately the provisions of the McNamara report. After visiting South Vietnam in May, Forrestal reported to Bundy that "the trend has definitely not yet turned in our favor" and that even Saigon was merely "still in the center of a doughnut of Viet Cong controlled territory." With South Vietnam spiraling out of control, Bundy and Forrestal now believed that the United States needed to escalate its own military role to save South Vietnam from communism. This period marked Forrestal's departure and Bundy's conversion from an ambivalent soft hawk to a committed hawk.[29]

Expanding the War

By the spring of 1964 Bundy and Forrestal were convinced that the United States had to take drastic action to provide South Vietnam the stability and security required to enact political, economic, and military reform. As Rostow had in 1961, they now believed there was no longer the luxury to pursue nonmilitary reform. Logically they both felt that the United States had to tackle the insurgency at its source—military pressure from the communists in Laos and, more important, the DRV. In Laos the 1962 Geneva Accords had done little to ease that country's turmoil or clarify the political situation, and in 1964 the communist Pathet Lao mounted a new campaign against the neutralist government of Souvanna Phouma. A right-wing coup in April, which failed when the United States refused to support it, further confused things. Taking advantage of the situation, the Pathet Lao pressed their offensive. Moreover, the North Vietnamese continued to use a huge swath of territory in eastern Laos as part of the famed Ho Chi Minh Trail, through which they supplied the NLF with weapons, supplies, and cadres. To the Johnson administration the Pathet Lao's strength posed a grave threat not only to Laos but, more important, also to South Vietnam itself.

Thus they both now conceived of a geographically wider war, although Forrestal remained more cautious than Bundy. As early as December 1963, to curtail the DRV's use of the Ho Chi Minh Trail, Forrestal had encouraged Johnson to expand "carefully controlled intelligence operations across the Laotian border" and suggested that the operations be run by the CIA rather than the U.S. military. He also thought that American troops should be sent to the Thai frontier with Laos.[30] But although he was prepared to recommend intelligence operations and an enlarged U.S. military presence in Southeast Asia, he was not yet willing to countenance cross-border military operations into Laos itself, a measure which the JCS and the Khanh government strongly recommended. On April 1 Forrestal explained to Bundy that Laos and Cambodia—a more stable, ostensibly neutral nation that also found itself unwittingly and unavoidably hosting a portion of the Ho Chi Minh Trail— were in another of their political "periodical states of jelly," and so now was "not the time to press against either of these countries." Forrestal's ulterior motive, however, was to establish a firm diplomatic foundation for military strikes against the DRV. The rationale for avoiding action in Laos and Cambodia was "particularly true if we have any hope of laying a political base for direct pressure against the North. It is going to be difficult enough to lay such a base without also having to face the screams of the rest of the world that we are beating on two small and supposedly neutral countries."[31]

Bundy, on the other hand, did not shrink from recommending small-scale military operations along the Laotian and Cambodian borders with South Vietnam or even into those countries themselves. Although he agreed that the main threat came from North Vietnam, he argued that it was both foolish and illogical to treat Laos and Vietnam as separate military theaters simply because they were separate countries. Over Rusk's objections Bundy declared to a full NSC meeting that "we could not separate the political and military chapters on Laos and South Vietnam. We will have to crank in any Laos scenario" to American military planning.[32] The Khanh regime, Bundy pointed out to Johnson, was clamoring for action against Vietnamese communist positions in Laos and Cambodia. Bundy even hinted to Dobrynin that Cambodia would not be indefinitely immune from American and South Vietnamese military pressure should the Ho Chi Minh Trail remain open. Short of actual combat operations—Johnson would sanction armed reconnaissance flights that could fire only if fired upon—Bundy thought that a large multinational contingent, perhaps an armed United Nations peacekeeping force, placed along the Laotian and Cambodian borders with South Vietnam could also be effective in cutting of access to the Ho Chi Minh Trail.[33]

Bundy and Forrestal did agree that any action over Laos would be a tactic only within a much larger strategy of directly attacking the DRV. The North had always represented the more important and enticing target. Along with Laos, the NSC staff had been considering striking the DRV since December 1963. Forrestal, moreover, proposed that the notoriously hawkish Walt Rostow be placed in charge of planning various pressures against the North. Early in the new year Bundy joined Rusk, McNamara, and McCone in advising Johnson to approve a program of covert operations—directed by Americans and implemented by South Vietnamese—against the DRV. The Special Group for Counterinsurgency, of which Bundy was a member, would then monitor the implementation of the program. This program for covert operations, known by its code name OPLAN-34A (Operations Plan 34A), would be responsible in August 1964 for helping to provoke the Tonkin Gulf crisis and the next serious escalation of the war in Vietnam.[34]

With the situation in South Vietnam continuing to worsen in the winter of 1964, Bundy and Forrestal believed that an improvement in the American performance would be irrelevant if the DRV were allowed to infiltrate the South without punishment. Moreover, they thought that action against the North would also boost the flagging morale of the South Vietnamese, whose best political and military efforts would be vital if the insurgency were to be defeated. Along with organizational reform and a change of personnel in the American decision-making team, Bundy emphasized that "stronger courses of action" against the DRV were essential. "The gut question here," he wrote Johnson in preparation for a meeting with Rusk and McNamara and after reading similar conclusions by Forrestal, "is whether and how we can bring pressure on North Vietnam." By the beginning of March, McNamara and the JCS, with considerable assistance from William Bundy, had devised a comprehensive military plan for action against the North. McGeorge Bundy, who charged Forrestal with drawing up the domestic political and diplomatic components of military escalation, promoted the Pentagon's plan to a wary Johnson. "I think it would be useful today," he suggested on March 3, "for you to explore with McNamara his own increasing concern that we simply cannot count on our current policies to carry us through the year without stronger steps of some sort."[35]

On March 31 Forrestal presented Bundy with a political scenario to support military action against the North and an anticipated schedule—with diplomatic aspects correlated to fit U.S. military action—of how the escalation should proceed. Forrestal, who confessed that "I am somewhat more worried by those who argue for a bugout in Southeast Asia than I am by the adherents of Rostow," devised the scenario to accommodate both covert support for South Vietnamese action and overt American strikes against the DRV.[36] The elaborate plan, which culminated in naval and air bombardment of North Vietnam, followed the carefully calibrated escalatory procedure of which the Kennedy and Johnson administrations were so fond. Forrestal designed the scenario so that each step in the process would gradually increase pressure on the DRV to cease its support of the insurgency. The switch from covert support for South Vietnam to overt American military action "can be made either suddenly or slowly," Forrestal wrote, "depending upon the array of military actions from which we choose." For this final phase he recommended that the administration seek a congressional resolution of support for U.S. military action and send private warnings to China and the Soviet Union. Eventually, Forrestal predicted, the United States would find itself at another Geneva conference on Indochina, where it could negotiate on behalf of a stable South Vietnam on terms of their own choosing. To maximize the American and South Vietnamese position he concluded that "if, as it should be, our measure of compliance is a reduction in the insurgency, rather than DRV promises, it is possible that military pressures might have to be continued over a period of several months and perhaps even longer."[37]

Despite the tough stance outlined in his scenario, Forrestal was not yet completely convinced of the need for such a drastic military strategy; but neither was he willing to consider a political solution for South Vietnam, such as neutralization. Faced with a significantly expanded conflict, Forrestal sought to continue existing American policy for as long as South Vietnam could bear. Others were not so unwilling to resort to force. Lodge, for example, had been continually pressing Washington to consider initiating military strikes against the DRV. Forrestal, however, could not be swayed entirely. "The point to keep in mind," he reminded Bundy in April after reading some of Lodge's recent cables, "is that almost any of the actions suggested by Lodge, but not yet implemented, could start a chain of escalation for which we are not yet prepared." Forrestal's reaction indicates a resigned acceptance of initiating further military action—"yet implemented" and "yet prepared" are the key phrases—if the situation in South Vietnam deteriorated to the point of collapse. In the interim he advised that the United States step up its efforts in political reform and counterinsurgency. Along these lines he thought that Khanh could make a series of mobilization speeches to rally his people or introduce a new program to improve the lives of the peasantry in areas of rural South Vietnam where the influence of the NLF was thought to be curtailed. Such a program would, Forrestal predicted, highlight "as many of the aspects of the better life as we and the GVN can contrive. The point is to emphasize as dramatically as we can the difference between life in a government cleared area and life in a VC dominated area." But by now Bundy, who was generally more receptive to expanding the war than Forrestal, had little faith in such soft hawk measures and instead stressed that continuing deterioration could warrant U.S. military action against the North.[38]

The situation in South Vietnam did indeed continue to deteriorate. Forrestal, who accompanied McNamara and Taylor for yet another visit to Saigon, discovered this for himself in May. Exasperated by the lack of progress in the war and the Americans' apparent unwillingness to expand their own effort, Khanh began calling publicly for punitive bombing of the North. Johnson, equally exasperated by the lack of progress and by the distinct lack of tact in Khanh's bellicose speeches, sent the McNamara-Taylor mission to South Vietnam to sound out Khanh and see what could be done to improve things in the short term without resorting to a major expansion of the war. Johnson was at this time commencing a presidential election campaign and did not want the escalation of war in Vietnam to pose any political problems. Above all the administration would not allow South Vietnam to fall to the communists, and it would if necessary increase America's own military role to prevent this from happening.

Forrestal presented Bundy with a report of his findings from South Vietnam on May 26. A slight improvement in some regions of the country could not disguise the fact that the war, if not quite a lost cause, was certainly not being won. In particular Saigon had come under heavy communist pressure, which Forrestal found to be "very depressing." Khanh had not been successful in attracting the loyalty of either the Buddhists (Khanh was, like Diem and Nhu, a Catholic) or the politicians. "Consequently," Forrestal noted, "political bickering among factions in the French fashion continues." The effect of this political instability was tremendous, as was the lack of a coordinated Vietnamese effort in the countryside. In addition the American team in South Vietnam continued to suffer from a debilitating lack of centralization and organization. Only MACV, owing to the efforts of its deputy commander, General William C. Westmoreland, showed signs of improvement. Forrestal again recommended that the American team in Saigon be reorganized under a change of personnel. As a result of what he saw, he recommended that the "United States must take a fairly dramatic step soon against the North, not only to respond to Hanoi's actions in Laos and increased Viet Cong activity in Vietnam, but also to develop a sense of urgency in GVN civil and military personnel. A bit of a shock is needed." Although he granted that the "shock" treatment might be more than the patient could handle, he believed more strongly that time was on their side: "I am convinced that the structure will get weaker, rather than stronger, if we do nothing." Finally, and perhaps most important, Forrestal noted that only the Americans could alleviate the crisis. In the Kennedy era he had believed that the South Vietnamese ultimately had to assume the brunt of the responsibility. However, under the conditions existing in 1964 the United States had to wrest control of the war effort from the South Vietnamese. "Eventually," Forrestal conceded, "this may mean an increase in both the American military and civilian presence in the country-side." But unlike the previous year, Forrestal was now willing to run this risk.[39]

Forrestal found in his boss a ready and extremely receptive audience. Judging it "a very sensitive and private report . . . which I think you will find of real interest," Bundy forwarded the Forrestal report to McNamara, George Ball, William Bundy, Assistant Secretary of Defense John T. McNaughton, and State Department official William H. Sullivan. Bundy also sent the report to Johnson and recommended that the president use it as a basis for private discussion with a group of Republican Senators.[40] "I've got an extremely good memorandum from Forrestal," he excitedly told Johnson over the phone the following day. "He thinks we ought to be ready to move a little bit, mainly the Vietnamese. On the other hand, readiness to do more [*sic*]. He believes really that that's the best way of galvanizing the South, that if they feel that we are prepared to take a little action against the center of this infection, that that's the best way." With prodding from Bundy, Forrestal summarized his findings for Johnson in a separate memo in which he concluded: "What I think is needed fairly soon . . . is action by the United States in some part of Southeast Asia which gets across forcefully to the Vietnamese a sense that we believe Communist insurgency can be contained and that we will do whatever is required to insure this."[41]

Unknown to Forrestal, Bundy had come to precisely the same conclusion while Forrestal was in South Vietnam. In a May 22 paper for Johnson, Bundy informed the president that a "small, tightly knit group meeting at my call" had arrived at a number of tentative conclusions. Bundy used these findings to recommend that the United States assume a greater role in waging the war in South Vietnam. "The object of this exercise is to provide . . . the tall American at every point of stress and strain. This cannot be done overnight, but for the first time there is agreement that we must prepare a means to do it." Bundy also suggested that Johnson consider approving a plan to begin hitting the DRV. "The theory of this plan is that we should strike to hurt but not to destroy, and strike for the purpose of changing the North Vietnamese decision on intervention in the south." Intelligence assessments of probable Soviet and Chinese reaction to American escalation and the drafting of a congressional resolution also proceeded under the direction of Bundy, NSC staff member and CIA liaison officer Chester L. Cooper, and George Ball. The resolution, Bundy wrote, "is essential before we act against North Vietnam, but . . . it should be sufficiently general in form not to commit you to any particular action ahead of time." Sullivan, working temporarily under Bundy, also concurred with Forrestal's views that the politicomilitary effort in the South needed Americanization, and that a political solution was desirable but only if preceded by heavy and continuous military pressure against the DRV.[42]

Bundy encompassed the thoughts of Forrestal, Sullivan, McNamara, and Rusk, as well as his own, in a memo outlining the "basic recommendations" for Johnson. "It is recommended," he wrote, "that you make a Presidential decision that the U.S. will use selected and carefully graduated military force against North Vietnam." He based this recommendation on three premises: that the United States "cannot tolerate the loss of Southeast Asia to Communism"; that without escalatory measures both South Vietnam and Laos would probably be lost to the communists; and that in the end escalation might not be required because the appearance of American military preparations action would deter the communists, thus giving "the best present chance of avoiding the actual use of such force." Treating all of Indochina as a single theater of war and attacking the DRV would probably not, Bundy stressed, provoke Soviet or Chinese intervention. He followed this advice with an outline of the probable course of events that would follow should Johnson accept this basic recommendation. The ten steps included another Honolulu conference, a vigorous diplomatic offensive at the UN, consultation with America's allies in Southeast Asia, the passing of a congressional resolution, strikes against the DRV, and, ominously, the "first deployments toward Southeast Asia of U.S. and, hopefully, allied forces." Bundy advised that the "deployments be on a very large scale, from the beginning, so as to maximize their deterrent impact and their menace." A subsequent draft of the projected courses of action provided for swifter and stronger Americanization of the war effort.[43]

If the genesis of Bundy's Vietnam policy can be traced to the formation of his worldview from the 1930s to the 1950s, and if the proximate motivators of this policy surfaced during the debate over the future of the Diem regime in the fall of 1963—or perhaps even earlier, during the debate over the Taylor-Rostow report in November 1961—the winter and spring of 1964 marked the period of crystallization in his thinking. His advice to Johnson was now characterized by an action-reaction phenomenon: as the situation in South Vietnam worsened, the United States needed to respond quickly; this action was then usually matched by escalation from the communists and an accompanying worsening of the political and military situation in the South. And yet for Bundy, South Vietnam possessed an intrinsic importance worth protecting at almost any cost. The United States would simply have to pay higher and higher costs, now established as a much deeper military role. From the reorganization of the American team in Saigon and the rejection of the neutralization of South Vietnam, to the inclusion of Laos and possibly Cambodia in American military planning and the bombing of North Vietnam and the possibility of introducing U.S. troops to South Vietnam, Bundy escalated his own advice to a reluctant Johnson as the situation seemed to warrant. In doing so he facilitated the Americanization, in both political and military terms, of the war in South Vietnam.

Like Walt Rostow before him, Forrestal left the NSC staff for the State Department in July 1964 to become Rusk's Special Assistant for Vietnam Affairs. By this time he had become deeply pessimistic and disillusioned about Vietnam. Although he had come to favor limited air strikes against the DRV, the increasingly military character of the American presence in Vietnam troubled him, mainly because it was beginning to overshadow the social, political, and economic aspects of the conflict. "What we are dealing with," Forrestal wrote John McNaughton in May, "is social revolution by illegal means, infected by the cancer of Communism." He complained that he had often heard American officials say that we "must win the war first, and then we can get on with the problem of social reform . . . I believed this too," he continued,

> until after the third or fourth trip to Vietnam. But the problems are not separable. The Viet Cong know this. It is why they are winning. To the extent we manage our economic assistance, our military action, and our political advice so as to perpetuate a social and economic structure which gave rise to the very problem we are fighting, we will fail to solve the problem.[44]

As pessimistic as his warning was, Forrestal still could not bring himself to doubt the basic U.S. commitment to a noncommunist South Vietnam, nor did he call for American disengagement. Under a departing memo to Bundy, which he felt should be passed on to Johnson, Forrestal forwarded a CIA intelligence assessment which concluded that China was committed irrevocably to the North Vietnamese cause and that much of the DRV's intransigence stemmed from Chinese pressure. China's belligerence, Forrestal believed, "shows the greater significance of Vietnam."[45]

The Summer of 1964

Two aspects of American escalation occupied Bundy's energies during the fateful summer of 1964. In political terms the administration felt it needed to secure congressional approval in the form of a joint resolution to provide a domestic foundation for expanded military action. It was Rostow who first floated the idea of a congressional resolution in December 1963. He raised it again the following February in a series of memoranda to Rusk, and Forrestal seconded the initiative in a March 31 memo to Bundy.[46] Douglass Cater, a White House aide, wrote Bundy in May that in Vietnam, the "Communists base their strategy on the premise that the free nations are soft and irresolute . . . We cannot allow them to make such a miscalculation." A resolution, Cater argued, would "make our determination crystal clear" both at home and abroad. In a cable to Bundy from Saigon, Lodge contended that a resolution "will give [Khanh] a shot in the arm." Clearly Bundy had been listening to Forrestal, Cater, and Lodge, and by June he was one of the foremost proponents of a joint resolution. He feared that domestic backing for an enlarged war would not be easy to maintain without such a grant of support from Congress, but in a "crash situation," such as an attack on Americans in Vietnam, obtaining a resolution would be relatively easy. And aside from providing safety from domestic opposition, Bundy told a White House meeting that a resolution would be instrumental "in conveying our purpose in Southeast Asia."[47]

In the second week of June, Bundy formally recommended to Johnson that the administration seek a congressional resolution if the situation warranted. In other words, he warned, unless a crisis erupted it would not be wise to provoke an unnecessary debate on Vietnam by requesting a resolution during the election campaign. Johnson, who ran against archconservative Republican nominee Barry Goldwater as a moderate, agreed completely. But Bundy did stress that "the U.S. will wish to make its position on Southeast Asia as clear and strong as possible in the next five months." He argued that the benefits were primarily international: the South Vietnamese would receive a much needed boost in morale, and American determination and domestic unity would be displayed before friend and foe alike. A congressional resolution, in short, would "give additional freedom to the Administration in choosing courses of action" to wage the war. The main disadvantages of not seeking a resolution were the opposite of the advantages: American commitment and authority would be called into question and the administration's decision making would be more constrained. Bundy concluded that the administration did not absolutely need a resolution, but that it would be wise to seek one if a crisis situation emerged. Forrestal concurred with Bundy's assessment and, based on the "increasingly fragile" political scene in Saigon stemming from "worries about our intention and determination," he strongly recommended that the administration push for a resolution, to be followed by strikes against communist positions in Laos. Bundy also drafted a set of guidelines for military escalation should a reluctant Johnson not wish to pursue explicit congressional support through a joint resolution. Significantly, he envisioned a "shift of [the] U.S. role from advice toward direction" of the conflict, including "limited ground troop movements."[48]

In the absence of a congressional resolution, Bundy also focused on other means of improving the situation in South Vietnam. Throughout the winter and spring of 1964 he and Forrestal had encouraged Johnson to find a replacement for Lodge as quickly as possible. Lodge's own wish to leave in June made finding his replacement an urgent priority. Bundy suggested six possible candidates, including McNamara, Robert Kennedy, and himself. In nominating himself, Bundy was not being immodest. He admitted that he was a poor judge of his own attributes and lacked the experience of running either an embassy or a war, but he did stress his relevant experience with Vietnam. "I think I do understand the issues," he insisted to Johnson. "I know I care about them. I speak French and have a heavy dose of the ways of thinking of all branches of the U.S. team in South Vietnam."[49] If the United States and South Vietnam were to win the war a new ambassador was essential. "I continue to believe unrepentantly that this is the single most important job you have to fill before the election," he wrote Johnson a few days later. "You know my list, and I promise you there is not a name that I would not remove from that list on any theory that the individual is more valuable to you where he is." Bundy was appalled by Johnson's eventual choice, Maxwell Taylor. Thanks to the influence of Rostow, Komer, Robert Johnson, and Forrestal, Bundy perceived Vietnam as a dual military and political conflict, and believed that the military half of the war would best be won by applying counterinsurgency and sociopolitical reform in addition to conventional tactics. Although he had begun to favor military measures over nonmilitary initiatives, he also thought Taylor could not perform both roles. In a tense telephone conversation with Johnson, Bundy confessed that "I myself do not believe that in fact [Taylor has] ever understood that war."[50]

Bundy, however, felt that he understood the war very well. He also believed that he understood, better than most, what would win the war. By the end of June it was clear that Johnson did not want to unsettle his election campaign by attacking the DRV or seeking a congressional resolution in the absence of a severe and sudden crisis. American officials continued to declare their determination, publicly reemphasize the commitment to South Vietnam, and warn the North Vietnamese that American patience was not inexhaustible, but they would still need to come up with more tangible methods of alleviating South Vietnam's plight. As Bundy argued metaphorically to Johnson, "an ounce of progress is worth a pint of propaganda and a peck of threats."[51] In the absence of striking the North or going to Congress, Bundy had come to believe that an "ounce of progress" would only come from the augmentation of the American military presence in South Vietnam itself. Combined with his belief that Americans in South Vietnam should take a more executive role in waging the war, it is clear that Bundy believed in the Americanization of the war at the expense of the soft hawk concepts to which he had subscribed since 1962.

Bundy had recommended increasing the number of American troops in South Vietnam before, most notably during the debate over the Taylor-Rostow report. But within the NSC staff the issue had since been superseded mainly by planning for air strikes against the DRV and socioeconomic, political, and counterinsurgency measures in the South. Although Bundy again raised the issue of more troops with the president in March 1964, he did not give the matter his fullest attention until July, after Johnson had ruled out a bombing campaign against North Vietnam. Events on the ground in South Vietnam forced Bundy to think more and more about sending U.S. troops. Upon a request from Bundy, for example, CIA Deputy Director Ray S. Cline wrote an extremely sensitive intelligence assessment concluding that South Vietnam could just barely survive, for no longer than another six months, without a significantly enhanced American effort in the summer and fall of 1964. Bundy and Johnson were the only recipients of this assessment. After Taylor assumed his ambassadorial duties in Saigon he reported that the number of NLF guerrillas and the pace of their activities were on the rise, and that

Washington needed to respond by increasing the number of U.S. troops in South Vietnam to 21,000; Bundy readily agreed.[52] When news of the troop increase leaked to United Press International, Bundy dismissed any potential damage. After all, the increase of U.S. forces did not represent a change, he felt. "I think myself that the news of this small reinforcement is in fact consistent with our policy for pacification in South Vietnam," he reassured Johnson, and argued that the publicity would even enable the administration to advertise its resolve. Bundy reported to Johnson that Khanh's position in Saigon seemed to be stabilized by the announcement of American reinforcements. Finally, he also urged McNamara to reinitiate Pentagon cooperation with the CIA in the training of Montagnards—indigenous tribes living in the isolated mountain highlands of central Vietnam—for "counter-guerrilla activity."[53]

During this military and economic planning, Bundy had not been paying close attention to OPLAN-34A, the joint American–South Vietnamese covert operation designed systematically to harass the DRV.[54] On August 2, two and a half days after U.S. Navy ships carrying South Vietnamese personnel had attacked a North Vietnamese island in the Tonkin Gulf, DRV torpedo boats fired upon the USS *Maddox,* an American destroyer conducting intelligence operations along the North Vietnamese coast. Although the attack came as a shock, Bundy did not think it warranted an American reprisal. "This would all pass over," he told Rusk the next day. But on August 4 the USS *C. Turner Joy,* another destroyer sent to the Tonkin Gulf for support, apparently also came under fire from DRV torpedo boats.[55] Bundy, who had strongly pushed for the introduction of a congressional resolution in the event of a crisis, now saw the incidents in the Tonkin Gulf as the perfect opportunity to do so. The U.S. destroyers, he declared to Johnson, had been "wantonly attacked," while the "new action by Hanoi shows pretty clearly who it is that is really disturbing the peace of the area." He also encouraged Johnson not to listen to UN Secretary General U Thant's objections to a retaliatory bombing; he even later rebuffed U Thant's arguments directly to the secretary general himself. Although the DRV attacks did not pose a substantial military challenge, they did provide an ideal pretext to implement a program of military action against North Vietnam. The incidents also provided the opportunity for introducing the congressional resolution. Thus, when Cater confessed at a White House meeting that the "logic that troubled him was how an attack on US forces specifically justified a resolution in favour of maintenance of freedom in [Southeast] Asia," Bundy replied that "perhaps the matter should not be thought through too far. For his own part, he welcomed the recent events as justification for a resolution the Administration had wanted for some time."[56]

The Johnson administration quickly secured its resolution of congressional support for military action in Vietnam. With only two dissenting votes cast in both houses, Congress adopted the Tonkin Gulf Resolution, drafted partly by Bundy, on August 7. Congressional approval followed closely on the heels of retaliatory bombing raids against military targets in the DRV. The administration was enacting the very program of political and military action on which Bundy and Forrestal had worked for months: militarily, the United States attacked the DRV and established a precedent for further retaliatory strikes; politically, the administration secured explicit and overwhelming domestic support; and internationally, the United States demonstrated its resolve and, as Forrestal believed, the limited nature of its ambitions by keeping the extent of retaliation to a minimum. These measures would quickly prove to be the building blocks for the complete Americanization of the war in Vietnam a year later.

This period also marked the transition in Bundy's own role from adviser to advocate. Whereas in the first half of 1964 he often pressed Johnson to act in a certain way toward Vietnam, Bundy without exception followed the president's direction. After the Tonkin Gulf incidents and resolution, against the backdrop of the perennially deteriorating situation in South Vietnam, Bundy devoted his energies to persuading Johnson to go even further in Vietnam. In the wake of the Tonkin Gulf incidents he reassured a troubled Walter Lippmann that the conflict was still as much political as military. Although this was true in the strictest sense—South Vietnam could never remain independent without political stability and support from its own people—Bundy's reassurance, coming while he was in the midst of urging Johnson to escalate the American side of the conflict, seems somewhat disingenuous. Whereas Bundy once believed that sociopolitical and counterinsurgency measures were sufficient to win the war, after the Tonkin Gulf incidents he felt that only the direct application of American military power could do the job. Bundy's confidence that U.S. forces could win the war was relatively high. Despite evidence that the United States needed to proceed cautiously so as not to instigate Chinese intervention, he believed that "we could handle them."[57]

For Bundy, then, it would be war. "Our only really serious international problem is South Vietnam," he explained to Johnson at the end of August, "but that could hardly be more serious . . . The larger question is whether there is any course of action that can improve the chances in this weakening situation." There was such a course, and he consequently suggested the adoption of a number of measures, including naval harassment, air strikes in Laos, a major increase in the U.S. naval presence in the Tonkin Gulf, and the establishment of American military bases in South Vietnam to be guarded by U.S. Marines. "A still more drastic possibility which no one is discussing at the moment," he concluded,

> is the use of substantial U.S. armed forces in operations against the Viet Cong. I myself believe that before we let this country go we should have a hard look at this grim alternative, and I do not at all think that it is a repetition of Korea. It seems to me at least possible that a couple of brigade-size units put in to do specific jobs about six weeks from now might be good medicine everywhere.

A few days later Bundy asked his brother William, the assistant secretary of state for Far Eastern affairs, some "quite amateurish questions" about the capacity of South Vietnam and its armed forces to absorb large numbers of U.S. ground troops.[58] McGeorge Bundy was preparing the way for American combat soldiers to fight in South Vietnam. He no longer concerned himself with soft hawk reforms and counterinsurgency. He now concentrated on simply winning the war.

CHAPTER 7

Bundy the Advocate: The Rush to War

Although the Gulf of Tonkin crisis temporarily settled America's policy toward Vietnam, it only unsettled Bundy. Although stability and progress in South Vietnam were not to his mind impossible, they continued to remain elusive. Since 1961 the pattern of Bundy's thinking on Vietnam had followed the pattern of developments in South Vietnam: as the situation deteriorated he advocated a strong American reaction and deeper intervention. As the situation deteriorated further through the fall of 1964 and into the winter of 1965, he would push more and more for the United States to come to South Vietnam's rescue. Although Bundy did not want the United States to become embroiled in a major Asian land war, ultimately he thought there was no other choice and did not shrink from an escalated American military role in Vietnam.

The previous ten months marked Bundy's emergence as one of Lyndon Johnson's key foreign policy advisers. By the summer of 1964 only Dean Rusk or Robert McNamara could rival him in terms of power and prestige within the administration. These ten months also saw his interest in Vietnam eclipse other matters of foreign policy, such as Europe or nuclear strategy, on which he had earlier concentrated. But this period also saw Bundy self-consciously limit his role to that of an adviser. He would steer policy in a certain direction, but always the one in which Johnson himself ultimately wanted to travel. Bundy never imposed his own view onto American policy. But after the Tonkin Gulf incidents, with the situation in South Vietnam worsening steadily, with Johnson indecisive, and with Bundy absolutely certain that the United States had to act, he pressed vigorously for more drastic measures to prevent the collapse of noncommunist Saigon. He had undergone the transformation from adviser to advocate.

Converting the Heathens

Although it had stabilized somewhat, the situation in South Vietnam remained grave in September 1964. General Nguyen Khanh had foolishly ushered in a period of political chaos by attempting to seize absolute power in the wake of the Tonkin Gulf crisis. In so doing he alienated virtually every major faction in South Vietnamese politics and, forced to retreat, he retained nominal power only by accommodating the powerful Buddhist faction and promising to include more civilians in his cabinet. The unceasing jostling for power and the political uncertainty arising from it would continue to plague Saigon for nearly a year. Although the situation was bad, Bundy felt it could have been much worse. "The fabric of the Khanh Government is wearing thin," he wrote Johnson on September 24, "and yet it does seem to remain true that the military balance can be held at least for the present." The existence of a balance was partly due, Bundy believed, to the resumption of OPLAN-34A, the covert military and intelligence campaign conducted jointly by the Americans and South Vietnamese against the coast of North Vietnam, and heightened anti-infiltration measures along the Ho Chi Minh Trail through Laos and Cambodia. He informed Johnson that these measures, although relatively modest, were "the best we can design for the central purpose of thickening the fabric of the Khanh government in the next two months." It was, he pointed out, strictly a short-term solution, "but you should know that in the longer perspective nearly all of us are agreed that substantially increased pressure against North Vietnam will be necessary if we are not to face the prospect of a gradual but increasingly inevitable break-up of our side in South Vietnam." Bundy promulgated the short-term plan in NSAM 314. A longer-term plan would have to await further developments.[1]

Bundy was certain that the administration would not have to wait for very long. His colleagues reinforced this notion by sending him gloomy assessments and analyses. From Ambassador Taylor in Saigon, Bundy learned that many South Vietnamese blamed American intervention for their troubles, news which seemed to mirror developments during the chaotic final days of the Diem regime a year earlier. From the CIA, he learned that "the signs of deterioration are so many and so clear . . . that the odds now favor a continuing decay of South Vietnam will and effectiveness in [the] coming weeks, sufficient to imperil the political base for present US policy and objectives in South Vietnam." And from John McNaughton, he discovered the military trend to be so dire that "risky US action [is] needed now." According to the Pentagon, not only was the government in Saigon ineffectual—who actually headed it did not seem to matter—but the ARVN could not defeat the communists and suffered from a high rate of desertion. Even a skeptical Michael Forrestal, now at the State Department, wrote that "it is of utmost importance to maintain, and gradually increase, pressures against the North in order to bring about a change in their estimate of speedy success in their efforts to take over South Vietnam." As specific measures, Forrestal recommended an increase in OPLAN-34A and cross-border operations into Laos in which American advisers would participate.[2]

It was clear to Bundy that the United States would need to resort to a much larger war effort to stave off defeat, but it was less clear that Johnson shared his view. In the fall of 1964 Bundy thus began his own campaign to convince the president of the need for military escalation. "On Vietnam," he suggested to Johnson in preparation for a meeting with the bureau chiefs of various news agencies and newspapers, "I think you may wish to give a hint of firmness. It is a better chance than even that we will be undertaking some . . . action in the Laotian corridor and even in North Vietnam within the next two months, and we do not want the record to suggest even remotely that we campaigned on peace in order to start a war in November. The middle course we are on," he reminded a wary Johnson, "could well require pressure against those who are making war against South Vietnam." In preparation for a presidential speech and press conference, Bundy supplied speechwriter Richard Goodwin with some hypothetical questions and answers on foreign policy. In response to the question, "What can we do to end the war in Vietnam?" Bundy thought it best that the President not answer the question directly. "This is the hardest single problem we have right now," he wrote, "and it has no easy answer." The conflict had exacerbated South Vietnam's already fragile social and political strains and made the construction of a South Vietnamese society nearly impossible. But America could not quit. It had a duty, sustained "for 10 years, under three Presidents . . . to support those who are resisting the aggressive terrorists." As the violence grew, so "our response has grown, but we have been very careful to avoid any recklessness or unjustified intervention. Our business is to help an independent government and people to help themselves, and to do it without growing weary, and without recklessness, and without retreat."[3]

Aside from Johnson, others in the administration needed convincing; failing that, their voices would be either silenced or drowned out. George Ball, for example, had consistently opposed the American commitment to Vietnam since the internal debate over the Taylor-Rostow report. He had kept some distance from Vietnam policy since, but the Tonkin Gulf incidents and congressional resolution prompted his concern once again. Working mostly on his own and at night to maintain secrecy, Ball wrote a comprehensive opposition paper to Vietnam policy. "I did not know where we were headed," he later reflected, "but it was clear the war was getting out of hand." Ball's exhaustive analysis, which totaled sixty-seven single-spaced pages, echoed many of the arguments of Chester Bowles, Walter Lippmann, Mike Mansfield, the editorial board of the *New York Times,* and others. South Vietnam was not an able ally, Ball warned, and the already appalling state of the war effort would only get worse. Expansion of the war would be a futile and extremely dangerous step. Perhaps the most insightful of Ball's arguments, and certainly the most novel, was that rather than reinforcing American credibility throughout the world, the pursuit of a misguided commitment to an unsustainable, authoritarian ally would merely damage America's reputation. Ball argued forcefully that now was the time for the administration to bring about a cease-fire, enter into negotiations with the DRV, and quit South Vietnam altogether.[4]

Ball completed the memo on October 5 and, because he had "a very strong conviction that I should never treat with the President on an ex parte basis," distributed it to Bundy, Rusk, and McNamara the same day. According to Ball, McNamara was "absolutely horrified" that the under secretary of state had committed such thoughts to paper and treated the memo "like a poisonous snake." After two meetings, Bundy, Rusk, and McNamara convinced Ball not to send the memo to Johnson. This articulate dissent from an influential insider represented a much more dangerous threat than the diffuse, and often inconsistent, opposition from critics outside the administration. And, as Fredrik Logevall has noted, had "the memorandum been less cogent, less incisive, these men probably would have been much more willing to pass it on to Johnson." In order to facilitate escalation, Bundy needed a quiet, compliant Ball, and he used the election campaign to justify the stifling of any internal opposition. As early as March 1964 Bundy had told Ball that "anything that could be said to keep discussion down on Vietnam would be helpful." In October, ostensibly on the same grounds, he urged Ball to keep his dissent to himself. Although Rusk and McNamara joined Bundy in their opposition to Ball, it was ultimately Bundy's duty, as the Special Assistant and thus the president's gatekeeper on foreign policy, to ensure that Johnson received a wide range of opinions on any given issue. The election campaign was merely used as a ruse to prevent disagreement from reaching the president. After the election Bundy continued to suppress Ball's memo, and Johnson did not read it until Ball bypassed the Special Assistant and sent it to Johnson through presidential aide Bill Moyers in February 1965.[5]

Some of America's closest allies, usually more loyal than the French, also began to question its policy on Vietnam. The British in particular had always kept their misgivings quiet, recognizing Washington's consistent support for London's own precarious finances and difficult position in Malaysia. But by the end of 1964, with a Labour government newly elected in London, British unease about Vietnam started to grow. The fact that even the British disagreed did not, however, lead Bundy to question the commitment to South Vietnam. In preparation for a meeting between Johnson and journalists from the *Manchester Guardian*, Britain's leading liberal newspaper, Bundy suggested to Johnson that "you will probably want to leave no doubt . . . of the conviction of the U.S. that [South Vietnam] really is a place where the interests of all free nations are the same." British anxiety over Vietnam, Bundy wrote before a December visit from Prime Minister Harold Wilson, "does not necessarily mean that we should not hit them hard" on the issue of increased British aid to South Vietnam, even though such aid would probably not be forthcoming. Instead of moderating American policy in the face of opposition from one of the nation's most steadfast allies, Bundy believed that it was time to rely predominantly on America's ability to lead. After all, he told Johnson, "it is hard to treat a thing as our problem for 10 years and then try to get other people to take on a share of it." The United States would simply have to go it alone.[6]

In an encore that was surely beginning to try the White House's patience, Senator Mike Mansfield also expressed serious misgivings about the war. In response to testimony from Taylor before the Senate Foreign Relations Committee in December, Mansfield carefully outlined all of his concerns in another memo to Johnson. Unlike other members of the Committee, Mansfield did not shrink from putting his dissent directly to his former Senate colleague. "We remain on a course in Viet Nam which takes us further and further out on the sagging limb," Mansfield argued. The situation in South Vietnam was now characterized by "a graver deterioration" and "a growing boldness in the Viet Cong." Ngo Dinh Diem and Duong Van Minh—Khanh's predecessors—had at least possessed some semblance of political legitimacy, but the turmoil in Saigon now meant that the United States was faced with "putting together makeshift regimes in much the same way that the French were compelled to operate in 1952–54." The war was quickly becoming an American war. If the situation continued "in the present pattern," he predicted, "we are sooner or later going to have to face up to the fact that the preponderant responsibility for what transpires in South Viet Nam really rests with us even as it once had with the French." Mansfield then issued a prophetic warning: "If a significant extension of the conflict beyond South Vietnam should occur," especially to China, "then the prospects are appalling." Instead, he advised Johnson to stop the spread of war in Indochina, support neutralist forces in Laos, encourage other Western countries to open substantial trade links with Hanoi, and explore the possibility of bilateral negotiations with China.[7]

As he had done with Mansfield's previous memoranda, Johnson had Bundy draft a rebuttal a week later. Bundy's dismissive response was, he told Johnson, "designed to treat [Mansfield] gently. We could get into a stronger debate, but I doubt if it is worth it." He noted, rather disingenuously, that while there existed a "difference in emphasis" between Mansfield and the administration, there was "no difference in fundamental purpose . . . What seems frugal to us may seem too much to him, but this is not a difference in principle." Bundy then answered each of Mansfield's points in turn. On the possibility of expanding the war, he noted that "it would be a mistake to make a commitment against any U.S. action of any kind beyond the borders of South Vietnam." On the encouragement of trade between American allies and the DRV, Bundy alluded to "what Hanoi is doing in South Vietnam," which categorically prevented a "policy of Free World friendliness to North Vietnam." He agreed with Mansfield's exhortation to improve relations with China, but he also pointed out that Beijing currently had no interest in a rapprochement with the United States. On the nature of the American commitment, Bundy reiterated an argument that the administration continued to make publicly: "No matter what course is taken, it seems likely to us that we face years of involvement in South Vietnam," a prospect the nation must face up to. What the United States must do, Bundy concluded, is follow a middle course: "We do not want a big war out there, and neither do we intend to back out on a 10-year-long commitment."[8]

Reaching the Fork in the Road

As Bundy knew and Mansfield did not, the administration had already decided to discard this middle course and expand America's role in fighting the war. Shortly after trouncing Republican candidate Barry Goldwater in the November 1964 presidential election, Johnson established the Vietnam Working Group, an interagency task force under the aegis of the NSC charged with devising a future diplomatic and military policy toward Vietnam. William Bundy chaired the Working Group, which included other midechelon figures like Forrestal, McNaughton, CIA official Harold P. Ford, and JCS operations officer Vice Admiral Lloyd Mustin. McGeorge Bundy was a nonparticipating member who, like Rusk and McNamara, was one of "the principals" who interceded only when they felt it necessary. NSC staffers Chester Cooper and James C. Thomson acted more as observers to the proceedings than as full participants. The Group's sole purpose was to generate a policy that would win the war in Vietnam.[9]

The Working Group proposed three options. All envisioned negotiations with the DRV, albeit strictly on American terms, as the eventual goal. Option A presented more of the same, essentially to follow the present course without significant change. Considering that the sole purpose of the Working Group was to devise ways of improving existing policy, this was not really an option at all. Option B represented what William Bundy and McNaughton termed the "fast/full squeeze": the implementation of a rapid series of heavy military pressures directly against the North to compel a halt to its support for the NLF. If the first option was too soft, Option B seemed too hard. The Working Group thus made good use of a traditional bureaucratic trick, the "Goldilocks principle": in between the two extremes of the first two alternatives, Option C seemed just right. Basically a combination of Options A and B, this third proposal called for a gradual increase in military pressure against the DRV, beginning with reprisal air strikes in response to specific communist provocations. Option C was a classic enunciation of flexible response: by slowly ratcheting up the pressure, the United States would control the pace of the conflict and could apply further military pressure as needed. Under this scenario, the DRV and the NLF would become convinced of the futility of their cause, cease the insurgency in the South, and sue for peace. But, as the authors of the Pentagon Papers pointed out, over the course of November "these options converged and the distinctions between them blurred." Thus Option A was bolstered to include some additional pressures against the North, the ultimate goal of negotiations was removed from Option B, and the pace of military action quickened in Option C. The middle course, Option C, had come to resemble the most extreme course, the original Option B. A diplomatic solution or complete disengagement does not seem to have been seriously considered.[10]

As one of the Working Group's overseers, Bundy's opinion carried much weight regarding which option would be adopted. From the start he made it clear that he favored Option C, the plan steadily to increase military pressure

against the DRV. In theory Option C was open-ended, as it would only fulfill its task when the communists abandoned their goal. This is why Bundy
preferred it to Option B—as always, the third way seemed to provide more
flexibility and discretion. For Bundy the deteriorating situation in South Vietnam unequivocally ruled out Option A. He had just spent the previous three
months trying to convince anybody who would listen that the United States
needed to do more in Vietnam. At a November 19 NSC meeting Bundy indicated that Option C had become the early consensus choice. "Unless the President indicated otherwise," he told his colleagues, "the present thrust towards
C would undoubtedly continue." A week later, shortly before Johnson was to
make his decision on the Working Group's three options, Bundy wrote the
president to urge the adoption of Option C. Taylor had indicated his support
for it, Bundy stressed, and most officials in Washington concurred. The plan
that Johnson eventually approved on December 2 was, typically, a compromise. Option B was discarded, and Options A and C became Phases I and II of
an integrated program. Existing policy would continue and the implementation of sustained pressure against the DRV would have to wait for another
communist provocation or a sudden deterioration of conditions in South
Vietnam.[11]

It did not shock Bundy to learn that the situation in South Vietnam did
indeed continue to deteriorate. On December 10 Cooper reported that the
Buddhists had undertaken a "concerted" effort to overthrow the government
of Prime Minister Tran Van Huong, the leader of the moment. "External
threats," militarily from the NLF and politically from the neutral Cambodians
(who felt it wise to tilt toward the winning side, the communists) and internal
"political agitation" increasingly plagued Saigon. A week later Bundy reported
to Johnson that "the military situation [is] not good and not hopeless." A
week after that, having read a report by J. Blair Seaborn, the Canadian Com-
missioner to the ICC who occasionally acted as Washington's messenger to
Hanoi, Bundy informed Johnson "of the general conclusion that the situation is going steadily but slowly against us" in South Vietnam.[12] Prospects did
not improve in the new year. By the middle of January, political intrigue
seemed to reach a critical mass even for Saigon, as Khanh renewed his bid
for total control of the government. Khanh's machinations, Bundy warned
Johnson, did not allow the administration to "move forward with some confidence." He also discovered from Cooper and Thomson that the United States
was more isolated internationally on the issue of Vietnam than ever before.
The "more flags" initiative—a State Department program monitored and

largely created by the NSC staff, designed to secure further military and economic assistance from U.S. allies, and particularly favored by Johnson—was failing abjectly.[13] And in what must have been one of the more disturbing pieces of information, the British Foreign Office quoted Chen Yi, the Chinese Foreign Minister, as declaring "that the end in South Viet Nam was now near" and that "things were going very well" in Vietnam.[14]

If things were going very well for the Chinese, they must be going very badly for the Americans. By January 1965 Bundy did not need the Chinese Foreign Minister to tell him that South Vietnam was verging on total collapse. The indicators were too numerous not to notice, especially for Bundy, who had detected the signs for nearly a year. Once again he endeavored simultaneously to stiffen Johnson's resolve and to promote an increased military role for the United States. To gird the nation for a wider war, he strongly believed that Johnson should be as clear with the public as possible. In a draft of a major presidential foreign policy address, possibly to be included in the 1965 State of the Union speech, Bundy defined the war in Vietnam as a difficult but ultimately worthwhile struggle that would likely escalate despite America's best intentions. Although "the Communists have made gains," there was "no reason for despair. This is not a one-year struggle. But we must do better in 1965." And while the United States would never expand the war without justification,

> neither are we bound to give to the aggressors any guarantee against joint and necessary reprisal for their repeated acts of war against free men in South Vietnam. What has been ordered from outside South Vietnam can be punished outside South Vietnam, by all the laws of nations, and by the elemental rule that men are answerable for what is done at their command. The aggressor in Hanoi knows his guilt, and the world knows it too.
>
> . . . What we do and what we forbear to do, in reprisal, must be governed by our own judgment of what helps to end the aggression itself. It is the end of the aggression, not punishment for its own sake, which is our steady object.

A major presidential declaration was required to shore up support at home and abroad, from St. Louis to Saigon. As Bundy put it to Johnson shortly afterwards, "My own view is that . . . it is absolutely essential to maintain a posture of firmness today. I believe that without firm U.S. language, the danger of further erosion in Saigon is bound to grow."[15]

With this in mind Bundy moved to strengthen the U.S. military posture in South Vietnam, in effect to begin ascending the ladder of escalation from Phase I to Phase II. Against the advice of Thomson, who feared that the American effort had already assumed too military a character, Bundy urged the adoption of reprisal air strikes against the DRV in response to specific communist provocations directed at Americans in South Vietnam. In a January 7 cable to Taylor in Saigon, which Bundy drafted, Johnson stated that Washington was now "inclined to adopt a policy of prompt and clear reprisal" in addition to detailed planning for sustained pressure against the North, although Johnson left undefined the exact timing for the implementation of these plans.[16] Disturbed by NLF attacks against American personnel in November and December—the NLF attacked a U.S. airfield at Bien Hoa two days before the election and bombed an Army barracks in Saigon on Christmas Eve—Taylor had been a persistent proponent of reprisal air strikes. It was largely his advice that prodded the Working Group to stiffen its three policy options. On January 9 Cooper secured Bundy's approval of specific bombing targets in the DRV and of using U.S. bases in Thailand from which to launch the bombing raids. Referring to a particular target, Cooper predicted: "If we can really knock it out we will slow down [the DRV and NLF] build-up and give a loud and clear signal to Hanoi at the same time."[17]

It is somewhat ironic that both Taylor and Cooper expressed grave reservations about sending American ground troops to South Vietnam. Taylor preferred sustained bombing to soldiers "for fear that their presence might lead the South Vietnamese to slacken their efforts." For similar reasons Cooper argued that a sustained bombing campaign would not be as effective as more precisely targeted attacks. "We should not underestimate the risk of bombing the North," he warned in a paper for Bundy. "Aside from the risk of greatly expanded hostilities, there is the considerable risk" that the war could become completely Americanized. Cooper assumed that air strikes against the DRV were designed to curb its support for the insurgency and improve the American "negotiating posture." "If this be so," he warned in an echo of Forrestal, "then the war must still be fought and victories achieved in South Vietnam."[18]

Bundy had no such qualms. He had already suggested to Johnson in August 1964 that a sizable contingent of U.S. troops in South Vietnam would help to improve the situation there. Bundy did not fear the rush to war that sustained bombing would inevitably unleash. By stemming DRV support for the NLF and sustaining the flagging morale of Saigon, bombing would save the South; if troops were required to augment this plan, then so be it. Nonetheless, if

Bundy disagreed with Cooper and agreed with Taylor about the desirability of a sustained bombing campaign, he disagreed with Taylor and agreed with Cooper about the timing of its implementation. In other words, Phase II could wait for the time being.[19] It was not yet necessary to augment the U.S. effort significantly. "We can always emphasize that while avoiding a 'wider war' and ignominious withdrawal, we are constantly at work trying to strengthen our program there on every front," Bundy told Johnson before a meeting with the press.[20]

But Bundy also realized that doing more of the same could not stave off a noncommunist collapse indefinitely. With this in mind, he told Johnson that he needed to meet with Rusk and McNamara to reevaluate the "whole SEA problem." After a series of NLF victories, and intelligence analyses demonstrating that the flow of supplies from North to South was increasing steadily, it was obvious that South Vietnam's condition was critical.[21] As McNamara recalled, "South Vietnam seemed on the brink of total collapse," which forced him to "conclude, painfully and reluctantly, that the time had come to change course." In a separate memo to Johnson, Bundy gave some hint of his belief that only American power could salvage the situation. Despite the carnival of political intrigue and scheming endemic to South Vietnamese politics, Bundy confessed that "there is strong feeling which I share that this back-and-forth in the government in Saigon is a symptom, not the root cause of our problem." The root cause was to be found north of the 17th parallel.[22]

Bundy discussed all these issues with Rusk and McNamara on January 27. The resultant "fork-in-the-road" memo, which Bundy wrote on behalf of himself and McNamara in anticipation of a subsequent meeting with Johnson, has become one of the landmark documents of American decision making in the Vietnam era. Bundy certainly did not pull any punches in his most vigorous push yet for an expanded American effort in Vietnam. "What we want to say to you," the substantive part of the memo began, "is that both of us are now pretty well convinced that our current policy can lead only to disastrous defeat." The administration had been waiting for a viable government to take power in Saigon and provide stability, but the wait had been, and would likely continue to be, in vain. He and McNamara, Bundy wrote, "are persuaded that there is no real hope of success in this area unless and until our own policy and priorities change." The basic problem was one of morale, caused mainly by "the spreading conviction there that the future is without hope for anti-Communists." NLF victories and growing confidence were crippling American prestige, he warned in a reference to the Bien Hoa and Christmas Eve raids, since "our best friends have been somewhat discouraged by our own inactivity in the face of major attacks on our own installations." The United States could no longer stand aside without damaging its credibility. "Meanwhile," he continued bluntly, the Vietnamese, both Northern and Southern, "see the enormous power of the United States withheld, and they get little sense of firm and active U.S. policy. They feel that we are unwilling to take serious risks." Just as worryingly, the evaporation of confidence and resolve had afflicted American personnel in South Vietnam as well.[23]

The memo then framed the choice before Johnson in the starkest terms possible. Because he wanted to be clear, Bundy did not even bother to utilize the Goldilocks principle to make his recommendation seem more palatable. Indeed, the "just right" option was no longer feasible. "Bob and I believe," Bundy asserted,

> that the worst course of action is to continue in this essentially passive role which can only lead to eventual defeat and an invitation to get out in humiliating circumstances.
>
> *We see two alternatives.* The *first* is to use our military power in the Far East and to force a change of Communist policy. The *second* is to deploy all our resources along a track of negotiation, aimed at salvaging what little can be preserved with no major addition to our present military risks. Bob and I tend to favor the first course.
>
> Both of us understand the very grave questions presented by any decision of this sort. We both recognize that the ultimate responsibility is not ours. Both of us have fully supported your willingness, in earlier months, to move out of the middle course. We both agree that every effort should still be made to improve our operations on the ground and to prop up the authorities in South Vietnam as best we can. But we are both convinced that none of this is enough, and that the time has come for harder choices.

Bundy also moved to isolate Rusk, who very strongly supported the basic commitment to South Vietnam but also remained wary of an open-ended military commitment:

> You should know that Dean Rusk does not agree with us. He does not quarrel with our assertion that things are going very badly and that the situation is unraveling. He does not assert that this deterioration can be stopped. What he does say is that the consequences of both escalation

and withdrawal are so bad that we simply must find a way of making our present policy work. This would be good if it was possible. Bob and I do not think it is.

"A topic of this magnitude," Bundy concluded, required still further discussion, "but McNamara and I have reached the point where our obligations to you simply do not permit us to administer our present directives in silence and let you think we see real hope in them."[24]

While direct, Bundy's memo was neither manipulative nor an inaccurate assessment of how he, Rusk, and McNamara perceived the issue. Rusk agreed with the contents of the memo and felt that it reflected his views faithfully. McNamara later described it as a "short but explosive" document that needed to be written because he and Bundy "believed events were at a critical juncture, and we wanted the president to know how that affected our thinking." Bundy himself later admitted that such a blunt, categorical memo was "an unusual thing." He had now carried the debate—which until then had been between himself and either Mansfield, the *New York Times*, Lippmann, Ball, Bowles, Galbraith, or the British and French—to the top, as far as it could possibly go. The president's top two foreign policy advisers had in effect given him an ultimatum to take the plunge into a much wider war on the Asian mainland.[25]

Crossing the Rubicon: Pleiku and Sustained Reprisal

Still Johnson hesitated, at least outwardly. Both options—complete and inevitably humiliating disengagement or a major, Americanized war—seemed unthinkable, although the president was now leaning toward the latter. In the fork-in-the-road memo, Bundy had given Johnson an extremely difficult decision to make. But rather than commit himself, Johnson decided to send Bundy to South Vietnam for another look. Sending Bundy to Saigon had originally been Taylor's idea three weeks before, "because of Bundy's perceptiveness in such matters and the fact that he has been physically detached from the local scene and hence would have an objectivity which an old Vietnamese hand would lack." Cooper and Douglass Cater had also suggested to Johnson that a Bundy mission be sent to Saigon for a reassessment. To be sure, the Special Assistant's trip to South Vietnam was not Johnson's method of exploring a diplomatic settlement, or of effecting a positive change in the Saigon government, or even of attempting to see if the current policy was unworkable. "In Saigon," the *New York Times* reported, Bundy "will be the eyes and ears of President Johnson." But the man acting as the president's eyes and ears had already seen and heard what he needed to. He had made up his mind even before departing the United States. Johnson knew this perfectly well from the regular stream of hawkish memoranda Bundy had sent him over the last six months. In sending a Bundy delegation, instead of one headed by Rusk or Ball, Johnson wanted to be sure that all of his options had been exhausted before moving militarily against North Vietnam. Just as important, he also sought to provide himself with political cover in the event of escalation by appearing to have exhausted all the options in Vietnam.[26]

Johnson cabled Taylor on January 27, the same day Bundy and McNamara brought him to the fork-in-the-road, to inform the ambassador of Bundy's mission to South Vietnam. "I want you to know," Johnson said in a cable drafted by Bundy and highly reminiscent of the extreme rhetoric of both the 1947 Truman Doctrine and Kennedy's 1961 inaugural address, "that once we get the dependents out of there, I am determined to make it clear to all the world that the U.S. will spare no effort and no sacrifice in doing its full part to turn back the Communists in Vietnam." In mentioning that he sought Taylor's advice, the president also alluded to the still undefined military "courses of action" the United States would take against North Vietnam. The only variable left to determine was what sort of military action it would be: retaliation limited to specific provocations by communist forces, or a larger, continuous aerial campaign unrelated to specific provocations but loosely and thematically tied to the general pattern of communist aggression. The choice, then, was between implementing a limited or an open-ended version of Phase II. Bundy had not come to a decision before departing for Saigon. Taylor was not so ambivalent. He advised the White House that a North Vietnamese attack on Americans in Vietnam, followed quickly by U.S. reprisals, "would offer a priceless advantage to our cause here. I hope that in approving the [Bundy] mission that this thought is uppermost in our minds."[27]

Bundy's main concern was the South Vietnamese political situation, tenuous even for Saigon, and how it would affect American military planning. This issue was vital, for many in Washington felt that a stable, viable South Vietnam government was necessary for major military action against the DRV. With this in mind, Bundy encouraged Taylor to try to effect a modicum of political stability, even if it were through the mercurial General Khanh. But Bundy was also unconvinced that political stability was necessary for military action. He confided to Taylor that the "central aspect of [the] current situation is the present and future prospect for [a] 'stable government.'

Present directives make such a government an essential prerequisite for important additional U.S. major action, but we now wonder whether this requirement is either realistic or necessary." "In general," he wrote Taylor in a separate cable, "I am primarily interested in coming away with a sense of what kind of pressures you and your senior subordinates feel can be effectively applied to the VC and Hanoi . . . Do we in fact need a stable government in order to proceed aggressively and effectively with pacification?" The distinction is important. Previously, bombing had been thought of as a tool to punish the DRV for supplying and directing the NLF; now it was thought by some American officials also to be an antidote to Saigon's many political ills, especially its low morale. From his queries to Taylor, it is clear that Bundy had begun to approve of bombing the North to save the South.[28]

Bundy was thrilled to be on his way to South Vietnam. Surprisingly, for someone who wielded so much authority over America's Indochina policy, Bundy had never visited Southeast Asia, and he clearly relished the opportunity. "This is as good a moment as any," he wrote Johnson shortly after he was asked to visit South Vietnam, "to say . . . how proud I am that you are willing to entrust this particular mission to me." The mission itself was to assume a relatively low profile. Bundy should not, Cooper strongly advised, appear to be visiting Saigon in advance of a major shift in U.S. policy. He even suggested that some members of the mission travel ahead of the rest of the group in order to dampen some of the excitement the trip would inevitably cause. To this end Bundy asked Taylor if they could "avoid extended organized briefings . . . The more time we can spend in very small groups on these central problems the better." White House Press Secretary George Reedy told the media that "no urgent crisis" forced the president to send Bundy, and that the mission was simply "a continuation of regular consultations with Mr. Taylor."[29] Before both domestic and international observers, the administration did not want to appear to be pushed hastily into a drastic change of policy should Bundy indeed recommend one upon his return.

However, before the Bundy mission had even left Washington, the administration was faced with a major and entirely unexpected complication. Under Nikita Khrushchev, who sought "peaceful coexistence" with the West, the USSR had provided the Vietnamese communists with plenty of rhetorical support but little in the way of military or economic aid. Although the ouster of Khrushchev in October 1964 had little to do with Indochina, his removal offered the new leadership in Moscow a chance to increase its Vietnamese profile and vie with Beijing for the leadership of the communist movement in Southeast Asia.[30] Concurrent with the Bundy mission, Alexei Kosygin,

Khrushchev's successor as Premier of the USSR, was visiting Hanoi. The CIA concluded that Moscow's decision to send "an unusually strong delegation" to accompany Kosygin "underscores both the USSR's desire to regain influence with the North Vietnamese and its concern over the possibility of escalation in the Indochina conflict." The timing of the Kosygin mission was shaped, according to the CIA, by a "general feeling that the US may be impelled to adopt more far-reaching military measures in an attempt to check the erosion in South Vietnam." Komer similarly warned Bundy that the Kosygin trip was a Soviet attempt to "re-engage in Southeast Asia" and edge out the Chinese. "I wish I saw a decent way to warn them off," he concluded gloomily. Others believed the Kosygin mission was an explicit threat, directed not at the PRC but at the United States. CIA Director John McCone argued that although the Soviets would caution the DRV not to provoke the United States unnecessarily, Kosygin would "encourage Hanoi to intensify what they were doing now in the way of subversion, political action and guerrilla activities." Similarly, the *Wall Street Journal* intoned on its February 4 front page that the Soviets were issuing "a warning to the U.S. to leave South Vietnam alone," while the *Chicago Tribune* declared, more reasonably, that the Soviet Premier was delivering "a warning to the United States against extending the Viet Nam conflict to North Viet Nam."[31]

The Bundy mission flew from Washington on Air Force 3 and arrived in Saigon on the morning of February 4. In addition to the Bundy, who was most senior, five other officials made the journey: Cooper; McNaughton; Leonard Unger, a deputy to William Bundy at the State Department's Division of Far Eastern Affairs; General Andrew Goodpaster, assistant to the chairman of the JCS and a former adviser to President Eisenhower; and Jack A. Rogers, McNaughton's deputy. For Bundy the crucial problem was the political situation in Saigon. "The keynote was local knowledge," William Bundy recalled, "and the trip was particularly focused on politics, with all the team to see as many groups as possible on their own—Buddhists, students, and politicians outside government, as well as the inevitable Khanh." The perennial struggle for power among the ARVN generals, Buddhists, Catholics, and religious sects influential in South Vietnamese life, and how this struggle affected the war effort, were paramount. Khanh, who continued to grasp for absolute power but could never retain it, was perhaps still the single most authoritative figure in Saigon. He had, however, also incurred the enmity of Taylor.[32]

Bundy, on the other hand, had identified the Buddhists as "the central problem" even before he left for South Vietnam. The intensity of Saigon's political intrigue astonished him. "The current situation among non-Communist forces gives all the appearance of a civil war within a civil war," he apprised McCone shortly after arriving. Ironically, considering his opposition to Diem, Bundy did not care much about Khanh's political shortcomings. Managing consistently to hold on to power while prosecuting the war against the NLF had now become the predominant job requirement, and he was certain that the Buddhists did not possess it. The outstanding impression of South Vietnamese politics he had gleaned from his trip, Bundy later told former President Eisenhower, was "the little experience of government which South Viet-Nam has had." He singled out the Buddhists, who "have had no experience in taking responsibility. Theirs has been an opposition role." While Khanh was indeed "very Asian and devious politically," he stressed that on military matters Khanh had never deceived the Americans.[33]

Taylor's determined opposition to Khanh also troubled Bundy. Just as it had with Diem, the issue divided the Americans in Saigon from the administration in Washington. Taylor cabled Bundy on February 3 that "you may be arriving just in time to witness some very important governmental developments . . . [and] we may give you an interesting time. In any case you will find as a specific item high on your agenda: Can [Washington] do business with a Khanh government? We shall expect you to defend the affirmative as we will be on the side of the negative." This was true enough, and Bundy's visit only aggravated his relationship with Taylor. They had of course had their differences over whether to deploy ground troops to South Vietnam, with Taylor strongly against and Bundy just as strongly in favor. But Bundy also confirmed his faith in Khanh and refreshed his distrust in Taylor's abilities as ambassador. "It is my strong sense," he reported to Johnson after returning, "that Max Taylor does not in fact have the political sensitivity needed to provide continuing and constructive advice to the struggling factions in Saigon. Moreover, his personal bridges with Khanh are damaged beyond repair." Because he felt "confident that we can do better by backing [Khanh] and advising him than by trying to get him thrown out," the Taylor-Khanh rift was not an insignificant problem, particularly as it had the potential to impinge upon future U.S. military planning. Bundy even advised Johnson to replace Taylor "once we get fairly squared away on a course of military action."[34]

Bundy's preference for Khanh did not stem from respect for the general or hope that he could turn back the communist tide. The worsening political situation in Saigon and collapsing military effort in the rest of South Vietnam convinced him that the United States would have to augment its own military role. Stable or not, Washington needed a government in Saigon with a semblance of permanency, and Bundy thought Khanh alone could provide it. He reiterated to McCone that while a stable government was preferable before beginning further U.S. military action, "getting it is something else again." Bundy also made sure to provide the South Vietnamese, especially Khanh, with ample moral support on behalf of the United States. In a public statement he declared to the people of South Vietnam: "I can tell you plainly that the United States remains determined to work in partnership with you for the defeat of these aggressors so that your families can sleep in peace . . . and so that a brave and independent people can continue on the path of freedom and development." Toward the end of his trip Bundy repeated these public words of encouragement. The United States, he promised, "has a deep commitment to the common effort against terror and aggression in Vietnam and the U.S. has every intention of maintaining full partnership" with Saigon. And in private conversation with Khanh, Bundy revealed that Washington "was willing to consider appropriate means for bringing pressure on North Vietnam, but this would be feasible only if it involved [a] frank and loyal partnership with a stable and reasonably popular" government in Saigon. Military strikes, he stressed, "would be taken against the North only insofar as they support the . . . U.S. policy objective of winning the war in the South." He concluded his conversation with Khanh by stressing the "President's determination to continue to assist Vietnam."[35]

The United States was given an opportunity to prove its determination when the NLF launched an attack against a U.S. air base at Pleiku in the central highlands of South Vietnam on February 7. As part of a comprehensive assault, NLF guerrillas also carried out raids against the South Vietnamese airfield at Tuy Hoi and villages near Nha Trang. These other raids received virtually no attention from American officials or the press; instead, focus remained entirely fixed on the eight American fatalities, 126 casualties, and extensive damage to the military installations and aircraft at Pleiku. Reaction in the United States was shrill. An unusually large banner headline that spanned the width of the *Chicago Tribune*'s front page blared: "Reds Kill 8 GIs, Wound 62." The Sunday *San Francisco Chronicle*'s main headline, almost three inches tall, was little different: "Big Viet Attack: Heavy Yank Losses." Even the normally staid *New York Times* used abnormally strong language in declaring on its front page, "Seven G.I.'s Slain in Vietcong Raid; 80 Are Wounded."[36]

The attack coincided with the Bundy mission's final day in South Vietnam. The NLF raid shocked U.S. officials, despite the fact that Allen Whiting of INR had predicted such an attack during Bundy's visit. With little doubt U.S.

officials blamed the North Vietnamese for the attack. And with little hesitation they perceived the assault as both a challenge and an opportunity. "I think," McNamara said at a press conference, "it was a very clear challenge and test of our political purpose and strength of will." In Bundy's view Hanoi had dramatically escalated "a contest of force, violence, morale, will and purpose." It was very important to determine that the DRV had been behind the attack, for it was sure to bear the brunt of any U.S. retaliation. "I can tell you this extremely clearly," Bundy said to the press upon returning to Washington, "that no one in South Vietnam . . . is in the smallest doubt as to where the primary impetus, impulse, power and direction for the efforts of the Communists in the south is coming from. Everyone there knows and it is known with a depth that forbids doubts or discussion really that this is coming in the last analysis from Hanoi." William Bundy told a hastily arranged meeting with ambassadors from SEATO member-states that "the North Vietnamese action" at Pleiku was "intended as a clear test of will and as such . . . called for urgent and appropriate retaliatory action."[37] Subsequent revelations, however, have called into question this assumption. In 1997 Dang Vu Hiep, a North Vietnamese adviser attached to the NLF units that staged the raid, disclosed that the NLF had acted entirely on its own, that this was not unusual, and that the guerrillas who attacked Pleiku had been unaware that Bundy was in South Vietnam. Although Dang's confession that the highly organized NLF units did not even know of the Bundy mission is somewhat suspect, there is little reason to doubt his assertion that the NLF acted alone, without either the prior approval or knowledge of Hanoi.[38]

In Washington, Johnson convened an emergency NSC meeting, where support for immediate air strikes was virtually unanimous. Even Ball agreed that "action must be taken." Johnson, however, stipulated that he first needed "a recommendation from Saigon." Bundy, who hoped that "those so-and-so's in Washington" had grasped the situation as he had, was eager to provide such a recommendation.[39] In a series of telephone calls from Saigon with Deputy Secretary of Defense Cyrus Vance in Washington, Bundy urged the immediate bombing of specific military targets in the DRV. Vance relayed Bundy's advice to Johnson during the NSC meeting. "Bundy," Vance said of one of the subsequent calls, "stressed again the need for a rapid decision." The retaliatory U.S. strikes, aptly code-named Flaming Dart I, hit their targets in North Vietnam on the evening of February 7.[40]

But if agreement for an immediate, limited reprisal was unanimous, approval for a program of continuous bombing of North Vietnam, or even of secondary reprisals, was not. The Bundy mission was certainly in favor.

McNaughton—a friend and disciple of the military theorist Thomas Schelling and in many respects the mission's grand strategist—cabled McNamara and Vance shortly after the Pleiku raid that he and Bundy had been working on and had already discussed with Taylor and General Westmoreland, now the MACV commander, the "theory of a graduated reprisal program." The concept, McNaughton summarized, would be that of a continuous aerial campaign "which, through a measured, controlled sequence of actions against the DRV, brought sufficient pressure to bear on the DRV to persuade it to stop its intervention in the South." The United States would also publicly stress that the program was designed only to protect the South, rather than to conquer or subjugate the North. "Not much of a government is required for [Saigon] to play its role," McNaughton wrote; the program would "probably inspire the South Vietnamese to more effective efforts."[41]

Civilian leaders were not the Pentagon's only proponents of sustained, gradually increasing attacks on the DRV. U.S. military officials also hoped that the Pleiku reprisal would mark a turning point toward a more intensive, comprehensive war effort. The Joint Chiefs had been pushing vigorously for reprisal air strikes since the NLF bombed a Saigon hotel that housed American officers in December. After Bundy had left Vietnam, Westmoreland told the British Ambassador to Saigon, Gordon Etherington-Smith, "that he personally hoped that attacks on the North would continue" with intensifying ferocity. Westmoreland was confident that U.S. "raids will have a deterrent effect and that this can be exploited by slowly increasing the pressure." Admiral Ulysses S. Grant Sharp, the commander-in-chief of U.S. forces in the Pacific, agreed. He cabled the JCS from his headquarters in Hawaii: "Now that we have retaliated for [the] attack on Pleiku we should take this opportunity to step up, on a continuing basis, military pressure against the DRV." Like McNaughton, Sharp believed that continuous, rather than limited, bombing would serve the dual purpose of crippling the North's support for the insurgency and bolstering the capabilities of the South.[42]

The U.S. Embassy in Saigon also supported the new policy. Even before the Pleiku attack, Taylor's deputy, U. Alexis Johnson, professed that the "only solution" to South Vietnam's political and military problems was "to adopt a more aggressive policy towards the north, involving military action as envisaged for phase 2." Taylor was as relieved as he was pleased that the administration was finally heeding his advice. As he wrote his son after Flaming Dart, "I have been working and waiting for a year and a half to get to this point." He strongly applauded sustained reprisal as a "significant new step which we should take enthusiastically and with a visible clearing of the boards for possible future action." In conversation with Nguyen Xuan Oanh, temporarily the premier of South Vietnam, Taylor stressed that he "hoped that [Saigon] would be thinking of ways to exploit these reprisals to maximum effect, and to demonstrate that a new and encouraging element had been added to the war." Robust official statements from Washington about the need to defend South Vietnam and the culpability of the North, Taylor reported, "provide in my view a good foundation for embarking on a graduated reprisal program to bring increasing pressure on the DRV to cease its intervention in SVN, as discussed here at some length with Bundy and his party." While Taylor may have needed some reassurance about Washington's political will, he needed none about the Air Force's abilities to pound the North Vietnamese. Some time later, when Etherington-Smith asked him what would happen if Hanoi refused to yield to American bombing, Taylor replied "that this would make things very simple, because Hanoi and the North would be destroyed."[43]

Others, however, strenuously objected to additional bombing of the DRV. Ball; Ambassador at Large and renowned Soviet expert Llewellyn "Tommy" Thompson; and Mansfield, who attended many of the NSC meetings during this period, all argued that Kosygin's presence in Hanoi made any further retaliatory strikes—even those previously scheduled but postponed due to bad weather—imprudent and possibly dangerous. Ambassador Dobrynin warned Thompson in a private discussion that Moscow would consider any more American strikes to be "a deliberate provocation." At one NSC meeting Thompson duly "issued a word of caution" to his less wary colleagues that "further strikes would cause the Soviets to move." The warnings of both Ball and Thompson received support from a State Department assessment concluding that because of the air strikes, Moscow "will feel that it has received a direct insult and challenge because of Kosygin's presence in Hanoi. The Soviets will probably feel that their prestige has been seriously damaged and that they must take some positive action to save face." Concerned as ever with the prospect of an enlarged conflict that could involve China, Mansfield sent Johnson yet another dissenting memo to argue that if the United States goes "too far in North Vietnam we would be in a far worse position than we were in Korea."[44]

Such doubts were in short supply in South Vietnam. On the day of the attack, Bundy, Taylor, and Westmoreland traveled to Pleiku to see the devastation for themselves. The heavy damage and loss of life rattled the nerves of the normally unflappable Bundy. Westmoreland recalled sardonically that once Bundy "smelled a little gunpowder he developed a field marshal psychosis." Upon visiting the ruined base, the General was surprised that the civilian Bundy "seemed appalled at the shambles the attack had made of the advisory compound." By all accounts Bundy was uncharacteristically moved by what he saw at Pleiku. Fascinated, Johnson loved hearing stories out of Saigon that the former Harvard dean had lost his cool and, in a typically rib-ald analogy, compared his Special Assistant at Pleiku to "the preacher's son, very proper and priggish, who had gone to a whorehouse" and been shocked by what he saw. Francis Bator, the senior international trade and economics expert on the NSC staff, recalled that "the standard theory was that it was dur-ing Pleiku that he sort of caught religion on Vietnam. He always thought it was all a bit foolish. I'm not so sure—not on the basis of what he said, but I saw his face when he came back from Pleiku, literally when he walked into the Situation Room office, and I had a sort of sense that perhaps he'd become more emotionally caught up in it."[45] Cooper, who accompanied Bundy to Pleiku, remembered vividly the Americans "killed or wounded in the attack. We flew up and saw the aftermath. It had quite an impact on all of us, espe-cially on Mac Bundy." Seymour Topping, a *New York Times* reporter based in Saigon who was also at the military hospital, recalled that Bundy "looked pale and shaken" as he visited the wounded. As Vice President Hubert H. Humphrey later wrote: "It may be that what Bundy cabled moved Johnson more than would have been normal. Ordinarily, he was factual, never tried to plead a personal point of view. At Pleiku, he became, for the moment, an advocate."[46]

The cable to which Humphrey referred was actually a lengthy memo, written for Johnson on the return plane journey to Washington. Accompa-nied by a detailed attachment by McNaughton on the specifics of a "program of sustained reprisal," the Pleiku report is possibly the single most important document Bundy ever wrote. He had not, however, anticipated writing such a seminal document. Before Bundy flew to Saigon, the British Embassy in Washington reported to London that in Bundy's deliberations with Taylor, Phase II "might" be discussed. On February 4, the day on which the mission arrived in Saigon, he spoke to William Bundy over the phone and guessed that "we will not return with urgent and immediate requirements for deci-sion making meetings because of the continuing fluidity of the local situation here." Two days later he sent a cable to his brother to say that the mission would draft its report en route back to Washington. The mission's final day in Saigon, to be spent in the field, "should give additional color to [our] con-clusions which will contain few major surprises. [The] overall impression is that important decisions are necessary but that there is time in which to make them." That day, of course, turned out to be an inspection of the devastation at Pleiku, where the vivid "additional color" changed everything. Bundy's prior ambivalence about when to bomb the DRV dissipated amid the smoke and ruin of Pleiku. At the White House, Johnson told those at the emergency NSC meetings that any decision on a program of continuous bombing would await Bundy's return.[47]

Bundy's report was fundamentally a reiteration of the fork-in-the-road memo, albeit in less ambiguous language. Abject pessimism about South Vietnam was tempered by guarded optimism about the potential impact of an increase in America's role. "The situation in Vietnam is deteriorating, and without new U.S. action defeat appears inevitable," Bundy's memo began. "There is still time to turn it around, but not much." Southeast Asia remained intrinsically vital to the security of the United States, but a new consideration was the collapse of American credibility should South Vietnam itself collapse. "The stakes in Vietnam are extremely high," he continued. "The American investment is very large, and American responsibility is a fact of life which is palpable in the atmosphere of Asia, and even elsewhere. The international prestige of the United States, and a substantial part of our influence, are directly at risk in Vietnam." The South Vietnamese could not save themselves, so there was "no way of negotiating ourselves out of Vietnam" without triggering the fall of Saigon. Continuing his monetary metaphor he stressed that "any negotiated U.S. withdrawal today would mean surrender on the installment plan." McNaughton's attached program of sustained reprisal thus offered the most "promising course available, in my judgment . . . The events of the last twenty-four hours have produced a practicable point of departure for this policy of reprisal." Moreover, Flaming Dart I had not only served to punish the North Vietnamese; it had also possibly "catalyzed" Saigon to improve its own efforts. "If so, the situation may be at a turning point."[48]

Upon praising the "outstanding men" and "mainly right and well directed" implementation of American policy in Vietnam, Bundy captured the nonetheless gloomy mood in Saigon by highlighting the "nervousness about the determination of the U.S. Government" among the Vietnamese. Because of this, to "be an American in Saigon today is to have a gnawing feeling that time is against us." After noting at some length that political and rural reform—particularly concerning pacification in the countryside away from Saigon—were also crucial to success, Bundy moved to the heart of his message to Johnson:

The prospect in Vietnam is grim. The energy and persistence of the Viet Cong are astonishing. They can appear anywhere—and at almost any time. They have accepted extraordinary losses and they come back for more. They show skill in their sneak attacks and ferocity when cornered. Yet the weary country does not want them to win.

There are a host of things the Vietnamese need to do better and areas in which we need to help them. The place where we can help most is in the clarity and firmness of our own commitment to what is in fact as well as in rhetoric a common cause. There is one grave weakness in our posture in Vietnam which is within our own power to fix—and that is a widespread belief that we do not have the will and force and patience and determination to take the necessary action and stay the course.

This is the overriding reason for our present recommendation of a policy of sustained reprisal. Once such a policy is put in force, we shall be able to speak in Vietnam on many topics and in many ways, with growing force and effectiveness.

One final word. At its very best the struggle in Vietnam will be long. It seems to us important that this fundamental fact be made clear and our understanding of it be made clear to our own people and to the people of Vietnam. Too often in the past we have conveyed the impression that we expect an early solution when those who live with this war know that no early solution is possible. It is our own belief that the people of the United States have the necessary will to accept and to execute a policy that rests upon the reality that there is no short cut to success in South Vietnam.[49]

McNaughton's annex, entitled "A Policy of Sustained Reprisal," outlined in great detail exactly the course of bombing the Bundy mission envisioned. "We believe that the best available way of increasing our chance of success in Vietnam is the development and execution of a policy of *sustained reprisal* against North Vietnam—a policy in which air and naval action against the North is justified by and related to the whole Viet Cong campaign of violence and terror in the South." Sustained reprisal carried risks, the paper conceded. "Yet measured against the costs of defeat in Vietnam, this program seems cheap. And even if it fails to turn the tide—as it may—the value of the effort seems to us to exceed its cost." This generalized bombing program "would remove the difficulty involved in finding precisely matching targets in response to specific atrocities." McNaughton was proposing that the United States bomb, and keep bombing, the DRV with or without specific communist provocations. The Bundy memo and McNaughton annex together represented the launch of a full-scale Asian war involving the United States as a belligerent. McNaughton acknowledged that Hanoi, the NLF, and even Beijing would probably in turn escalate their own war effort. "These are the risks of any action," he admitted, "but we believe them to be acceptable." Moreover, in addition to hindering the DRV's support for the insurgency, sustained reprisal would also dramatically improve the sinking morale of the South Vietnamese. As with Bundy's memo, the annex noted that the attack on Pleiku had created "an ideal opportunity" to launch a program of sustained reprisal. "Conversely, if no such policy is now developed, we face the grave danger that Pleiku, like the Gulf of Tonkin, may be a short-term stimulant and a long-term depressant."[50]

Even though he had participated in one of the Pentagon's two SIGMA war games in 1964, simulations suggesting that bombing the North would have little positive effect on the war, Bundy pushed vigorously for the adoption of sustained reprisal upon his return to Washington. At an NSC meeting the following day, Republican Everett Dirksen, the Senate Minority Leader, asked Bundy what the impact would be should the United States simply disengage from South Vietnam. Invoking a psychological version of the domino theory, he replied that "there would be a strong feeling in the nations of Southeast Asia that we had failed to carry out our policy of assisting the Vietnamese to continue as an independent state." Such a failure, he emphasized, would resonate beyond Southeast Asia, "even to the extent of affecting the morale in Berlin." Bundy agreed with McCone that what was now required was the full implementation of Phase II—in other words, the program of sustained reprisal. He briefed the meeting on his trip and placed particular stress on the general state of decay in South Vietnam. In comments designed to sway the uncertain, he reminded everyone of the "disappointment in SVN that the Tonkin Gulf incident, which gave a great lift, was not pursued further and this caused the SVN leaders to look over their shoulders at what was really the U.S. intention and long-range purpose." A day later Bundy wrote Mansfield to dispel the Senator's mounting concern. "Unfortunately stating the difficulties does not solve them," he admonished the Senate Majority Leader and Asia expert. "We made a vastly heavier sacrifice in Korea—and one which was fully justified—and yet the stakes there were certainly not greater than those that are now on the table in Southeast Asia."[51]

The architects of sustained reprisal needed no additional impetus when the NLF staged another raid against Americans in South Vietnam on February 10. A bomb at a hotel accommodating U.S. military personnel in the coastal city of Qui Nhon killed twenty-three, making it the single worst attack on Americans in Vietnam. Bundy notified Johnson about the attack and said that he and McNamara felt "very strongly" about using South Vietnamese casualties to "tie them in" more intimately to the war effort. Only Ball, Thompson, and Humphrey thought that the retaliation, codenamed Flaming Dart II, should at least wait until Kosygin had departed East Asia (from Hanoi the Soviet premier had gone on to visit North Korea and, very briefly and acrimoniously, Beijing).[52] Bundy disagreed and "pointed out that we cannot put ourself [sic] in the position of giving the Russians control over our actions by their moving Soviet diplomats from one place to another. If we take no action, the Soviets may think we are in fact a paper tiger." Following Pleiku, the explosion at Qui Nhon offered a perfect opportunity to shift policy into Phase II. Against opposition from Ball and Thompson, Bundy "expressed support of immediate action," argued that American policy had "turned the corner," and declared that "we were on the track of sustained and continuing operations against the North." Johnson authorized Flaming Dart II, and on February 11 U.S. Air Force jets bombed North Vietnam for the second time in four days. Two days later Johnson approved the policy of sustained reprisal, known as Rolling Thunder, in a cable to Taylor. From its inauguration on March 2, 1965 (it was delayed during February due to poor weather) until Johnson's resignation speech of March 31, 1968, Rolling Thunder proved to be a staple of America's military effort and the source of widespread devastation in North Vietnam.[53]

But internal opposition to sustained reprisal continued nonetheless, particularly from the State Department. There was nothing inevitable about the adoption of sustained reprisal and the widening of the war it undoubtedly entailed. Thomas Hughes, the Department's INR Director, drafted an intelligence analysis specifically to counter the arguments in Bundy's sustained reprisal memo. "Incomprehensibly to me," Hughes wrote Ball, Bundy's conclusions had not seriously dealt with potential responses from China and the Soviet Union. Bundy had also neglected well-known intelligence assessments by INR, the CIA, and the Defense Intelligence Agency, which all concluded that any boost to South Vietnamese morale from American bombing would be temporary and that world opinion, even among U.S. allies, would come down heavily against sustained bombing. Hughes, moreover, knew Humphrey personally and knew that the Vice President had become very nervous about expanding the war. On February 13—the day Johnson formally approved Rolling Thunder—Hughes, armed with the relevant memos, cables, and intelligence analyses, tracked down Humphrey in Georgia. Sharing a deep skepticism about America's military prospects in Vietnam, the two men wrote a powerful, prescient opposition to the extension of the war. Humphrey passed the resultant memo, which carefully detailed the domestic political risks inherent to a course of escalation, to Johnson on February 17. Another Humphrey memo followed two weeks later, which prompted an irate Johnson to ban the vice president from the administration's decision-making councils on Vietnam for a year.[54] In addition, Ambassador to the UN Adlai Stevenson sent Johnson his own views about the folly of war in Vietnam and the desirability of negotiations. Bundy summarily dismissed Stevenson's memo and recommended that Johnson do the same. "Our position is not one in which we should now look as if we were hunting negotiations," he advised Johnson. "Both the Communists and our friends in Saigon would interpret such a proposal as a sign of weakness and readiness to withdraw."[55]

At the same time, George Ball intensified his own dissent. While Hughes and Humphrey were writing their opposition piece in Georgia, Ball submitted one of his own. By stating at the outset that he had discussed the memo with Bundy, McNamara, and Tommy Thompson, Ball later claimed he had "shifted my tactics" to "gain my colleagues' agreement to a forecast of future dangers, giving the President . . . a collective view that would show him some of the mine fields we would be risking." Clearly making use of the intelligence assessment Hughes had provided him, Ball outlined the hazards of a war that might come to involve China or the Soviet Union and of the adverse world reaction American bombing would inevitably provoke. Using his colleagues's positions, Ball roughly sketched out the two sides of the internal debate over open-ended escalation: on one hand, Bundy and McNamara believed that American military pressures against the DRV should increase gradually, without constraints, until the survival of a viable noncommunist South Vietnamese state was assured; on the other, Ball and Thompson urged the president to "be prepared and alerted . . . to accept a cease-fire under international auspices short of the achievement of our total political objectives." And toward the end of February, Bill Moyers handed Johnson Ball's uncommonly long memo of the previous October. Neither of Ball's memoranda, however, seemed to have any effect on Vietnam policy.[56]

Unease also emerged from outside the administration, especially from members of Congress. As expected, during NSC meetings and through private memoranda, Mansfield led the congressional charge against sustained reprisal.[57] But Bundy faced a greater storm of opposition from Capitol Hill when Johnson sent him to meet five Democratic Senators, including Eugene

McCarthy and Frank Church, in Humphrey's office on February 18. Bundy expected the Senators to form a "united front" to support the war, but the Senators, offended by Bundy's "arrogant manner," declined the political advice and instead expressed their growing anxiety. After Bundy left, Humphrey, who had been largely silent throughout the meeting, exclaimed approvingly: "You boys don't scare easily, do you?" Despite the obvious signs of political and military deterioration in South Vietnam, Bundy exuded optimism at the meeting. Unnerved by Bundy's lack of candor, in addition to that of McNamara and Rusk, Senator McCarthy, whose antiwar presidential campaign would topple Johnson three years later, commented that the administration's handling of the Vietnam issue made him "inevitably begin to raise some questions and have some doubts."[58]

Skepticism in the press also became more noticeable. Walter Lippmann had privately disagreed with the bombing, Bundy reported to Johnson, and would thus "need missionary work" to keep him from opposing the war openly. A few days later Bundy met with Lippmann to reassure him that "we were not planning any immediate all-out bombardment of Hanoi." In response to Lippmann's inquiries about the possibility of a peace conference, Bundy "gave him a lecture to the effect that calling a conference now was no way to get an honorable settlement." Lippmann maintained that the administration should not be afraid of using "the tools of diplomacy" in its policy. "I said that I fully agreed," Bundy recalled for Johnson's benefit, "as long as it was understood that one of the major tools of diplomacy was the 7th Fleet." In closing Bundy warned the venerable columnist that "the very word 'conference' sounded suspiciously like surrender in Southeast Asia right now."[59] Just as it seemed that Bundy had subdued one opponent, another reappeared. During dinner with the Bundy mission the night before the attack, Topping of the *New York Times* argued that bombing would not work, could even be counterproductive, and that the United States should instead withdraw. Bundy replied simply, "we cannot do that." And in a lead editorial on Flaming Dart I, the *New York Times* wondered "why we are fighting this war on the other side of the globe in alliance with a people whose sympathies toward us are doubtful." It was understandable, the editorial continued, for the United States to retaliate for one or two specific provocations. But sustained bombing was "not a substitute for a policy . . . What the Johnson administration now has to explain is where we go from here."[60]

The comments from McCarthy and the *Times* were indicative of an emerging schism between the administration and its critics over the truth behind the war. Many members of Congress and the media simply no longer believed administration officials' diagnoses of the Vietnam problem or their prescriptions to cure it. And the administration, inadvertently or otherwise, exacerbated the problem. Contrary to his numerous overwhelmingly pessimistic assessments for the president, of which the February 7 sustained reprisal memo was only the most notable, Bundy gave what Charles Mohr of the *Times* called a "highly optimistic" press conference in Washington, saying that the tide in South Vietnam was turning steadily against the communists.[61] Bundy even claimed to an increasingly dubious press that "the month of January has probably been the most successful in the entire war." An editorial in the normally supportive *Washington Post* picked up on these statements to criticize "McGeorge Bundy's repeated attempts to sidetrack reporters' questions," a tactic which the paper saw as an "embarrassing addendum" to "many recent examples" in which administration officials had "deliberately sought to misinform the public." As his conversation with Lippmann further demonstrates, Bundy had begun to wade into the ethical morass that came to be known as the credibility gap. Although Bundy had consistently advised Johnson to be publicly as open as possible on Vietnam, the manner in which he and the administration handled the implementation of sustained reprisal caused the credibility gap to widen.[62]

The administration also faced pressure from three of its traditional allies. The French, who knew all too well the frustrations of interminable war in Vietnam, unsurprisingly posed further problems. French Foreign Minister Maurice Couve de Murville flatly told Bundy that Paris was "fearful" about the U.S. decision to escalate the Vietnam conflict. When Couve suggested that American action be confined to the South as a preliminary maneuver toward de-escalation, Bundy replied that Washington "had to take account of the very heavy role and responsibility of Hanoi and of the problem of morale which is created when there is increasing violence against our people and the Vietnamese, with no visible response." He also told the French Foreign Minister "that we did not think it was helpful for the French to make public calls for a conference." In a meeting between Johnson and Couve later that day, Bundy commented that the "difference was that France seems to think that there can be no solution to the problem of stable government in South Vietnam while the United States remains there, while we think that there can be no solution if we leave." He thought the French were not being at all helpful and, as Bundy wrote to Johnson in early March, "at some point we may wish to indicate that the road to a settlement does not run through Paris."[63]

Moreover, the British were also finding it very difficult to support a wider war. Bundy suggested that Johnson offer public gestures of consultation and closeness, plus private reassurances, to Prime Minister Wilson in exchange for a British promise on Vietnam "not to advocate negotiations and not to go back on their existing announced approval of our present course of action."[64] And, like the British, the Canadians worried about the destabilizing effects of an indefinite bombing campaign. Although they were limited, Ottawa found the Flaming Dart reprisals "disturbing" and the escalating violence as "dramatic evidence" that Vietnam was beyond America's ability to repair. Prime Minister Lester Pearson, a Nobel Peace Prize winner, told the House of Commons that the best solution was an international peace conference on Vietnam.[65]

American retaliation for Pleiku marked a turning point for Soviet policy as well. As Thompson, Ball, and Mansfield had warned, the Soviets were furious that the United States would bomb the DRV while Kosygin was still in Hanoi, even though the strikes were limited to an area far from the North Vietnamese capital. Because of the Sino-Soviet rivalry and its fledgling détente with the United States, the Soviet Union did not want Indochina to become embroiled in a major war. The reprisal for Pleiku, however, not only infuriated and worried the Soviets, it also embarrassed them before the Chinese, lest Moscow be seen as giving less than it should to its fraternal communist ally in Hanoi. Flaming Dart I brought the Soviet Union directly into the conflict for the first time, although not as a belligerent, and destroyed its leaders' hopes to avoid an internationalization of the conflict. In its official newspaper, *Pravda,* Moscow depicted the reprisal strikes as "marauding raids" and declared that "the Soviet Union, together with its allies and friends, will be forced to take further measures to guard the security and strengthen the defense capacity" of the DRV. Another Soviet statement described the U.S. reprisals as "piratical."[66] Kosygin's anger and disappointment did not fade. In 1967 he complained to Tommy Thompson, by then ambassador to Moscow, that the USSR had wanted to prevent the spread of war but that the United States "started bombing North Vietnam when he was in Hanoi. He brought this up," Thompson reported, "in [the] context of [the] importance of mutual confidence." Although Hanoi had not directed the NLF attack on Pleiku, the perception, in Ball's phrase, was that the Soviets had been "mouse-trapped by Hanoi . . . The North Vietnamese action has put the Russians on the spot." Soviet aid for the Vietnamese communists' cause would now increase dramatically.[67]

But perhaps the most threatening challenge to sustained reprisal, as far as Bundy was concerned, came from within his own staff. Until Pleiku, neither

Chester Cooper nor James Thomson had expressed much disagreement with Bundy's approach to Vietnam. Both began work on the NSC staff in 1964 believing, to some degree, in the necessity of maintaining a noncommunist South Vietnamese state. Both were extremely well qualified for their jobs. And, intriguingly, both underwent a transformation from soft hawk to dove in early 1965.

Cooper had served with the Office of Strategic Services (OSS) in China during World War II. In 1947 he joined the CIA, the successor agency to the OSS. Throughout the 1950s he worked under William Bundy as an analyst on Asia, including Indochina, at the CIA's Office of National Estimates. Like Michael Forrestal, Cooper was also quite close to Averell Harriman, who, in a letter of recommendation to Bundy, described Cooper as "a man of wide experience in his field, and I find his judgment sound and well balanced." It was no coincidence that in 1965 Harriman himself began to revert from a soft hawk back to a dove, and in 1966 Cooper assisted Harriman on a special presidential project to explore the possibility of a negotiated peace with North Vietnam. Nonetheless, prior to joining the NSC staff Cooper had supported the commitment to South Vietnam along soft hawk lines. Cooper was originally attached to the NSC staff on detail from the CIA, but his position on Bundy's staff became permanent in 1964.[68]

Thomson was a Chinese expert, born in the United States but raised in China and Japan by American missionary parents. After taking undergraduate degrees at Yale and Cambridge, he went on to study for a Ph.D. in Chinese history at Harvard under the renowned Sinologist John King Fairbank. By coincidence, Thomson had also worked for William Bundy, but at the State Department's Division of Far Eastern Affairs rather than the CIA. In Chester Bowles, to whom he had been an assistant in the late 1950s, Thomson had a powerful and fervently dovish mentor. During the 1960 election campaign Thomson worked with Hughes, another future dove, as a member of Bowles's staff. To Rusk, Bundy described the independently minded Thomson as a "gifted young man, but not perfectly suited to the bureaucracy. My hunch is that in due course he should go back to academic life."[69] Originally Thomson had been a soft hawk, a fierce critic of the Ngo family, and a supporter of their removal. "People in our government are finally doing the right things and thinking the right thoughts, albeit many years too late," he wrote Bowles in September 1963 as Forrestal, Lodge, and Hilsman were in the midst of their campaign to remove the Ngos. "One major astonishment: Cabot Lodge has been absolutely superb from the moment of his arrival at the post; tough, decisive, with a clear sense of purpose" in combating Diem and Nhu. "Anyway, virtually all . . . now agree that we are finished there unless the Ngos are ousted. ('No Nhus is good news.')"[70]

The similarities between Cooper and Thomson are striking. Before joining the NSC staff, both had worked under William Bundy, himself a primary architect of U.S. policy toward Vietnam, which afforded them a glimpse of how policy was made and implemented. Both had expressed somewhat tepid and untested soft hawk support for a noncommunist South Vietnam in the early 1960s. And to temper their hawkish surroundings while working for the Bundy brothers, both could rely on eminent administration veterans Harriman and Bowles for dovish counsel. Of the two, Thomson would become the more vocal critic on Vietnam in 1965—within a year Bundy began to refer to him as "Mao Tse-Thomson."[71] And both began to harbor severe doubts when faced with sustained reprisal.

Thomson had not traveled to South Vietnam as a member of the Bundy mission and had to rely on the mission's reports to gauge how policy toward Vietnam would change as a result of Pleiku and sustained reprisal. Much of what he read bothered him. "In reflecting on Mac's report and its Annex," he wrote Cooper the day of the attack on Qui Nhon, "I am troubled by some far-reaching questions." Thomson did not question the wisdom of a limited retaliation for the specific attack on Pleiku; rather, his "doubts focus on the suggested policy of systematic and continuous reprisals against the North." A possible war with China and the lack of solid domestic backing for a war in Asia particularly worried him. But what bothered Thomson most was the notable lack of exploration of diplomatic possibilities to solve the crisis. "Finally, what has happened to the concept of 'negotiation' so earnestly pursued by our more thoughtful journalistic and Congressional critics, and previously pursued by many thoughtful people here at State?" Cooper evidently agreed, for he and Thomson encouraged Bundy to prod Johnson into making a speech to emphasize America's peaceful, limited intentions in Vietnam and to affirm that Americans recognized and applauded the nationalist, rather than communist, aspirations of Southeast Asia. "Such a speech would be an antidote to overly alarmist reactions to Vietnam at home and abroad," they urged. Cooper and Thomson suggested that the president could say that "Asia is in *revolution*" and that Americans "welcome the spirit of revolutionary search that infuses each of the nations of Asia." With its benign view of revolutionary change in Asia and its veiled call for a rapprochement between the United States and the DRV, and indeed China, it is no surprise that Bundy did not pass the draft speech on to the president.[72]

Another coup in Saigon on February 19—the third encouraged by the U.S. Embassy—removed Khanh from the circles of South Vietnamese power permanently. But it also demonstrated that the goal of political stability in Saigon would be elusive. Because one of the primary reasons for launching sustained reprisal was to bring about political stability, the coup greatly deepened Thomson's concern. "Certainly the wide-spread public impression of air strikes as a desperation move—as a *substitute* for political stability in Saigon—will be compounded by this most recent power grab," he wrote Bundy immediately following the coup in a memo provocatively subtitled "One Dove's Lament." With the prospect of Chinese intervention in mind, Thomson stressed that he continued "to believe that a policy of sustained reprisals against the North entails greater risks than we have any right to take in terms of our world-wide interests." Although he probably dealt his cause a fatal blow by invoking the editorial views of the *New York Times*, Thomson boldly declared that the "only rational alternative remains negotiations" and that the president should enlist the help of UN Secretary General U Thant, the Vatican, and "the thoughtful press." It was, Thomson argued passionately,

> vital that we not lose our perspective: in South Vietnam we have slipped into a gross overcommitment of national prestige and resources on political, military, and geographic terrain which should long ago have persuaded us to avoid such a commitment. Our national interest now demands that we find ourselves a face-saving avenue of retreat—that we marshal our imaginations and those of other powers—to discover such an avenue.[73]

Cooper echoed Thomson's concern shortly after. The peace movement in South Vietnam had gathered momentum because of the U.S. bombing, he told Bundy, and neither political, military, nor pacification efforts had improved in the wake of the reprisals. What troubled Cooper most was the lack of contingency planning for political crises—diplomatic and negotiated solutions had been particularly neglected—mostly due to the excessive attention on military matters. He urged Bundy to slow the pace in making military decisions. "What is needed now is more walking and less running," Cooper warned. "Perhaps a bit of just plain sitting would be useful."[74]

While dissension in the ranks of his own staff took hold, for the moment Bundy himself entertained no doubts. With the draft speech, Cooper and Thomson had provided Bundy with a sophisticated analysis of the nature of the Vietnam conflict, but he was not interested. Without qualification he believed in the necessity of preserving South Vietnam's independence, and that the people of South Vietnam did not want to live otherwise. Once this belief had been established in his own mind, the tenets of his worldview roughly guided his policy. His belief in the applicability of military power made him an architect of Rolling Thunder. His fear of appeasement instilled in him a contempt for negotiations with the DRV, NLF, and Chinese. His answer to Thomson's query about the conspicuous absence of a search for a negotiated solution was thus: "The pressure for negotiations," Bundy wrote Johnson toward the end of February, "is coming mostly from people who simply do not understand what that word means in Asian ears right now. If the U.S. proposes negotiations or even indicates a desire for them, the word in Saigon will be that we are getting out. And the consequences of that rumor would be very severe for our whole position."[75] The third tenet of Bundy's worldview, anticommunism, justified the whole enterprise in his mind. And the absence of a nuclear threat to South Vietnam or the United States meant there was little to check Bundy's hawkish views. Once he had helped to bring this process about, Bundy expended much energy in defending sustained reprisal against its many critics.

That February, in an attempt to blend these beliefs with a reassurance that American intentions were indeed limited, Bundy tried his own hand at a major presidential address on Vietnam:

> The aggressor will no longer be allowed to export death and destruction at no cost to himself . . . We have been patient with your calculated use of fear against your neighbor and we fear that you have misunderstood us.
>
>   . . . The United States knows that in any action which requires the use of force, there is need for care and prudence. We have shown that care and prudence throughout the last twenty years. We have had to deal with threats to peace in many parts of the world, and we have had to prove our good sense under many provocations. Through all that time we have been the world's strongest power, and through all that time we have been first in the responsible search for peace. As we now take resolute but limited action against a particularly destructive form of aggression, we feel it right to call attention to our claim upon your confidence. We have nothing to hide and we are eager for talks—our purpose is peace.[76]

Bundy's purpose was indeed peace, but not peace at any price. As with Cooper and Thomson's draft speech, but for different reasons, Bundy's proposed address was never given. Johnson was not yet ready to announce publicly such significant change in policy.

The attack on Pleiku and the American response to it rank as the most significant turning point in the escalation of the conflict in Vietnam. The Flaming Dart reprisals led directly to the Rolling Thunder bombing campaign. When such a deep commitment of U.S. power and prestige failed to turn the tide of war, Johnson had little recourse but to send ground troops. After Pleiku, an inevitably humiliating withdrawal was no longer a credible option. A decade later Cooper shrewdly compared Pleiku to the assassination of the Austrian Archduke Franz Ferdinand that triggered the outbreak of the First World War. More important, Cooper also admitted that until the Bundy mission to South Vietnam, U.S. policy remained fluid. War was likely, but the "get-out option was by no means academic." While Bundy and Cooper were in South Vietnam, Johnson "was still pausing warily" and waiting to hear what Bundy thought. Had the NLF "laid low" and not attacked, Bundy would not have written his sustained reprisal report and the United States may have been able to avert war. What if, Cooper asked, the communists "had not made the awful miscalculation that they could frighten Lyndon Johnson out of Vietnam" and had instead sought negotiations? Perhaps war would still have broken out, but "*without* Pleiku, it is at least conceivable that the decision could have gone the other way."[77]

As Bundy himself acknowledged during the internal deliberations over sustained reprisal, after Pleiku the administration "had turned a corner and changed our policy" by launching Rolling Thunder. In February 1965 the American war in Vietnam would change irrevocably. The bombing campaign did not stunt the growth and success of the insurgency; nor did it punish the DRV enough to halt its support for the NLF; nor did it permanently boost the morale and political stability of the South. When all of this became apparent, after the commitment of so much American prestige, the administration had little choice but to escalate further to prevent the collapse of South Vietnam. The next logical step was the introduction of large numbers of regular U.S. ground troops, a process that began, slowly but steadily, in March. By that time Bundy himself had begun quietly to entertain doubts about the existing pattern of escalation, but it was much too late. Cooper later commented that the American reaction to Pleiku was "the straw that broke the camel's back. Once the bombers were sent north, there was no turning back." It was also clear that the attack on Pleiku simply provided a pretext to implement a decision toward which many in the administration, including Bundy, were already leaning. Shortly after Bundy's return from South Vietnam, a reporter asked him what the difference was between the Bien Hoa and Christmas Eve assaults and Pleiku. Why did the administration ignore the former two and yet respond violently to the latter? "Pleikus," Bundy replied in words that would later come to haunt him, "are like streetcars"—in other words, due to their frequency and predictability, one can be boarded when needed.[78] Whichever metaphor one chooses, it is clear that during February 1965 the United States passed a turning point from which there was little chance of return.

CHAPTER 8

Bundy Ambivalent:
Rolling Thunder, Student Unrest,
and the Decision to Commit Troops

Rather than defeating the communists and solving the Vietnam dilemma, sustained reprisal acted as a precursor to a much more significant and fundamental expansion of the war. When Rolling Thunder failed to coerce Hanoi or stabilize Saigon, the introduction of U.S. ground forces was the next logical progression in the escalation and Americanization of the Vietnam War. To Bundy this came as something of a shock, for he had conceived of sustained reprisal as a means to achieve, at a relatively small political and military cost, the sustainability of South Vietnam. The spring and summer of 1965 thus marked a somewhat confusing time for him, and in his policy recommendations he vacillated between the approval of deploying ground troops and the promotion of further nonmilitary measures as methods to improve the situation in Vietnam. At times he even toyed with the idea of negotiating with the North Vietnamese, and he listened with closer attention to recommendations from the NSC staff to that effect. Bundy was now unsure about his own hawkish advice, although he still believed firmly in the need to sustain the U.S. commitment to South Vietnam. It is thus unsurprising that during this period he shifted ground once again to become something of a soft hawk.

What is surprising is the extent to which Bundy explored, and encouraged Cooper and Thomson to explore, the prospects for a negotiated settlement to the conflict. Diplomatic initiatives and ongoing military maneuvers, however, made for an uneasy mix. In a rough draft for a presidential address on Vietnam, Bundy jotted down that Johnson should highlight the "fact that this is a campaign consciously planned and directed in Hanoi," the decade-long "record of American support and assistance," the "appropriate, fitting, and measured" pattern of American military action, and the "importance of meeting this type of challenge—Vietnam [is] the best place." But he also wanted

Johnson to say that an eventual settlement "can occur in many different ways, ranging from a full-dress peace conference to a tacit understanding. The U.S. is not fussy about the ways and means of settlement." The United States, Bundy stressed in a well-worn phrase, "wants no wider war."[1] In the end the Johnson administration could not sustain such inherently contradictory and unstable policies. With U.S. air power being used so prominently and troops being deployed to South Vietnam, when the contradictions became too great to manage Bundy was left with little choice but to recommend additional escalatory measures. Withdrawal, tantamount to an admission of failure, was simply no longer an option.

The Soft Hawk Returns

Bundy would not have had to entertain such previously unthinkable notions about peace conferences and tacit settlements if Rolling Thunder was success-ful or if South Vietnam's political and military capabilities improved. Instead, it was immediately apparent that both efforts were failing. On March 16, only two weeks after Rolling Thunder began, Bundy received a CIA assessment that concluded that the NLF, and the DRV's ability to supply it, were proving to be much more resilient and adaptable than anticipated. A week later an unidentified CIA official informed Cooper that the "situation in South Vietnam has deteriorated to such an extent that our political-military position has become precarious." Sustained reprisal had neither bolstered the morale of Saigon nor blunted the determination of Hanoi, the analysis concluded, while the NLF just kept getting stronger and bolder.[2] Additional intelligence analy-ses at the end of April and the beginning of June confirmed the continuation of this trend. In a note attached to the front of one such analysis, Cooper wrote, "Mac: On the gloomy side—but they are probably right."[3]

American air power, it seemed, could not win the war by itself. Bundy was not yet certain that U.S. troops could do so either; Cooper and Thomson were certain that they could not. But while Cooper and Thomson were also qui-etly contemplating life with a reunified, communist Vietnam, Bundy was not. Instead he pushed his staff to examine additional soft hawk measures that would improve both the American and South Vietnamese war efforts. Iron-ically, considering his strong advocacy of punitively bombing the DRV as early as December 1963, it was former Ambassador to Saigon Henry Cabot Lodge who catalyzed Bundy's thinking. In a March 8 memo, which he sent to Bundy in hope that the Special Assistant would forward it to the president, Lodge outlined a plan to improve the situation in South Vietnam. Rural pacification, economic development, and political reform, rather than sustained bombing, were the keys to victory; these nonmilitary measures were also the strengths of the NLF and DRV, which is why they were winning the war. "Communist subversion-terrorism," Lodge wrote, "is the great unsolved problem in South Vietnam . . . It is, in a sense, a bigger threat than the nuclear, where we have superiority and a well understood procedure." To coordinate these matters more effectively, he strongly recommended that Johnson establish an office on Vietnamese pacification and counterinsurgency in Washington under the direction of a single powerful individual. He also suggested that the South Vietnamese police force be increased significant, that the American personnel and their efforts in Vietnam be decentralized to create greater independence and initiative, that the Buddhist clergy be employed to deliver surplus food, and that the U.S. Embassy provide greater support for educational, cultural, and religious activities throughout South Vietnam. Finally, and perhaps most significantly, Lodge argued for a "Plan for the Development of Southeast Asia, comparable in scope to the Marshall Plan and in addition to what we are doing already." Such a redevelopment plan would be focused on the Mekong River, and would include not only Vietnam but the whole of Southeast Asia.[4]

After reading the memo, with its allusion to the Marshall Plan that doubtless struck a chord, Bundy telephoned Lodge to praise his "most valuable, interesting, and constructive paper." More important, Bundy sent the memo with an endorsement to Johnson the same day.[5] Lodge had also given Cooper an advance draft of the memo. Cooper, who had never believed that sustained reprisal would defeat the NLF, praised the memo but thought that it did not go far enough, that it should be "somewhat more pointed." In his own subsequent effort to provide a program for a nonmilitary soft hawk strategy, he borrowed heavily from Lodge's recommendations. Although he would not halt the bombing of selected targets in the North and would consider the introduction of a small number of U.S. troops to patrol South Vietnam's borders to limit infiltration through Cambodia and Laos, Cooper stressed that the war could ultimately be won only through a combination of unconventional military tactics, such as psychological warfare and counterinsurgency, and nonmilitary, largely economic initiatives. "Why can't we be the insurgents?" he asked plaintively. To his plan, Cooper added the decentralization of the American effort in Vietnam with the creation of a "Mr. Pacification" to monitor the effort from Saigon and a "Mr. Big" to oversee the implementation of these measures in each contested South Vietnamese province. He also recommended that the administration take the initiative to start negotiations with the DRV.[6]

The climax of these efforts came in early April, when Johnson gave a major speech on Vietnam at Johns Hopkins University. Much of the impetus and organization for this speech came from Bundy, who toward the end of March began to emphasize to the president the importance of nonmilitary measures. "The war in South Vietnam can be won only if military actions are supplemented by those which will give the people a stake in the promise and fruits of an effective, stable, non-Communist government," he wrote in a summary of the various proposals floating around Washington. Quite deliberately and shrewdly, Bundy sought to appeal to Johnson's progressive instincts by conflating the Great Society with the need for social reform in Vietnam.[7] Others echoed his advice. William Bundy, for example, forwarded to the NSC staff work on economic rehabilitation and development in Indochina by his economic deputy, Robert Barnett.[8] McGeorge Bundy also sought guidance on the Johns Hopkins address from Lippmann, who thought that Johnson should make a speech outlining his version of a "Wilsonian 14 points on Southeast Asia."[9] Cooper came up with the notion of a "Southeast Asia Development Association," open to any communist, neutralist, or noncommunist nation as a means of halting the Vietnam conflict peacefully and maintaining American influence in the region through economic rehabilitation. Because of its incorporation of all these new elements, Bundy anticipated that the Johns Hopkins speech would mark a turning point in the war. At the end of March he told Johnson that it "may well be the most important foreign policy speech you have yet planned."[10]

Johnson's address on April 7 offered the two Vietnams a billion-dollar redevelopment package based around the Mekong River, but it did nothing to blunt the communists' drive to win outright power. Hanoi responded the next day with its own "Four Points," a plan for the settlement of the Vietnam conflict based on the NLF's participation in South Vietnamese politics and immediate American withdrawal. It was a quick and unequivocal repudiation of Johnson's Mekong development proposal. Hanoi's unhesitating opposition to the Johns Hopkins speech removed much of the momentum behind Bundy's new approach. Once again, the crossroads at which U.S. policy found itself posed a stark choice between further military escalation and a search for an imperfect negotiated solution. If Bundy's vacillation between the soft hawk and hawk options can be seen as a battle between the legacies of, respectively, Michael Forrestal and Walt Rostow, the choice now facing him represented one between his own long-standing hawkish beliefs and the increasingly dovish counsel of his principal Vietnam advisers, Cooper and Thomson. The extent to which Bundy was now ambivalent is illustrated by his toleration of his staff's previously heretical search for a negotiated solution.

Thomson was particularly insistent on exploring the prospects of a "détente with North Vietnam," even if it meant the neutralization of both Vietnams, and even though Bundy had already dismissed such a plan as a disguised form of surrender. Cooper nonetheless twice joined Thomson in these efforts. The first was to press for a presidential pledge to commit the United States to a specific negotiating agenda, possibly involving the UN, rather than Johnson's rather undefined and "now familiar" promise "to go anywhere at any time, etc." The second effort was their strong recommendation to commit the United States to an international conference on Cambodia, much like the 1961–1962 Geneva Conference on Laos.[11]

Although he would never change his mind on the importance of South Vietnam's noncommunist status, the urgings of Cooper and Thomson, delivered against the backdrop of a perpetually deteriorating situation in South Vietnam, did have an impact on Bundy. The United States should agree to a Cambodian conference and send word privately to Hanoi that the administration was ready "to discuss larger issues," Bundy wrote Johnson on April 23. "At the same time," the administration should "slow down our bombing . . . to improve the atmosphere for talks." In words he himself would have rebuked just a few months before, Bundy wrote that the "basic assumption is that we want to get the war to the Conference table. We do not know if Hanoi is willing to negotiate, but we want to make it as easy for them to do so as possible." A decrease in the bombing would possibly facilitate an answer, and if the DRV responded negatively the administration could resume its current bombing level to greater propagandistic effect. "We should also make a real peace effort before putting in many more ground troops," he argued prophetically. "It is a lot easier to disengage planes than ground troops."[12] In the following months, Bundy and Cooper continued to impress upon Johnson the case for diplomatic negotiations.[13]

Campus and Caribbean Revolt

The failure of sustained reprisal, the continuing political instability in South Vietnam, and the arguments of Lodge, Cooper, and Thomson all contributed to altering the way in which Bundy viewed Vietnam. But these were not the only influences. Public opposition to the war emerged in full force at this time, especially on university campuses in the form of "teach-ins"—extracurricular seminars in which academic experts would vent antiwar frustrations to their students. Because the movement was initially concentrated among a handful of elite universities in the Northeast and Midwest with which Bundy had enjoyed close contact, the real question is not whether this nascent dissent affected Bundy, but how. To what extent did the campus controversy alter his perception of the war in Vietnam? Although he was generally dismissive of academic opposition, he was also sensitive to the adverse impact it could have on broader public opinion. "They were a bunch of undergraduates and that was a breed I knew," he recalled thirty years later. But they were passionate, articulate, and motivated, and he acknowledged that the "worst thing you could do to them was ignore them." "Articulate critics," he warned Johnson at the time, "have stimulated extensive worry and inquiry in the nation as a whole." While Bundy was confident that he and his colleagues could counter the academics' arguments, he worried about the origins, nature, and impact on public opinion, at home and abroad, of this particular source of dissent.[14]

Moreover, because he had been involved in academia for so long, at such a high level, and at such prestigious and well-connected institutions, the universities' anger over the war would have been uncomfortably personal. "After all," Bundy himself said of the campus protestors, "these are my people." Although he received several supportive letters from Henry Kissinger—then a Harvard professor and occasional consultant to the NSC staff—more critical antiwar letters from other former Harvard colleagues, such as John Kenneth Galbraith and Stanley Hoffman, doubtless made a profound impression. Galbraith in particular was an old and respected friend.[15] Just as important, and certainly more painful, Bundy also experienced difficulty at home with some members of his family over their emerging opposition to the war.[16]

Nonetheless, despite his doubts about some of the Pentagon's methods, he still very much believed in basic policy toward Vietnam; and perhaps stung by the growing anger from those to whom he was personally and intellectually closest, he wanted a chance to justify the war to his critics. This approach was also in line with the administration's strategy to counter academic opposition, code-named Operation Target: College Campus, run jointly by the NSC staff and Jack Valenti of the White House. As Cooper told a diplomat at the British Embassy, the administration was targeting the "vocal minority of malcontents" who might "give the wrong impression to the world as a whole and also possibly lead astray a large number of people in the U.S."[17] Bundy made the mistake, however, of disdaining the first opportunity to come his way, thereby antagonizing and provoking the very people he hoped to court. In refusing an invitation to a forum at Washington University in St. Louis, Bundy simply repeated the official line: "The center of the problem in South Viet Nam is to ensure the right of the people there to peaceful self-determination, and that is the purpose of the United States." Had he been in a position "as a professor of Government" to grade the invitation, he concluded acidly, "I would not be able to give it high marks." Unfortunately for Bundy, the exchange was reprinted in the pages of *Time* magazine.[18]

Thus the issue was now as much personal as it was political. Bundy accepted the professors' next invitation and agreed to debate George Kahin, a Southeast Asian specialist from Cornell, at the National Teach-In in Washington on May 15. By now the meeting of minds from the White House and the academy had been poisoned by the bitterness of the exchange in *Time*. Expectations for a clash were high. The *Washington Post* observed that in this "intellectual heavyweight championship match . . . combative emotions on both sides have been honed to a razor edge."[19] Bundy, however, did not participate; Johnson forced him to withdraw at the last minute. Quite understandably, Johnson was not keen on the idea of his Special Assistant for National Security Affairs seeking out and debating opponents of the administration, thereby providing critics with publicity and legitimacy. Instead Johnson sent Bundy to the Dominican Republic, where U.S. Marines had recently intervened.[20] To compensate for his absence, a month later Bundy spoke to students at Harvard about U.S. policy toward Vietnam.[21] That month he also agreed to debate the renowned international relations scholar Hans Morgenthau on national television. Although he clearly won the debate over an uncharacteristically browbeaten Morgenthau, Bundy's aggressive debating tactics came across as mean spirited. When he broke from the agreed debating format to quote from a past sampling of Morgenthau's erroneous predictions, the moderator, Eric Sevareid of CBS News, interceded by saying that "this has become something of a personal confrontation."[22]

Indeed it had. Coming after his difficult mission to South Vietnam in February and the inability of sustained reprisal to blunt the communist insurgency, Bundy's experience with the academic teach-in movement marked a particularly sour moment in his tenure as Special Assistant. That he agreed to participate in the National Teach-In only on the condition that the organizers promise to assume "direct responsibility for seeing to it that no one would stamp, chant, march, or immolate himself in response to Bundy's presence" illuminates just how sensitive the issue had become and just how warily Bundy treated it.[23] But despite these precautions, or perhaps because of them, he failed to impress his critics and won few plaudits for trying. His letter to the professors at Washington University, his last-minute cancellation for the National Teach-In, and his exchange with Morgenthau struck three more blows to the administration's credibility. Students at the National Teach-In hissed during the announcement that Bundy would not show; one participant recalled that Bundy's absence "had a powerful effect in further undermining the authority of the government's position." Students protested Bundy's Harvard appearance with placards that read: "When Will Bundy Pay for His War Crimes?"[24] Moreover, his relationship with the president suffered severe damage. Bundy's willingness to participate in the teach-in without first checking with Johnson infuriated the President. "I think it's awful . . . for Mac Bundy to be debating," he complained to Bill Moyers shortly before ordering Bundy to withdraw from the May National Teach-In. "[It] leaves the impression in the world that we're divided." Johnson later confided to Abe Fortas that he was losing confidence in Bundy's judgment and told Moyers that he was going to ask Bundy to resign.[25] Years later, Bundy acknowledged that his central role in the teach-ins severely strained his relationship with Johnson.[26]

Many of the students and professors demonstrating the war did so on pacifistic or anti-imperialist grounds. Driven unwittingly by larger demographic, social, and economic patterns and reacting consciously to the issues of nuclear holocaust, decolonization, war, and racial injustice, the students who protested the Vietnam War and contributed to the sociological ferment of "the Sixties" would have opposed almost any American conflict at the time.[27] While Bundy was concerned about their potential political impact, he thought the student unrest could be contained. There was, however, another element of antiwar dissent that Bundy found just as threatening because it did not emerge from the counterculture and was thus respectable: realism. His debate with Morgenthau, a professor of political science and modern history at the University of Chicago, brought to the fore the realist critique of U.S. policy toward Vietnam. Morgenthau was (and still is) considered the modern founder of the realist school of international relations theory. At the time he was also renowned as one of the country's leading foreign policy experts. Morgenthau's realism argued that states were concerned primarily with maintaining security and, in order to do so, motivated by a drive to attain, protect, and use power. Whether communist or capitalist, democratic or totalitarian, fundamentally all states behaved the same in the international system. In turn, the international system itself was predicated on anarchy; within this anarchy, states had to fend for themselves. And the system was beyond reform. Because it was beyond reform, it was also beyond control, and states that attempted to impose control were doomed to fail.[28]

Morgenthau and other realists, such as Walter Lippmann and George F. Kennan, emphasized above all else that the United States needed to distinguish between vital and peripheral interests. And South Vietnam, they argued, was most certainly a peripheral interest. By waging a large-scale and destructive war to defend this peripheral interest, the United States was damaging its international prestige, credibility, and reputation for sound judgment. Morgenthau said as much in his debate with Bundy, among other venues. Americans, Morgenthau wrote in his 1965 antiwar book, *Vietnam and the United States*, were generally "unaware" of the "nature and the greatness of our power"; in dealing with Vietnam, they had "become negligent of its limits. Thus our judgments are at odds with empirical reality."[29] Similarly, Lippmann argued publicly in 1963 that the "price of a military victory in the Vietnamese war is higher than American vital interests can justify."[30] Kennan, the principal architect of containment, felt likewise. In addition to the established credentials of these critics—they were not, after all, "a bunch of undergraduates"—it was the rational basis of their opposition that posed biggest threat to the administration's position. The respectable antiwar faction also brought Bundy's justifications for war, and their flaws, into sharper relief.[31]

Aside from a readiness to use military force, Bundy had, of course, inherited what Kennan pejoratively called the "legalistic-moralistic approach" from Henry Stimson.[32] Bundy was no realist: he had always disagreed with realism's perceived amorality and with its acknowledgment of America's limitations. But now the United States was running into a firm wall of such limitations. In the face of the ongoing debacle in Vietnam and the failings of a policy that was as much his as anybody else's, Bundy's arguments in support of the war acquired a curiously circular, illogical ring to them. The rationalism of Morgenthau and Lippmann stood in stark contrast. Time and again, in public and in private, Bundy argued that the United States had to fulfill its obligation to South Vietnam simply because it existed, whatever its merits. Thus in his televised debate with Morgenthau, Bundy claimed flatly that "we have a commitment, matured through time, made for good reasons, and sustained for the same reasons."[33] He had made precisely the same argument countless times in private. The enormous, and constantly growing, gap between his own arguments and beliefs and those of his critics was becoming impossible to bridge. As a result the fabric of some of his close friendships, such as that with Lippmann, began to fray.[34]

Bundy's last-minute, hastily arranged role during the crisis in the Dominican Republic also put strain on both his duties as Special Assistant and his relationship with Johnson. On April 28, after a coup in the Dominican Republic that seemed to portend a possible communist takeover, Johnson sent four hundred U.S. Marines to the capital, Santo Domingo, ostensibly to protect American lives and property. These hundreds were the first in a massive deployment that would send nearly 25,000 U.S. troops there. Although Bundy was not paying any particular attention to the Dominican Republic, or to the Caribbean in general, Johnson decided that his Special Assistant would be more useful trying to negotiate a settlement with the warring factions in Santo Domingo than he would be debating college students in Washington. Bundy agreed that the administration must confront potentially communist-inspired instability in the Western Hemisphere with the strongest possible measures. He did not particularly mind going to the Dominican Republic, even though he knew that Johnson had sent him simply to avoid the National Teach-In, and throughout the crisis he agreed with the president's snap decision to send in the Marines.[35] Bundy had in fact already been pushing Johnson to make use of exactly such a crisis situation to "put the Russians and Latin Americans on notice that the U.S. would not accept a second Castro in this hemisphere."[36] Initially the difficulties Bundy and Johnson experienced during the Dominican crisis had little to do with politics or ideology. Rather, by questioning one another's judgment during the crisis, they exacerbated the personal tensions that had first emerged over the teach-in.

The first source of trouble was one that did not normally affect Bundy: a lack of influence with the president. The problem was that while Bundy was the highest-ranking U.S. official in a delegation that arrived in the Dominican Republic on May 14, Johnson listened instead to Under Secretary of State for Economic Affairs Thomas Mann, a member of the Bundy mission. "Well now, really honestly," Johnson told Fortas not long after the Bundy mission had gone to the Dominican Republic, "I have more confidence in Mann's judgment than I do in Bundy's." General Bruce Palmer, who commanded the U.S. forces in the Dominican Republic, also maintained an independent line of communication to the White House. Bundy's recent ambivalence about Vietnam policy specifics (and not about policy in general), and especially his decision to participate in the National Teach-In, increasingly led Johnson to question his judgment on other matters. Bundy's diminished authority during his mission both reflected and aggravated this tension.[37]

Johnson's growing distrust of Bundy's judgment resulted in the second source of trouble. As the leader of the mission to the Dominican Republic, it was up to Bundy to bring the warring factions to a peaceful, negotiated settlement that would be amenable to American interests and thus make future use of the Marines unnecessary. After leading several days of intense talks with both sides, Bundy thought he had achieved exactly such a result. On May 18 he reached a settlement that would have placed Silvestre Antonio Guzman Fernandez in power, although Bundy could not guarantee Guzman's anticommunist credentials. Mann, supported by Rusk, was not convinced that Bundy had concluded a good deal. Partly due to pressures on the ground in Santo Domingo, but largely because Johnson trusted Mann over Bundy and Guzman, the deal collapsed.[38] With his authority diminished, albeit temporarily, the Dominican crisis marked the beginning of the end of Bundy's tenure as Johnson's Special Assistant.

Toward the July Troop Decision

Rolling Thunder was still not going well. Political stability and basic internal security still did not exist in South Vietnam. Bundy's two key advisers on Vietnam, Cooper and Thomson, were close to open revolt against the administration's policy. The prevailing opinion of the community in which Bundy had spent almost his entire life, the university, was turning against the war, often bitterly so. And, quietly, Bundy had differed with Johnson over the Dominican crisis. Given all these developments within a relatively short span of time, it is not at all surprising that Bundy had become deeply ambivalent on Vietnam. It was perhaps former British Foreign Secretary Patrick Gordon Walker, visiting Washington for talks with "the Big Three" in June 1965, who best summed up Bundy's feelings on the war in a report to London:

> Rusk: "The war is going well."
> McNamara: "The war is not going well."
> . . . On the Viet-Nam war in general Bundy took a line somewhere between Rusk and McNamara.[39]

What is surprising, however, is that Bundy was only ambivalent and had not altered his fundamental view of the Vietnam conflict more drastically. Despite these recent troubles, Bundy still believed steadfastly in the U.S. commitment to maintain a noncommunist South Vietnam. His ambivalence covered some of the administration's tactics, not its overall strategy or purpose.

Bundy would only contemplate negotiations, for example, if they could secure the continued survival of an independent South Vietnam—if they could be a different means to achieve the same end. If they looked only to bring about a face-saving withdrawal from Indochina, he wanted no part of them. Bundy knew that the Vietnamese communists felt similarly about conceding their ultimate goal of national reunification, so although negotiations were unlikely to produce any actual progress, their invocation could still be used as a valuable propaganda tool. Thus although his desire for a peaceful solution to the conflict on American terms was certainly sincere, Bundy also tended to perceive the call for negotiations, he told Johnson, as "a tactical matter" designed simply "to pin the rose of aggression on the Communists." Bundy also outlined to Johnson a variation of the strategy that the DRV would later call "fighting while negotiating." When the United States was "ready to talk," he explained, "we do not at all mean that we are ready for a cease-fire. The fact is that we expect our own military action to continue unless we see a prospect of a better situation in the South than we have now." Bundy was thus willing to sanction the expansion of military activities while Washington simultaneously probed for opportunities to bring the conflict to the negotiating table. To this end he believed that the rigid restrictions on bombing Hanoi, the capital, and Haiphong, the DRV's main harbor and a frequent destination for Soviet and Chinese freighters, should be relaxed. "I myself am more attracted than Rusk and McNamara by the notion of an occasional limited attack inside the Hanoi perimeter—probably in the Haiphong port area," he wrote to Johnson at the beginning of June.[40]

The trouble, as Bundy well knew, was that the situation in South Vietnam only continued to crumble. The very concept of negotiations, if they were to assure South Vietnam's political and territorial integrity, rested mainly on the premise that the communists could not prevail militarily. But facts on the ground continued to prove that this was an illusion. Moreover, neither the United States nor the DRV was willing to enter into negotiations and risk losing at the conference table what both believed they were still able to win on the battlefield. Bundy may have been pessimistic about Rolling Thunder specifically, but he did not believe that the U.S. military could be defeated generally. Under these grim circumstances in the spring and summer of 1965, diplomacy, as Bundy well recognized, was not yet a viable option. And so, if the United States was to persevere it would need to escalate its own military role tremendously. After Rolling Thunder this could only mean the introduction of large numbers of U.S. soldiers. In addition to the approximately twenty thousand U.S. troops already in South Vietnam, Johnson approved a request from Westmoreland to send two battalions of Marines to protect the U.S. air base at Danang. After sustained reprisal the Marines who waded ashore on March 8 represented the second significant step in the Americanization of the war. Bundy had never before been averse to sending American troops to Vietnam. But in the spring of 1965 he hesitated, now uncertain of such a radical departure.

U.S. ground troops could greatly enhance the American position in South Vietnam. As Bundy argued to Johnson shortly after the deployment of the Marines to Danang, "our eventual bargaining position . . . will be improved and not weakened if the United States presence on the ground increases in the coming weeks." Moreover, the ARVN "is not really effective," and the ratio of ARVN to NLF forces remained inadequate.[41] Having promulgated another increase in the American military presence on April 6 in NSAM 328, Bundy still thought that yet more troops, perhaps another six battalions, should be added. And in June, responding to the continued deterioration in Vietnam, he enjoined McNamara to find "more dramatic and effective actions in South Vietnam" to shore up the noncommunist position. But as Bundy and the rest of the administration would find out shortly, McNamara's "dramatic and effective" program meant the deployment to Vietnam of many more American soldiers than anyone had previously imagined.[42]

McNamara's solution was more than Bundy was willing to countenance. On July 1, in response to yet another request for more troops from Westmoreland, McNamara submitted to the president an outline of a program for the drastic expansion of the American military role in Vietnam.[43] The sheer size and scope of the plan shocked Bundy, who had previously envisioned a more limited U.S. role, based on a smaller increase in troops, intensified air power, lower-intensity military measures such as counterinsurgency and pacification, and more soft hawk initiatives. Bundy had warned Johnson in April that it would be "easier to disengage planes than ground troops." Yet according to the McNamara program, which represented the most radical plan for the escalation of the war since Bundy's sustained reprisal memo, such a commitment of troops was the only plausible method of ensuring the survival of a noncommunist South Vietnam. Before submitting the program to Johnson, McNamara circulated a draft version throughout the administration, and Bundy held little back in criticizing the early draft.

Bundy noted that the plan proposed to double the number of ground troops, triple the bombing rate, and initiate a naval blockade of Vietnam. These increases came at a time, he felt, "when our troops are entirely untested in the kind of warfare projected" and "the value of the air action we have taken is sharply disputed." The plan focused too much on the North "at a time when nearly everyone agrees the real question is not in Hanoi, but in South Vietnam. My first reaction is that this program is rash to the point of folly." The NLF would not accommodate the U.S. military by fighting more conventionally, he warned; in turn this would render such a vast increase in American troops useless and therefore unnecessary. The evident weakness of Saigon revealed "a slippery slope toward total US responsibility and corresponding fecklessness on the Vietnamese side." In opting for such rapid escalation, McNamara and many others in the administration had ignored other, less costly, methods of halting the insurgency, such as sealing off South Vietnam by establishing barriers along the Ho Chi Minh Trail and across the Demilitarized Zone that separated the two Vietnams at the 17th parallel. But Bundy's main concern was the inevitable Americanization of the war under the McNamara plan:

> The paper also omits examination of the upper limit of US liability. If we need 200 thousand men now for these quite limited missions, may we not need 400 thousand later? Is this a rational course of action? Is there any real prospect that US regular forces can conduct the anti-guerrilla operations which would probably remain the central problem in South Vietnam?
>
> ... Any expanded program needs to have a clear sense of its own internal momentum. The paper does not face this problem. If US casualties go up sharply, what further actions do we propose to take or not to take? More broadly still, what is the real objective of the exercise? If it is to get to the conference table, what results do we seek there? Still more brutally, do we want to invest 200 thousand men to cover an eventual retreat? Can we not do that just as well where we are?[44]

The obvious irony, which escaped Bundy's attention, is that the failure of his own "expanded program," as outlined in his sustained reprisal memo of February, had created the "internal momentum" that led directly to the McNamara program. And in worrying about the political stability of Saigon, Bundy had apparently forgotten that this had been his own rationale in advocating sustained reprisal.

Unsurprisingly Ball also objected to the McNamara program, and he quickly submitted a rebuttal to the secretary of defense. South Vietnam was a lost cause that had reached a critical threshold, he argued. A presidential decision was needed now, preferably one that halted any further escalation and initiated negotiations with the DRV. More unexpectedly, both Rusk and William Bundy also expressed misgivings about the McNamara proposal. Rusk agreed that the "integrity" of the American commitment to South Vietnam "is the principal pillar of peace throughout the world." But, much like his opinion in the January fork-in-the-road memo, he felt that the current effort could be made more effective without adding to it substantially. Similarly, William Bundy proposed a "middle way course" between the McNamara program of escalation and the Ball proposal to negotiate and eventually withdraw. The military should enact those force-level increases already approved and intensify the bombing campaign (but not extend it to Hanoi and Haiphong), while Johnson should defer any additional measures, such as those outlined by McNamara, until it was clear that the modest increases were not working. "In essence," he summarized, "this is a program to *hold on* for the next two months, and *to test* the military effectiveness of US combat forces and the reaction of the Vietnamese army and people to the increasing US role."[45]

In his capacity as Special Assistant—as the president's gatekeeper of foreign policy—it was McGeorge Bundy's job to gather and present these contrasting arguments to Johnson. And as his own reaction to the McNamara plan demonstrates, Bundy did not favor an open-ended U.S. ground commitment in South Vietnam. But neither was he a newly converted or closet dove. He may have become a reluctant warrior, but he was a warrior nonetheless. Like Rusk and William Bundy, he still believed in the basic American commitment to South Vietnam, and he emphatically did not believe in withdrawal. When he forwarded the responses to McNamara's plan, his advice to Johnson conveyed these beliefs. "My hunch is that you will want to listen hard to George Ball and then reject his proposal," he advised in a covering memo. "Discussion could then move to the narrower choice between my brother's course and McNamara's." For Bundy, despite his recent tolerance of the dovish arguments of Cooper and Thomson, the ultimate choice for America was not between escalation and withdrawal, but between massive escalation and limited escalation. The struggle to maintain a noncommunist regime in Saigon was in the end much too important to relinquish without a fight.[46]

The failings of Rolling Thunder, and the enormous commitment of American prestige by launching such a course, left Johnson with little choice but to escalate yet again. Perhaps without realizing it, Johnson had in fact already made the decision to commit troops when he adopted Bundy's program of sustained reprisal the previous February. The course upon which Johnson now decided was a typical politically motivated hedge—the appearance of William Bundy's middle way of limited escalation, but actual acceptance of something much closer to McNamara's program of massive escalation. The famous NSC meetings of late July 1965, were conducted before a president who had already made up his mind. As William Bundy later wrote of the meetings: "By that time . . . the main decisions had been made, and Ball's main arguments considered and rejected."[47] Johnson, for example, sent McNamara to South Vietnam in July for another look before any formal decisions were reached. But two days before McNamara's return, Bundy sent the president a memo detailing the implementation of specific military increases according to the July 1 McNamara program.[48]

Bundy had over the past six months largely brought this about, even though he questioned the extent of the plan proposed by McNamara and accepted by Johnson. Still, massive escalation was preferable to ignominious withdrawal, and Bundy supported the new course. Cooper, Thomson, and fellow NSC staff member Richard C. Bowman maintained that the president should give nonmilitary measures and diplomatic initiatives more of a chance to succeed before additional troops were committed to South Vietnam. Cooper even submitted a counterpart program of diplomatic maneuvers to accompany the military provisions of the McNamara plan.[49] But if Bundy agreed with them, he kept such reservations to himself amid the inexorable drift toward the Americanization of the war. "The military recommendations, as usual, are in pretty good order," he informed Johnson before the first of the major NSC meetings. "On the political side, we have hard problems, also as usual." Despite the bleak situation facing them, Bundy felt that the administration had little choice but to confront the "hard problems" and commit itself even further to the survival of noncommunist South Vietnam.[50]

At a July 21 NSC meeting Bundy reaffirmed his own commitment to the cause and pressed for his colleagues to do the same. Only Ball presented a serious obstacle, and Bundy had little difficulty in brushing aside the under secretary of state's by-now routine concerns. To Ball's argument that the DRV was settling in for a protracted guerrilla war, and that Hanoi and Beijing "are taking the long view," Bundy replied: "I agree with the main thrust of McNamara . . . The difficulty in adopting [Ball's argument] now would be a radical switch without evidence that it should be done." Most important for Bundy, the call for disengagement "goes in the face of all we have said and done." He maintained that Ball's "whole analytical argument gives no weight to [the] loss suffered by [the] other side," even though Bundy knew very well about the inability of sustained reprisal to halt the insurgency or compel Hanoi to sue for peace. Bundy also stressed the need to approach Vietnam as they would any other major war. "We need to make clear that this a somber matter—that it will not be quick—no single action will bring quick victory." But even against these difficulties, with the latest increase in troops it was also "clear that we are not going to be thrown out." When Ball replied that his "problem is not that we don't get thrown out, but that we get bogged down and don't win," Bundy countered, "I would sum up: The world, the country, and the [South Vietnamese] would have alarming reactions if we got out." According to Cooper, who also attended the meeting, Bundy argued that the shift in policy advocated by Ball would be "disastrous." In an echo of his own sustained reprisal recommendations of February, Bundy then stressed that he "would rather maintain our present commitment and 'waffle through' than withdraw." A week later Johnson announced at a press conference that he had authorized the deployment of fifty thousand additional U.S. ground troops to South Vietnam. Thanks in large part to Bundy, the conflict in Vietnam had now become an American war.[51]

CHAPTER 9

Bundy Resilient: The Bombing Pause and the Continuing Search for a Successful Policy

In the spring and summer of 1965 Bundy's commitment to the overall goal of protecting and preserving a noncommunist South Vietnam had not wavered, but his belief in the ability of U.S. military power, both in the air and on the ground, to defeat the insurgency had. Yet in July, once President Johnson had made it clear that he was willing to meet Westmoreland's request for more troops, Bundy ignored his own concerns about the "folly" of the McNamara-Westmoreland plan for escalation and temporarily set aside his doubts. However, only a few months later, with the major decisions on the war already behind him, Bundy could not prevent his apprehension from resurfacing. Increasingly his own view on Vietnam was diverging sharply. Although he still felt strongly that the national security of the United States was tied to that of South Vietnam, and therefore that the Vietnam War was a necessary one, he no longer believed that the Johnson administration was pursuing this goal in the best possible way. No longer the advocate who urged Johnson to adopt the punitive use of air power, Bundy's approach to Vietnam remained, as it had been the previous spring, one of ambivalence.

A number of factors contributed to the return of Bundy's doubts. Most important, the war was not going very well. The Rolling Thunder bombing campaign, which Bundy had worked assiduously to bring about, had not forced the North Vietnamese to abandon their goals nor had it galvanized the South Vietnamese. The July troop decision had Americanized the war; now the South Vietnamese had even less incentive to contribute to the defense of their own country. Both decisions, moreover, greatly contributed to the rise of antiwar sentiment at home and abroad. Bundy had spent the past four years shaping a policy that would save South Vietnam. Now, in the late summer and fall of 1965, not only was the policy not working, it was becoming deeply unpopular both at home and abroad. For once Bundy did not have an answer, and for the first time his confidence, in himself and in the president, wavered. As he admitted to Johnson in October, "the more we learn of the problem the harder the job looks." "Some of us are greatly concerned by the possibility that what began as a Vietnamese war with U.S. assistance may end as a U.S. war with only passive Vietnamese cooperation," he wrote a few days later in a cable he drafted for Lodge and Westmoreland but never sent. "Some of us also wonder whether we adequately understand what is now happening in Vietnam."[1] This was not the sort of military campaign Bundy had envisioned.

But although Bundy began to entertain doubts about how the war was being waged, he never doubted the necessity of the war itself. He still thought it vital to defeat the Vietnamese communists, and he differed with his colleagues only over how to wage the war. He disagreed with some of the means but never the end. He was often quite worried about how the administration approached the conflict. In November, for example, he warned Johnson that a

> still deeper question . . . is the question of our underlying purpose in Vietnam. Are we seeking a negotiated solution after which the superior political skill of the Communists would eventually produce a Commie takeover? Or are we determined to do all that is necessary to establish and sustain a genuinely non-Communist South Vietnam?

But after presenting this delicate and almost heretical choice, he reassured Johnson that he would "incline to the latter position" even though "costs continue to grow."[2]

This was not simple blind faith. Bundy believed that for every problem there was a political or military solution: for the ineffectiveness of Rolling Thunder and the diplomatic difficulties it caused, there was a bombing pause; for the dangerous reliance on U.S. troops, there were incentives to impel the South Vietnamese to do more of the fighting; and for the political difficulties posed by the consistently inept and authoritarian rule from Saigon, there was, as in the days of confronting Diem, a push for political and economic reform. His ambivalence deepened and sharpened, but instead of despairing and recommending withdrawal, he looked to make the policy work. He was resilient in the face of great difficulties. If he ever doubted the entire venture itself, he kept those misgivings strictly to himself.

The Soft Hawk Returns . . . Again

Since McNamara's most recent trip to South Vietnam in June, Bundy had quietly expressed deep misgivings over the direction U.S. military strategy was taking. Although he had played an instrumental role in shaping this very strategy—particularly the adoption of sustained reprisal in the form of the Rolling Thunder bombing campaign—by August 1965 Bundy was certain that the larger the American military presence grew, the less effective it would be. As his advocacy of bombing and consistent support for sending a limited number of U.S. troops to South Vietnam indicates, Bundy never doubted that the defeat of the Vietnamese communists would require an enormous military effort from the United States. But although he was always prepared to make a heavy military commitment, he did not wish to Americanize the war completely. And he never completely abandoned his conviction that nonmilitary measures were an integral part of the war effort. Even in the midst of the great July troop decisions, he reminded Johnson that they still needed "a good political punch to go with our military decisions." Now, with the U.S. war effort under McNamara and Westmoreland growing at an alarmingly rapid pace, Bundy began to spend much of his time, as he informed Johnson, "looking at ways of beefing up our non-military efforts in Vietnam." This marked another return to the soft hawk flock that Forrestal had once made the centerpiece of U.S. policy.[3]

Such measures naturally included large-scale economic and political reform, which had been Forrestal's main goals. But above all Bundy sought to make the war effort more effective and less cumbersome at the local level. After the deployment of U.S. troops, he was less concerned with grand, and largely cosmetic, political gestures than with waging the war on a smaller scale. He wanted to compete directly with the "superior political skill of the Communists" and beat them at their own game. The first problem was the lack of attention in Washington for such an initiative. Throughout the fall Bundy prodded Johnson to make soft hawk projects more integral to the overall effort. Although the NSC staff and the State Department worked on such projects, Bundy believed that "only when the President makes such statements did they get any substantial coverage." Moreover, while the growing American military presence in Vietnam may have been necessary, it made success on the political front much more difficult. A sustained and earnest nonmilitary effort would also deflect criticism, growing both in volume and in vehemence, from "world opinion and forthcoming student demonstrations" at home. It was therefore essential to launch a comprehensive soft hawk program and to provide maximum publicity for its implementation.[4]

Aside from the propaganda value of nonmilitary initiatives, Bundy believed that success would not come strictly from applying America's armed might. Once the buildup in aerial bombing and ground forces over the previous spring and summer had failed decisively to defeat the NLF or curb its support from North Vietnam, thus demonstrating that the communist insurgency would not simply fade away, the potential for the military alone to win the conflict had run up against its natural limits. The U.S. military's presence was required to maintain security, but by itself it could not be victorious. In a stalemate with no easily discernible front line, the war would be won or lost over the allegiance of the Vietnamese people. In October Bundy noted to Johnson that "the Viet Cong are no longer able to achieve a military victory," due primarily to the fact "that the U.S. military commitment is now clearly established." This had not, however, led to much success since "most Vietnamese remain fence-sitters," as yet uncommitted but ready to support whoever could ensure local security. Daily, local interests, such as property damage, land reform, and inflation, loomed much larger than ideological ones. The American effort, Bundy believed, needed to emphasize this aspect of the conflict better. The military campaign was sufficient—perhaps overly so—but other elements of the war effort were not. "In my office," he told Johnson later the same day, "we are thinking about ways of reorganizing our nonmilitary effort so as to really put it on a level with the extraordinary achievement of the Army."[5] One of his suggestions was to increase the role of the ARVN and South Vietnamese police forces in rural pacification while the U.S. military took care of the military struggle. Another was to sponsor the creation of the American Southeast Asia Foundation, which would stimulate and organize the flow of private American aid to South Vietnam.[6]

While Bundy was convinced that U.S. policy toward Vietnam had become too militarized, he was not particularly adept at devising his own soft hawk program as a solution. In a reprise of his working relationship with Forrestal, who had provided the substance that he would subsequently promote, Bundy relied on others to forward specific soft hawk proposals. In his capacity as Special Assistant, he would then recommend these proposals to Johnson.

Once again Bundy's principal ally in this endeavor was Henry Cabot Lodge, who began his second term as ambassador to Saigon in August 1965. The American military effort in Vietnam, Lodge feared, was in danger of winning military battles even as it simultaneously was losing the overall war.

Lodge had become particularly alarmed after reading a memo by Edward Lansdale, whom Lodge wanted to coordinate a new counterinsurgency program, that was bluntly critical of U.S. strategy. Although his reputation was not as high as it had been under Kennedy, and although his unconventional approach was deeply distrusted by the military, Lansdale was still widely regarded as one of the most knowledgeable Americans on Vietnam. "Personally, I don't see how the Communists can be defeated without these positive steps," he warned Lodge. Although the United States could wage war against the communists, it "cannot defeat them short of genocide unless our side puts the war on a political footing." The NLF and DRV, Lansdale continued, were conducting a more effective campaign because they realized that war is as much about politics as it is about troops and bombs. "This is a strict rule the enemy borrowed from Clausewitz," Lansdale argued. "Lenin, Mao, Ho, and Giap have been clear and firm on this basic rule. The Viet Cong have obeyed it amazingly well. Our side has broken this rule over and over again. It is being broken daily right now." Lodge sent the memo to Bundy, who promptly forwarded it to the president. Bundy also seconded Lodge's proposal to hire Lansdale to launch a new counterinsurgency effort. "Lansdale appears quite ready to take over MACV," Bundy admitted to Johnson, "and yet he's not all wrong." Lansdale headed to Saigon shortly after.[7]

From Washington, Bundy did his best to ensure that the administration was behind its men in Saigon. Often he simply endorsed Lodge's recommendations that concentrated specifically on political, economic, and other nonmilitary initiatives.[8] In a State Department directive from Rusk to Lodge, Bundy added the phrase "and winning more positive popular support" to a section on how to help improve political leadership in Saigon. And in a meeting toward the end of September with the president, McNamara, and Ball, Bundy urged that they grant Lodge's request for emergency shipments of rice and that a continuing program for rice exports to South Vietnam be implemented. Nobody at the meeting commented on the irony that the Vietnamese needed to import what should have been their most lucrative export crop.[9]

Bundy received support from Cooper too. While Bundy straddled the hawk and soft hawk positions, Cooper was nominally a soft hawk who often advocated dovish policies, such as disengagement under the cover of negotiations. Increasingly doubtful that a military solution could work, he began to tilt toward pulling out of Vietnam. Johnson, however, had made it clear that withdrawal was no longer a serious option; and since his frequent dovish advice did not stem from a total aversion to war or from an overall rejection of containment, Cooper strove to find an approach that might succeed and also limit the burgeoning conflict. Although he wanted to reverse the militarization of U.S. policy, he was not prepared to resign over the war, and so his only alternative was to seek acceptance of his views within the confines of existing policy. Unlike Bowles or Thomson, who by comparison were quite radical, Cooper was a reformer. The war in Vietnam, he stressed to colleagues, "represents a difficult and brand new type of warfare," which Americans "may not know how to fight." His favorite example was the military's reliance on air power, which he strongly criticized as excessive. Too often, bombing missions directed against the communist guerrillas resulted in civilian casualties and the destruction of peasant villages. This presented "a deeply important problem that goes beyond public relations. At issue here is how the war should be fought." The bombing of villages, even when they provided temporary shelter for the NLF, was not only ineffective, it was also counterproductive: ineffective because the NLF was rarely significantly affected, counterproductive because civilian casualties only increased support and recruitment for the communists. "Our object," Cooper warned, "is not so much to destroy an enemy as to win a people."[10]

As the Johns Hopkins speech the previous April had demonstrated, a soft hawk approach dovetailed with the president's ambitions, both at home and in Southeast Asia. Although Johnson had committed the United States to a major war in Vietnam, he had done so reluctantly. He was more comfortable with domestic politics and progress than with diplomacy and war, and he was eager to transplant the Great Society elsewhere. If a program of progressive reform similar to the Great Society could be applied to the conflict in Vietnam, it would enable Johnson to avoid both a messy foreign war and an impending domestic battle.[11] With its members unconvinced that arms alone could win the war and unanimously supportive of increasing nonmilitary aid and urging the South Vietnamese to reform, and with a receptive president and ambassador to Saigon, Bundy and the NSC staff had an opportunity to concentrate their energies on devising and implementing a soft hawk program. Thus the interagency Vietnam Planning Group for 1965, which Cooper chaired, shifted its focus from searching for a diplomatic settlement on terms favorable to the United States and South Vietnam to "the problem of building a more popular and effective political infrastructure" in Saigon.[12] Throughout the fall the NSC staff, including Bundy himself, monitored the progress of various nonmilitary initiatives designed to win the war, including counterinsurgency, police enforcement, economic assistance and anti-inflationary measures, democracy promotion, psychological warfare, and agricultural reform.[13]

While Bundy and his staff were confident that these American-sponsored soft hawk initiatives would help turn the tide in their favor, through a prolonged learning period they eventually realized that the turning point was still quite distant. In October, after he and Cooper had been working steadily on a nonmilitary program, Bundy boasted to Johnson that the range of such projects was "wide and comprehensive" and that "in essence, we are making perceptible progress on a broad front." Although tough problems remained—such as communications within South Vietnam, a growing number of refugees, a shortage of skilled labor, and a paucity of bureaucratic talent in Saigon—Bundy was "convinced that each of these are being tackled aggressively." Cooper was more cautious after conducting a reassessment the following month. Success would come, but slowly. "The very nature of the non-military struggle in Vietnam," he told Bundy, "is such that we cannot realistically expect dramatic progress from one month to the next." Solid evidence of improvement in both the American and South Vietnamese efforts provided hope, but the problems inherent to the conflict in Vietnam remained tremendously difficult. Neither the United States nor South Vietnam could be impatient. "Much is being done," Cooper emphasized. "Much more has yet to be done."[14]

However, deteriorating political support in the United States for the war and the continuing erosion of security and stability in South Vietnam combined to make patience an unaffordable luxury. Although dissent from the universities, galvanized by the teach-ins, had crested in the spring and abated over the summer break, it reemerged as students returned to campus in the fall. In Saigon, Ky and Thieu seemed to provide temporary relief from the constant rise and fall of governments, but few in Washington had much confidence that their regime could withstand the communist challenge. And as Bundy came to realize, despite the growing U.S. military role in the war, the Vietnamese communists were no closer to defeat than they had been a year earlier. The bloody Battle of Ia Drang, fought between regular North Vietnamese forces and the U.S. Army in mid-November, resulted in heavy casualties for both sides and, despite Westmoreland's optimism, seemed to offer a cautionary tale. The Americans held the disputed territory in the central highlands of South Vietnam and killed thousands of North Vietnamese troops, but it was a pyrrhic victory that demonstrated how fiercely the communists would fight and how much they were willing to commit to the battle against the technologically superior U.S. military.[15]

Thus by December, when he would join forces with McNamara to urge Johnson to adopt a unilateral bombing pause, Bundy would yet again invert the logic that he had used in 1962 and 1963 to argue that counterinsurgency and nonmilitary reform would complement the military campaign: success on the battlefield, he now claimed, was a prerequisite for the implementation of soft hawk programs. No longer were these two aspects of the war effort mutually dependent; success of the nonmilitary program was now contingent upon victorious fighting. While Bundy had continued to straddle the hawk and soft hawk positions, he began once again to tilt more toward the former. Throughout the fall he had, for example, supported Westmoreland's overall military strategy and requests for more ground forces. He had also opposed a renewed diplomatic offensive to test the viability of a negotiated solution.[16] But now, with the end of the year approaching and little progress to show for the military buildup, there was a different appeal. When forwarding a December report on soft hawk initiatives to Johnson, Bundy cautioned that "we have to understand that unless and until there can be military victories, this program is irrelevant. Moreover, we are making major non-military efforts now which should produce results with victories, although they will come to nothing with them." After recommending projects such as additional economic aid, improvements in national health care, educational initiatives, intensified propaganda, and a more comprehensive rural pacification effort, he warned bluntly that "with or without this stronger non-military program, we face major immediate military and diplomatic decisions."[17]

Toward the Bombing Pause

The most important of these decisions was whether to initiate a pause in the bombing campaign. Although it had demonstrated that the United States was not going to quit Vietnam, Rolling Thunder was not at all close to fulfilling either of the goals Bundy had set for it in February: boosting the morale of the South Vietnamese and coercing the North Vietnamese to halt their support for the insurgency. And although the deployment of regular U.S. ground troops to South Vietnam had prevented a sudden collapse in South Vietnam, it was clear that neither the NLF nor the DRV was ready to capitulate. As the Battle of Ia Drang showed, the communists were willing and able to make tremendous sacrifices to win the war. By doing so they had made it clear that they could match any American escalation of the war. With both the non-military and military campaigns caught in an impossible dilemma—neither could work without the other succeeding and neither was succeeding—Bundy was willing to explore new tactics.

Initially, however, Bundy's willingness came reluctantly. As on other matters, such as a negotiated settlement or soft hawk initiatives, it was Cooper who pushed him to consider a bombing pause. On August 5, months before McNamara—who would come to be identified as the strongest proponent of a pause—supported it, Cooper suggested to Bundy that a pause would have several advantages. Politically the United States would gain valuable leverage by making it "abundantly clear that we have *voluntarily* held back our vast power." U.S. bombing had given the North Vietnamese—and by extension the Soviets and Chinese—an enormous propaganda weapon; an extended pause would reverse its effectiveness by demonstrating American magnanimity. And the fact that a pause would occur alongside a buildup of ground forces "should minimize a possible interpretation of 'weakness.' " Such a pause, reflecting U.S. strength, would facilitate would-be negotiators, such as Ghanaian President Kwame Nkrumah; appease wary allies, such as Britain, Japan, and Canada; and neutralize important international critics, such as UN Secretary-General U Thant, India, and Yugoslavia. It would also provide the Soviets, who quietly sought to contain the fighting, with an opportunity to press Hanoi into talks with the United States. And if the North Vietnamese did not respond favorably to a pause, a resumption in bombing, and even additional escalatory measures, could be justified more easily. The rigidity of the bombing campaign was damaging the United States politically, which was, in turn, constraining the U.S. war effort. "We need to de-fuse this issue," Cooper stressed, "in order to free our hands." A pause would have the same effect on the administration's domestic critics.[18]

Bundy remained unconvinced. Part of the reason may have been that Cooper, with the support of Thomson and others on the NSC staff, was promoting a bombing pause as a means to end the war quickly. They were much more pessimistic than Bundy about the war and about America's prospects to bring about a settlement conducive to South Vietnam's survival. To Cooper a bombing pause was really a device to stimulate negotiations, a development to which Bundy was still steadfastly opposed. As Cooper confessed to Bundy on the same day of his bombing pause memo, "I can't resist the opportunity to cast an affirmative vote" on whether to make contact with the NLF. Cooper suggested Algiers as the best place to begin direct secret talks with the communist guerrillas of South Vietnam.[19] Shortly afterward, Cooper and Thomson urged Bundy to consider negotiating with Hanoi using the Soviets as intermediaries. Cooper reiterated the point a month later, stating that the North Vietnamese were sending oblique but genuine signals that they were now interested in exploring grounds for talks with the United States. Even Robert Komer, a hawk who within a year would become Johnson's special assistant for Vietnamese pacification, warned the president not to disdain third-country peace initiatives.[20] Cooper's strongest wish, he told Bundy in a reference to the likely site of any future negotiations, was that "if the time comes when Hanoi says 'Geneva here we come,' we will be going to."[21]

But as long as such arguments were anathema to Bundy, so too was any notion of a bombing pause. His stance on negotiations had not changed much over the preceding four years: they were only feasible when the United States and South Vietnam could negotiate from a position of strength. Back in March he told *The Times* of London in comments that were not for attribution and were immediately disavowed by the State Department, that even after a negotiated settlement American forces would remain in South Vietnam "to stabilize the situation" just as they were doing in South Korea. His view had not changed by the fall. The American military position in South Vietnam, he told his friend Philip Geyelin of the *Wall Street Journal*, "was still too weak to allow negotiations in any real sense of the term." Ultimately the fundamental status of South Vietnam as a noncommunist state was nonnegotiable; this was, after all, the very issue that had caused the war in the first place. For Bundy negotiations were simply another tactic in the struggle to prevent Vietnam from becoming reunited under communist rule.[22]

Because their positions had already been discounted, it did not matter to Bundy what the NLF or DRV proposed. The road to peace, he believed, did not run through Hanoi or wherever the NLF was basing itself at the time. For example, in a conversation that fall with a skeptical Joseph Kraft, the *New York Times* reporter, Bundy "tackled Kraft once again on his know-it-all view that the Viet Cong are the key to peace in South Vietnam." As Bundy told Johnson in preparation for an interview with NBC News in which the subject of negotiations was bound to come up, "we certainly mean to stay there [in South Vietnam] as long as we are needed to prevent a take-over by force or terror under any cloak." The NLF had not abandoned the fight, so nor should the United States. The communists "certainly do not seem to be ready for negotiation. So we and the people of [South] Vietnam have to keep on our steady course of resistance. We [should] also keep it very clear indeed, before all the world, that we are ready for negotiations the moment that others are." Bundy himself publicly reiterated these points and disparaged the idea of a bombing pause a week later in an interview with CBS News. He did not anticipate true negotiations, in which each party compromises its position until a settlement is reached; rather, he envisioned a process in which the NLF and DRV would recognize unequivocally the American and South Vietnamese fundamental position on South Vietnam's right to noncommunist independence. He agreed wholeheartedly with Lodge's "important" view, which the Ambassador sent to the president through Bundy, that "we *can* succeed in warding off communist aggression . . . [and] should therefore stress the need for warding off the aggression, for getting a satisfactory 'outcome,' and not lay so much stress on diplomatic settlements which we probably are not going to be able to get." Since neither side believed in talks with any sincerity, and since neither side was yet willing to compromise on any of the basic issues that had provoked war in the first place, both the conflict and Bundy's opposition to negotiations continued. Mainly because he distrusted the Vietnamese communists, Bundy was not yet convinced that such a drastic maneuver as a bombing pause was necessary or wise.[23]

He did not, however, rule it out altogether. After he read Cooper's August 5 memos on the bombing and on making contact with the NLF, Bundy told Johnson that although a pause not a bad idea, it was not yet a good one either. "[A] long pause at a time of relative U.S. strength seems to me more sensible than a short one now."[24] If implemented and exploited correctly, a pause could have political, diplomatic, and even military advantages. With this in mind, and despite his lingering doubts about its efficacy, Bundy kept the idea of a pause simmering while preventing it from boiling over. In his capacity as Special Assistant he continued to solicit opinion on a pause from Rusk, Lodge, and McNamara in addition to his own staff.[25]

In the meantime Bundy did nothing to disguise his opposition. "McNamara tends to favor a pause," he informed Johnson. "Rusk and I tend to be opposed until we get some signal from someone that a pause would have results in matching action by Hanoi."[26] Nearly two weeks later, after McNamara had begun to push firmly for a pause, a cynical Bundy suggested to the president that the secretary of defense, a "man who has to present next year's defense budget," was simply following his bureaucratic instincts, while Secretary of State Rusk was the "man who has to cope with an effort by the Communists to embarrass us by ambiguous responses." Bundy argued against the pause because, as he put it, "I am more concerned with the diplomatic aspects than with the military budget." He was also concerned that "if we pause, we may seem to admit that our bombing is the cause of the trouble, and this is simply not so." Bundy's view, moreover, was well known within the administration. McNamara confided to George Ball, another supporter of a pause, that Bundy did not agree with them.[27]

McNamara need not have worried. Only a few days after he and Ball discussed the Special Assistant's stance on a bombing pause, Bundy changed his mind. By this time, against the advice of the Joint Chiefs, McNamara had made a pause the centerpiece of the Pentagon's Vietnam strategy for 1966. Characteristically he advocated for a pause with great logic and persistence, the effects of which were beginning to convince a previously skeptical Bundy. A few weeks earlier John McNaughton, McNamara's most trusted adviser, sent Bundy his official assessment, prepared originally for the secretary of defense, of a bombing pause's potential. After explaining why Rusk was still opposed to McNamara's plans, McNaughton stated bluntly that "State is wrong with respect to the Pause." A pause, he stressed, offered the best chance to improve the U.S. military and diplomatic posture in Vietnam: "I hate to miss the small chance [a pause] offers to turn this thing around." McNaughton's views would have had considerable significance for Bundy: McNaughton had visited South Vietnam with Bundy in February and had helped draft the Bundy mission's key recommendations; he was also one of the Johnson administration's most respected members and was widely recognized for his integrity and intelligence. However, McNaughton would not have had much influence had McNamara not agreed with him. McNamara relied on McNaughton heavily and trusted him deeply, particularly on Vietnam policy. When McNaughton spoke people in the administration, even at Bundy's rarefied level, listened. Supported by McNaughton, McNamara kept pushing, and gradually Bundy found himself more and more convinced.[28]

Once again Bundy found himself holding the balance of bureaucratic power at a key moment in the war. Rusk and the State Department were vigorously opposed to a pause; McNamara and the Pentagon's civilian leadership were strongly supportive. For now, President Johnson remained unmoved by McNamara's arguments, but he did not reject a pause entirely. Thus in a manner strikingly similar to the Kennedy administration's indecision over what to do with Diem in the fall of 1963, to the Johnson administration's debate over bombing in February 1965, and to the debate over deploying ground troops in spring and summer of 1965, whichever way Bundy decided would ultimately determine the administration's course. Although he had argued against a pause, up to the end of November Bundy could not make up his mind definitively. "I think McNamara will turn out to be right," he told Johnson early that month, "but I also agree with Rusk." Bundy did agree with McNamara that for strategic reasons a decision was needed before the new year, preferably in the weeks before Christmas. Ironically, Bundy explained to Johnson, a pause would make it easier to escalate the war afterward. "If we are going to have major additional reinforcements in January, we almost surely need to take some political steps in December. One such step may be a pause in bombing (McNamara clearly favors such a pause)." If Johnson was persuaded by this reasoning and wanted a pause, Bundy wrote the following week, "we must begin to plan for it very promptly."[29]

Tactically a pause made sense. As Cooper had argued to Bundy in August, temporarily freezing Rolling Thunder would provide the administration with a fillip diplomatically and some breathing room domestically. If the North Vietnamese reacted positively to the pause, it would signal their vulnerability to bombing, and any negotiations that followed would doubtless be on American terms. And if the pause failed—if neither Hanoi nor Moscow responded favorably (nobody expected Beijing to cooperate)—the administration would be justified in resuming, even intensifying, Rolling Thunder. An unsuccessful pause would certainly make it more difficult for the war's critics, both at home and abroad, to oppose the deployment of more U.S. troops to Vietnam. This vital point was brought home by British Foreign Secretary Michael Stewart, who told an intrigued Bundy in October that not only did the bombing, rather than ground troops, provide "Communist front organizations in Britain with their main propaganda weapon," it was also causing moderate public opinion to swing against the U.S. war effort. Thus when he finally did come out in favor of a pause, Bundy stressed continually that it should be a tactical pause for appearances—designed to improve the administration's diplomatic and military standing, expand its options, and prepare the way for additional escalatory measures—rather than a strategic pause—designed to bring the war to an end on the best terms available instead of the best terms desirable. In July, just prior to the major internal debates on further troop deployments, Bundy had searched in vain for an answer to the difficult problem: "How do we combine a peace offensive with stepped-up military action?" With a bombing pause, he seemed to have found an answer. "My own conviction," Bundy wrote to Johnson at the beginning of December, shortly after he had changed his mind to support the pause, "is still that the best preparation for the tough programs of January is a peace offensive in December, and that the pause is the necessary centerpiece of that effort."[30]

By November other factors were making a pause seem more palatable. Not only were the myriad nonmilitary programs failing to turn the tide, as Bundy had already concluded, but it was increasingly clear that the bombing campaign itself was not at all successful.[31] Bundy had suspected as much as early as the spring, but by the fall he and the NSC staff had much more solid evidence of sustained reprisal's shortcomings. While it hadn't failed abjectly, neither had it inflicted sufficient damage to compel the DRV to cease its support for the NLF in the South. According to a CIA appraisal in October, which Bundy received and read, economic losses due to the bombing of North Vietnam "are still small." Rolling Thunder had inflicted tremendous physical damage, but to little effect: "There continues to be no basic change in Hanoi's attitude toward the war." Hanoi was still determined "to press on with the war in South Vietnam despite the continuing attrition of the air war and the increase of US troops in the south." Popular support for the war had not diminished, and the activities of the North Vietnamese military had not been hampered significantly. Temporarily halting Rolling Thunder therefore posed little, if any, risk to overall strategy.[32]

All these factors—pressure from Cooper, McNamara, and McNaughton; the lack of significant progress in both the nonmilitary programs and the military campaign; and the evident political advantages—led Bundy to change his mind toward the end of November. He announced his conversion at a particularly crucial moment in the deliberations over a bombing pause: when McNamara's campaign was at its height, when planning for a December pause was still feasible, and when President Johnson had not yet firmly made up his mind. In a November 27 memo entitled "Once more on the pause," Bundy came out for the first time in favor of a pause. This was not simply a mild recommendation, a fulfillment of his duties as Special Assistant. He argued unequivocally that a pause "is such an important question that I think you may want to look at it once again." In a manner similar to the fork-in-the-road memo of the previous January, Bundy addressed Johnson on behalf of himself and McNamara. They had "the impression that your mind is settling against a pause, but we both believe that the matter is too important to be decided without making sure that the question has been explored to your satisfaction." As in January, Bundy moved to isolate Rusk in a bid to tilt the balance in his and McNamara's favor: "I have mentioned our concern to Dean Rusk and while he is still against a pause at present, he has encouraged me to raise the matter with you once more."[33]

Claiming that recent developments made it more plausible to halt the bombing temporarily, Bundy made it clear that he envisioned a pause as a tactic that would give the administration a freer hand to wage the war. A pause would fulfill several political goals. First, by "proving our good faith," it would neutralize criticism that the administration was disinterested in any negotiations. Second, as the fighting at Ia Drang and Westmoreland's subsequent requests for further reinforcements demonstrated, "we may have to look forward to a pretty grim year." By showing that "our determination to seek peace is equal to our determination on the battlefield," a failed pause would go a long way to convince skeptics that the administration had little choice but to escalate. A pause would have the same mitigating effect on the third factor: the war was proving to be more costly than anyone had anticipated, and the White House would need to ask Congress to appropriate additional funds to meet Westmoreland's requests. Finally, potential third-party peace advocates, such as British Prime Minister Harold Wilson, were threatening actively to seek a settlement. Such endeavors would only complicate matters for the United States, but for political reasons the White House could not distance itself from them and be seen as a saboteur of peace. "We will spike [Wilson's] guns and those of everyone else like him" if Johnson accepted a pause. Overall, Bundy stressed, the domestic and international arguments for a pause were "substantially stronger," evidenced by the fact that "my own judgment has shifted over toward McNamara." He concluded by highlighting the political advantages to a pause: "It is quite true, as I have argued before, that the bombing is not what started the trouble, but it is also true that we have a great interest in proving our own good faith as peace lovers."[34]

The similarities between this memorandum and the January 27 fork-in-the-road memo are striking: in both Bundy teamed up with the secretary of defense to isolate the more cautious and reticent secretary of state, in both Bundy presented Johnson with a stark choice between equally unpalatable options, and in both Bundy portrayed the war as not going well and argued that Johnson must adjust its strategy to avoid a serious erosion of the U.S. position. Although the rhetoric of the fork-in-the-road memo is much more shrill and alarmist, both documents are similar in their aim. The ultimate purpose of both memos—to present Johnson with a preferred option that would help win the war—was identical. The key difference is that in January Bundy had urged the president to escalate America's role in the conflict; in November he pushed Johnson temporarily to de-escalate. The recommendation to pause the bombing, however, was not designed to prepare for an American withdrawal. Quite the opposite was true. Indirectly, Bundy's version of the bombing pause was also an escalatory measure.

Now that he had joined forces with the pro-pause faction, Bundy threw all of his weight behind the effort. If it were to be plausible and have any chance of success, Bundy felt that Soviet participation was essential. Should the pause lead to negotiations, Moscow would probably be in the best position to prod Hanoi into making concessions. Should the pause fail, involving the Soviets would co-opt them and hopefully mute their criticism. Shortly before writing his conversion memo, Bundy sat down to discuss Vietnam, among other matters, with Anatoly Dobrynin, the Soviet ambassador. Dobrynin promised Bundy that the Soviet Union would do all it could to temper Hanoi's demands, provided there was a "renewed and longer pause" than the previous one in May. Unsurprisingly, one of Bundy's key points in his seminal memo of November 27 was that "there is growing evidence that we can count on quiet but strong Soviet diplomatic support in pushing Hanoi toward the conference table during another pause." Later, in forwarding the record of a conversation among Rusk, Dobrynin, and Soviet expert Llewellyn Thompson, Bundy informed Johnson that it appeared "that the Soviets would make an effort to move things onward during the pause." Combined with a similar pledge to Rusk by the Hungarians, Johnson found the prospect of using communists to contain communists an enticing one.[35]

Aside from encouraging Soviet participation, Bundy began a constant campaign to endorse the bombing pause and plan for its implementation. These efforts were intended to convince President Johnson, who remained skeptical and had not yet given his approval for a pause. Bundy enlisted the support of key White House aides Bill Moyers and Joseph Califano to urge Johnson to adopt a pause. All three of them, Bundy reported to Johnson on December 2 while the president was vacationing at the LBJ Ranch in Texas, believed that only a pause would appease Congress enough to gain its support for Westmoreland's request to have more troops in the new year. A pause would prove the administration's eagerness to secure peace while at the same time help to prepare "a solid base for the chosen level of later military action." Lest Johnson think that his Special Assistant had gone soft on the war, Bundy was careful to emphasize that "a pause should be quite hard-nosed" by making it clear that a lack of progress during the cessation of bombing would give the United States "a fully free hand" to intensify its military operations afterward. The next day Bundy cabled Johnson with his judgment that "we shall almost surely wish to proceed energetically on Westmoreland's course in South Vietnam," and that a pause was the best form of preparation for this. The "long and the short of it," Bundy continued, was that "the international advantages outweigh the international traps." The day after that Bundy informed Johnson that "opinion in favor of a pause continues to grow" in Washington. "We think this is the best single way of keeping clear that Johnson is for peace, while Ho is for war." A new element to the strategy was to exploit potential divisions among the Vietnamese communists: by dealing only with the DRV and not the NLF, a pause leading to talks "would drive a sharp wedge between Hanoi and the Communists in South Vietnam." It was, Bundy promised, a no-lose gambit. If Johnson decided in favor of a pause, "either the infiltration [from the North to the South] would stop, or we would have a perfectly legitimate and internationally defensible reason for renewed bombing at a time of our choice." "My own basic reason for supporting the pause," he wrote Johnson on another occasion, "is simply that we are going to have to do these other tough things in January . . . I think the peace-lovers will support our January actions a whole lot more if there has been a pause beforehand." Bundy and the NSC staff also drafted for the president's use a comprehensive, point-by-point list of diplomatic, political, and military advantages to a pause.[36]

Bundy's analysis betrayed his fundamental misunderstanding of the war and how it was perceived by critics at home and throughout the world. Domestic criticism of the war had been galvanized by the bombing; it was seen as one of the causes, rather than a symptom, of the Vietnam problem. Moreover, most of the developing world, communist and noncommunist alike, blamed the United States for perpetuating the conflict. Much of the industrialized world, including key American allies, privately blamed the communists for instigating the conflict but could not understand why the fate of South Vietnam was so important to the United States. As McNamara himself recognized two years later, people were particularly horrified by images of the world's wealthiest and most technologically advanced nation systematically pulverizing one its poorest and least developed. West Germans, for example, equated the American bombing of Vietnam with the allied firebombing of Dresden in World War II. To much of the world it was Rolling Thunder, not Hanoi's intransigence, that was the problem.[37]

Despite Stewart's warning in October, Bundy still did not appreciate just how unpopular the bombing was and that a temporary pause would bestow only ephemeral gains. He was certain that a bombing pause would serve as a political masterstroke that would dampen dissent and enable the administration to escalate as it wished. Thus he spent as much time promoting the kind of pause he envisioned as he did debating the merits of the pause itself. As Dobrynin had told him, and as he himself had argued to Johnson on several occasions, Bundy thought a pause would only work if it was sustained over several weeks. He also encouraged Johnson to make a concerted effort to sell the pause, and America's good faith in finding a settlement, to as many countries as possible through a major diplomatic initiative during the bombing halt. Unlike McNamara, Bundy did not believe that a comprehensive cease-fire across Vietnam, in the air and on the ground, should accompany the pause. At present, the political risks were much too high. A cease-fire, Bundy warned, "carries unacceptable costs with the troops in the field" and with public opinion at home. Westmoreland was certain to reject it, as were Republicans and conservative Democrats. Bundy feared criticism from former President Eisenhower in particular. Militarily the U.S. forces in Vietnam were unprepared to participate in a cease-fire. In a memo appraising the president of McNamara's cease-fire proposal, Bundy added: "I continue to think we are not ready for this one yet." Later the same day, in a small meeting with Johnson, Rusk, McNamara, and Ball, Bundy tersely challenged the secretary of defense's idea of a cease-fire: "Not now. It takes time." Moreover, while a bombing pause would not hurt the war effort because the bombing was not all that successful, Bundy did want to relinquish the initiative on the ground. "I'm more optimistic," he told McNamara. "Our military is hurting them."[38]

Above all, to have any political impact a pause had to last long enough to provide Hanoi with plenty of time to decide and prove to critics that the United States was serious about ending the war. Bundy believed that a long pause, announced with great publicity, would accrue much more political and diplomatic capital than a brief, purely symbolic one. "We ought to examine the question of a continuous pause," Bundy said at another intimate meeting between the key decision makers and President Johnson. "We could get a major political advantage from this." To Rusk's objections that a pause should be a brief—a day or two at most—and quiet diplomatic affair, Bundy retorted that "you won't hear in that time frame . . . I don't see where it leads us." Once the pause began, on December 24, Bundy maintained the pressure on Johnson to extend the pause. Even Maxwell Taylor, he told the president shortly before the new year, was in favor of a longer pause. Taylor, Bundy wrote, "thinks the political reward of a solid pause is worth it at this stage."[39] The publicity Bundy hoped would accompany the pause would maximize the political credit the administration would receive. Following Bundy's advice and, more important, his own instincts, Johnson sent high-level emissaries to important world capitals—such as Averell Harriman to Warsaw, Belgrade, Tokyo, and eight other cities; and Ambassador to the UN Arthur Goldberg to London, Paris, and Rome—to inform friends and convince foes that the United States was exploring every option in the pursuit of peace. Bundy himself traveled to Ottawa to brief Prime Minister Lester B. Pearson and enlist Canada's support in finding a peaceful settlement. After all, how would the United States gain political points if nobody apart from a few diplomats, working behind the scenes, knew that a pause was even occurring? Bundy therefore supported his colleagues, such as George Ball and Goldberg, who sought to discover openings to Hanoi via the UN, Moscow, and Vientiane.[40]

The problem with Bundy's approach was that it was designed not to seek an end to the war but to earn the administration political plaudits, diplomatic leverage, and time to prepare the military for an intensification of the war. Cooper, whose chief priority was to find a settlement to the war, raised this issue with Bundy before pause began. Is the pause, he asked pointedly, "to be one motivated by considerations of domestic and foreign opinion, or is it motivated by a desire to exploit fully whatever chance there may be that negotiations could soon emerge (an 'image' pause or a 'probing' pause)?" Cooper was worried that Johnson "would call for negotiations publicly but avoid them in fact," a cynical ploy that would "consciously and deliberately . . . pass up an opportunity for a political resolution of the Vietnam problem." Because of this he strongly advised that a pause be implemented quietly and pursued privately.[41] Bundy rejected Cooper's advice. In search of political and military gains, rather than negotiations, he preferred an "image" pause to one that was "probing." As Bundy explained in guidelines drafted for Lodge and Westmoreland, should Saigon complain about the pause, "it should be made clear that the massive commitment of US power to SVN requires the overwhelming support of the American people and broad understanding internationally."[42]

The Pause and Its Limits

As Bundy had anticipated, and even planned for, the pause failed to produce a diplomatic breakthrough. Begun on December 24, 1965, as a limited initiative that President Johnson expected to last no longer than a few days, the cessation of the Rolling Thunder bombing campaign eventually became the centerpiece for the administration's efforts to convince its critics, at home and abroad, that it was only the communists who stood between the United States and a peaceful settlement. Bundy for one did not believe that the pause would ever lead to productive negotiations. During the internal debate over whether to pause the bombing, he had supported it for reasons of politics and propaganda, and he continued to do so as the pause stretched into January. As he told Johnson on January 24 after informing him of Hanoi's tepid reaction, "We began the pause without thinking there was much chance that it would get a better response than all this. We began because there was real and honest concern among our friends, and even among many of our people who expressed with eloquence their belief that we should try it and see." A few days later he bluntly reminded his colleagues during an NSC meeting that "we did not expect any serious response to the pause" from the Vietnamese communists. Unsurprisingly, by the middle of January Bundy was pushing strongly for a resumption in bombing. Rolling Thunder duly resumed on January 30, 1966.[43]

The decision to resume bombing was not a difficult one, and Bundy supported it fully. The majority of intelligence emerging from Vietnam certainly clarified things. As hopeful as the indistinct and cryptic contact with North Vietnamese and Soviet diplomats was, it could not disguise the fact that the DRV was appearing to take advantage of the lull in bombing by sending troops and supplies to the South. At Bundy's request the CIA provided the NSC staff with continuous assessments of communist reactions to the pause. The CIA concluded that whereas the NLF had curtailed its military activities, the DRV had increased markedly its rate of infiltration to the South. The CIA also informed Bundy that the pause had produced scant movement among European and Asian communist countries on any of the key issues surrounding the war and that the North Vietnamese themselves were preparing to wage a protracted but intensified guerilla war.[44] Bundy in turn warned Johnson that the "attitude of Hanoi has been one of public and private denunciation and of feverish effort to take advantage of the pause to repair and retrain and resupply." In a subsequent meeting he argued that all of their available intelligence concluded that any extension of the pause "will strengthen the will of the enemy."[45]

The lack of an encouraging substantive response from Hanoi, or even from Moscow, inflicted the most damage on the viability of continuing the pause. This fact, combined with the evidence that the communists were regrouping and reinforcing, convinced Bundy that the pause should end. Although he was prepared to support Harriman, Ball, and Goldberg in their quest for a breakthrough, he was unwilling to do so indefinitely. Moreover, Bundy felt that many promising leads that had emerged in the first few weeks of the pause were at best ephemeral and oblique or at worst intentionally misleading and confusing. And if the administration promised to explore all of the leads fully, Hanoi could tie down the American war effort indefinitely by hinting at concessions or suggesting that talks were imminent. By late January, as the pause was nearing thirty days, Bundy's patience had eroded completely. The pause, he admonished Ball and Harriman, has "proved that we have done all we can do—and the other nations in the world know this." In case the Canadians had not got the message during his visit to Ottawa, Bundy reiterated the point over the Canadian ambassador's objections to a resumption in bombing during a meeting at the Canadian Embassy.[46] Bundy was especially disparaging about the fitful and elliptical exchange between the U.S. ambassador to Rangoon, Henry A. Byroade, and a North Vietnamese diplomat in Burma, telling Johnson unequivocally that "the man from Hanoi has nothing to say." Bundy even dismissed one promising lead, from Laos, that he had previously encouraged. "Odds are nine to one nothing will happen," he said at a meeting with Johnson, McNamara, Rusk, and Ball. Rather than chase any potential lead, it was now more important for the United States to resume bombing. After all, as Bundy had put it earlier in the month when he decided against sending an official letter from Johnson to Ho, if the president went out of his way to explore every opening, it "would almost surely be misread in Hanoi as a sign of U.S. weakness."[47]

In November and December 1965 Bundy had worked diligently to bring about a pause; in late January 1966 he worked just as hard to end it. The effort to convince the president and the rest of the administration to resume the bombing was not, however, nearly as difficult as it had been to convince them to adopt it in the first place. Johnson had always been skeptical and had approved the pause after much deliberation and with great reluctance. Bundy also found that many influential people, both inside and outside the government, agreed that the pause should end, among them McNamara, Rusk, Westmoreland, McNaughton, Taylor, Clark Clifford, John McCloy, and Robert A. Lovett. Even Cooper, who had pushed vigorously for the pause to extend to the middle of February, ruefully concurred that Johnson had little choice but to abandon the search for peace and resume Rolling Thunder.[48]

Intelligence on communist activity and a lack of diplomatic progress convinced Bundy that the pause was not working. Just as important, his original reasons in favor of a pause—particularly the international and domestic political benefits of demonstrating the administration's peaceful intent—had been fulfilled, and a cessation of the bombing was no longer useful. As an architect of the administration's policy of sustained reprisal, moreover, Bundy believed that bombing was an essential tactic in the war, despite its failings. "One thing the bombing has done," he said during an NSC meeting, "is to serve as an umbrella for 200,000 men." Thus Bundy was arguing from a position of strength, and he had little trouble convincing Johnson of his case. As early as January 10 Bundy argued that the administration should publicize the fact that the communists were taking advantage of the pause. Such publicity, he stressed, would "clear the way for bombing resumption." Two weeks later Bundy was satisfied that the pause had outlasted its usefulness. He told Johnson that the question of "whether to resume bombing . . . should clearly be answered in the affirmative." To facilitate the renewal of Rolling Thunder, he urged the president to initiate a publicity campaign to convince Americans and foreign governments of the administration's sincerity in trying to find a peaceful settlement. He also advised that the State Department should be "doing everything we can to close all the circuits" of diplomacy that had emerged during the pause.[49]

Concurrent to Bundy's push to end the bombing pause was his equally vigorous push to improve the nonmilitary effort both in Washington and South Vietnam. While the failure of the pause meant that an intensification of the war was necessary, it also meant that soft hawk initiatives would also assume a greater role. This was the message Bundy emphasized most frequently during the pause. One of his strongest recommendations was the appointment to Saigon of a U.S. official in charge of pacification and the appointment of a counterpart in Washington. A pacification director, Bundy told Johnson, "needs to learn to think of himself as the field commander for pacification in the same way that Westmoreland is the field commander for the war . . . The truth is . . . that the broad front of pacification is absolutely equal in importance to the more familiar and more advertised business of fighting organized enemy units."[50] He also seconded Lodge's suggestion that the Peace Corps be sent to South Vietnam.[51] Bundy believed the soft hawk effort to be so important as to warrant its own section in the president's State of the Union speech; he even included an appropriate passage in a draft of the speech:

> [The] work for stability and education and health and relief is just as important as the fight against the invader. Our economic aid program in Vietnam is now becoming the largest we have anywhere. Rice for the hungry; schoolbooks for the children; shelter for the refugees; these are all part of a policy of hope for the people of South Vietnam . . . Our efforts for the people there have expanded greatly in the last year. They will expand again in 1966.[52]

"My basic conviction," Bundy told Johnson shortly after, is that nonmilitary programs "are very much more important than bombing the North. This is why I think the State of the Union should keep attention focused on the effort in the South."[53]

On January 31 Bundy pulled all of these arguments together in a rare press conference to announce and defend the decision to resume bombing. Blaming the North Vietnamese for prolonging the war, he warned the nation not to expect a quick victory. Because "there is no readiness for talks or peace in Hanoi," he told the assembled reporters, the United States would have to "go forward with determination and with strength" and "persevere for as long as was necessary." Since it was unclear "whether the government regime in Hanoi understands this determination," the United States could only "go about our business" in prosecuting the war, in prodding the communists diplomatically, and in soft hawk programs such as "political reconstruction and pacification and economic and social efforts in South Vietnam." Bundy mentioned that both the NLF and the DRV used the pause to supply their forces and reinforce their numbers in the South. This was because of Hanoi's underestimation of American resolve. "I think if they did understand it adequately and fully," he declared, "they would see the advantage from their point of view . . . of moving towards a peaceful settlement. They aren't ready to do that. It follows that they still have hopes which make them unwilling to settle for anything but their version of total victory." Significantly, according to Bundy the communist insurgents in the South whom the DRV was supporting escaped culpability. They were merely agents of the DRV's will. Responding to a question about who controlled the insurgency, Bundy replied that "a decision in Hanoi would be decisive . . . If there were a decision in Hanoi for the course of peace . . . then the peace could in fact be restored." Bundy's goal was to portray U.S. policy as passive—in that American and South Vietnamese goals were limited, static, and defensive—and reactive—in that the American war effort was only in response to North Vietnam's aggressive designs of conquest. Curiously, then, the decision to resume bombing was not for Washington to make.[54]

Whether this was Bundy's actual belief remains unclear. But what is clear is that the bombing pause was never intended to be a genuine attempt to bridge American and communist differences to secure a political, peaceful settlement to the war. It was instead a propaganda offensive designed to promote a peaceful image for the Johnson administration. As Cooper recalled with some bitterness:

> In retrospect the prospects for negotiations were dim in early 1966 . . . The style and method adopted in December and January were plainly unsuitable. Where finely tooled instruments were required, we used a sledgehammer. Where confidential and careful advance work was necessary, we proceeded with the subtlety of a Fourth of July parade. Where a dramatic, surprise proposal may have stirred Hanoi's interest, we made a public spectacle of every melodramatic move. Instead of maximizing the effect of our . . . peace package, we buried it in the razzmatazz of sudden, noisy, and florid VIP trips. In short the President was acting like a ringmaster of a three-ring circus, rather than as the focal point of a carefully worked out exercise in diplomacy.[55]

This was all, of course, exactly according to Bundy's plan.

From the White House to the Ford Foundation

On November 7, 1965, John J. McCloy, a family friend and chairman of the board of the Ford Foundation, offered Bundy the organization's presidency. Based in New York, Ford was the country's largest and wealthiest philanthropic institution and a pillar of the Establishment into which Bundy had been born and raised. With his social and government connections, his administrative experience from Harvard and Washington, and his renowned intelligence, Bundy seemed to be the perfect choice to head Ford. The presidency of the Ford Foundation, in turn, was powerful and prestigious enough to tempt him away from the Johnson administration. Bundy informed Johnson of McCloy's offer the next day and subsequently arranged with Johnson, Rusk, and McNamara to continue as Special Assistant and prepare for a successor until the end of February 1966.[56]

By this time Bundy had doubtless tired of President Johnson's overbearing personality. Although Bundy was no prude, Johnson's scatological humor and psychological games eventually wore thin. To take one example, Johnson had once questioned Bundy's masculinity because of his fondness for playing tennis; to take another, Johnson once humiliated Bundy by asking the Special Assistant to conduct a conversation while the president was sitting on the toilet. Much as he still believed in his work, Bundy was also exhausted with his official duties and worn down by Washington. Even before McCloy approached him with the offer from Ford, a weary Bundy had quietly asked Harvard president Nathan Pusey if the university would take him back as a professor.[57] Nonetheless, Bundy's remarkable January 31 press conference underscored the optimism and determination he felt about Vietnam immediately prior to leaving Washington for the Ford Foundation. In retrospect many of his colleagues believed that Bundy left the White House in silent protest over Johnson's handling of the war. Many historians have since concurred.[58] But Bundy's words and deeds during his last few months in Washington demonstrate that this was not the case at all. He was, in fact, rather optimistic about the war's progress. Whatever his true reasons for quitting, he did not leave the Johnson administration over differences on Vietnam.

Despite the failure of the pause, and of the peace offensive that formed its centerpiece, in early 1966 Bundy was more optimistic about America's ability to defeat the communist insurgency in South Vietnam than he had been in a long time. He had anticipated the lack of diplomatic progress that came to characterize the pause, so there was little cause for disillusionment. But what also emerged during the pause was intelligence indicating that the NLF had been suffering more than anyone had previously known. In January both the Pentagon and the CIA informed Bundy that the NLF was reeling from unexpectedly high casualties and low morale. South Vietnam itself also seemed to be doing better. Even Thomson, the NSC staff's lone outright dove, informed Bundy that in South Vietnam the programs for pacification, economic reform, political stability, and counterinsurgency had all improved significantly.[59] Little wonder that Bundy was feeling bullish in a conversation on January 20 with Walter Lippmann. Lippmann, an incredulous Bundy reported to Johnson afterwards, "genuinely believes it is a civil war, and that it was not started by Hanoi." Lippmann also argued that "the best answer is to let the place go

Communist as gracefully as possible." Bundy replied confidently that Lippmann was simply "looking at our troubles and not the troubles of the enemy, and that there is a good deal of evidence that the Viet Cong were hurting and that the balance was less unfavorable than [Lippmann] assumed." A month later, only a week before he left the administration, Bundy confessed to Johnson: "I am more optimistic than Bob McNamara" about America's chances in Vietnam.[60]

Bundy was not pessimistic about the war. Nor did he ever doubt the reasons for American intervention. With his intention to resign and move to the Ford Foundation a matter of public record by November 14, 1965, there was no need for him to assume any major responsibilities on Vietnam, particularly if he now disagreed with U.S. policy. But this was exactly what he did in twice volunteering to go to South Vietnam to discuss with Lodge the various soft hawk programs that they both envisioned.[61] It is difficult to imagine a true dissenter, such as Ball, volunteering for such a task. Accompanied by Vice President Humphrey, Secretary of Agriculture Orville Freeman, and Harriman, Bundy traveled to South Vietnam on February 9, 1966. This visit contrasted starkly to the Bundy mission a year before when, after the devastating attack on U.S. forces in Pleiku, Bundy returned to Washington in a darkly pessimistic frame of mind. In February 1966 Bundy was buoyed by signs of progress in both the military and nonmilitary campaigns. "My own strong feeling," he told the NBC news program *Meet the Press* after returning from Saigon, "is that there is more reason to be hopeful about the eventual result there now than there was a year ago." He contrasted the "downward course a year ago" with the "upward course now." On the show Bundy even rebuked his friend (and Johnson's nemesis) Senator Robert F. Kennedy for suggesting that the NLF be admitted into a South Vietnamese neutralist, coalition government.[62]

What is most striking about Bundy's reaction to his trip, and what is most revealing about his sincerity, is that there was no difference between his views in public and in private. Unlike in 1965, when his private pessimism dramatically contradicted his public optimism, in 1966 he was consistently optimistic. "The general atmosphere here is enormously better than it was a year ago," he wrote Johnson while still in Saigon. He reiterated his criticism of neutralism in a private letter to Kennedy and drafted instructions for Lodge and Westmoreland to tell the South Vietnamese to ignore Kennedy's comments and "be assured that our position on the NLF has not changed . . . What we hope you can communicate to [Saigon], in short, is a full understanding of both our own firmness and determination and of the real problems created by critics here who seize upon any minor difference to exploit."[63] Bundy told Johnson of the tremendous progress in pacification; only the problem of management and coordination from Washington remained unresolved. What he found especially encouraging was "the clear evidence of gradually improving performance by [South] Vietnamese troops." Unlike the year before, there was now little reason to fear an imminent communist takeover. "In sum," Bundy concluded buoyantly, "all the real military indicators are favorable . . . [and] the deployments of 1965 have been a magnificent success." In virtually every facet of the war it seemed clear to Bundy that the United States was winning and the communists were losing.[64]

Bundy, then, was no quiet critic or closet dove. He remained as convinced of America's mission in Southeast Asia in 1966 as he had been in 1961. If his resignation was submitted as a form of protest against the president's Vietnam policy—a policy Bundy, as much as anyone else, had shaped over the preceding five years—it was known only to Bundy himself. "The truth is that in Southeast Asia we are stronger than China," Bundy wrote to himself in a private memo intended for his personal records. "If the basic questions of interest, right, and power are assessed, the casualties and costs are to be accepted." This was a rhetorical blend of might and right that Henry Stimson could not have put better himself. Years later Bundy told an interviewer that he did not want to resign "in a way that criticized the decision" on Vietnam, not out of loyalty to the president or due to fear of Johnson's considerable wrath, but "because I agreed with the basic decision."[65]

Bundy's conscience, then, did not force him to leave. Tempted by an offer of the presidency of one of America's great philanthropic organizations, enticed by a move to New York, frustrated with President Johnson's personality, and doubtless exhausted, mentally and physically, by his strenuous duties as Special Assistant, Bundy justifiably felt he had done all he could in Washington. But he did not regret the policy he had helped to build. In his letter of resignation, undated but tendered in early December 1965, Bundy specifically praised the war in Southeast Asia:

> There are dangers ahead, as there are dangers that we have put behind us. In Vietnam a hard and testing struggle continues. But you have set a course there that is both right and brave, and I know our country will continue in its understanding support of both your resolution and your steady search for peace.[66]

To the end, Bundy remained a true believer.

Even more telling was the administration's search, nearly a year later and after Bundy had settled into his position at the Ford Foundation, for a replacement for Ambassador Lodge. With the war absorbing much of the country's attention and resources, running the U.S. Embassy in Saigon had become something much greater than a mere ambassadorship. It was a post, in the view of the administration, somewhat equal in importance and stature to a cabinet official. Robert Komer, recently promoted from the ranks of the NSC staff to Special Assistant to the president for pacification, told Johnson that the new ambassador should be "a top manager who can run a $20–25 billion show, make the military perform, and quietly lead [Saigon] by the nose. It also means, if we want early results, *an insider who already knows his Vietnam.*" It went without saying that the new ambassador should also believe in his work. After reminding Johnson that "your choice for Vietnam might well be the single most important appointment you make in 1967–68," Komer ranked the ideal candidates in descending order of preference and qualifications. At the very top of the list was the name of McGeorge Bundy.[67]

Johnson would hardly have been surprised by Komer's recommendation. Although he and Bundy had had their minor policy differences and major personality differences, at a January 1967 NSC meeting Johnson mentioned Bundy's name as one of the preferred candidates to replace Lodge.[68] Over a period of five years, from January 1961 to February 1966, Bundy had molded America's policy toward Indochina according to his own belief that stemming the communist advance in Vietnam was integral to U.S. national security. In these efforts he was aided and abetted by the NSC staff; without their help, Bundy's views on Vietnam would not have had as much of an impact within the Kennedy and Johnson administrations. Bundy's departure from government in 1966 was not an anguished protest over the president's misguided approach to Vietnam but a career move, a professional decision. He may have had enough of President Johnson, but he had never quit on America's commitment to South Vietnam.

Epilogue: Legacies

A few years after he left the Johnson administration, Bundy agreed to an interview on Vietnam with the journalist and chronicler of presidential elections Theodore H. White. Doing research for his forthcoming book, *The Making of the President, 1968,* White wanted to know exactly what went wrong in Vietnam, when, and why. Meeting in the top floor lunchroom at the Ford Foundation's headquarters in New York, Bundy carefully answered questions about several of the most important and controversial events of his time in Washington: the Tonkin Gulf crisis, the fork-in-the-road memo, his first trip to South Vietnam and the attack at Pleiku, the decision to Americanize the war, and the thirty-seven-day bombing pause. They spoke for quite some time, but not in great detail. Later that day White typed up his notes from the interview. "A satisfactory conversation," he concluded. "But just barely so. Mac [seemed] largely disturbed. He'd been all through it. But like a man in a storm—he could tell you about moments in the storm, about decisions under stress, but he couldn't see the whole storm or what we had gotten into."[1]

Although he thought he had given away little to White, Bundy had inadvertently revealed everything. The war in Vietnam had indeed left indelible, painful scars. Nearly two years of running the largest and most influential philanthropic foundation in the world had not salved his wounds. Bundy certainly regretted his part in committing the United States to its most divisive and difficult war in a century, but he also regretted that he had not been able to see the disaster coming. Most of all he regretted the fact that it was he who had made the mistake. In 1991, after victory in the Gulf War, President George H. W. Bush triumphantly declared, "By God, we've kicked the Vietnam syndrome once and for all!"[2] While Bush's pronouncement was perhaps premature, Bundy himself could never vanquish his own personal Vietnam syndrome.

Aside from the profound impact of the war itself, the other legacy Bundy bequeathed to American foreign policy was the creation of the National Security Adviser's position. As we have seen, prior to Bundy the post was essentially clerical and, in terms of actual policymaking, relatively meaningless. Bundy first augmented, then consolidated, and then wielded his power with unprecedented self-assurance. In much the same way that he governed Harvard University in the 1950s, he blended administrative responsibilities and bureaucratic authority with an active role in substantive policymaking. By the end of 1961 Dean Bundy of Harvard had basically become Dean Bundy of the White House. Perhaps no other bureaucratic change of the past forty years has had such momentous consequences for the conduct of America's foreign relations.

The War's Legacy

Although he was famously reticent about the subject, Bundy came to regret his role in escalating and waging the Vietnam War. The gradual erosion of his own support for the war mirrored the trend in domestic public opinion during the three years after he quit the Johnson administration in February 1966. When he left Washington to head the Ford Foundation, he still believed in the necessity and rightness of the commitment to South Vietnam; the war played little part in convincing him to resign. Nonetheless, it was clear that his five years in Washington had been a heavy psychological burden.

Once he was free from his direct ties to Vietnam policy and from his obligations to the president, Bundy slowly began to see the war in a different light. To be sure, at first he maintained a belief that the war should be fought and could be won. In two private memos to Johnson in May and October 1967, for example, he strongly cautioned against de-escalating the war to pursue negotiations. Bundy was subsequently inducted into the famed group of Wise Men, an esteemed bipartisan collection of elder statesmen whom Johnson consulted in moments of crisis. In a November 1967 meeting they recommended that Johnson stand fast in Vietnam. Even after Secretary of Defense McNamara, who by this time had privately turned against the war, told the Wise Men that perhaps the country's "efforts since 1961 have been a failure," Bundy admonished Johnson to emphasize "the 'light at the end of the tunnel' instead of battles, deaths and danger. . . . I think it is logical to say that we in the Administration do not expect negotiations in the next year."[3] Withdrawing from Vietnam, he argued, was both "impossible" and "undesirable."

He echoed this private advice with a very public article in *Foreign Affairs* that strongly reaffirmed his own belief in the war's necessity. But, true to soft hawk form, shortly afterwards Bundy also urged Johnson to jettison West-moreland's blunt, heavy-handed, and quite visible strategy of "search and destroy" that was causing so much public discomfort with a war "that is more political in character than any in our history except the Civil War."[4]

The shock of the Tet Offensive in January and February 1968 shook Bundy's faith in the war just as it did for millions of other Americans. Tet finally shattered the illusion of difficult but gradual progress that had largely kept U.S. policy moving forward since the mid-1950s. In turn, the Tet Offen-sive demonstrated to Bundy that the policy he had shaped for five years had failed, and he began to turn against the policy itself. Meeting in March, essen-tially the same group of Wise Men advised Johnson to wind down America's involvement in Vietnam. It is no small irony that it was Bundy, as the group's spokesman, who told Johnson that the administration "must begin to take steps to disengage." Bundy followed this private counsel with public warn-ings. In October 1968 he told an audience at DePauw University in Indiana that although the "basic decision of 1965, to stand and fight in South Vietnam, was right," the war was now preventing the country from pursuing "other great national tasks" and should therefore end as soon as possible. In a May 1970 speech to students at the University of Texas at Austin, he strongly crit-icized the Nixon administration's decision to invade Cambodia as militarily unnecessary and domestically provocative. At the Council on Foreign Rela-tions a year later, Bundy referred elliptically to the need for "extrication from Vietnam" as the first essential step in the rejuvenation of the U.S. military. Two years later, even though he would not assist the *New York Times* in its own defense, Bundy took the stand as a witness in the Pentagon Papers case on behalf of his former colleague, the antiwar radical Daniel Ellsberg, who had leaked the Papers to the *Times* and was charged with exposing state secrets. According to Ellsberg's codefendant, Anthony Russo, Bundy was "the only volunteer we've had. He wanted to come here and confess." And in 1978 he bluntly reminded readers of the journal *Daedalus* that since World War II Americans "have had time for many blunders, the worst of them in Southeast Asia." Clearly, Bundy harbored serious doubts about the Vietnam War.[5]

But how extensive were these doubts? How deeply did they reach? Had Bundy, as one newspaper commented at the time, begun "to shed some of his hawkish plumage"? He had, but only partially. Despite his public initiatives against the continuation of the conflict, not once did Bundy actually reject the underlying rationale and justness of the war in Vietnam. Instead he simply accepted that intervention had failed to deter and defeat the communists and recommended that the United States quit. In 1964, Bundy mused fifteen years later, Johnson and his advisers could not "foresee how large the struggle would eventually become." On the contrary, had they been able to estimate the hazards accurately, they "would have acted differently at every stage." Or, as he told the *MacNeil/Lehrer NewsHour* in 1985, the United States lost the war simply due to the "extraordinary determination and skill and dedication of Hanoi," which "constituted a force vastly greater in enduring effectiveness than we were ever able to find or encourage in our friends in South Vietnam." Had the war ended in victory and ensured the independence of a noncommunist South Vietnam, it is highly unlikely that Bundy would have subsequently repudiated it. In other words, he never questioned the war; he only acknowledged its outcome.[6]

It was not until decades later, in the years shortly before his death in September 1996, that Bundy would turn more fully to confront the war. Perhaps inspired by McNamara's Vietnam War confessional, *In Retrospect,* and aided by a research assistant, Bundy began to write a memoir of his own role in the war. Although he admitted that he "had a part in a great failure," he stressed that he never intended for the war to become so large, unwieldy, and overly reliant on the U.S. military. Bundy wanted "more explanation" to the public, "more congressional participation," and more on the part of Saigon—in other words, "a less open-ended commitment." In the memoir Bundy also defended his decision to facilitate a policy in which he did not wholeheartedly believe by stressing the value of loyalty. The president's men simply fulfilled a duty to their boss. Johnson knew of Bundy's misgivings, but nonetheless "prefers his course. I help him. That's an indispensable part of what the White House staff is for."[7] At first glance, Bundy's memoir—which remained unfinished at the time of his death—seems to be an act of contrition. However, it has more in common with his statements at DePauw, the University of Texas, and the Council on Foreign Relations than it does with a total renunciation of the war. It is, to paraphrase James Thomson, Bundy's soft hawk lament, amounting to something less than a disavowal of the war's aims. The memoir is certainly an act of contrition, but it does not seem to regret that the Vietnam War happened at all. He expressed remorse about the war's outcome, not its outbreak.

This is not to say that Bundy always accepted the war as necessary or wise. What he did say on the war is reflective of his reticence on such issues, which in turn is reflective of his personality, social standing, and upbringing. He did regret the war—he just never said so explicitly. More indicative of his feelings about Vietnam is the fundamental shift of his political views after he left the Johnson administration. He had always been a nominal conservative and moderate Republican. He had been, much like his mentor Henry Stimson, a progressive conservative who believed that gradual change is the best antidote to social upheaval and chaos. Yet in 1966, contrary to the cliché about young conservatives not having a heart and old liberals not having a brain, somewhat late in life Bundy moved swiftly from right to left in the ideological spectrum. Perhaps his time as an adviser to Lyndon Johnson, one of the most ambitiously progressive presidents in the nation's history, swayed Bundy. Perhaps he was simply lured by the radical tenor of "the Sixties." While these two influences were surely important, it seems more likely that Bundy regretted his role in the escalation of the war and perceived liberal deeds as his way of doing penance for his sins in Vietnam.

Consider Bundy's tenure as president of the Ford Foundation. From March 1, 1966, he was responsible for distributing the charitable funds of the world's wealthiest philanthropic institution. Given Bundy's background, it would not have been unreasonable to assume that he would favor the foundation's traditional recipients of funding, such as universities, traditional cultural institutions, and established aid organizations. In fact, in one his first major decisions Bundy did approve an unprecedented grant to help endow and revamp Wolfson College at Oxford University, the special project of his friend Isaiah Berlin. And at a time when the foundation was forced to cut back on its generosity, he also decided to continue to provide funding for the Congress for Cultural Freedom, a well-connected anticommunist association of European intellectuals.[8]

But Bundy also steered the Ford Foundation onto a completely new, and quite revolutionary, course. The social projects he supported at home and some of the international projects he favored abroad provided a dramatic break from the normal recipients of Ford grants. Under Bundy's direction, and much to the chagrin of his establishment friends, in the United States the foundation facilitated the decentralization of the New York City public school system, a move strongly favored by the city's black community and just as strongly opposed by higher-income white Protestants and Jews. Ford also disbursed funding to the Cleveland chapter of the Congress on Racial Equality and to the Southern Regional Council to assist their drive to enlarge voter registration among blacks. At Bundy's insistence, the foundation officially amended its funding policy specifically to target those Americans who had not usually been the recipients of its largesse—in this case, visible minorities (especially African-Americans) and the urban poor. He also hired minorities and labor leaders for key positions at the foundation. Abroad, Ford radically decreased its emphasis on Europe and increased its activities in Africa, Latin America, and Asia. Overall, however, Bundy uncharacteristi- cally placed a much higher value on progressive domestic reform than on international affairs, an outlook that was reflected in the foundation's donor policy. These dramatic changes at the Ford Foundation reflected Bundy's personal priorities.[9] And it was clear that he sought escape from being under the shadow of Vietnam. As Waldemar Nielsen, a former Ford Foundation officer, put it, Bundy "came to the foundation determined to put as much distance as possible between himself and the horror of the Far East."[10]

Bundy demonstrated his newly developed left-of-center outlook elsewhere, too. On a variety of salient, controversial issues, Bundy found himself quite vigorously articulating a radical stance. In a robust public defense of affirma- tive action programs in higher education, for example, he decried America's "terrible" and "destructive inheritance" of racism. He also called for energy conservation and the development of alternative sources of energy. At a time when many liberals were abandoning the Democratic Party over the left's embrace of the Palestinian cause, he publicly suggested that it was up to Israel to be less belligerent toward the Palestinians, and not the other way around. And, most startling from someone who had often been on the hawk- ish side of crises in Southeast Asia and Latin America, after the Soviet invasion of Afghanistan in 1979 he declared, presciently, that "in the Third World the losses of one superpower are not necessarily the gains of the other, and it is a mistake to act as if expressions of Moslem outrage over Afghanistan are some- how a score for 'our side.'" If neoconservatives are those who have migrated politically from the left to the right, then Bundy must be considered one of the nation's pioneering neoliberals.[11]

Consider, finally, the controversy surrounding Bundy's appointment to New York University's History Department in 1979. Twenty-four NYU faculty members vigorously protested Bundy's hiring on the grounds that his role in the Vietnam War made him an unsuitable educator and colleague, if not a war criminal. So it was an enormous surprise for these NYU professors to discover that on departmental issues, they and Bundy were usually in total agreement, liberals to a fault. Perhaps no other development better symbol- izes both the indelible stigma of the Vietnam legacy and Bundy's efforts to overcome the war without directly confronting it.[12]

The intriguing question is not whether Bundy lost faith in the Vietnam War, but why. After escalating America's role in the conflict for four years, and then helping to orchestrate the U.S. war campaign for nearly another two, what caused Bundy to criticize an endeavor of major significance that had occupied so much of his efforts and emotion over such a long period of time? The answer has as much to do with the collapse of Bundy's ideologically based worldview as it does with the collapse of the U.S. war effort in Vietnam. Bundy had inherited, from mentors such as Stimson, an ideological worldview that denounced isolationism, fascism, and communism, embraced gradual American-inspired progress (so long as it accorded with U.S. interests), and believed in U.S. exceptionalism. He never doubted or questioned these precepts, which comprised an ingrained belief system that he knew instinctively and applied reflexively. The belief system itself was based on values that had been directly inherited from eminent predecessors (such as Stimson and Dean Acheson) and consecrated by historical precedent. Bundy received this wisdom without ever realizing it as such. Indeed, in 1963, while in thrall to these ideological premises, he claimed that on matters of foreign affairs Americans were simply a pragmatic, passive people "dominated by events."[13]

Prior to World War II, Americans had encountered great difficulty in determining exactly how to use their potentially overwhelming, and constantly growing, national power in the world. This was especially true regarding American interests in the Pacific, which did not seem to be as clear as those in Latin America or Europe. The early Cold War, particularly after the communist rise to power in China in 1949 and the outbreak of the Korean War in 1950, seemed to solve this problem by providing American policy with a purpose. Henry Kissinger, in the guise of historian rather than statesman, has observed that "moral maxims were real" to American leaders during the early Cold War, and that the United States felt compelled to resist communism "in the name of principle, not in defense of a sphere of interest; America had exerted itself in order to remedy an insult to a universal cause, not over a challenge to the local status quo."[14] This sense of purpose, or ideology, sharpened the strategy of containment as it applied to Asia. Containing communism in Europe and Japan proved to be so successful that its extension to Southeast Asia seems now, in retrospect, to have been inevitable. As one critic, Senator Walter George, noted prophetically in 1947 in response to the ideological clarity of the Truman Doctrine: "I do not see how we are going to escape going into Manchuria, North China, and Korea and doing things in that area of the world. When we make a policy of this kind we are irrevocably committing ourselves to a course of action, and there is no way to get out of it next week or next year. You go down to the end of the road."[15] In America's case, the end of the road was in Vietnam.

Most important, this ideological worldview provided Bundy (and many of his colleagues, such as Michael Forrestal) with familiar solutions to unfamiliar problems. Thus reflexive anticommunism seemed to clarify the incoherence of the postcolonial Vietnamese civil war. Vietnam became simply another player in the Cold War game with the Soviet Union and China. As we have seen, from 1961 to 1966 Bundy consistently recommended that Presidents Kennedy and Johnson stand fast in Vietnam; in turn, this advice was based on a perception that the conflict in Vietnam was somehow tied directly to the fate of American national security. Historians have rightly argued that during the Cold War, Soviet, Chinese, and German communists could have pursued obviously disastrous policies, such as a command economy or forced collectivization, only out of blind ideological devotion.[16] Similarly, the enormous gap between American rhetoric and reality during the Vietnam War could only be bridged by adherence to a rigid ideological conception of the world and how it works. After all, why else would the Kennedy and Johnson administrations pursue such a clearly unsuccessful policy in pursuit of such clearly flawed aims? This was the true measure of the Stimsonian legacy.

The war forced Bundy to scrutinize this dogma for the first time. As his political conversion from center-right to solidly left demonstrates, he found it wanting, if only partially. That Bundy could so quickly dispense with the shibboleths of his ideological worldview reflects the underlying superficiality of his conviction. He had inherited it, but it was not his own. Kissinger, who worked briefly for Bundy during the Kennedy administration, noted perceptively in his memoirs that it "was Bundy's misfortune to begin governmental service at a time of upheaval within the very institutions and groups that should have served as his fixed reference points. He was thus perpetually finding himself on the fashionable side, but at the very moment that fashion began to wane."[17] Although Bundy was saddled with ideological baggage, he lacked the true conviction that would have sustained his ideological worldview through the anguish of losing the Vietnam War.

An instructive contrast is Rostow, who not only worked for Bundy but succeeded him in 1966. Unlike Bundy, Rostow possessed an ideological worldview that was not simply based on received wisdom. His outlook was similar to Bundy's, but it was based on true faith. He was, in a word, devout. Unsurprisingly, Rostow never repudiated the war; in fact he continued to be as stridently hawkish after the war as he had been during it. His memoirs, published in 1972, staunchly defended American policy in great detail at a time when most Americans, hawk and dove alike, simply wanted to forget Vietnam and its conflict. He has also argued that a U.S. military victory was not at all unfeasible and would have been possible had Johnson escalated faster, harder, and sooner than he did. But Rostow not only defended the war—he also claimed that by "buying time" for the other countries of the region to strengthen themselves against the communist threat, the United States had in fact won the struggle politically and economically.[18]

Both were brilliant, disciplined men. The key difference between them is class. Bundy was born to wealth, power, and privilege and was expected to follow family tradition and attend Yale. Rostow attended public schools and relied on scholarships to attend Yale. Whereas Bundy, as a scion of the Establishment, unconsciously inherited his foreign policy worldview from its most illustrious practitioners, Rostow had to deliberately construct his. Rostow's was genuine, Bundy's superficial. Thus whereas Bundy's ideologically based worldview crumbled under the weight of unfulfilled expectations over Vietnam, Rostow's remained impervious to these same pressures. Within the ranks of the NSC staff, the contrast between the postwar reactions of Bundy and Rostow was mirrored by that between Michael Forrestal and Robert Komer. Although Forrestal, like Bundy, had inherited his views of the world and America's place in it at birth, Komer developed his intellectually and independently. Forrestal's commitment was weak and Komer's was strong for this very reason, and it helps to explain that although they all helped escalate the war in Vietnam, Bundy and Forrestal came to regret their actions while Rostow and Komer did not.

The National Security Adviser's Legacy

Bundy's other lasting influence was the creation of the powerful new position that has come to be known as the National Security Adviser. The history of the Adviser's role in the foreign policy process must be divided into "B.B." and "A.B."—Before Bundy and After Bundy—such was his influence. In effect but not in name, Bundy was the first National Security Adviser, rather than a mere Special Assistant for National Security Affairs, but several of those who have followed in his footsteps have been even more powerful. Along with the Vietnam War itself, this is the second part of the Bundy legacy.

The most celebrated of these successors, and the one who made the role famous, was Henry Kissinger, Richard Nixon's Adviser and foreign policy architect. But rather than work with the secretaries of state and defense, Kissinger supplanted them by conducting foreign policy exclusively from the White House. To do so, Nixon and Kissinger resorted to a level of secrecy and deception that would have shamed even Lyndon Johnson. The result was spectacular, both negatively and positively. While Kissinger alienated Secretary of State William Rogers and Secretary of Defense Melvin Laird, to name only the most prominent and obvious of his victims, he also formed an extremely close and effective partnership with President Nixon. And although Kissinger's virtual monopoly on policymaking led in large part to fiascos such as the Cambodian incursion, the secret bombing of Laos and Cambodia, the overthrow of Salvador Allende and the rise of the dictator Augusto Pinochet in Chile, and U.S. support for Pakistan in the war with India over Bangladeshi independence, it also enabled Nixon and Kissinger to establish relations with communist China, secure meaningful détente and nuclear arms control with the Soviet Union, and settle the October 1973 Arab-Israeli war. Even Bundy, who was not a great admirer of Kissinger, admitted grudgingly in 1979 that Kissinger's "method and style had some advantages in the extrication from Vietnam."[19]

Zbigniew Brzezinski, Jimmy Carter's Adviser who had argued in favor of the war alongside Bundy during the June 1965 televised debate with Hans Morgenthau, continued and in many ways exacerbated the tensions that Kissinger had introduced. Brzezinski's internecine bureaucratic warfare with Secretary of State Cyrus Vance poisoned and often skewed the Carter administration's approach to foreign policy. Kissinger and Rogers had had an equally adversarial relationship, but it mattered less due to Kissinger's intimacy with Nixon. In other words, while nobody doubted Kissinger's supremacy over foreign policy in the Nixon administration, Brzezinski and Vance struggled with one another for ascendancy in the Carter presidency. Brzezinski gained a decisive advantage in late 1979, but by that time the damage done to Carter's foreign policy was irreparable. The confused, vacillating American response to the crises over energy and in Afghanistan and Iran, and how they led to the collapse of détente with the Soviet Union, reflected this internal power struggle. Vance resigned in protest in 1980, ostensibly in response to the botched rescue of the American hostages in Iran but in reality due to his own waning influence with the president.

In terms of effectiveness as both a facilitator and a formulator of foreign policy, the nadir of the Adviser occurred during the presidency of Ronald Reagan. Since its creation in 1961, the position had been a fairly stable appointment: Kennedy had only one (Bundy), Johnson two (Bundy and Rostow), Nixon one (Kissinger), Ford two (Kissinger and Brent Scowcroft), and Carter one (Brzezinski). Seven Advisers served under Reagan, a figure that illustrated his exceedingly informal and chaotic decision-making structure. The Reagan administration achieved several foreign policy triumphs, but none carried an NSC imprimatur. More tellingly, the Lebanese crisis and the Iran-Contra scandal were largely the products of the NSC staff, particularly Robert C. McFarlane (who, like Rostow and Scowcroft, served as Deputy Adviser before becoming the National Security Adviser). The main problem with Reagan's Advisers was that they lacked a direct, productive relationship with the president. Despite their myriad faults, Kissinger and Brzezinski usually acted in the president's interest and almost always possessed his confidence. Reagan's Advisers competed not only with powerful secretaries of state and defense, but sometimes with the Oval Office itself. In a 1989 interview with the *Crimson,* the Harvard student newspaper, Bundy argued that it was vital for the incoming Bush administration to "clear the air" of the secrecy that had marred national security policymaking in the Reagan era.[20]

Since then, a measure of stability has returned to the role of the Adviser and the NSC staff. President George H. W. Bush formed a tight bond and smooth working relationship with his capable Adviser, Brent Scowcroft, who was also respected by the secretary of state, James A. Baker, and the secretary of defense, Dick Cheney. Although in some respects it lacked a certain dynamism, the result was a relatively coherent foreign policy. President Bill Clinton's two Advisers, Anthony Lake and especially Sandy Berger, also enjoyed the president's favor. It was no coincidence that Berger's closer relationship with the president produced more success and stability in Clinton's second term. By dealing with the various executive departments and agencies judiciously yet retaining an independent voice in the making of foreign policy, both Scowcroft and Berger came closest to resembling Bundy.

It is perhaps still premature to pass judgment on Condoleezza Rice's bureaucratic performance as George W. Bush's first National Security Adviser. At the very least, her record was mixed. She obviously held (and, now as secretary of state, continues to hold) the president's trust, but she did not necessarily have Secretary of State Colin Powell's or Secretary of Defense Donald Rumsfeld's. It is also clear that she perceived her role, as an honest and integral gatekeeper for the White House on foreign policy, much as Bundy did his. With the possible exceptions of Bundy (under Kennedy), Scowcroft, and Berger, Rice enjoyed perhaps the most symbiotic relationship with the president of any Adviser since 1961. Contrary to recent criticism of her, it is not the Adviser's job to act as a "policy referee" to "forge consensus" among battling Cabinet secretaries—that is the president's task alone.[21] The system can only work if the Adviser holds the trust and commands the attention of the president; and even then, as Rice's experience demonstrates, powerful secretaries of state and defense and a strong-willed vice president, combined with extraordinary international crises, can sometimes drown out the Adviser's voice and obscure her role. And yet, as Rumsfeld grumpily discovered when Rice seized control of Iraq and Afghanistan policy in the fall of 2003, it was unwise to underestimate her skill at bureaucratic warfare.[22] One component of the Adviser's duties is to present the president with all of the relevant policy alternatives. The other is to make recommendations of his or her own. This dual role, of both shaping and steering foreign policy, is a tremendously influential one. Because of it, Advisers can use the system to tilt the balance of foreign policymaking in the direction they favor. This is the very essence of acting as the National Security Adviser, and it does not seem to have escaped Rice. Whether her successor and former deputy, Stephen Hadley, will exploit the full potential of the Adviser's dual role as both maker and broker of American foreign policy remains to be seen.[23]

Almost exactly forty years after Bundy created this powerful new institution, a half dozen of his successors gathered at the Woodrow Wilson Center in Washington to discuss the roles and responsibilities of the National Security Adviser. All of them agreed that the Adviser possessed a rare and potent combination of policymaking influence and bureaucratic authority. Berger remarked that it "is one of the only jobs I know that is both a line job and a staff job." The Adviser is "in a sense the foreign policy chief of staff." Brzezinski observed that the Adviser's power uniquely flowed not only from bureaucratic prerogatives but also from a personal relationship with the president. And when asked whether the Adviser should be an honest broker or a policy advocate, McFarlane noted: "You can't escape being both."[24] Each of Bundy's successors defined their role in terms of power over the foreign policymaking process, both in formulation and implementation. Unlike the secretary of state or defense, the Adviser's bureaucratic terrain crosses departmental boundaries. It is this duty as the gatekeeper of foreign policy that often allows the National Security Adviser to hold the bureaucratic balance of power and thus shape the foreign policy of a presidential administration.

What this esteemed group did not mention, and what has largely been forgotten, is that it was McGeorge Bundy who made it all possible. As he neared the end of his time in Washington, he reflected on the changes he had wrought and how they would evolve. "The NSC existed in some form before I got here and it will exist in some form after I go," he told *Newsweek* magazine in characteristically terse fashion. "But whether we have written in water, sand or stone, I really can't say."[25] One cannot blame Bundy for the intrigues of Kissinger and Brzezinski any more than one can credit him for the discretion of Scowcroft and Berger. What is clear, however, is that neither Kissinger nor Scowcroft, nor any of the National Security Advisers since March 1966, would have been able to function had it not been for Bundy. Since then the exact manner in which American foreign policy has unfolded has been shaped by different personalities and changing national priorities—this aspect of his job Bundy necessarily wrote in water and sand. But the basic institutional parameters in which foreign policy has been conducted have remained relatively unchanged. These powers he wrote in stone.

In 1995 McNamara praised Bundy as "by far the ablest national security adviser I have observed over the last forty years."[26] As secretary of defense from 1961 to 1968 and subsequently president of the World Bank until 1981, McNamara could claim to be a good judge of such things. The National Security Adviser's job is to act as both policy formulator and facilitator by providing a link between the White House and the executive's various foreign policy departments and agencies. And according to these criteria Bundy performed his job well.

As an administrator Bundy was unswervingly loyal to Presidents Kennedy and Johnson—perhaps, as some critics charge, even too loyal—and usually ensured that they were aware of competing viewpoints within their administration.[27] The fact that Rusk, McNamara, Ball, and Rostow all viewed Bundy's role approvingly is powerful evidence that he operated as few of his successors would—as an honest broker. His record as a policymaker, on the other hand, is mixed. Despite initially being on the losing (hawkish) end of debates over the Bay of Pigs, Berlin, and the Cuban missile crisis, in each case Bundy eventually swung his considerable influence behind the more moderate, successful policy. His efforts in the Dominican Republic were unsuccessful but farsighted, and his perennial campaign to reduce the risk of nuclear danger was as courageous as it was necessary. Thus, despite occasional imprudent advice that was never actually implemented, Bundy functioned as an able, respected, and successful National Security Adviser. His overall record, however, has been ultimately and irrevocably tarnished by his role in causing and continuing the Vietnam War. This singular disaster continues to overshadow his other accomplishments. It is unfortunate, but apt, that this should be so, for Bundy's role in marginalizing internal dissent and shaping escalation was crucial to the escalation of the war. Without his efforts, the war would not have unfolded as it did; indeed, it may not have unfolded at all.

NOTES

BIBLIOGRAPHY OF PRIMARY SOURCES

INDEX

Notes

Abbreviations

CF	Country File
CFR	Council on Foreign Relations Archives, Mudd Library, Princeton University
CHRON	Chronological File
CUOH	Oral History Research Office, Butler Library, Columbia University, New York
D&A	Departments and Agencies Series
DSB	*Department of State Bulletin*
FO	Foreign Office File
FRUS	*Foreign Relations of the United States*
HC	*Harvard Crimson*
JFKL	John F. Kennedy Library, Boston
LBJL	Lyndon B. Johnson Library, Austin
LOC	Library of Congress, Washington, D.C.
M&M	Meetings and Memoranda Series
McGB	McGeorge Bundy
Memcon	Memorandum of Conversation
MHS	Massachusetts Historical Society, Boston
MP	Memos to the President
MVN	Meetings on Vietnam
NAC	National Archives of Canada, Ottawa
NARA	National Archives and Records Administration, College Park, Md.
NSCF	National Security Council File
NSF	National Security File
NYRB	*New York Review of Books*
NYT	*New York Times*
NYTM	*New York Times Magazine*
OH	Oral History
PP	Pentagon Papers (Senator Gravel Edition)
PREM	Prime Minister's Files
PRO	Public Record Office, Kew, Surrey, United Kingdom

RG   Record Group
RSS   Regional Security Series
SAE   Studies on Aid to Europe
SEA   Southeast Asia
SEP   *Saturday Evening Post*
SM   Staff Memoranda
T&C   Trips and Conferences
Telcon   Telephone Conversation (Transcript)
UGA   Dean Rusk Oral History Collection, University of Georgia, Athens
VPFE   Vice President's Trip to the Far East
YDN   *Yale Daily News*

Introduction

1. *HC,* January 5, 1961. Thanks to George W. Bush, Hal's transformation from way-ward Prince to King Henry V is back in fashion as an analogy. See, for example, Niall Ferguson, "The Monarchy of George II," *Vanity Fair,* September 2004, 382–388, 411–414; and John Lewis Gaddis, *Surprise, Security, and the American Experience* (Cambridge, Mass., 2004), 92.
2. Alexandra Robbins, *Secrets of the Tomb: Skull and Bones, the Ivy League, and the Hidden Paths of Power* (Boston, 2002), 127.
3. Gore Vidal, "Real Class," *NYRB,* July 18, 1974, 12.
4. The only biography of Bundy is Kai Bird, *The Color of Truth: McGeorge Bundy and William Bundy, Brothers in Arms* (New York, 1998). The only scholarly examina-tion of Bundy's role is Lloyd C. Gardner, "Harry Hopkins with Hand Grenades? McGeorge Bundy in the Kennedy and Johnson Years," in *Behind the Throne: Ser-vants of Power to Imperial Presidents, 1898–1968,* ed. Thomas J. McCormick and Lloyd C. Gardner (Madison, Wis., 1993), 204–231. The first to cover Bundy in any real depth was David Halberstam, "The Very Expensive Education of McGeorge Bundy," *Harper's,* July 1969, 21–41.
5. Karl Marx, "The Eighteenth Brumaire of Louis Bonaparte," in *The Marx-Engels Reader,* ed. Robert C. Tucker (New York, 1978), 595.
6. Frank Ninkovich, "Interests and Discourse in Diplomatic History," *Diplomatic History* 13 (Spring 1989), 139.
7. James Joll, "1914: The Unspoken Assumptions," in *The Origins of the First World War,* ed. H. W. Koch (London, 1972), 307–328.
8. Ernest R. May, "The Nature of Foreign Policy: The Calculated versus the Axiomatic," *Daedalus* 91 (Fall 1962), 662–667.
9. Alan Brinkley, *Liberalism and Its Discontents* (Cambridge, Mass., 1998), 165–166.
10. The most influential and persuasive account is Fredrik Logevall, *Choosing War: The Lost Chance for Peace and the Escalation of War in Vietnam* (Berkeley, 1999).
11. Janice Knight, *Orthodoxies in Massachusetts: Rereading American Puritanism* (Cam-bridge, Mass., 1994).
12. James Roger Sharp, *American Politics in the Early Republic: The New Nation in Crisis* (New Haven, 1993), esp. 5–8, 13–14.

13. Margaret MacMillan, *Peacemakers: The Paris Conference of 1919 and Its Attempt to End War* (London, 2001), 7.

14. Logevall, *Choosing War*, esp. xvi–xix.

15. Pierre Salinger, *With Kennedy* (Garden City, N.Y., 1966), 68.

16. Ernest R. May, *"Lessons" of the Past: The Use and Misuse of History in American Foreign Policy* (New York, 1973), 120–121. For a more recent example, which calls the war "virtually inevitable," see Charles E. Neu, *America's Lost War: Vietnam, 1945–1975* (Wheeling, Ill., 2005), xv. See also Mark Atwood Lawrence, *Assuming the Burden: Europe and the American Commitment to War in Vietnam* (Berkeley, 2005), 280.

17. See, for example, Joseph Buttinger, *Vietnam: The Unforgettable Tragedy* (New York, 1977); Larry Berman, *Planning a Tragedy: The Americanization of the War in Vietnam* (New York, 1982); Robert S. McNamara, *In Retrospect: The Tragedy and Lessons of the Vietnam War* (New York, 1995); and David Kaiser, *American Tragedy: Kennedy, Johnson, and the Origins of the Vietnam War* (Cambridge, Mass., 2000).

18. The bureaucracy outmaneuvering the president is one of the main arguments in Gareth Porter, *Perils of Dominance: Imbalance of Power and the Road to War in Vietnam* (Berkeley, 2005).

1. The Mentor

1. Larry Berman, *Lyndon Johnson's War: The Road to Stalemate in Vietnam* (New York, 1989), 196; Lloyd C. Gardner, *Pay Any Price: Lyndon Johnson and the Wars for Vietnam* (Chicago, 1995), 453.

2. See, for example, David Halberstam, *The Best and the Brightest* (New York, 1972), 50; David M. Barrett, *Uncertain Warriors: Lyndon Johnson and his Vietnam Advisers* (Lawrence, Kans., 1993), 22; Lloyd C. Gardner, "Harry Hopkins with Hand Grenades? McGeorge Bundy in the Kennedy and Johnson Years," in *Behind the Throne: Servants of Power to Imperial Presidents, 1898–1968,* ed. Thomas J. McCormick and Lloyd C. Gardner (Madison, Wis., 1993), 204–207; Gardner, *Pay Any Price,* 94; Michael H. Hunt, *Lyndon Johnson's War: America's Cold War Crusade in Vietnam, 1945–1968* (New York, 1996), 47; and Frank E. Vandiver, *Shadows of Vietnam: Lyndon Johnson's Wars* (College Station, Tex., 1997), 55.

3. Godfrey Hodgson, *The Colonel: The Life and Wars of Henry Stimson, 1867–1950* (New York, 1990), 4.

4. Kai Bird, *The Color of Truth: McGeorge Bundy and William Bundy, Brothers in Arms* (New York, 1998), 38.

5. Henry L. Stimson and McGeorge Bundy, *On Active Service in Peace and War* (New York, 1948), 343.

6. George F. Kennan, *American Diplomacy, 1900–1950* (Chicago, 1951), 95. Kennan also called this the "universalistic" approach to foreign relations. John Lewis Gaddis, *Strategies of Containment: A Critical Appraisal of Postwar American National Security Policy* (New York, 1982), 27–29.

7. Herbert Hoover, *The Memoirs of Herbert Hoover: The Cabinet and the Presidency, 1920–1933* (New York, 1951), 219.

8. Elting E. Morison, *Turmoil and Tradition: A Study of the Life and Times of Henry L. Stimson* (Boston, 1960), 654.

9. Frank Ninkovich, "Theodore Roosevelt: Civilization as Ideology," *Diplomatic History* 10 (Summer 1986), 221–245.

10. Stimson and Bundy, *On Active Service*, 101, 103–107, 584–591; Morison, *Turmoil and Tradition*, 250–251; Karen A. J. Miller, *Populist Nationalism: Republican Insurgency and American Foreign Policy Making, 1918–1925* (Westport, Conn., 1999), 87; Henry L. Stimson, "Bases of American Foreign Policy During the Past Four Years," *Foreign Affairs* 11 (April 1933), 388.

11. Winston Churchill, *The Second World War*, vol. IV, *The Hinge of Fate* (London, 1951), 719; Henry L. Stimson, "The Challenge to Americans," *Foreign Affairs* 26 (October 1947), 13; idem, "The Nuremberg Trial: Landmark in Law," *Foreign Affairs* 25 (January 1947), 179.

12. Stimson, "Bases," 389–390; Stimson and Bundy, *On Active Service*, 243–256, 261–262; memcon, April 4, 1932, *FRUS, Japan, 1931–1941*, I: 89; memcon, November 20, 1931, *FRUS, 1931*, III: 511; Christopher Thorne, *The Limits of Foreign Policy: The West, the League and the Far Eastern Crisis of 1931–1933* (London, 1972), 157–160, 299–300.

13. William Kamman, *A Search for Stability: United States Diplomacy Toward Nicaragua, 1925–1933* (Notre Dame, Ind., 1968), 100–101, 203–207; Robert H. Ferrell, *The Presidency of Calvin Coolidge* (Lawrence, Kans., 1998), 135–137; David F. Schmitz, *Henry L. Stimson: The First Wise Man* (Wilmington, Del., 2001), 50–61; Henry L. Stimson, *American Policy in Nicaragua* (New York, 1927), 91, 94.

14. Henry L. Stimson, "First-Hand Impressions of the Philippine Problem," *SEP*, March 19, 1927, 6; idem, "Future Philippine Policy Under the Jones Act," *Foreign Affairs* 5 (April 1927), 459–471; Stanley Karnow, *In Our Image: America's Empire in the Philippines* (New York, 1989), 251–252; H. W. Brands, *Bound to Empire: The United States and the Philippines* (New York, 1992), 140–141; Schmitz, *Henry L. Stimson*, 61–70.

15. Stimson and Bundy, *On Active Service*, 31–41, 91, 316; Harvey Bundy OH, 108–109, CUOH; Robert H. Ferrell, *The American Secretaries of State and Their Diplomacy: Frank B. Kellogg and Henry L. Stimson* (New York, 1963), 54–55; Kamman, *Search for Stability*, 103–105.

16. Stimson and Bundy, *On Active Service*, 101; Stimson, "Bases," 389; idem, *Democracy and Nationalism in Europe* (Princeton, 1934), 85–86; Bundy to Stimson, July 28, 1947, Stimson Papers, Reel 117, Yale University Archives; Stimson, "Challenge," 5–6.

17. Stimson and Bundy, *On Active Service*, 101–107, 297–316, 604–605; Stimson, *Democracy and Nationalism*, 86; Akira Iriye, *The Origins of the Second World War in Asia and the Pacific* (London, 1987), 66; Morison, *Tradition and Turmoil*, 463–478.

18. Stimson, "Challenge," 5–7; Bundy draft letter (from Stimson to Arthur Vandenberg), July 18, 1949; Stimson to Irving Ives and John Foster Dulles, July 18, 1949, Stimson Papers, Reel 121, Yale.

19. Alan Brinkley, *Liberalism and its Discontents* (Cambridge, Mass., 1998), 169–171; Christopher Thorne, *The Issue of War: States, Societies, and the Far Eastern Conflict of*

1941–1945 (London, 1985), 27; John W. Dower, *War Without Mercy: Race and Power in the Pacific War* (New York, 1986), 80, 82–83, 313, 344n14; Anders Stephanson, "Liberty or Death: The Cold War as US Ideology," in *Reviewing the Cold War: Approaches, Interpretations, Theory*, ed. Odd Arne Westad (London, 2000), 92; Stimson, "Challenge," 8; John Lewis Gaddis, *The United States and the End of the Cold War: Implications, Reconsiderations, Provocations* (New York, 1992), 11, 41; Stimson, "Nuremberg," 188.

20. Milton MacKaye, "Bundy of the White House," *SEP*, March 10, 1962, 84; *YDN*, October 3, 1938, 4; *YDN*, October 7, 1938, 2; *YDN*, November 23, 1938, 5.

21. Bird, *Color of Truth*, 64–65; *YDN*, November 23, 1938, 2; Gaddis Smith, "The Two Worlds of Samuel Flagg Bemis," *Diplomatic History* 9 (Fall 1985), 298; Richard M. Bissell, Jr., *Reflections of a Cold Warrior: From Yalta to the Bay of Pigs* (New Haven, 1996), 13–14; Peter Novick, *That Noble Dream: The "Objectivity Question" and the American Historical Profession* (New York, 1988), 247–248.

22. McGeorge Bundy, "They Say in the Colleges . . . ," in Stephen Vincent Benet, *Zero Hour: A Summons to the Free* (New York, 1940), 81–85, 112–113.

23. Bundy to Archibald MacLeish, September 26, 1940, MacLeish Papers, Box 4, LOC.

24. MacKaye, "Bundy," 82; Bird, *Color of Truth*, 79, 417n32; Kirk OH, 226, 242, 364, CUOH; Stimson Diary, February 12–13, 1945, Stimson Papers, Vol. I, Reel 9, 104–05, 107, 109, Yale; McGeorge Bundy, "Ultra Warnings," in *Assault on Normandy: First-Person Accounts from the Sea Services*, ed. Paul Stillwell (Annapolis, 1994), 29–31.

25. *YDN*, January 13, 1939, 2, 4; McGeorge Bundy, "A Letter to Twelve College Presidents," *Atlantic Monthly*, May 1945, 52 (emphasis in original).

26. Arthur M. Schlesinger, Jr., *A Life in the Twentieth Century: Innocent Beginnings, 1917–1950* (Boston, 2000), 224; Bird, *Color of Truth*, 69–70; Stimson and Bundy, *On Active Service*, 673; Henry L. Stimson, "The Decision to Use the Atomic Bomb," *Harper's*, February 1947, 97–107. For a critique of Stimson and Bundy's handling of the atomic controversy, see Barton J. Bernstein, "Seizing the Contested Terrain of Early Nuclear History: Stimson, Conant, and Their Allies Explain the Decision to Use the Atomic Bomb," *Diplomatic History* 17 (Winter 1993), 37, 45–55; and Gar Alperovitz, *The Decision to Use the Atomic Bomb and the Architecture of an American Myth* (New York, 1995), 448–497. Bernstein and Alperovitz criticize the decision to list Stimson as the sole author because doing so gave the *Harper's* article a measure of authority it might not have otherwise attained. See also James G. Hershberg, *James B. Conant: From Harvard to Hiroshima and the Making of the Nuclear Age* (New York, 1993), 291–301.

27. Stimson to Frederick Woodbridge, December 8, 1949, Stimson Papers, Reel 122, Yale; Stimson to Bundy, April 21, 1947, Reel 117, ibid.; Allen Klots to Elizabeth Neary, September 16, 1949, Reel 122, ibid.

28. Bundy to Frankfurter, August 1, 1946, Frankfurter Papers, Reel 18, LOC; Bundy to Stimson, July 28, 1947, Stimson Papers, Reel 117, Yale.

29. Bundy to Stimson, January 20, 1948, Reel 119, ibid.

30. Bundy to Stimson, April 26, 1948, Reel 119, ibid.; Bundy to Stimson, October 25, 1948, Reel 120, ibid.; Bird, *Color of Truth*, 101–113; Peter Grose, *Gentleman Spy:*

The Life of Allen Dulles (Boston, 1994), 289; Townsend Hoopes, *The Devil and John Foster Dulles* (Boston, 1973), 72; Robert D. Schulzinger, *The Wise Men of Foreign Affairs: The History of the Council on Foreign Relations* (New York, 1984), 136–141; *NYT*, September 11, 1950, 14; McGeorge Bundy, *The Pattern of Responsibility: From the Records of Dean Acheson* (Boston, 1951). The Oppenheimer Panel's final report of January 1953, "Armaments and American Policy," is found in *FRUS, 1952–54*, II: 1056–1091. Thirty years afterward, Bundy published an abridged version of the report in "Early Thoughts on Controlling the Nuclear Arms Race: A Report to the Secretary of State, January 1953," *International Security* 7 (Fall 1982), 3–27. See also McGeorge Bundy, *Danger and Survival: Choices About the Bomb in the First Fifty Years* (New York, 1988), 288–290, 674n119.

31. *HC,* January 5, 1961. See also Morton and Phyllis Keller, *Making Harvard Modern: The Rise of America's University* (New York, 2001), 190, 211–215; and McGeorge Bundy, "Were Those the Days?" *Daedalus* 99 (Summer 1970), 531–567.

32. See, for example, McGeorge Bundy, "The Attack on Yale," *Atlantic Monthly,* November 1951, 50–52; idem, "The Private World of Robert Taft," *The Reporter,* December 11, 1951, 37–39; and idem, "The Years of Indecision," *The Reporter,* October 13, 1953, 37–39.

33. Joseph Kraft, "The Two Worlds of McGeorge Bundy," *Harper's,* November 1965, 110; *HC,* May 20, 1965; Halberstam, *Best and the Brightest,* 56–57. Bundy received tenure as associate professor of government after Ralph Bunche, the diplomat and Nobel laureate, declined Harvard's offer of the same position. Brian Urquhart, *Ralph Bunche: An American Life* (New York, 1993), 236n.

34. Norman A. Graebner, *The New Isolationism: A Study in Politics and Foreign Policy since 1950* (New York, 1956).

35. Bundy to Lyndon B. Johnson, January 11, 1965, NSF/MP/McGB, Box 2, LBJL.

36. Bird, *Color of Truth,* 150.

37. Bundy, *Pattern of Responsibility,* viii; Bundy, "Letter," 52, 54; Bundy to Lippmann, February 1, 1948, Lippmann Papers, Box 59, Yale; McGeorge Bundy, "The Test of Yalta," *Foreign Affairs* 27 (July 1949), 618–629.

38. Bundy memorandum M-5, February 28, 1949, 7–8, 10–11, SAE, Box 243, CFR; Bundy memorandum M-16, July 13, 1949, 9, ibid. (emphasis in original).

39. Bundy, "Test"; Bundy, *Danger and Survival,* 217; Bundy to Acheson, undated, Acheson Papers, Box 4, Yale; Bundy to Oppenheimer, December 1, 1952, Oppenheimer Papers, Box 191, LOC; McGeorge Bundy, "To Cap the Volcano," *Foreign Affairs* 48 (October 1969), 7–8.

40. *NYT,* April 30, 1950, 8E; McGeorge Bundy, "November 1952: Imperatives of Foreign Policy," *Foreign Affairs* 31 (October 1952), 3, 12–13.

41. MacKaye, "Bundy," 84; Bird, *Color of Truth,* 152.

42. Bundy to Lippmann, June 6, 1949, Lippmann Papers, Box 59, Yale.

43. Bundy, "November 1952," 8, 13; Bundy, "Private World," 38–39; Bundy to Lippmann, February 1, 1948, Lippmann Papers, Box 59, Yale; Henry F. Graff, *The Tuesday Cabinet: Deliberation and Decision on Peace and War under Lyndon B. Johnson* (Englewood Cliffs, NJ, 1970), 48. The "caboose" remark became something of an embarrassment for Bundy, particularly after he was the subject of

a critical *New York Times* editorial. Bundy knew about the editorial ahead of time and tried unsuccessfully to persuade the *Times* to retract the offending quotation. Melvin Small, *Johnson, Nixon, and the Doves* (New Brunswick, N.J., 1988), 56–57.

44. Geoffrey Blainey, *The Causes of War*, 3rd ed. (London, 1988), 108.

45. Gaddis, *Strategies of Containment*, 39.

46. Bundy to Frankfurter, October 14, 1953, Frankfurter Papers, Reel 19, LOC; Bundy memorandum M-5, 7, SAE, Box 243, CFR.

47. Stimson and Bundy, *On Active Service*, 220–221; Bundy, "Letter," 53; Bundy, "Years," 38; Halberstam, *Best and the Brightest*, 56; Bundy, "November 1952," 7, 11; Bundy, *Pattern of Responsibility*, 24–25; idem, "Isolationists and Neutralists: A Sketch in Similarities," *Confluence* 1 (June 1952), 70.

48. Bundy, "They Say in the Colleges . . . ," 110.

49. Bundy memorandum M-5, 3, SAE, Box 243, CFR; Bundy to Harold Laski, July 13, 1949, Frankfurter Papers, Reel 19, LOC; Bundy memorandum M-16, 4, SAE, Box 243, CFR; Bundy, "Isolationists and Neutralists," 75. To friends, Bundy recommended Hannah Arendt, *The Origins of Totalitarianism* (New York, 1951), which is the classic statement of this stance. Bundy to Frankfurter, October 14, 1953, Frankfurter Papers, Reel 19, LOC.

50. McGeorge Bundy, "The Battlefields of Power and the Searchlights of the Academy," in *The Dimensions of Diplomacy*, ed. E. A. J. Johnson (Baltimore, 1964), 2–3; John Trumpbour, "Introducing Harvard: A Social, Philosophical, and Political Profile," in *How Harvard Rules: Reason in the Service of Empire*, ed. John Trumpbour (Boston, 1989), 8; McGeorge Bundy, "A Report from an Academic Utopia," *Harper's*, January 1962, 10–15; Robin W. Winks, *Cloak & Gown: Scholars in the Secret War, 1939–1961* (New York, 1987), 114–115, 447–448.

51. Bundy review essay, *American Political Science Review* 45 (June 1951), 534–536.

52. McGeorge Bundy, "Harvard and Government Security Policy," *School and Society*, July 5, 1955, 2; Ellen Schrecker, *No Ivory Tower: McCarthyism and the Universities* (New York, 1986), 88; Hershberg, *James B. Conant*, 635; Sigmund Diamond, "Veritas at Harvard," *NYRB*, April 28, 1977, 13–17; *Newsweek*, July 25, 1977, 77; Sigmund Diamond OH, 10–14, 17–19, 21–22, CUOH; Sigmund Diamond, *Compromised Campus: The Collaboration of Universities with the Intelligence Community, 1945–1955* (New York, 1992), 3–4, 17–23; Ellen Schrecker, *Many Are the Crimes: McCarthyism in America* (Princeton, 1998), 285; Keller, *Making Harvard Modern*, 204–205; Tom Wells, *The War Within: America's Battle over Vietnam* (Berkeley, 1994), 209; Bundy letter to the May 1965 National Teach-In, reprinted in *Teach-Ins: U.S.A.—Reports, Opinions, Documents*, eds. Louis Menashe and Ronald Radosh (New York, 1967), 153–155.

53. Hershberg, *James B. Conant*, 396–399; Bundy, "Harvard and Government Security Policy," 1; Keller, *Making Harvard Modern*, 202; *NYT*, March 16, 1955, 17; Bundy to Frankfurter, August 5, 1959, Frankfurter Papers, Reel 19, LOC. For his work on the Oppenheimer Panel, during which he was engaged in highly classified research and analysis, Bundy used an office in the appropriately secure facilities at MIT.

2. A Foreign Office in Microcosm

1. Dean Acheson, "The Eclipse of the State Department," *Foreign Affairs* 49 (July 1971), 603. Acheson admitted elsewhere that he would have resigned from an administration that included a Special Assistant as powerful as Bundy. James Chace, *Acheson: The Secretary of State Who Created the American World* (New York, 1998), 441.

2. *NYT*, November 13, 1960, Section 2, 15. See also Bundy's strong endorsement of presidential leadership in "Woodrow Wilson and a World He Never Made," *Confluence* 5 (Winter 1957), 283–285.

3. Milton MacKaye, "Bundy of the White House," *SEP*, March 10, 1962, 84; Vandenberg to Bundy, October 21, 1948, Allen Dulles Papers, Box 10, Princeton; *HC*, April 22, 1952; McGeorge Bundy, "The Test of Yalta." *Foreign Affairs* 27 (July 1949), 621; idem, "November 1952: Imperatives of Foreign Policy." *Foreign Affairs* 31 (October 1952), 6; idem, *The Pattern of Responsibility: From the Records of Dean Acheson* (Boston, 1951), viii; idem, "Woodrow Wilson and a World He Never Made," *Confluence* 5 (Winter 1957), 286.

4. Kai Bird, *The Color of Truth: McGeorge Bundy and William Bundy, Brothers in Arms* (New York, 1998), 36, 150; Bundy to Shriver, November 16, 1960, Schlesinger Papers, Box 8, JFKL; Ronald Steel, *Walter Lippmann and the American Century* (Boston, 1980), 523–524; *Newsweek*, March 4, 1963, 24; Benjamin C. Bradlee, *Conversations With Kennedy* (New York, 1975), 134; Kenneth P. O'Donnell and David F. Powers, *"Johnny, We Hardly Knew Ye": Memories of John Fitzgerald Kennedy* (Boston, 1972), 266; William P. Bundy, Vietnam memoir–unpublished manuscript, chs. 3, 5, LBJL.

5. Harry S Truman, *Memoirs*, vol. 2, *Years of Trial and Hope* (New York, 1956), 60; Dean Acheson, *Present at the Creation: My Years in the State Department* (New York, 1969), 733–734; Clark Clifford, *Counsel to the President: A Memoir* (New York, 1991), 164; Anna K. Nelson, "President Truman and the Evolution of the National Security Council," *Journal of American History* 72 (September 1985), 360–378; John Prados, *Keepers of the Keys: A History of the National Security Council from Truman to Bush* (New York, 1991), 29–32; Amy B. Zegart, *Flawed by Design: The Evolution of the CIA, JCS, and NSC* (Stanford, 1999), 57–75, 78–80; Andrew Preston, "The Little State Department: McGeorge Bundy and the National Security Council Staff, 1961–65," *Presidential Studies Quarterly* 31 (December 2001), 636–638.

6. Robert Cutler, "The Development of the National Security Council," *Foreign Affairs* 34 (April 1956), 448–449; Anna K. Nelson, "The 'Top of Policy Hill': President Eisenhower and the National Security Council," *Diplomatic History* 7 (Fall 1983), 307–326; I. M. Destler, "The Presidency and National Security Organization," in *The National Security: Its Theory and Practice, 1945–1960*, ed. Norman A. Graebner (New York, 1986), 229–232; Zegart, *Flawed by Design*, 80–83; Preston, "Little State Department," 638–639.

7. Henry M. Jackson, ed., *The National Security Council: Jackson Subcommittee Papers on Policy-Making at the Presidential Level* (New York, 1965); Prados, *Keepers of the*

Keys, 92–95; Preston, "Little State Department," 639–641. The Subcommittee's full report is *Organizing for National Security: Inquiry of the Subcommittee on National Policy Machinery of the Committee on Government Operations, United States Senate*, 3 vols. (Washington, D.C., 1961).

8. Kennedy press release, January 1, 1961, in Jackson, *National Security Council*, 302–303.

9. R. Johnson paper, undated, and Hirsch to Bundy, April 28, 1961, NSF/D&A/NSCF, Box 283, JFKL. On February 18, 1961, Kennedy officially abolished the OCB when he issued Executive Order 10920. The next day he released a statement explaining the order and his reasons for it. *FRUS, 1961–63*, VIII: 16n2; *Public Papers of the Presidents: John F. Kennedy, 1961* (Washington, D. C., 1962), 104–105.

10. Bundy to Rusk, February 3, 1961, *FRUS, 1961–63*, VIII: 23–24; Bundy to Dulles, March 10, 1961, NSF/McGB/CHRON, Box 398, JFKL.

11. Weber to Bundy, January 27, 1961, NSF/D&A/NSCF, Box 283, JFKL; Neustadt paper, Pre-Presidential Papers, Box 1072, JFKL; Bromley K. Smith, *Organizational History of the National Security Council During the Kennedy and Johnson Administrations* (Washington, D.C., 1988), 25.

12. Bundy to Kennedy, January 30, 1961, NSF/D&A/NSCF, Box 283, JFKL; Bundy OH, 16, UGA; Bundy to Jackson, September 4, 1961, NSF/McGB/CHRON, Box 398A, JFKL; Johnson paper, NSF/D&A/NSCF, Box 283, JFKL; Walt W. Rostow, *The Diffusion of Power: An Essay in Recent History* (New York, 1972), 167. However, the clerical support staff who worked for the NSC grew dramatically during the Kennedy presidency. As a result the actual number of people working on the NSC staff increased from 26 in the second Eisenhower administration to 56 in the Kennedy administration. John P. Burke, *The Institutional Presidency* (Baltimore, 1992), 17–18.

13. Benjamin Read OH, 36, JFKL; Michael V. Forrestal interview transcript by Joseph Kraft, April 8, 1964, 31–32 (transcript in author's possession; I am grateful to Kai Bird for providing me with a copy); Theodore C. Sorensen, *Kennedy* (New York, 1965), 372; Rostow, *Diffusion of Power*, 168; Zegart, *Flawed by Design*, 241.

14. Truman, *Memoirs*, 60.

15. Rostow OH, 43, JFKL; Carl Kaysen, interview with the author, March 12, 1999, Cambridge, Mass.; Forrestal interview with Kraft, April 8, 1964, 18; Kaysen OH, 5, JFKL; Sorensen, *Kennedy*, 330.

16. George Ball, *The Past Has Another Pattern: Memoirs* (New York, 1982), 172; Sorensen, *Kennedy*, 284; idem, *The Kennedy Legacy: A Peaceful Revolution of the Seventies* (New York, 1969), 82–83; Arthur M. Schlesinger, Jr., *A Thousand Days: John F. Kennedy in the White House* (Boston, 1965), 297, 421–423; Roger Hilsman, *To Move a Nation: The Politics of Foreign Policy in the Administration of John F. Kennedy* (Garden City, N.Y., 1967), 56, 561.

17. John E. Endicott, "The National Security Council: Formalized Coordination and Policy Planning," in *National Security Policy: The Decision-making Process*, ed. Robert L. Pfaltzgraff and Uri Ra'anan (Westport, Conn., 1984), 188.

18. Rusk lecture, February 1, 1960, vol. 34, Box 228, CFR; Dean Rusk, "The President," *Foreign Affairs* 38 (April 1960), 355–369; Warren I. Cohen, *Dean Rusk* (Totawa, N.J., 1980), 94–99; Thomas J. Schoenbaum, *Waging Peace and War: Dean Rusk in the Truman, Kennedy, and Johnson Years* (New York, 1988), 15–24, 257–259; Robert Dallek, *An Unfinished Life: John F. Kennedy, 1917–1963* (Boston, 2003), 314–316.

19. Rostow to Kennedy, May 6, 1961, NSF/RSS/SEA, Box 231, JFKL; Smith, *Organizational History*, 49–50; James N. Giglio, *The Presidency of John F. Kennedy* (Lawrence, Kans., 1991), 33; telcon, Ball and Kennedy, October 4, 1963, Ball Papers, Box 7, LBJL.

20. Nicholas Katzenbach, interview with the author, February 6, 1999, London.

21. Bundy to Johnson, January 21, 1965, NSF/MP/McGB, Box 2, LBJL.

22. Bundy OH, 3, UGA. On Rusk's legendary reticence, see also Cohen, *Dean Rusk*, 101–103; Schoenbaum, *Waging Peace and War*, 14–15; and David Halberstam, *The Best and the Brightest* (New York, 1972), 32–37, 62–63.

23. Bundy to Kennedy, March 15, 1961, *FRUS, 1961–63*, X: 158; Bird, *Color of Truth*, 195–197; W. Bundy, Vietnam memoir, 3: 26, LBJL.

24. Smith, *Organizational History*, 36–38; Schlesinger, *Thousand Days*, 269, 382; O'Donnell and Powers, *"Johnny,"* 277–278; anonymous to Kennedy, June 22, 1961, *FRUS, 1961–1963*, VIII: 108; Bundy to Shepard, July 11, 1961, NSF/McGB/CHRON, Box 398A, JFKL.

25. McGeorge Bundy, "The History-Maker," *Proceedings of the Massachusetts Historical Society* 90 (1978), 79; W. Bundy, Vietnam memoir, 3:3, LBJL.

26. Raymond L. Garthoff, *A Journey through the Cold War: A Memoir of Containment and Coexistence* (Washington, D.C., 2001), 122–123; Rostow's comments in W. Scott Thompson and Donaldson D. Frizzell, eds., *The Lessons of Vietnam* (New York, 1977), 140–141; Fowler to Dillon, May 5, 1961, and Lilly to Bundy, May 11, 1961, NSF/D&A/NSCF, Box 283, JFKL; Robert Cutler, *No Time for Rest* (Boston, 1966), 301.

27. Kaysen memo, July 3, 1961, NSF/M&M/SM/CK, Box 320, JFKL; anonymous to Kennedy, *FRUS, 1961–63*, VIII: 106–107; Bundy to Kennedy, May 16, 1961, NSF/McGB/CHRON, Box 398, JFKL.

28. Bundy to Johnson, December 11, 1964, NSF/Files-McGB/CHRON, Box 5, LBJL; Francis Bator, interview with the author, April 8, 1999, Cambridge, Mass. A useful corrective to the common misperception that LBJ was completely unskilled in foreign affairs is Thomas Alan Schwartz, *Lyndon Johnson and Europe: In the Shadow of Vietnam* (Cambridge, Mass., 2003).

29. Telcon, Moyers, Bundy, and Johnson, November 4, 1964, in Michael R. Beschloss, ed., *Reaching for Glory: Lyndon Johnson's Secret White House Tapes, 1964–1965* (New York, 2001), 112; telcon, Russell and Johnson, June 11, 1964, in idem, *Taking Charge: The Johnson White House Tapes, 1963–1964* (New York, 1997), 401; Max Frankel, "The Importance of Being Bundy," *NYTM*, March 28, 1965, 96; *Time*, June 25, 1965, 21; Aleksandr Fursenko and Timothy Naftali, *"One Hell of a Gamble": Khrushchev, Castro, and Kennedy, 1958–1964* (New York, 1997), 345; Bird, *Color of Truth*, 268.

30. Bundy to Johnson, November 23, 1963, NSF/Files-McGB/CHRON, Box 1, LBJL; Kraft, "Two Worlds," 112; Jack Valenti, *A Very Human President* (New York, 1975), 69, 80–81; Paul R. Henggeler, *In His Steps: Lyndon Johnson and the Kennedy Mystique* (Chicago, 1991), 74–75; Jeff Shesol, *Mutual Contempt: Lyndon Johnson, Robert Kennedy, and the Feud that Defined a Decade* (New York, 1997), 120–121. However, Johnson occasionally thought Bundy's real loyalties were indeed to Robert Kennedy. Thus Bundy often found himself acting as peacemaker between the two, to the satisfaction of neither. See telcon, Bundy and Johnson, April 9, 1964, in Beschloss, *Taking Charge*, 312; and telcon, Stephen Smith and Johnson, May 11, 1964, ibid., 344. But by the summer of 1965, Johnson believed that the exodus to RFK "started with Bundy." Telcon, Moyers and Johnson, July 1, 1965, in Beschloss, *Reaching for Glory*, 379.

31. Lloyd C. Gardner, *Pay Any Price: Lyndon Johnson and the Wars for Vietnam* (Chicago, 1995), 93–94; Bundy to Johnson, March 2, 1964, NSF/MP/McGB, Box 1, LBJL; McGeorge Bundy, "The Presidency and the Peace," *Foreign Affairs* 42 (April 1964), 364.

32. Bundy to Johnson, November 23, 1963, NSF/Files-McGB/CHRON, Box 1, LBJL; Bundy to Johnson, August 2, 1965, NSF/MP/McGB, Box 4, LBJL.

33. Robert H. Johnson, "The National Security Council: The Relevance of Its Past to Its Future," *Orbis* 13 (Fall 1969), 719; Richard Reeves, *President Kennedy: Profile of Power* (New York, 1993), 53; Rusk OH, 23–24, LBJL; *Time*, April 30, 1965, 18.

34. Rusk OH, 22, LBJL; David C. Humphrey, "Tuesday Lunch at the Johnson White House: A Preliminary Assessment," *Diplomatic History* 8 (Winter 1984), 81–82; Bundy to Valenti, July 27, 1964, NSF/Files-McGB/CHRON, Box 3, LBJL; Smith, *Organizational History*, 63; Rostow, *Diffusion of Power*, 358–359.

35. Forrestal OH, 17, 21–22, LBJL; Bator interview; Smith OH, 33, LBJL; Cooper to Bundy, January 22, 1965, NSF/CF/VN, Box 12, LBJL.

36. Schlesinger, *Thousand Days*, 208–209; Stewart Alsop, "The White House Insiders," *SEP*, June 10, 1961, 91; *Time*, May 7, 1965, 24; Michael Ignatieff, *Isaiah Berlin: A Life* (London, 1998), 263.

37. Charles A. Ritchie, *Storm Signals: More Undiplomatic Diaries, 1962–1971* (Toronto, 1983), 3, 75; *HC*, November 10, 1956; Ball, *Past Has Another Pattern*, 173; Hilsman, *To Move a Nation*, 45–46; James C. Thomson, Jr., "A Memory of McGeorge Bundy," *NYT*, September 22, 1996, E3; Lady Bird Johnson, tape-recorded diary, February 10, 1965, in Beschloss, *Reaching for Glory*, 177.

38. Rusk to Acheson, March 3, 1971, Acheson Papers, Box 27, Yale; Dean Rusk, *As I Saw It: A Secretary of State's Memoirs* (New York, 1990), 518–519; Glenn T. Seaborg, *Kennedy, Khrushchev, and the Test Ban* (Berkeley, 1981), 51; McNamara interview with the author, March 17, 1999, Washington, D.C.; Robert S. McNamara, *In Retrospect: The Tragedy and Lessons of the Vietnam War* (New York, 1995), 95; Ball, *Past Has Another Pattern*, 172–173; Garthoff, *Journey through the Cold War*, 124.

39. Rostow, *Diffusion of Power*, 169. This is what one scholar has called "the influence of mutual advice." Joseph G. Bock, *The White House Staff and National Security Assistant: Friendship and Friction at the Water's Edge* (Westport, Conn., 1987), 51.

40. Chester Bowles, *Promises to Keep: My Years in Public Life, 1941–1969* (New York, 1971), 360–361; Bowles OH, 842, CUOH; Bundy to Johnson, March 11, 1964, NSF/MP/McGB, Box 1, LBJL; U. Alexis Johnson, *The Right Hand of Power* (Englewood Cliffs, N.J., 1984), 315; Hilsman OH, 8, JFKL; Bundy OH, 4, UGA.

41. Carl Marcy OH, 195–96, Senate Historical Office Oral History Program, LOC; William C. Berman, *William Fulbright and the Vietnam War: The Dissent of a Political Realist* (Kent, Oh., 1988), 106; telcon, Moyers and Johnson, May 26, 1965, in Beschloss, *Reaching for Glory*, 341; Gregory Allen Olson, *Mansfield and Vietnam: A Study in Rhetorical Adaptation* (East Lansing, Mich., 1995), 141.

3. Learning to Fear the Bomb

1. Rostow OH, 43, JFKL; Kaysen interview with the author.

2. See especially George C. Herring, *America's Longest War: The United States and Vietnam, 1950–1975* (New York, 1979, and subsequent editions); Paul M. Kattenburg, *The Vietnam Trauma in American Foreign Policy, 1945–1975* (New Brunswick, N.J., 1980); John Lewis Gaddis, *Strategies of Containment: A Critical Appraisal of Postwar American National Security Policy* (New York, 1982), 237–273; and Lawrence Freedman, *Kennedy's Wars: Berlin, Cuba, Laos, and Vietnam* (New York, 2000), 284.

3. See, for example, Fred Halliday, *The Making of the Second Cold War*, 2nd ed. (London, 1986), 3–7; Vladislav Zubok and Constantine Pleshakov, *Inside the Kremlin's Cold War: From Stalin to Khrushchev* (Cambridge, Mass., 1996), 236–237; John Lewis Gaddis, *We Now Know: Rethinking Cold War History* (New York, 1997), 291–292; Marc Trachtenberg, *A Constructed Peace: The Making of the European Settlement, 1945–1963* (Princeton, 1999), 352, 379–382, 398–402; James G. Hershberg, "The Crisis Years, 1958–1963," in *Reviewing the Cold War: Approaches, Interpretations, Theory*, ed. Odd Arne Westad (London, 2000), 319–320; Jennifer W. See, "An Uneasy Truce: John F. Kennedy and Soviet-American Détente, 1963," *Cold War History* 2 (January 2002), 161–194; and Jeremi Suri, *Power and Protest: Global Revolution and the Rise of Détente* (Cambridge, Mass., 2003), 41–43.

4. McGeorge Bundy, "Shadow and Substance in 1980," in McGeorge Bundy and Edmund S. Muskie, *Presidential Promises and Performance* (New York, 1980), 43–44.

5. Not to be confused with the distinction between symmetrical and asymmetrical containment that is the analytical focus of Gaddis, *Strategies of Containment*. For a different account of how Vietnam acted as a spur to détente, see H. W. Brands, "Vietnam and the Origins of Détente," in *The Search for Peace in Vietnam, 1964–1968*, ed. Lloyd C. Gardner and Ted Gittinger (College Station, Tex., 2004), 371–390.

6. Wesley T. Wooley, "Learning to Fear the Bomb," in *Toward a World of Peace: People Create Alternatives*, ed. Jeanette P. Maas and Robert A. C. Stewart (Suva, Fiji, 1986), 311–324.

7. G. Pascal Zachary, *Endless Frontier: Vannevar Bush, Engineer of the American Century* (Cambridge, Mass., 1999), 362.

8. Henry L. Stimson and McGeorge Bundy, *On Active Service in Peace and War* (New York, 1948), 641–646; Elting E. Morison, *Turmoil and Tradition: A Study of the Life and Times of Henry L. Stimson* (Boston, 1960), 634–638; Gar Alperovitz, *The Decision to Use the Atomic Bomb and the Architecture of an American Myth* (New York, 1995), 429–436. It is interesting to note that John J. McCloy—an assistant secretary of war to Stimson, wartime colleague of Harvey Bundy, and friend and mentor to McGeorge Bundy—also developed an abhorrence of nuclear weapons. McCloy worked with the Truman, Eisenhower, Kennedy, Johnson, and Nixon administrations to curtail the potential use and existence of nuclear arms. See John J. McCloy, "Balance Sheet on Disarmament," *Foreign Affairs* 40 (April 1962), 339–359; Thomas Alan Schwartz, *America's Germany: John J. McCloy and the Federal Republic of Germany* (Cambridge, Mass., 1991), 26; Kai Bird, *The Chairman: John J. McCloy, The Making of the American Establishment* (New York, 1992), 261–264, 468–469, 500–517, 615–618; and Alan Brinkley, *Liberalism and its Discontents* (Cambridge, Mass., 1998), 201–202.

9. Scott D. Sagan, "SIOP-62: The Nuclear War Plan Briefing to President Kennedy," *International Security* 12 (Summer 1987), 35–39; Kurt Gottfried and Bruce G. Blair, eds., *Crisis Stability and Nuclear War* (New York, 1988), 52–54; Freedman, *Kennedy's Wars*, 47, 95–100.

10. Richard Reeves, *President Kennedy: Profile of Power* (New York, 1993), 179; Trachtenberg, *Constructed Peace*, 298. See also McGeorge Bundy, *Danger and Survival: Choices About the Bomb in the First Fifty Years* (New York, 1988), 322, 354. Despite Bundy's misgivings, and contrary to the Kennedy administration's public rhetoric, the SIOP, and therefore Eisenhower's strategy of massive retaliation, did not change after 1961. Francis J. Gavin, "The Myth of Flexible Response: United States Strategy in Europe during the 1960s," *International History Review* 23 (December 2001), 850–858.

11. Meeting notes, February 4, 1963, in editorial note, *FRUS, 1961–1963*, VIII: 463–464. See also the reiteration of this thought, in which he substituted "think-tank analysts" for "military planners," in McGeorge Bundy, "To Cap the Volcano," *Foreign Affairs* 48 (October 1969), 9–10.

12. Fred M. Kaplan, *The Wizards of Armageddon* (New York, 1983), 307–310, 313–314.

13. Schlesinger, *Thousand Days*, 459, 503; Desmond Ball, *Politics and Force Levels: The Strategic Missile Program of the Kennedy Administration* (Berkeley, 1980), 85; Freedman, *Kennedy's Wars*, 84; editorial note, *FRUS, 1961–1963*, VII: 236–237.

14. Draft guidelines for Kennedy, drafted by Bundy, October 27, 1961, NSF/McGB/MP, Box 405, JFKL; telcon, Rusk and Bundy, April 21, 1963, Rusk Records, Box 48, NARA; Schlesinger, *Thousand Days*, 487.

15. Kaysen to Kennedy, January 15, 1962, *FRUS, 1961–1963*, VII: 297–303; Bundy to Kennedy, January 17, 1962, ibid., 306; Kaysen to Bundy, October 31, 1962, *FRUS, 1961–1963*, V: 551; Raymond L. Garthoff, *A Journey through the Cold War: A Memoir of Containment and Coexistence* (Washington, D.C., 2001), 156–160; Nigel Ashton, *Kennedy, Macmillan and the Cold War: The Irony of Interdependence* (New York, 2002), 205.

16. See Glenn T. Seaborg, *Stemming the Tide: Arms Control in the Johnson Years* (Lexington, Mass., 1987), 43, 157, 399–400, for Bundy's role in the Johnson administration; Thomas Alan Schwartz, *Lyndon Johnson and Europe: In the Shadow of Vietnam* (Cambridge, Mass., 2003), 18.

17. Bundy, "To Cap the Volcano," 1, 9, 11; Daniel J. Kevles, "The Politics of Atomic Reality," *Reviews in American History* 18 (March 1990), 100; McGeorge Bundy et al., "Nuclear Weapons and the Atlantic Alliance," *Foreign Affairs* 60 (Spring 1982), 753–768; McGeorge Bundy, William J. Crowe, Jr., and Sidney D. Drell, *Reducing Nuclear Danger: The Road Away from the Brink* (New York, 1993), 5, 81–85, 98–102; Bundy, *Danger and Survival*, 595.

18. McGeorge Bundy, "Pearl Harbor Brought Peace," *Newsweek*, December 16, 1991, 8; Alperovitz, *Decision to Use the Atomic Bomb*, 494–495; Kai Bird, *The Color of Truth: McGeorge Bundy and William Bundy, Brothers in Arms* (New York, 1998), 96–98.

19. Charles Glaser, "Why Do Strategists Disagree about the Requirements of Strategic Nuclear Deterrence?" in Lynn Eden and Steven E. Miller, eds., *Nuclear Arguments: Understanding the Strategic Nuclear Arms and Arms Control Debates* (Ithaca, N.Y., 1989), 113–115.

20. Memo for the record, January 8, 1962, *FRUS, 1961–1963*, VII: 289–290; McGeorge Bundy, "The Next Steps Toward Peace: Some Notes on the Two-Legged Process," *DSB*, October 21, 1963, 625; Bundy speech, August 11, 1964, NSF/Files-McGB/CHRON, Box 3, LBJL; Bundy, "To Cap the Volcano," 11. See also Bundy, *Danger and Survival*, 603; and idem, "The Bishops and the Bomb," *NYRB*, June 16, 1983, 3–7.

21. Bundy, *Danger and Survival*, 532.

22. Gordon H. Chang, "JFK, China, and the Bomb," *Journal of American History* 74 (March 1988), 1287–1310; Kendrick Oliver, *Kennedy, Macmillan and the Nuclear Test-Ban Debate, 1961–63* (Basingstoke, U.K., 1998), 150–151; John W. Lewis and Xue Litai, *China Builds the Bomb* (Stanford, 1988), 192–193. Instead of isolating China, nuclear weapons gave it a measure of international respectability. Evelyn Goh, *Constructing the U.S. Rapprochement with China, 1961–1974* (New York, 2005), 66–67.

23. Bundy to Kennedy, November 8, 1962, *FRUS, 1961–1963*, VII: 598; memcon, January 10, 1963, in editorial note, *FRUS, 1961–1963*, XXII: 339; Gordon H. Chang, *Friends and Enemies: The United States, China, and the Soviet Union, 1948–1972* (Stanford, 1990), 261–262.

24. William Burr and Jeffrey T. Richardson, "Whether to 'Strangle the Baby in the Cradle': The United States and the Chinese Nuclear Program, 1960–64," *International Security* 25 (Winter 2000/01), 55.

25. Meeting notes, December 21, 1962, PREM 11/4229, PRO.

26. Memcon, Bundy and Dobrynin, May 17, 1963, *FRUS, 1961–1963*, V: 675; Burr and Richardson, "Whether to 'Strangle the Baby in the Cradle,'" 72–73.

27. Burr and Richardson, "Whether to 'Strangle the Baby in the Cradle,'" 76–83.

28. Memcon, Bundy and Dobrynin, September 25, 1964, *FRUS, 1964–1968*, XXX: 105; Chang, "JFK, China, and the Bomb," 1308; Goh, *Constructing the U.S. Rapprochement with China*, 28.

29. Schlesinger, *Thousand Days*, 251; *HC*, November 16, 1960. On the invasion, see Trumbull Higgins, *The Perfect Failure: Kennedy, Eisenhower, and the CIA at the Bay of Pigs* (New York, 1987); Thomas G. Paterson, "Fixation with Cuba: The Bay of Pigs, Missile Crisis, and Covert War Against Fidel Castro," in Thomas G. Paterson, ed., *Kennedy's Quest for Victory: American Foreign Policy, 1961–1963* (New York, 1989), 123–139; Michael R. Beschloss, *The Crisis Years: Kennedy and Khrushchev, 1960–1963* (New York, 1991), 90–151; Fursenko and Naftali, *"One Hell of a Gamble,"* 77–100; and Freedman, *Kennedy's Wars,* 123–146.

30. Bundy to Kennedy, February 8, 1961, *FRUS, 1961–1963,* X: 89; Bundy to Kennedy, February 18, 1961, ibid., 107; Fursenko and Naftali, *"One Hell of a Gamble",* 84; Zachary Karabell, *Architects of Intervention: The United States, the Third World, and the Cold War, 1946–1962* (Baton Rouge, 1999), 198–201; Bundy to Kennedy, March 15, 1961, *FRUS, 1961–1963,* X: 158; Stewart Alsop, *The Center: People and Power in Political Washington* (New York, 1968), 222; Richard N. Goodwin, *Remembering America: A Voice from the Sixties* (Boston, 1988), 176–177. For the Yale connection between Bundy and Bissell see Bird, *Color of Truth,* 59, 64. Bissell had also taught Rostow at Yale. Two months before the Bay of Pigs, Bundy recommended to Kennedy that Bissell be appointed deputy under secretary of state for political affairs, which Bundy described as "the key job" in the State Department. Bundy to Kennedy, February 25, 1961, NSF/McGB/MP, Box 405, JFKL.

31. Bundy to Kennedy, April 18, 1961, *FRUS, 1961–1963,* X: 272. Bundy maintained this position during Maxwell Taylor's internal investigation into the Bay of Pigs. Bundy to Taylor, May 4, 1961, ibid., 455–458; Richard E. Welch, Jr., *Response to Revolution: The United States and the Cuban Revolution, 1959–1961* (Chapel Hill, N.C., 1985), 83.

32. Halberstam, *Best and the Brightest,* 68; Bundy to Kennedy, May 5, 1961, *FRUS, 1961–1963,* X: 478; Bundy to Taylor, NSF/M&M/SGCI, Box 319, JFKL; memo of meeting, August 16, 1962, *FRUS, 1961–1963,* X: 940–941; memo for the file, August 21, 1962, ibid., 947–949.

33. The Cuban missile crisis is one of the most thoroughly studied episodes in recent American history. Excellent accounts include Raymond L. Garthoff, *Reflections on the Cuban Missile Crisis,* rev. ed. (Washington, D.C., 1989); Gaddis, *We Now Know,* 260–280; Fursenko and Naftali, *"One Hell of a Gamble",* 166–315; Mark J. White, *Missiles in Cuba: Kennedy, Khrushchev, Castro, and the 1962 Crisis* (Chicago, 1997); and Freedman, *Kennedy's Wars,* 161–237. Bundy himself wrote an authoritative history of the missile crisis in *Danger and Survival,* 391–462.

34. One major study has erroneously identified Bundy as one of "the doves" in the administration. James G. Blight and David A. Welch, *On the Brink: Americans and Soviets Reexamine the Cuban Missile Crisis,* 2nd ed. (New York, 1990), 153, 218.

35. Ernest R. May and Philip D. Zelikow, eds., *The Kennedy Tapes: Inside the White House during the Cuban Missile Crisis* (Cambridge, Mass., 1997), 63, 70, 94, 103, 142, 189–191, 195; Sheldon M. Stern, *Averting "The Final Failure": John F. Kennedy and the Secret Cuban Missile Crisis Meetings* (Stanford, 2003), 87–88, 91, 107, 115, 130–131, 250–251, 417–419; record of meeting, October 19, 1962, *FRUS,*

1961–1963, XI: 118–119; minutes of NSC meeting, October 20, 1962, ibid., 130–133; Fursenko and Naftali, *"One Hell of a Gamble"*, 266–267, 279; Sheldon M. Stern, *The Week the World Stood Still: Inside the Secret Cuban Missile Crisis* (Stanford, 2005), 48, 58, 64, 71–73.

36. Bundy to Ball, December 6, 1962, *FRUS, 1961–1963*, XI: 586–587; Frank Ninkovich, *The United States and Imperialism* (Oxford, 2001), 147; Stern, *Averting "The Final Failure"*, 260–261; Bundy to the NSC Standing Group, April 21, 1963, and attached paper by Bundy, both in *FRUS, 1961–1963*, XI: 774–778; Thomas A. Parrott memo, April 25, 1963, ibid., 784; memo for the record, June 19, 1963, ibid., 837; CIA paper, June 8, 1963, ibid., 828–834.

37. On the Berlin Crisis, see Vladislav M. Zubok, "Khrushchev and the Berlin Crisis (1958–62)," Working Paper 6, Cold War International History Project (Washington, D.C., 1993); Trachtenberg, *Constructed Peace*, 251–351; Freedman, *Kennedy's Wars*, 45–120; and Hope M. Harrison, *Driving the Soviets Up the Wall: Soviet–East German Relations, 1953–1961* (Princeton, 2003), 96–223.

38. Acheson to Kennedy, April 3, 1961: Bundy to Kennedy, April 4, 1961, and Bundy to McNamara, April 17, 1961: all in NSF/CF/Germany, Box 81, JFKL; memcon, July 12, 1961, *FRUS, 1961–1963*, XIV: 190; Acheson report, June 28, 1961, ibid., 138–159; Bundy to Kennedy, June 10, 1961, ibid., 108; Bundy to Kennedy, July 19, 1961, ibid., 216–218; Embassy in Washington, D.C., to Ottawa, December 22, 1961, RG25, Vol. 5088, File 4901–4940, Part 15, NAC; Rostow to Kennedy, June 26, 1961, NSF/CF/GER, Box 81A, JFKL.

39. Draft telegram, Arnold Heeney (Washington, D.C.), August 24, 1961, Heeney Papers, Vol. 1, NAC. Bundy sent an apologetic letter the next day, which is reprinted in Arnold Heeney, *The Things that are Caesar's: The Memoirs of a Canadian Public Servant* (Toronto, 1972), 171–172. Bundy to Sorensen, August 23, 1962, *FRUS, 1961–1963*, XV: 285.

40. Bundy to Kennedy, August 14, 1961, *FRUS, 1961–1963*, XIV: 330–331 (emphasis in original); Bundy to Kennedy, September 20, 1961, ibid., 429–431; and Bundy to Kennedy, October 2, 1961, ibid., 460–461; Reeves, *President Kennedy*, 212; *NYT*, August 15, 1961, 1, 9.

41. Bundy to Kennedy, May 29, 1961, NSF/McGB/MP, Box 405, JFKL; Trachtenberg, *Constructed Peace*, 325, 327; Bundy to Kennedy, November 20, 1961, *FRUS, 1961–1963*, XIV: 588–589; H. Basil Robinson to Ottawa, February 11, 1963, RG25, vol. 5088, File 4901–40, part 17, NAC.

42. Acheson report, June 28, 1961, *FRUS, 1961–1963*, XIV: 141; meeting notes, September 7, 1961, *FRUS, 1961–1963*, XIV: 398. Curiously, in his own history of nuclear weapons Bundy mistakenly portrays Acheson as opposed to the use, or even threatened use, of nuclear weapons during the Berlin crisis. Bundy, *Danger and Survival*, 372–376.

43. Kaysen to Bundy, July 7, 1961, Kaysen to Bundy, July 3, 1961, Kissinger to Bundy, July 7, 1961, Bundy to Kennedy, July 7, 1961, Kissinger to Bundy, July 14, 1961, and Schlesinger to Bundy, July 18, 1961, all in NSF/CF/Germany, Box 81A, JFKL; Isaacson, *Kissinger*, 111–112; Schlesinger, *Thousand Days*, 386–389;

Schlesinger to Kennedy, *FRUS, 1961–1963,* XIV: 173–176; Freedman, *Kennedy's Wars,* 68–69; Bundy to Kennedy, July 20, 1962, *FRUS, 1961–1963,* XV: 232–234; Trachtenberg, *Constructed Peace,* 296.

44. James G. Blight and Peter Kornbluh, eds., *Politics of Illusion: The Bay of Pigs Invasion Reexamined* (Boulder, Colo., 1998), 112–113; William Attwood, *The Twilight Struggle: Tales from the Cold War* (New York, 1987), 254, 260–263; memo for the record, November 5, 1963, *FRUS, 1961–1963,* XI: 878; memo for the record, November 12, 1963, ibid., 888–889; Arthur M. Schlesinger, Jr., *Robert Kennedy and His Times* (Boston, 1978), 551–554; Freedman, *Kennedy's Wars,* 240–242; Piero Gleijeses, *Conflicting Missions: Havana, Washington, and Africa, 1959–1976* (Chapel Hill, N.C., 2002), 23–25. For a contrary view, which argues that the Kennedy administration showed no inclination to soften its stance toward Castro's Cuba, see Stephen G. Rabe, "After the Missiles of October: John F. Kennedy and Cuba, November 1962 to November 1963," *Presidential Studies Quarterly* 30 (December 2000), 714–726. Johnson's caution may have stemmed from his suspicion that the Cubans had assassinated Kennedy to exact revenge for Operation Mongoose. Robert Dallek, *Flawed Giant: Lyndon Johnson and His Times, 1961–1973* (New York, 1998), 52–53.

45. This crucial distinction is made by Raymond L. Garthoff, *Détente and Confrontation: American-Soviet Relations from Nixon to Reagan,* rev. ed. (Washington, D.C., 1994), 28.

46. Bird, *Color of Truth,* 187; Raskin to Bundy, April 20, 1961, NSF/M&M/SM/Raskin, Box 323, JFKL (emphasis in original).

47. Schlesinger, *Thousand Days,* 900; Bird, *Color of Truth,* 247; See, "Uneasy Truce," 172; McGeorge Bundy, "The Best of All Possible Nuclear Worlds: A Review Essay," *International Security* 5 (Summer 1980), 176.

48. Bundy to Johnson, January 13, 1964, NSF/MP/McGB, Box 1, LBJL; Bundy to Rusk, March 26, 1965, NSF/CF/VN, Box 14, LBJL.

49. Komer to Bundy, November 23, 1964, *FRUS, 1964–1968,* XXX: 131.

50. Bundy to Goodwin, December 24, 1964, NSF/Files-McGB/CHRON, Box 5, LBJL.

51. Anatoly Dobrynin, *In Confidence: Moscow's Ambassador to America's Six Cold War Presidents* (New York, 1995), 146. See also Frank Costigliola, "Lyndon B. Johnson, Germany, and 'the End of the Cold War,' " in *Lyndon Johnson Confronts the World: American Foreign Policy, 1963–1968,* ed. Warren I. Cohen and Nancy Bernkopf Tucker (New York, 1994), 207.

52. Odd Arne Westad, "The Fall of Détente and the Turning Tides of History," in *The Fall of Détente: Soviet-American Relations during the Carter Years,* ed. Odd Arne Westad (Oslo, 1997), 19.

53. Garthoff, *Détente and Confrontation,* 588. On the Soviets' optimism that they were making progress in the developing world during the era of détente, see Christopher Andrew and Vasili Mitrokhin, *The World Was Going Our Way: The KGB and the Battle for the Third World* (New York, 2005).

54. Jussi M. Hanhimaki, "Ironies and Turning Points: Détente in Perspective," in Westad, *Reviewing the Cold War,* 330.

4. The Hawk

1. Walt W. Rostow, *The Stages of Economic Growth: A Non-Communist Manifesto* (Cambridge, U.K., 1960), 131. See also idem, *The United States in the World Arena: An Essay in Recent History* (New York, 1960), 415–430, 475–478; idem, "Ideas and Reality," *Confluence* 6 (Fall 1957), 199–214; and Kimber Charles Pearce, *Rostow, Kennedy, and the Rhetoric of Foreign Aid* (East Lansing, Mich., 2001).

2. Chester Bowles, *Promises to Keep: My Years in Public Life, 1941–1969* (New York, 1971), 345.

3. Townsend Hoopes, *The Limits of Intervention: An Inside Account of How the Johnson Policy of Escalation was Reversed* (New York, 1969), 20–21.

4. Robert S. McNamara, *In Retrospect: The Tragedy and Lessons of the Vietnam War* (New York, 1995), 235. See also Robert D. Schulzinger, "Walt Rostow: Cheerful Hawk," in *The Human Tradition in the Vietnam Era*, ed. David L. Anderson (Wilmington, Del., 2000), 46.

5. Rostow draft speech, September 20, 1956, Lippmann Papers, Box 99, Yale. See also Rostow, *Stages of Economic Growth*, 133–136, 145–167. Modernization theory has also been called development theory, but for purposes of clarity and consistency only the former will be used here. On modernization theory, see Irene L. Gendzier, *Managing Political Change: Social Scientists and the Third World* (Boulder, Colo., 1985), 1–18, 19n6; Michael H. Hunt, *Ideology and U.S. Foreign Policy* (New Haven, 1987), 159–162; D. Michael Shafer, *Deadly Paradigms: The Failure of U.S. Counterinsurgency Policy* (Princeton, 1988), 48–103; and Michael E. Latham, *Modernization as Ideology: American Social Science and "Nation Building" in the Kennedy Era* (Chapel Hill, N.C., 2000). For an insightful overview, see Nick Cullather, "Development? It's History," *Diplomatic History* 24 (Fall 2000), 641–653.

6. Rostow paper, August 15, 1961, NSF/M&M/SM/Rostow, Box 326A, JFKL.

7. W. W. Rostow, "Guerrilla Warfare in the Underdeveloped Areas," *DSB*, August 7, 1961, 234, 236. On the speech as a reflection of policy, see Douglas S. Blaufarb, *The Counterinsurgency Era: U.S. Doctrine and Performance, 1950 to the Present* (New York, 1977), 57.

8. Rostow to Acheson, December 18, 1956, Acheson Papers, Box 26, Yale; Latham, *Modernization as Ideology*, 176.

9. Rostow OH, 44, JFKL; Bundy to Rusk, McNamara, and Dulles, January 27, 1961, NSF/CF/VN, Box 193, JFKL; Lansdale to Gates, January 17, 1961, *United States-Vietnam Relations, 1945–1967*, Book 11 (Washington, D.C., 1971), 1–12.

10. Rostow to Bundy, January 30, 1961, NSF/CF/VN, Box 193, JFKL. For other accounts of the meeting, see record of meeting, January 28, 1961, *FRUS, 1961–1963*, I: 13–15; and Rostow, *Diffusion of Power*, 264–65. In his memoirs, Rostow mistakenly dates the meeting on February 2.

11. Rostow to Bundy, January 30, 1961, NSF/CF/VN, Box 193, JFKL.

12. On Komer and Vietnam after 1965, when he oversaw the counterinsurgency program, see Douglas Kinnard, *The War Managers* (Hanover, N.H., 1977), 93–106, 165; George C. Herring, *LBJ and Vietnam: A Different Kind of War* (Austin, 1994),

71–85; and Richard A. Hunt, *Pacification: The American Struggle for Vietnam's Hearts and Minds* (Boulder, Colo., 1995), 63–171.

13. Komer to Rostow, NSF/Komer Papers/VN, Box 447, JFKL (emphasis in original); Komer to Rostow, February 14, 1961, NSF/M&M/SM/Rostow, Box 325, JFKL.

14. Rostow paper, February 28, 1961, and Rostow to Kennedy, March 27, 1961, both in NSF/M&M/SM/Rostow, Box 325, JFKL.

15. Rostow to Kennedy, March 29, 1961, and Rostow to Kennedy, April 3, 1961, both in NSF/CF/VN, Box 193, JFKL.

16. Editorial note, *FRUS, 1961–1963*, I: 74; Gilpatric to Bowles, Bundy, and Dulles, April 17, 1961, NSF/CF/VN, Box 193, JFKL; "Presidential Task Force Program," April 22, 1961, *FRUS, 1961–1963*, I: 74–75; "A Program of Action to Prevent Communist Domination of South Vietnam," *US-VN Relations*, 11: 42–57; Gilpatric to Kennedy, May 3, 1961, plus attachment, May 1, 1961, *FRUS, 1961–1963*, I: 92–115.

17. Komer to Rostow, April 28, 1961, NSF/Komer/VN, Box 447, JFKL.

18. Komer to Rostow, May 3, 1961, NSF/M&M/SM/Komer, Box 321, JFKL (emphasis in original). See also Komer to Rostow and Bundy, May 4, 1961, *FRUS, 1961–1963*, I: 123–124.

19. Rostow to Kennedy, May 6, 1961, and Rostow to Kennedy, May 11, 1961, both in NSF/RSS/SEA, Box 231, JFKL.

20. Michael Cannon, "Raising the Stakes: The Taylor-Rostow Mission," *Journal of Strategic Studies* 12 (June 1989), 128.

21. Memcon, May 4, 1961, *FRUS, 1961–1963*, I: 115–123; Rostow to Kennedy, May 10, 1961, ibid., 131–132.

22. R. Johnson to Rostow, April 28, 1961, NSF/CF/VN, Box 193, JFKL.

23. Sorensen to Kennedy, April 28, 1961, ibid. Emphasis in original.

24. NSAM 52, May 11, 1961, *FRUS, 1961–1963*, 132–134; Bowles to Saigon, May 20, 1961, ibid., 140–143; Rusk to Saigon, April 16, 1961, NSF/T&C/VPFE, Box 242A, JFKL; Lyndon B. Johnson, *The Vantage Point: Perspectives of the Presidency, 1963–1969* (New York, 1971), 53.

25. Nolting (Saigon) to Rusk, May 15, 1961, and Nolting to Rusk, May 12, 1961, both in NSF/T&C/VPFE, Box 242A, JFKL; Johnson paper, undated, *FRUS, 1961–1963*, I: 149.

26. Rostow to Kennedy, March 29, 1961, and Rostow to Kennedy, April 12, 1961, NSF/CF/VN, Box 193, JFKL; Rostow to Kennedy, April 15, 1961, *FRUS, 1961–1963*, I: 72; Bundy to Johnson, May 30, 1961, NSF/RSS/SEA, Box 231, JFKL. Based on upon his own experience, Henry Kissinger has observed: "Such missions almost invariably signal that a decision has already been reached. No vice president is in a position to make an independent judgment about a decade-old guerrilla war in a visit of two or three days. Though his access to intelligence and reporting cables is usually extensive (depending on the president), he does not have staffs adequate for extensive analysis, and none for follow-up. Vice presidential overseas missions are generally designed to stake American prestige, or to supply credibility for decisions that have already been made." Henry Kissinger,

Diplomacy (New York, 1994), 649. Rostow and Bundy certainly had both purposes in mind.

27. Minutes of meeting, June 22, 1961, NSF/M&M/Special Group (CI), Box 319, JFKL.

28. Memcon, July 19, 1961, and Rostow to Kennedy, July 21, 1961, both in NSF/RSS/SEA, Box 231, JFKL; memcon, June 30, 1961, *FRUS, 1961–1963*, I: 192; Heeney to Ottawa, November 20, 1961, RG25, Vol. 4668, File 50052-A-13–40, Part 2, NAC; R. Johnson to Rostow, August 2, 1961, NSF/CF/VN, Box 194, JFKL.

29. Memcon, July 28, 1961, *FRUS, 1961–1963*, I: 254.

30. U. Johnson to Rostow, July 8, 1961, NSF/RSS/SEA, Box 231, JFKL; Rostow to Rusk, July 13, 1961, *FRUS, 1961–1963*, I: 206–207; Rostow to Kennedy, June 26, 1961, NSF/CF/Germany, Box 81A, JFKL.

31. Rostow to Kennedy, July 21, 1961, and memcon, July 19, 1961, NSF/RSS/SEA, Box 231, JFKL; Heeney to Ottawa, November 27, 1961, RG25, Vol. 4668, File 50052-A-13–40, Pt. 2, NAC.

32. Rostow to Kennedy, August 17, 1961, NSF/RSS/SEA, Box 231, JFKL.

33. Rostow to Kennedy, October 5, 1961, *FRUS, 1961–1963*, XXIV: 445.

34. Komer paper, May 9, 1961, NSF/RSS/SEA, Box 231, JFKL.

35. Komer to Rostow, August 2, 1961, NSF/Komer/VN, Box 447, JFKL; R. Johnson to Bundy, August 25, 1961, NSF/RSS/SEA, Box 231, JFKL.

36. Taylor OH, 21, JFKL.

37. In the international relations aviary, my ornithological categories have nothing to do with those from Graham T. Allison, Albert Carnesale, and Joseph S. Nye, Jr., eds., *Hawks, Doves, and Owls: An Agenda for Avoiding Nuclear War* (New York, 1985).

38. Rostow OH, 83–84, JFKL; Maxwell D. Taylor, *Swords and Plowshares* (New York, 1972), 222–223.

39. Rostow and Taylor to Kennedy, July 27, 1961, NSF/RSS/SEA, Box 231, JFKL.

40. Rostow to Kennedy, July 29, 1961, *FRUS, 1961–1963*, I: 256–257; Cottrell to Walter P. McConaughy, July 8, 1961, ibid., 201n2, 203; Rostow to Kennedy, August 4, 1961, NSF/CF/VN, Box 194, JFKL; Taylor OH, 20, JFKL; Rostow OH, 84, JFKL.

41. Cannon, "Raising the Stakes," 137; *PP*, II: 55, 73–80; editorial note, *FRUS, 1961–1963*, I: 380.

42. Hilsman, *To Move a Nation*, 421; Schlesinger, *Thousand Days*, 545.

43. CIA Special National Intelligence Estimate, October 5, 1961, Kent to Rostow, October 5, 1961, Tanham to Rostow, September 21, 1961, Lansdale to Rostow, October 6, 1961, and Bela Kiraly to Lansdale, undated: all in NSF/CF/VN, Box 194, JFKL.

44. R. Johnson to Rostow, October 10, 1961, NSF/CF/VN, Box 194, JFKL. See also R. Johnson to Rostow, October 14, 1961, *FRUS, 1961–1963*, I: 368–374; R. Johnson to Rostow, undated, ibid., 374–375.

45. Rostow to Taylor, October 16, 1961, ibid., 381–382.

46. W. Bundy, Vietnam memoir, 4:15, LBJL. See also Lansdale to Taylor, October 21, 1961, *FRUS, 1961–1963*, I: 412; and *PP*, II: 80–82.

47. Nolting to State Department, October 23, 1961, NSF/CF/VN, Box 194A, JFKL; *NYT*, October 13, 1961, 1, 16; *NYT*, October 14, 1961, 9.

48. Taylor, *Swords and Plowshares*, 228–229. See also Douglas Kinnard, *The Certain Trumpet: Maxwell Taylor and the American Experience in Vietnam* (Washington, D.C., 1991), 96–97.

49. Nolting to State Department, October 18, 1961, *FRUS, 1961–1963*, I: 391–392.

50. Memo for the record, October 20, 1961, *FRUS, 1961–1963*, I: 406; Rostow, *Diffusion of Power*, 275; *PP*, II: 85–87; Nolting to State Department, October 25, 1961, *FRUS, 1961–1963*, I: 431.

51. Taylor to Kennedy, November 3, 1961, *FRUS, 1961–1963*, I: 478. The entire report with appendices is in ibid., 477–532. William Bundy has written that it was understood within the administration that the covering letter was written by Rostow, and that it strongly implied that North Vietnam was vulnerable to air strikes and should be bombed by the United States. W. Bundy, Vietnam memoir, 4:17, LBJL. See also Taylor, *Swords and Plowshares*, 243.

52. Bowles paper, October 5, 1961, *FRUS, 1961–1963*, I: 322. Emphasis in original.

53. Bowles, *Promises to Keep*, 409.

54. Ball, *Past Has Another Pattern*, 365–366.

55. Meeting notes, November 9, 1961, *FRUS, 1961–1963*, I: 573; George Kahin, *Intervention: How America Became Involved in Vietnam* (New York, 1986), 136; MacDonald (Geneva to London), November 4, 1961, PREM 11/3739, PRO.

56. John Kenneth Galbraith, *Ambassador's Journal: A Personal Account of the Kennedy Years* (Boston, 1969), 243; Ormsby Gore to Alec Douglas-Home, November 13, 1961, PREM 11/4166, PRO.

57. Galbraith to Kennedy, November 13, 1961, and Rostow to Kennedy, November 13, 1961, NSF/CF/VN, Box 195, JFKL; Howard Jones, *Death of a Generation: How the Assassinations of Diem and JFK Prolonged the Vietnam War* (New York, 2003), 133; Galbraith (Saigon) to Kennedy, November 21, 1961, in *Letters to Kennedy: John Kenneth Galbraith*, ed. James Goodman (Cambridge, Mass., 1998), 89–94; Galbraith (New Delhi) to Kennedy, November 28, 1961, ibid., 95–97; Bird, *Color of Truth*, 221.

58. Memo for the record, November 6, 1961, *FRUS, 1961–1963*, I: 533; U. Alexis Johnson, *The Right Hand of Power* (Englewood Cliffs, N.J., 1984), 409–410; Frederick Nolting, *From Trust to Tragedy: The Political Memoirs of Frederick Nolting, Kennedy's Ambassador to Diem's Vietnam* (Westport, Conn., 1988), 36; Nolting OH, 9–10, JFKL.

59. Hilsman to Rusk, November 16, 1961, *FRUS, 1961–1963*, I: 620; Hilsman, *To Move a Nation*, 421–424; McGhee to Rusk, November 27, 1961, *FRUS, 1961–1963*, I: 672; McGhee to Bundy, November 21, 1961, NSF/M&M/SM/Rostow, Box 326A, JFKL; George C. McGhee, *On the Frontline in the Cold War: An Ambassador Reports* (Westport, Conn., 1997), 147–148.

60. Rusk to State Department, November 1, 1961, *PP*, II: 105; meeting notes, November 9, 1961, *FRUS, 1961–1963*, I: 573.

61. McNamara to Kennedy, November 8, 1961, *FRUS, 1961–1963*, I: 559–561; Rusk and McNamara to Kennedy, November 11, 1961, *PP*, II: 110–116; Dean Rusk, *As I Saw It: A Secretary of State's Memoirs* (New York, 1990), 432–433; McNamara, *In Retrospect*, 38–39; Johnson, *Right Hand of Power*, 409.

62. Rostow, *Diffusion of Power*, 275; memo for the record, November 6, 1961, *FRUS, 1961–1963*, I: 533–534. For the assessments see Rostow to Kennedy, November 11, 1961, ibid., 573–575; Rostow to Kennedy, November 14, 1961, ibid., 601–603; Rostow to Bundy, November 15, 1961, and Rostow to Kennedy, November 21, 1961, NSF/CF/VN, Box 195, JFKL.

63. Komer to Bundy, October 31, 1961, NSF/RSS/SEA, Box 231A, JFKL. Emphasis in original.

64. R. Johnson to Bundy, October 31, 1961, NSF/CF/VN, Box 194A, JFKL.

65. R. Johnson to Bundy, November 1, 1961, ibid.

66. R. Johnson to Rostow, November 14, 1961, *FRUS, 1961–1963*, I: 598–601. Emphasis in original.

67. Notes on Bundy lecture, May 22, 1956, Vol. 22, Box 226, CFR; Kahin, *Intervention*, 477n39.

68. Bundy to Kennedy, November 15, 1961, NSF/CF/VN, Box 195, JFKL. Emphasis in original.

69. Ibid.

5. The Soft Hawk

1. James N. Giglio, *The Presidency of John F. Kennedy* (Lawrence, Kans., 1991), 91.

2. Bundy to Bowles, July 18, 1961, Bowles Papers, Box 297, Yale; Bundy to Kennedy, November 15, 1961, NSF/CF/VN, Box 195, JFKL; Chester Bowles, "Toward a New Diplomacy," *Foreign Affairs* 40 (January 1962), 251. Ironically, considering their differing views on Indochina, earlier in the year Bowles had recommended Rostow for the head of the Policy Planning Staff (when Rostow joined in November, its status was elevated from a "Staff" to a "Council"). Bowles to Rusk, March 3, 1961, Bowles Papers, Box 300, Yale.

3. David Halberstam, *The Best and the Brightest* (New York, 1972), 208–209, 265, 285, 366–367, 376–377. For examples of historians, see Patrick Lloyd Hatcher, *The Suicide of an Elite: American Internationalists and Vietnam* (Stanford, 1990), 97; David DiLeo, *George Ball, Vietnam, and the Rethinking of Containment* (Chapel Hill, N.C., 1991), 59, 160; Kai Bird, *The Color of Truth: McGeorge Bundy and William Bundy, Brothers in Arms* (New York, 1998), 251–252, 279–280; John Prados, *The Blood Road: The Ho Chi Minh Trail and the Vietnam War* (New York, 1999), 89; A. J. Langguth, *Our Vietnam: The War, 1954–1975* (New York, 2000), 321; and Howard Jones, *Death of a Generation: How the Assassinations of Diem and JFK Prolonged the Vietnam War* (New York, 2003), 179, 220, 445. For an explicitly contrary view, see Leslie H. Gelb, *The Irony of Vietnam: The System Worked* (Washington, 1979), 149–150. Another account has even suggested that Forrestal underwent a reverse process, from dove to hawk. Noam Chomsky, *Rethinking Camelot: JFK, the Vietnam War, and US Political Culture* (Montreal, 1993), 94–95. For colleagues who later portrayed Forrestal as a neglected dove, see Theodore C. Sorensen, *The Kennedy Legacy: A Peaceful Revolution of the Seventies* (New York, 1969), 206; James C. Thomson, Jr., "Getting Out and Speaking Out," *Foreign Policy* 13 (Winter

1973–74), 52; Arthur M. Schlesinger, Jr., *Robert Kennedy and His Times* (Boston, 1978), 707, 722; Roger Hilsman, *The Politics of Policymaking in Defense and Foreign Affairs: Conceptual Models and Bureaucratic Politics* (Englewood Cliffs, N.J., 1987), 88, 90; idem, "McNamara's War—Against the Truth: A Review Essay," *Political Science Quarterly* 111 (Spring 1996), 161; and Harold P. Ford, *CIA and the Vietnam Policymakers: Three Episodes, 1962–1968* (Langley, Va., 1998), 56–57.

4. Bird, *Color of Truth,* 251n.

5. On James Forrestal and Harriman, see Townsend Hoopes and Douglas Brinkley, *Driven Patriot: The Life and Times of James Forrestal* (New York, 1992); Rudy Abramson, *Spanning the Century: The Life of W. Averell Harriman, 1891–1986* (New York, 1992); and Walter Isaacson and Even Thomas, *The Wise Men: Six Friends and the World They Made* (New York, 1986).

6. Forrestal biographical data, NSF/M&M/SM/Forrestal, Box 320, JFKL; Arnold A. Rogow, *James Forrestal: A Study of Personality, Politics, and Policy* (New York, 1963), 80–81; Melvyn P. Leffler, *A Preponderance of Power: National Security, the Truman Administration, and the Cold War* (Stanford, 1992), 5–6; Schlesinger to Bundy, January 5, 1962, NSF/M&M/SM/Forrestal, Box 320, JFKL; Hoopes and Brinkley, *Driven Patriot,* 92, 269, 480–481.

7. Michael V. Forrestal interview transcript by Joseph Kraft, April 8, 1964, 7–8 (transcript in author's possession; I am grateful to Kai Bird for providing me with a copy); Forrestal interview with Kraft, July 28, 1964, 75. Forrestal was certainly not unique. Unlike his more sophisticated views on Europe, for example, John Foster Dulles's positions on China were not based on travel, study, experience, or expertise. Ronald W. Pruessen, "John Foster Dulles and the Predicaments of Power," in *John Foster Dulles and the Diplomacy of the Cold War,* ed. Richard H. Immerman (Princeton, 1990), 39, 43–44.

8. Alan Brinkley, *Liberalism and its Discontents* (Cambridge, Mass., 1998), 166.

9. CBS News Interview with Forrestal, broadcast on December 21 and 22, 1971. I am indebted to Kai Bird for a copy of this transcript. Forrestal was not alone in his ignorance of Indochina: both Rostow and McNamara, for example, also claimed a fundamental lack of expertise in the issues they were chosen to manage. Before a Senate committee hearing on communism and the U.S. military, McNamara admitted that he had formed his own views on American foreign policy by reading back issues of *Foreign Affairs.* Deborah Shapley, *Promise and Power: The Life and Times of Robert McNamara* (Boston, 1993), 131. On Indochina, Rostow revealed in his memoirs: "When Kennedy had asked me about Laos on January 9, [1961,] in Boston, I told him I simply didn't know enough about the situation to give him a judgment. He seemed relieved at my candor." Walt W. Rostow, *The Diffusion of Power: An Essay in Recent History* (New York, 1972), 284.

10. Francis X. Winters, *The Year of the Hare: January 25, 1963–February 14, 1964* (Athens, Ga., 1997), 32. For an excellent account that illustrates that American officials supported only those Vietnamese who were to some degree Westernized, see Seth Jacobs, *America's Miracle Man in Vietnam: Ngo Dinh Diem, Religion, Race, and U.S. Intervention in Southeast Asia, 1950–1957* (Durham, N.C., 2004).

11. NSAM 119, Bundy to Rusk and McNamara, December 18, 1961, *FRUS, 1961–1963*, VIII: 231; NSAM 124, Bundy to Rusk and McNamara, January 18, 1962, *PP*, II: 660–661. See also Bundy to Taylor, February 14, 1962, *FRUS, 1961–1963*, VIII: 248.

12. Memcon, April 6, 1962, *FRUS, 1961–1963*, II: 309; U. Alexis Johnson, "The United States and Southeast Asia," *DSB*, April 29, 1963, 636.

13. Forrestal interview with Kraft, April 8, 1964, 6, 16–17.

14. Roger Hilsman, *To Move a Nation: The Politics of Foreign Policy in the Administration of John F. Kennedy* (Garden City, N.Y., 1967), 6, 52–53, 57; idem, *American Guerrilla: My War Behind Japanese Lines* (McLean, Va., 1990); Arthur M. Schlesinger, Jr., *A Thousand Days: John F. Kennedy in the White House* (Boston, 1965), 212, 341; Theodore C. Sorensen, *Kennedy* (New York, 1965), 118; Trench (Washington) to London, September 11, 1963, FO 371/170112, PRO; memcon, August 29, 1963, Hilsman Papers, Box 3, Folder 22, JFKL.

15. State Department press release of Hilsman speech, September 18, 1962, FO 371/166722, PRO.

16. Hilsman paper, February 2, 1962, *FRUS, 1961–1963*, II: 76, 78. See also Hilsman's comments in memcon, February 9, 1961, ibid., 114–115; and David Kaiser, *American Tragedy: Kennedy, Johnson, and the Origins of the Vietnam War* (Cambridge, Mass., 2000), 153–155.

17. Forrestal to Kennedy, May 2, 1962, *FRUS, 1961–1963*, II: 370; Bagley to Taylor, May 18, 1962, ibid., 408–409; Forrestal to Bundy and Kaysen, August 18, 1962, from a collection of W. Averell Harriman's papers privately held by Kai Bird. For the story behind the acquisition of these papers, see Bird, *Color of Truth*, 15, 410; and idem, "Disinterring Truth in a Dungeon," *NYT*, December 5, 1998, B9. I am grateful to Kai Bird for allowing me to copy and use material from this collection.

18. Forrestal to Kennedy, September 28, 1962, NSF/CF/VN, Box 196A, JFKL; Mark Haefele, "John F. Kennedy, USIA, and World Public Opinion," *Diplomatic History* 25 (Winter 2001), 80–81.

19. Jones, *Death of a Generation*, 241; Forrestal to Bundy, October 4, 1962, NSF/M&M/SM/Forrestal, Box 320, JFKL; Forrestal to Kennedy, April 16, 1962, NSF/CF/VN, Box 196, JFKL; Bagley to Taylor, April 26, 1962, *FRUS, 1961–1963*, II: 345–346; CIA intelligence summary, July 12, 1962, and Desmond FitzGerald to Bundy, July 12, 1962, NSF/CF/VN, Box 196A, JFKL.

20. Philip E. Catton, "Counter-Insurgency and Nation Building: The Strategic Hamlet Programme in South Vietnam, 1961–1963," *International History Review* 21 (December 1999), 919–925; Hilsman, *To Move a Nation*, 431–435.

21. Hilsman paper, February 2, 1962, *FRUS, 1961–1963*, II: 78; Forrestal to Kennedy, May 2, 1962, ibid., 369.

22. CIA intelligence summary, July 12, 1962, NSF/CF/VN, Box 196A, JFKL; Brubeck to Bundy, October 4, 1962, NSF/RSS/SEA, Box 231A, JFKL; Forrestal to Bundy and Kaysen, August 18, 1962, NSF/CF/VN, Box 196A, JFKL.

23. Bundy to Forrestal, May 7, 1962, and Forrestal to Bundy, May 8, 1962, NSF/M&M/SM/Forrestal, Box 320, JFKL.

24. Bagley to Taylor, November 12, 1962, *FRUS, 1961–1963,* II: 728–729; Hilsman to Harriman, December 19, 1962, ibid., 789–792.

25. Forrestal to Bundy, May 29, 1962, ibid., 431; Forrestal to Kennedy, June 20, 1962, ibid., 463–466.

26. Forrestal to Kaysen, August 6, 1962, NSF/CF/VN, Box 196A, JFKL.

27. Galbraith to Kennedy, April 4, 1962, *FRUS, 1961–1963,* II: 297–298. Galbraith had also written Kennedy to complain about South Vietnam in March. Galbraith to Kennedy, March 2, 1962, in James Goodman, ed., *Letters to Kennedy: John Kenneth Galbraith* (Cambridge, Mass., 1998), 98–100.

28. Galbraith to Kennedy, April 4, 1962, *FRUS, 1961–1963,* II: 297n1; Kaiser, *American Tragedy,* 156; memcon, May 1, 1962, *FRUS, 1961–1963,* II: 367.

29. Bowles to Bundy, April 5, 1962, Bowles Papers, Box 297, Yale; Bowles to Kennedy, April 4, 1962, *FRUS, 1961–1963,* II: 299–303.

30. Bowles to Komer, April 5, 1962, Bowles Papers, Box 298, Yale; Bowles to Forrestal, April 5, 1962, and Bowles to Kaysen, April 20, 1962, Bowles Papers, Box 297, Yale; memcon, April 6, 1962, *FRUS, 1961–1963,* II: 309–310.

31. Bowles to Kennedy, June 13, 1962, ibid., 448–451; speech draft, June 13, 1962, Bowles to Bundy, June 14, 1962, and James C. Thomson, Jr., to Forrestal, July 31, 1962, Bowles Papers, Box 297, Yale.

32. Chester Bowles, "Is Communist Ideology Becoming Irrelevant?" *Foreign Affairs* 40 (July 1962), 561; Bowles to Rusk, July 12, 1962, *FRUS, 1961–1963,* II: 516–519.

33. Komer to Kaysen, June 7, 1962, NSF/M&M/SM/Komer, Box 322, JFKL (emphasis in original); Komer to Bundy, July 13, 1962, NSF/RSS/SEA, Box 231A, JFKL (emphasis in original); Komer to Kaysen, July 11, 1962, NSF/Komer/VN, Box 447, JFKL (emphasis in original).

34. Bowles, *Promises to Keep,* 410–414; Howard B. Schaffer, *Chester Bowles: New Dealer in the Cold War* (Cambridge, Mass., 1993), 234–235.

35. Bowles to Kennedy, March 7, 1963, *FRUS, 1961–1963,* III: 136–140; Bowles (Manila) to Rusk, July 10, 1963, ibid., 482–483; Bowles to Bundy, July 19, 1963, ibid., 518–521.

36. Forrestal to Bundy, May 5, 1962, NSF/CF/VN, Box 196, JFKL (emphasis in original); Wood to Nolting, August 7, 1962, *FRUS, 1961–1963,* II: 580–581; Forrestal to Kennedy, June 20, 1962, ibid., 466.

37. Forrestal interview with Kraft, August 14, 1964, 116; Forrestal to Bundy, July 31, 1962, *FRUS, 1961–1963,* XXIV: 882.

38. Forrestal to Bundy, December 3, 1962, Harriman/Bird Papers.

39. Forrestal to Bundy, July 31, 1962, *FRUS, 1961–1963,* XXIV: 882; Forrestal to Bundy, August 8, 1962, NSF/M&M/SM/Forrestal, Box 320, JFKL.

40. Forrestal to Bundy, October 13, 1962, NSF/M&M/SM/Forrestal, Box 320, JFKL; Robert Dallek, *An Unfinished Life: John F. Kennedy, 1917–1963* (Boston, 2003), 665.

41. Forrestal to Harriman, December 3, 1962, Harriman Papers, Box 461, LOC; Frederick Nolting, *From Trust to Tragedy: The Political Memoirs of Frederick Nolting, Kennedy's Ambassador to Diem's Vietnam* (Westport, Conn., 1988), 96.

42. Memo for the record, January 2, 1963, *FRUS, 1961–1963*, III: 3–4; Hilsman OH, 20, JFKL; Hilsman, *To Move a Nation*, 460–461; memo for the record, January 1963, Hilsman Papers, Box 3, Folder 11, JFKL. See also Hilsman memo, January 1963, *FRUS, 1961–1963*, III: 7–11; Hilsman memo, January 1963, ibid., 14; and Hilsman, *American Guerrilla*, 272–273.

43. Bundy to Forrestal, undated, NSF/M&M/SM/Forrestal, Box 320, JFKL; Hilsman and Forrestal to Kennedy, January 25, 1963, *FRUS, 1961–1963*, III: 49–60; Forrestal to Bundy, January 15, 1963, NSF/M&M/SM/Forrestal, Box 320, JFKL.

44. Forrestal interview with Kraft, August 14, 1964, 127; Felt to Taylor, March 9, 1963, NSF/CF/VN, Box 197, JFKL.

45. Forrestal to Kennedy, February 1, 1963, *FRUS, 1961–1963*, III: 95.

46. Forrestal to Kennedy, February 4, 1963, ibid., 97. Forrestal told Kennedy that the meeting to discuss Wheeler's report "was a complete waste of your time for which I apologize."

47. Forrestal to Harriman, February 8, 1963, ibid., 105–106; Hilsman to Harriman, February 12, 1963, Hilsman Papers, Box 6, JFKL.

48. Memo for the record, March 6, 1963, NSF/CF/VN, Box 197, JFKL; Forrestal to Harriman, Bundy, and Kaysen, March 8, 1963, *FRUS, 1961–1963*, III: 142–143; Forrestal to Harriman, March 11, 1963, Harriman Papers, Box 461, LOC.

49. Forrestal to Kennedy, January 28, 1963, *FRUS, 1961–1963*, III: 64; editorial note, ibid., 132–133; Forrestal to Kennedy, May 10, 1963, ibid., 291.

50. Memcon, February 26, 1963, Harriman Papers, Box 461, LOC.

51. Carl von Clausewitz, *On War*, ed. Michael Howard and Peter Paret (Princeton, 1976), 87.

52. Bundy speech, March 29, 1963, Lippmann Papers, Box 59, Yale.

53. William J. Rust, *Kennedy in Vietnam* (New York, 1985), 102.

54. Forrestal interview with Kraft, April 8, 1964, 49. Forrestal originally protested Lodge's appointment because he felt that Lodge, a consummate politician, would simply continue Nolting's policy of compromise and conciliation. Ibid., 47–51; Forrestal interview with Kraft, August 14, 1964, 145–147. However, others on the NSC staff had always been supportive of Lodge. Komer, for example, had once suggested that Lodge succeed Arthur Dean as the Kennedy administration's chief nuclear arms control negotiator. Komer to Bundy, January 5, 1962, NSF/M&M/SM/Komer, Box 322, JFKL. For Bundy's positive assessment of Lodge, see Anne E. Blair, *Lodge in Vietnam: A Patriot Abroad* (New Haven, 1995), 155. Forrestal would soon agree with Komer and Bundy, and the NSC staff quickly formed a powerful alliance with Lodge.

55. Hilsman to Ball, August 6, 1963, *FRUS, 1961–1963*, III: 555; Richard Reeves, *President Kennedy: Profile of Power* (New York, 1993), 311; memcon, June 17, 1963, Lodge Papers, Part II, Reel 17, Confidential Journal, MHS. See also meeting notes, November 9, 1961, *FRUS, 1961–1963*, I: 573; and Abramson, *Spanning the Century*, 606–609.

56. *PP*, II: 233; memo for the record, undated, Lodge Papers, Part V, Reel 19, Vietnam Papers, MHS; Trueheart (Saigon) to Rusk, August 21, 1963, *FRUS, 1961–1963*, III: 595.

57. CIA intelligence memo, August 23, 1963, and McCone to Bundy, August 23, 1963, NSF/CF/VN, Box 198A, JFKL; Blair, *Lodge in Vietnam*, 43, 168n52; Forrestal to Kennedy, August 24, 1963, *FRUS, 1961–1963*, III: 625.

58. Ball to Lodge, August 24, 1963, ibid., 628.

59. Hilsman, *To Move a Nation*, 487; idem, "McNamara's War," 157; Forrestal to Kennedy, August 24, 1963, *FRUS, 1961–1963*, III: 627; memo for the record, August 24, 1963, ibid., 630. Forrestal later claimed that he had secured Taylor's approval of the cable through Marine General Victor Krulak. Forrestal interview with Kraft, August 14, 1964, 154.

60. Taylor, *Swords and Plowshares*, 292; *Time*, October 4, 1963, 33; Robert S. McNamara, *In Retrospect: The Tragedy and Lessons of the Vietnam War* (New York, 1995), 54–55; Rust, *Kennedy in Vietnam*, 119; Lodge, cf earlier Vietnam memoir, Pt. 2, Chap. 2, 2, Lodge Papers, Pt. VIII, Reel 26, MHS.

61. Hilsman, *To Move a Nation*, 488; Hilsman OH, 34–35, JFKL.

62. Stanley Karnow, *Vietnam: A History*, rev. ed. (New York, 1991), 304.

63. Forrestal to Kennedy, August 26, 1963, *FRUS, 1961–1963*, III: 649–650; Forrestal to Bundy (including CIA intelligence analysis), August 26, 1963, NSF/CF/VN, Box 198A, JFKL; Forrestal to Kennedy (including CIA intelligence analysis), September 2, 1963, NSF/CF/VN, Box 199, JFKL. "This is not hard stuff," Forrestal wrote on a memo disparaging Diem and Nhu. Memo for record, August 27, 1963, *FRUS, 1961–1963*, III: 665n1.

64. Forrestal to Kennedy, August 27, 1963, *FRUS, 1961–1963*, III: 658–659; Forrestal to Kennedy, August 28, 1963, Harriman/Bird Papers; Forrestal to Kennedy, September 4, 1963, NSF/CF/VN, Box 199, JFKL.

65. Memcon, August 29, 1963, *FRUS, 1961–1963*, IV: 28; memcon, August 29, 1963, Hilsman Papers, Box 4, JFKL. See also memcon, August 27, 1963, *FRUS, 1961–1963*, III: 664; memcon, August 28, 1963, *FRUS, 1961–1963*, IV: 3–5; memcon, August 28, 1963, NSF/M&M/MVN, Box 196, JFKL. According to this record of a meeting with Kennedy, it was Bundy who toughened up an original draft of new instructions for Lodge. Rusk to Lodge and Harkins, August 28, 1963, *FRUS, 1961–1963*, IV: 16.

66. Bundy's momentary indecision stemmed from a nagging uncertainty whether the departure of Diem would indeed improve the situation in South Vietnam. Like many other U.S. officials, he feared that the chaos that would likely erupt in the event of a coup would harm the war effort. He briefly considered and rejected two alternatives: giving Diem another chance to prove himself, which was favored by McNamara and Taylor; or securing a face-saving international diplomatic settlement leading to American withdrawal and the political neutralization of Vietnam, which Bowles had repeatedly advocated and France was at the time promoting. On the former, see telcon, Rusk and Bundy, August 31, 1963, *FRUS, 1961–1963*, IV: 68; Bundy to Kennedy, September 2, 1963, ibid., 95–97; and memcon, September 6, 1963, Hilsman Papers, Box 4, JFKL. On the latter, see telcon, Rusk and Bundy, August 31, 1963, *FRUS, 1961–1963*, IV: 61, in which Bundy momentarily seemed to follow Rusk's lead. There is no further evidence to support the notion that Bundy sought a diplomatic solution to the war.

67. Memcon, August 31, 1963, *FRUS, 1961–1963*, IV: 75; memcon, September 10, 1963, NSF/M&M/MVN, Box 316, JFKL; *Time*, October 4, 1963, 33; telcon, Rusk and Bundy, August 29, 1963, Rusk Records, Box 48, NARA; memo of meeting, September 11, 1963, *FRUS, 1961–1963*, IV: 174–175. For Bundy's instructions to Forrestal and Hilsman, see memcon, September 10, 1963, *FRUS, 1961–1963*, IV: 170–171. The papers are found in Hilsman draft paper, September 11, 1963, Hilsman Papers/VN, Box 4, JFKL; Hilsman paper, September 11, 1963, *FRUS, 1961–1963*, IV: 177–180; Hilsman paper, September 11, 1963, ibid., 180–181; and Forrestal paper, September 11, 1963, ibid., 181–183. Bundy used these papers as the basis for general discussion for a full NSC meeting on September 11. See memcon, September 11, 1963, ibid., 185–190.

68. It is therefore inaccurate to portray Bundy as having "suddenly moved into a leading role" on Vietnam policy only at the end of October 1963. Kaiser, *American Tragedy*, 268.

69. Telcon, Rusk and Bundy, September 11, 1963, *FRUS, 1961–1963*, IV: 176; memcon, September 11, 1963, ibid., 187; memo of meeting, September 11, 1963, ibid., 192–193; LeRoy Ashby and Rod Gramer, *Fighting the Odds: The Life of Senator Frank Church* (Pullman, Wash., 1994), 168–170; telcon, Bundy and Ball, September 24, 1963, Ball Papers, Box 7, LBJL.

70. Forrestal to Bundy, September 16, 1963, *FRUS, 1961–1963*, IV: 235–236; telcon, Rusk and Bundy, September 18, 1963, Rusk Records, Box 48, NARA; draft telegram, Forrestal, NSF/CF/VN, Box 200, JFKL; Kennedy to Lodge, September 18, 1963, *FRUS, 1961–1963*, IV: 256–257; memcon, September 29, 1963, NSF/CF/VN, Box 200A, JFKL. Under the CIP, the United States exported to South Vietnam commodities such as sugar, tobacco, or dried foods to be sold on the local market. The local currency, the South Vietnamese piastre, was then removed from circulation. The purpose was to encourage economic growth while keeping inflation under control; this also protected Saigon's foreign exchange reserves. As the United States funded the entire project, the program was a political and economic boon for the Diem regime. According to Forrestal, suspending the CIP "seemed the best thing to do because it affected the elite, the merchants and the business community with whom Diem was deeply in league." Forrestal interview with Kraft, August 14, 1964, 166.

71. McNamara and Taylor to Kennedy, October 2, 1963, *FRUS, 1961–1963*, IV: 336–346.

72. Bundy to Lodge, October 5, 1963, ibid., 379.

73. Bundy to Lodge and Harkins, October 24, 1963, ibid., 429; Bundy to Lodge, October 25, 1963, ibid., 437; draft telegram, October 25, 1963, NSF/CF/VN, Box 201, JFKL.

74. Bundy to Lodge, October 29, 1963, *FRUS, 1961–1963*, IV: 473–475; Jones, *Death of a Generation*, 404; Bundy to Lodge, October 30, 1963, *FRUS, 1961–1963*, IV: 500–502.

75. Memcon, October 29, 1963, Hilsman Papers, Box 4, JFKL; Bundy memo, October 29, 1963, NSF/McGB/MP, Box 405, JFKL; Bundy to Lodge, October 30, 1963, *FRUS, 1961–1963*, IV: 502.

76. Memo of meeting, November 1, 1963, ibid., 518; telcon, Rusk and Bundy, November 2, 1963, Rusk Records, Box 49, NARA.

77. Memo of meeting, November 4, 1963, *FRUS, 1961–1963*, IV: 556; memo of meeting, November 2, 1963, NSF/M&M/MVN, Box 317, JFKL.

6. Bundy the Adviser

1. Forrestal (Saigon) to Bundy, November 22, 1963, NSF/CF/VN, Box 202, JFKL; David Kaiser, *American Tragedy: Kennedy, Johnson, and the Origins of the Vietnam War* (Cambridge, Mass., 2000), 282–283.

2. Bundy to Forrestal (Saigon), November 22, 1963, NSF/CF/VN, Box 202, JFKL. For a good description of Bundy during these few days, see Kai Bird, *The Color of Truth: McGeorge Bundy and William Bundy, Brothers in Arms* (New York, 1998), 265–268.

3. The apogee of this argument is found in John Newman, *JFK and Vietnam: Deception, Intrigue, and the Struggle for Power* (New York, 1992). See also the more sophisticated Kaiser, *American Tragedy;* Howard Jones, *Death of a Generation: How the Assassinations of Diem and JFK Prolonged the Vietnam War* (New York, 2003); and Robert Dallek, *An Unfinished Life: John F. Kennedy, 1917–1963* (Boston, 2003), 664–686. For an overview of the historical controversy, see Fredrik Logevall, "Vietnam and the Question of What Might Have Been," in *Kennedy: The New Frontier Revisited,* ed. Mark J. White (New York, 1998), 19–62. Bundy left behind an unfinished manuscript of a memoir on Vietnam when he died in 1996. In it he intended to demonstrate Johnson's centrality and inflexibility toward the decision making on Vietnam, and that Kennedy would have acted and decided very differently. Bird, *Color of Truth,* 402–403, 461n21.

4. McGeorge Bundy, "The History-Maker," *Proceedings of the Massachusetts Historical Society* 90 (1978), 84.

5. Dean Rusk, *As I Saw It: A Secretary of State's Memoirs* (New York, 1990), 440–442; William P. Bundy, "Kennedy and Vietnam," in *The Kennedy Presidency,* ed. Kenneth W. Thompson (Lanham, Md., 1985), 241–284; Chester L. Cooper, *The Lost Crusade: America in Vietnam* (New York, 1970), 417–419; and Bobby Kennedy's comments in Larry Berman, "NSAM 263 and NSAM 273: Manipulating History," in *Vietnam: The Early Decisions,* ed. Lloyd C. Gardner and Ted Gittinger (Austin, 1997), 183–184.

6. Melvin Small, *Johnson, Nixon, and the Doves* (New Brunswick, N.J., 1988), 40; Richard Reeves, *President Kennedy: Profile of Power* (New York, 1993), 660–661.

7. Bundy to Johnson, June 1, 1964, NSF/MP/McGB, Box 2, LBJL.

8. Memo of meeting, October 7, 1963, *FRUS, 1961–1963*, IV: 387; NSAM 263, Bundy to Rusk, McNamara, and Taylor, October 11, 1963, ibid., 395–396; Rusk to Lodge, October 5, 1963, ibid., 371–379; William Conrad Gibbons, "Lyndon Johnson and the Legacy of Vietnam," in Gardner and Gittinger, *Vietnam,* 138. The troop withdrawal statement has predictably caused great historical controversy and is one of the main evidentiary bases for the theory that Kennedy would not have sent ground troops to Vietnam. For example, see Newman, *JFK and Vietnam,* 407–412.

For an opposing view see Berman, "NSAM 263 and NSAM 273," 177–180, 185–188.

9. NSAM 273, Bundy to Rusk, McNamara, et al., November 26, 1963, *FRUS, 1964–1968,* I: 637–640. Bundy's earlier draft, written on November 21 for Kennedy's signature, did not explicitly mandate planning for military strikes against the DRV as contained in paragraph 7 of the final, approved version, but its language and meaning are essentially the same. See draft NSAM, November 21, 1963, NSF/CF/VN, Box 202, JFKL. On the difference in the text, but not the meaning or result, between the two drafts of NSAM 273, see Gibbons, "Lyndon Johnson," 141–144, 155n71.

10. Bundy to Johnson, December 2, 1963, and Bundy to Johnson, December 12, 1963, NSF/MP/McGB, Box 1, LBJL; minutes of meeting, December 12, 1963, *FRUS, 1961–1963,* IV: 705.

11. CIA report, December 16, 1963, and Forrestal to Bundy, December 17, 1963, NSF/CF/VN, Box 1, LBJL; memo, Forrestal to McNamara, February 14, 1964, *FRUS, 1964–1968,* I: 77. The best account of the Hamlets' failings is Philip E. Catton, *Diem's Final Failure: Prelude to America's War in Vietnam* (Lawrence, Kans., 2002), 117–183, 194–198, 204–208.

12. Memcon, November 20, 1963, *FRUS, 1961–1963,* IV: 623–624.

13. Forrestal to Johnson, December 11, 1963, ibid., 698–700; Forrestal to Bundy, February 2, 1964, NSF/CF/VN, Box 2, LBJL. On defoliation, see Forrestal to Bundy, March 2, 1964, NSF/CF/VN, Box 2, LBJL.

14. Memcon, November 22, 1963, *FRUS, 1961–1963,* IV: 625; Bundy to Johnson, December 9, 1963, ibid., 693.

15. Bundy to Johnson, January 9, 1964, NSF/Files-McGB/CHRON, Box 1, LBJL.

16. Memo for the record, March 30, 1964, *FRUS, 1964–1968,* I: 197; telcon, Bundy and Johnson, May 20, 1964, in Michael R. Beschloss, ed., *Taking Charge: The Johnson White House Tapes, 1963–1964* (New York, 1997), 359; Reeves, *President Kennedy,* 284; Forrestal to Bundy, March 30, 1964, *FRUS, 1964–1968,* I: 200. The book was Roger Trinquier, *Modern Warfare: A French View of Counterinsurgency* (New York, 1964).

17. Fredrik Logevall, *Choosing War: The Lost Chance for Peace and the Escalation of War in Vietnam* (Berkeley, 1999), 67; Forrestal to Bundy, November 7, 1963, NSF/CF/VN, Box 202, JFKL.

18. Forrestal to Bundy, November 13, 1963, NSF/CF/VN, Box 202, JFKL. Emphasis in original.

19. Forrestal to Bundy, November 14, 1963, *FRUS, 1961–1963,* IV: 601; Forrestal to Bundy, December 10, 1963, NSF/CF/VN, Box 1, LBJL.

20. Memcon, December 16, 1963, Harriman Papers, Box 461, LOC.

21. Mansfield to Johnson, January 6, 1964, *FRUS, 1964–1968,* I: 3. See also Mansfield to Johnson, December 7, 1963, *FRUS, 1961–1963,* IV: 691–692.

22. Bundy to Johnson, January 9, 1964, *FRUS, 1964–1968,* I: 8–9 (emphasis in original); Bundy to Johnson, January 6, 1964, ibid., 14–15 (emphasis in original).

23. Mansfield to Johnson, February 1, 1964, NSF/CF/VN, Box 1, LBJL.

24. Telcon, Bundy and Johnson, February 6, 1964, in Beschloss, *Taking Charge*, 226; Bundy to Johnson, February 10, 1964, *FRUS, 1964–1968*, I: 67.

25. Forrestal to Bundy, March 9, 1964, NSF/CF/VN, Box 2, LBJL; Johnson to Bohlen, March 24, 1964, *FRUS, 1964–1968*, I: 191; draft telegram, Johnson to Lodge (drafted by Bundy), March 20, 1964, NSF/Files-McGB/CHRON, Box 2, LBJL.

26. Bundy to Johnson, March 4, 1964, NSF/MP/McGB, Box 1, LBJL; Forrestal to Bundy, April 20, 1964, NSF/CF/VN, Box 3, LBJL. And indeed it was not. See "Johnson's Way," *NYT*, April 26, 1964, E1. See also Logevall, *Choosing War*, 140–141.

27. Telcon, Bundy and Johnson, February 6, 1964, in Beschloss, *Taking Charge*, 226.

28. Bundy to Johnson, March 13, 1964, *FRUS, 1964–1968*, I: 146; Bundy to Johnson, March 14, 1964, ibid., 148; Bundy memo, March 20, 1964, NSF/Files-McGB/CHRON, Box 2, LBJL.

29. McNamara to Johnson, March 16, 1964, *FRUS, 1964–1968*, I: 153–167; NSAM 288, Bundy to Rusk and McNamara, March 17, 1964, ibid., 172–173; Forrestal to Bundy, May 26, 1964, ibid., 386.

30. Forrestal to Johnson, December 11, 1963, *FRUS, 1961–1963*, IV: 700; Forrestal to W. Bundy, May 1, 1964, Harriman Papers, Box 461, LOC.

31. Forrestal to Bundy, April 1, 1964, NSF/CF/VN, Box 3, LBJL.

32. NSC Meeting, May 24, 1964, *FRUS, 1964–1968*, I: 370.

33. Bundy to Johnson, June 2, 1964, NSF/MP/McGB, Box 2, LBJL; memcon, July 11, 1964, NSF/Files-McGB/CHRON, Box 3, LBJL; memo, Bundy to Johnson, May 29, 1964, NSF/CF/VN, Box 5, LBJL.

34. Forrestal to Johnson, December 11, 1963, *FRUS, 1961–1963*, IV: 699; Forrestal to Bundy, February 4, 1964, NSF/CF/VN, Box 2, LBJL; Bundy to Johnson, January 7, 1964, *FRUS, 1964–1968*, I: 4–5.

35. Bundy to Johnson, February 4, 1964, *FRUS, 1964–1968*, I: 60; Forrestal to Bundy, February 4, 1964, NSF/CF/VN, Box 2, LBJL; Bundy to Johnson, March 3, 1964, NSF/Files-McGB/CHRON, Box 2, LBJL. On the Pentagon's plan, see George Kahin, *Intervention: How America Became Involved in Vietnam* (New York, 1986), 208–211; and Kaiser, *American Tragedy*, 299–305.

36. Forrestal to Bundy, March 18, 1964, NSF/CF/VN, Box 2, LBJL. The remark is not insignificant. When Forrestal succeeded Rostow on the NSC staff, Kennedy told him that "Walt is a fountain of ideas; perhaps one in ten of them is absolutely brilliant. Unfortunately, six or seven are not merely unsound, but dangerously so. I admire his creativity, but it will be more comfortable to have him creating at some remove from the White House." Townsend Hoopes, *The Limits of Intervention: An Inside Account of How the Johnson Policy of Escalation was Reversed* (New York, 1969), 21.

37. Forrestal to Bundy, March 31, 1964, *FRUS, 1964–1968*, I: 206–207; Forrestal paper, undated, ibid., 207–213.

38. Forrestal to Bundy, April 28, 1964, *FRUS, 1964–1968*, I: 271; Forrestal to Bundy, May 5, 1964, NSF/CF/VN, Box 4, LBJL; Bundy to Lodge, May 7, 1964, *FRUS, 1964–1968*, I: 297n4.

39. Forrestal to Bundy, "May 26, 1964, ibid., 385–388.

40. Bundy to McNamara et al., May 27, 1964, NSF/CF/VN, Box 5, LBJL; Bundy to Johnson, May 27, 1964, *FRUS, 1964–1968*, I: 385n1; Bundy to Johnson, May 26, 1964, ibid., 390.

41. Telcon, Bundy and Johnson, May 27, 1964, in Beschloss, *Taking Charge*, 371; Forrestal to Johnson, May 29, 1964, *FRUS, 1964–1968*, I: 397.

42. Bundy to Johnson, May 27, 1964, NSF/MP/McGB, Box 1, LBJL; Sullivan to Bundy, May 21, 1964, and Sullivan to Bundy, May 22, 1964, NSF/CF/VN, Box 4, LBJL.

43. Bundy to Johnson, May 25, 1964, *FRUS, 1964–1968*, I: 374–377; Bundy paper, May 26, 1964, NSF/Files-McGB/CHRON, Box 2, LBJL.

44. Forrestal to McNaughton, May 1, 1964, in Bird, *Color of Truth*, 280.

45. Forrestal to Bundy, undated, NSF/CF/VN, Box 5, LBJL. The CIA cable quoted, in part, a high-ranking Chinese official in Nanjing as saying: "It is just a matter of time before all of Vietnam is Communist. The delay in gaining the final victory is according to plan and serves to undermine the prestige of the American imperialists by highlighting their ineffectiveness in full view of all the world. What can the United States do? Nothing at all." CIA intelligence cable, June 25, 1964, ibid.

46. Andrew L. Johns, "Opening Pandora's Box: The Genesis and Evolution of the 1964 Congressional Resolution on Vietnam," *Journal of American–East Asian Relations* 6 (Summer-Fall 1997), 178, 180; Forrestal paper, undated, *FRUS, 1964–1968*, I: 212.

47. Johns, "Opening Pandora's Box," 189; Lodge to Bundy, June 13, 1964, NSF/CF/VN, Box 5, LBJL. See also Cooper, *Lost Crusade*, 235 (about to join the NSC staff, Cooper was posted to the U.S. Embassy in Saigon at the time); and record of meeting, June 10, 1964, *FRUS, 1964–1968*, I: 490–491.

48. Draft memo, Bundy, June 10, 1964, *FRUS, 1964–1968*, I: 493–496; Forrestal to Bundy, June 15, 1964, NSF/CF/VN, Box 5, LBJL; Bundy paper, June 15, 1964, *FRUS, 1964–1968*, I: 517.

49. Bundy to Johnson, June 6, 1964, ibid., 472–473. That Bundy volunteered himself was undoubtedly a reflection of his willingness to accept a challenge, a belief in dedicated public service, and a commitment to Vietnam policy rather than, as one historian has written, disenchantment with his role as Special Assistant. Kaiser, *American Tragedy*, 328.

50. Bundy to Johnson, June 10, 1964, NSF/MP/McGB, Box 2, LBJL; telcon, Bundy and Johnson, June 15, 1964, in Beschloss, *Taking Charge*, 408–409.

51. Bundy to Johnson, June 25, 1964, NSF/Files-McGB/CHRON, Box 3, LBJL.

52. Telcon, Bundy and Johnson, March 2, 1964, in Beschloss, *Taking Charge*, 263; Cline OH, 21–22, LBJL; Taylor to Rusk and McNamara, July 15, 1964, *FRUS, 1964–1968*, I: 547–548; Bundy to Johnson, July 16, 1964, NSF/CF/VN, Box 6, LBJL.

53. Bundy to Johnson, July 15, 1964, Bundy to Johnson, July 27, 1964, and Bundy to McNamara, June 6, 1964, ibid.

54. Edwin E. Moise, *Tonkin Gulf and the Escalation of the Vietnam War* (Chapel Hill, N.C., 1996), 19.

55. Telcon, Bundy and Rusk, August 3, 1964, in editorial note, *FRUS, 1964–1968*, I: 602; telcon, Bundy and Ball, August 3, 1964, Ball Papers, Box 49, Princeton. The *Turner Joy* "apparently" came under fire because no conclusive proof for the attack could be produced at the time, and it has since emerged that no attack on the night of August 4 even occurred. This does not, however, mean that the United States deliberately staged the phantom incident or faked evidence to say that one had occurred. Rather, it appears that the Johnson administration acted precipitously on the basis of inconclusive evidence. See Moise, *Tonkin Gulf,* xi–xiii, 203–207.

56. Bundy to Johnson, August 5, 1964, NSF/MP/McGB, Box 2, LBJL; Bundy to Johnson, August 5, 1964, in David M. Barrett, ed., *Lyndon B Johnson's Vietnam Papers: A Documentary Collection* (College Station, Tex., 1997), 73; memcon, August 6, 1964, *FRUS, 1964–1968*, I: 644–645; memo for record, August 5, 1964, *FRUS, 1964–1968*, I: 631–632. See also David Halberstam, *The Best and the Brightest* (New York, 1972), 414. Bundy later claimed that he had cautioned Johnson against proceeding too quickly, both militarily and politically. See Bundy's comments in Ted Gittinger, ed., *The Johnson Years: A Vietnam Roundtable* (Austin, 1993), 31–33.

57. Bundy to Johnson, August 21, 1964, NSF/MP/McGB, Box 2, LBJL; memo for record, August 5, 1964, *FRUS, 1964–1968*, I: 632. The State Department intelligence estimate of a Chinese response is in Hughes to Rusk, July 20, 1964, NSF/CF/VN, Box 6, LBJL. China was indeed considering intervening in the Vietnam War, much as it did in the Korean War in 1950, should the United States invade the DRV. Qiang Zhai, *China and the Vietnam Wars, 1950–1975* (Chapel Hill, N.C., 2000), 122–156; Chen Jian, *Mao's China and the Cold War* (Chapel Hill, N.C., 2001), 221.

58. Bundy to Johnson, August 31, 1964, *FRUS, 1964–1968,* I: 723–724; Bundy to W. Bundy, September 2, 1964, NSF/CF/VN, Box 8, LBJL.

7. Bundy the Advocate

1. Bundy to Johnson, September 24, 1964, NSF/MP/McGB, Box 2, LBJL; Bundy to Johnson, September 8, 1964, *FRUS, 1964–1968*, I: 746–747; NSAM 314, Bundy to Rusk and McNamara, September 10, 1964, ibid., 758–760.

2. Bundy to Johnson, October 1, 1964, NSF/MP/McGB, Box 2, LBJL; CIA intelligence memo, passed from Marshall Carter to Bundy, September 28, 1964, NSF/CF/VN, Box 9, LBJL; McNaughton paper, passed from McNamara to Bundy, November 7, 1964, NSF/CF/VN, Box 10, LBJL; Forrestal to McNaughton, passed from Forrestal to Bundy, September 24, 1964, NSF/CF/VN, Box 9, LBJL.

3. Bundy to Johnson, October 1, 1964, NSF/MP/McGB, Box 2, LBJL; Bundy to Goodwin, October 19, 1964, NSF/Files-McGB/CHRON, Box 4, LBJL.

4. George Ball, *The Past Has Another Pattern: Memoirs* (New York, 1982), 380; Ball to Bundy, Rusk, and McNamara, NSF/CF/VN, Box 9, LBJL.

5. Ball OH, 16, LBJL; Fredrik Logevall, *Choosing War: The Lost Chance for Peace and the Escalation of War in Vietnam* (Berkeley, 1999), 246; telcon, Bundy and Ball, March 2, 1964, Ball Papers, Box 49, Princeton; Ball, *Past Has Another Pattern*, 383, 392.

6. Bundy to Johnson, December 2, 1964, NSF/Files-McGB/CHRON, Box 5, LBJL; Bundy to Johnson, December 5, 1964, *FRUS, 1964–1968*, I: 981–982. On the weakening of the "special relationship' between London and Washington, due partly to the Vietnam War, see Alan Dobson, "The Years of Transition: Anglo-American Relations, 1961–1967," *Review of International Studies* 16 (July 1990), 239–258.

7. Gregory Allen Olson, *Mansfield and Vietnam: A Study in Rhetorical Adaptation* (East Lansing, Mich., 1995), 137; Mansfield to Johnson, December 9, 1964, Mansfield Papers, Box 103, Folder 13, K. Ross Toole Archives, University of Montana, Missoula.

8. Olson, *Mansfield and Vietnam*, 138; Bundy to Johnson, December 16, 1964, *FRUS, 1964–1968*, I: 1010–1012.

9. Editorial note, *FRUS, 1964–1968*, I: 812–813; Logevall, *Choosing War*, 255–260; David Kaiser, *American Tragedy: Kennedy, Johnson, and the Origins of the Vietnam War* (Cambridge, Mass., 2000), 353–356; W. Bundy, Vietnam memoir, 18:4, LBJL.

10. *PP*, III: 114; George Kahin, *Intervention: How America Became Involved in Vietnam* (New York, 1986), 246–254; Logevall, *Choosing War*, 268–274.

11. Memo for the record, November 19, 1964, *FRUS, 1964–1968*, I: 915; Bundy to Johnson, November 28, 1964, NSF/Files-McGB/CHRON, Box 5, LBJL; Kahin, *Intervention*, 252.

12. Cooper to Bundy, December 10, 1964, *FRUS, 1964–1968*, I: 993–994; Bundy to Johnson, December 17, 1964, and Bundy to Johnson December 23, 1964, NSF/CF/VN, Box 11, LBJL. On Seaborn, whose missions to Hanoi Bundy helped organize, see Logevall, *Choosing War*, 156–163, 208–210; and Andrew Preston, "Balancing War and Peace: Canadian Foreign Policy and the Vietnam War, 1961–1965," *Diplomatic History* 27 (Winter 2003), 94–103.

13. Bundy to Johnson, January 12, 1965, NSF/MP/McGB, Box 2, LBJL; Cooper and Thomson to Bundy, January 15, 1965, NSF/CF/VN, Box 12, LBJL. The origins of what became the "more flags" campaign can be traced to the first year of the Kennedy presidency, when Kennedy charged Bundy with finding a way to get Filipino soldiers to fight in Vietnam. Kennedy to Bundy, July 10, 1961, and Kennedy to Bundy, August 14, 1961, Presidential Office File/SM, Box 62, JFKL; R. Johnson to Kaysen, December 13, 1961, NSF/CF/VN, Box 195A, JFKL. Bundy suggested Johnson resurrect the initiative in June 1964. Bundy paper, June 15, 1964, *FRUS, 1964–1968*, I: 517; Bundy to Johnson, June 25, 1964, ibid., 531. See also Stanley Robert Larsen and James Lawton Collins, Jr., *Vietnam Studies: Allied Participation in Vietnam* (Washington, 1975), 3.

14. British Embassy (Beijing) to London, January 12, 1965, passed to Bundy January 25, 1965, NSF/CF/VN, Box 12, LBJL. The telegram also quoted Chen Yi as saying that he "saw no need for direct Chinese intervention" because of the favorable

trend. However, this may have been Beijing's way of deterring U.S. escalation by reassuring the Americans that, despite its vitriolic rhetoric, China's own goals in Indochina were limited. Qiang Zhai, *China and the Vietnam Wars, 1950–1975* (Chapel Hill, N.C., 2000), 137–139.

15. Draft speech, Bundy to Johnson, undated, NSF/Files-McGB/CHRON, Box 5, LBJL; Bundy to Johnson, January 4, 1965, *FRUS, 1964–1968,* II: 7–8.

16. Thomson to Bundy, December 4, 1964, NSF/CF/VN, Box 11, LBJL; Johnson to Taylor, January 7, 1965, *FRUS, 1964–1968,* II: 40–41. The drafting information is in editorial note, ibid., 39.

17. Taylor paper, undated, *FRUS, 1964–1968,* I: 948–955; Taylor paper, November 27, 1964, ibid., 960–961; *PP,* III: 290; Maxwell D. Taylor, *Swords and Plowshares* (New York, 1972), 326–334; Robert Buzzanco, *Masters of War: Military Dissent and Politics in the Vietnam Era* (New York, 1996), 176–180; Cooper to Bundy, January 9, 1965, and Cooper to Bundy, January 7, 1965, NSF/CF/VN, Box 12, LBJL.

18. Taylor, *Swords and Plowshares,* 333; Cooper paper, January 6, 1965, *FRUS, 1964–1968,* II: 34.

19. Bundy to Johnson, January 14, 1965, *FRUS, 1964–1968,* II: 54.

20. Bundy to Johnson, January 7, 1965, NSF/Files-McGB/CHRON, Box 6, LBJL.

21. Bundy to Johnson, January 26, 1965, *FRUS, 1964–1968,* II: 84; telcon, Rusk and Bundy, January 23, 1965, Rusk records, Box 52, NARA.

22. Robert S. McNamara, *In Retrospect: The Tragedy and Lessons of the Vietnam War* (New York, 1995), 166; Bundy to Johnson, January 26, 1965, *FRUS, 1964–1968,* II: 89.

23. Bundy to Johnson, January 27, 1965, ibid., 95–96.

24. Ibid., 96–97. Emphasis in original.

25. Dean Rusk, *As I Saw It: A Secretary of State's Memoirs* (New York, 1990), 447; McNamara, *In Retrospect,* 166–167; William Conrad Gibbons, *The U.S. Government and the Vietnam War: Executive and Legislative Roles and Relationships,* Part III: January–July 1965 (Princeton, 1989), 47.

26. Bundy's comments in Ted Gittinger, ed., *The Johnson Years: A Vietnam Roundtable* (Austin, 1993), 47; Lyndon B. Johnson, *The Vantage Point: Perspectives of the Presidency, 1963–1969* (New York, 1971), 123; Taylor to Johnson, January 6, 1965, *FRUS, 1964–1968,* II: 24; Cooper paper, January 6, 1965, ibid., 36; Cater to Johnson, January 26, 1965, NSF/CF/VN, Box 12, LBJL; *NYT,* February 2, 1965, 1–2.

27. Johnson to Taylor, January 27, 1965, *FRUS, 1964–1968,* II: 98–99; Taylor to Rusk, January 31, 1965, ibid., 115.

28. Bundy to Taylor, January 28, 1965, ibid., 104; Bundy to Taylor, January 30, 1965, ibid., 114; Bundy to Taylor, February 1, 1965, ibid., 121–122.

29. Bundy to Johnson, January 27, 1965, NSF/MP/McGB, Box 2, LBJL; Cooper to Bundy, January 29, 1965, NSF/CF/VN, Box 12, LBJL; Bundy to Taylor, January 30, 1965, *FRUS, 1964–1968* II: 114; *NYT,* February 2, 1965, 1; *San Francisco Chronicle,* February 2, 1965, 10.

30. Ilya V. Gaiduk, *The Soviet Union and the Vietnam War* (Chicago, 1996), 3–21; Eva-Maria Stolberg, "People's Warfare versus Peaceful Coexistence: Vietnam and the

Sino-Soviet Struggle for Ideological Supremacy," in *America, the Vietnam War, and the World,* ed. Andreas W. Daum, Lloyd C. Gardner, and Wilfried Mausbach (New York, 2003), 248–249.

31. CIA intelligence memo, February 1, 1965, *FRUS, 1964–1968* II: 118–120; Komer to Bundy, February 1, 1965, NSF/CF/VN, Box 13, LBJL; memo for the record, February 3, 1965, *FRUS, 1964–1968,* II: 130; *Wall Street Journal,* February 4, 1965, 1; *Chicago Tribune,* February 5, 1965, 2.

32. W. Bundy, Vietnam memoir, 22:7, LBJL; Taylor, *Swords and Plowshares,* 329–335.

33. Bundy's handwritten comments at the bottom of Bundy and Cooper to Johnson, January 13, 1965, NSF/CF/VN, Box 12, LBJL; Bundy to McCone, February 4, 1965, *FRUS, 1964–1968,* II: 141; memo of meeting, February 17, 1965, ibid., 306–307.

34. Taylor to Bundy, February 3, 1965, Westmoreland papers, Box 5, Folder 13, LBJL; Bundy to Johnson, February 14, 1965, NSF/MP/McGB, Box 2, LBJL. On the tensions between Bundy and Taylor over the issue of U.S. troops, see also H. R. McMaster, *Dereliction of Duty: Lyndon Johnson, Robert McNamara, the Joint Chiefs of Staff, and the Lies that Led to Vietnam* (New York, 1997), 201–203, 207–208, 252–253. Bundy led the administration's criticism of Taylor for not effecting a more positive change in Saigon's political atmosphere. Thanks to Bobby Kennedy, Taylor was not unaware of the criticism. Taylor, *Swords and Plowshares,* 335; Douglas Kinnard, *The Certain Trumpet: Maxwell Taylor and the American Experience in Vietnam* (Washington, D.C., 1991), 149.

35. Bundy to McCone, February 4, 1965, *FRUS, 1964–1968,* II: 141; *San Francisco Chronicle,* February 4, 1965, 12; Taylor to Rusk, February 6, 1965, NSF/CF/VN, Box 13, LBJL; Taylor to Rusk, February 6, 1965, *FRUS, 1964–1968,* II: 153–154.

36. *Chicago Tribune,* February 7, 1965, 1; *San Francisco Chronicle,* February 7, 1965, 1; *NYT,* February 7, 1965, 1.

37. Kahin, *Intervention,* 277; McNamara news conference, February 7, 1965, NSF/CF/VN, Box 13, LBJL; *The Times* (London), February 9, 1965, 9; Bundy press briefing, February 8, 1965, NSF/CF/VN, Box 13, LBJL; Harlech (Washington) to London, February 7, 1965, FO 371/180594, PRO.

38. Robert S. McNamara et al., *Argument Without End: In Search of Answers to the Vietnam Tragedy* (New York, 1999), 173–174, 188–189, 205–208. The DRV treated their Soviet patrons in much the same way. Despite their best efforts, Soviet officials could not get the North Vietnamese to divulge virtually anything sensitive. "Vietnamese comrades," a Soviet diplomat in Hanoi complained in December 1964, "do not want to share with us any information, particularly concerning specific questions of the situation in South Vietnam, the NLFSV's activity and its plans for the future." Gaiduk, *Soviet Union and the Vietnam War,* 28–29.

39. Meeting notes, February 6, 1965, *FRUS, 1964–1968,* II: 156–157. Only Mansfield, whom Johnson had invited to attend the NSC meeting, demurred. Bundy quoted in *New York Herald Tribune,* February 14, 1965.

40. Memo for the record, February 7, 1965, *FRUS, 1964–1968,* II: 160–164; Johnson, *Vantage Point,* 124; *PP,* III: 302.

41. McNaughton to McNamara and Vance, February 7, 1965, *FRUS, 1964–1968*, II: 165–166; Lawrence Freedman, "Vietnam and the Disillusioned Strategist," *International Affairs* 72 (January 1996), 133–151.

42. McMaster, *Dereliction of Duty*, 200–202, 209; Etherington-Smith (Saigon) to London, February 10, 1965, FO 371/180594, PRO; Sharp to JCS, February 7, 1965, NSF/CF/VN, Box 13, LBJL; U.S. Grant Sharp, *Strategy for Defeat: Vietnam in Retrospect* (San Rafael, Calif., 1978), 61–62.

43. Etherington-Smith (Saigon) to London, February 1, 1965, FO 371/180539, PRO; Kinnard, *Certain Trumpet*, 147; Taylor to Rusk, February 7, 1965, NSF/CF/VN, Box 13, LBJL; Taylor to State Department, February 9, 1965, *FRUS, 1964–1968*, II: 206; Etherington-Smith (Saigon) to London, March 13, 1965, FO 371/180595, PRO.

44. Memo for the record, February 7, 1965, *FRUS, 1964–1968*, II: 169–170; memcon, February 7, 1965, ibid., 173; memo for the record, February 8, 1965, ibid., 194; Tyler to Ball, February 8, 1965, ibid., 198; Mansfield to Johnson, February 8, 1965, ibid., 205.

45. William C. Westmoreland, *A Soldier Reports* (Garden City, N.Y., 1976), 138–139; David Halberstam, *The Best and the Brightest* (New York, 1972), 521; Bator interview with the author. See also McMaster, *Dereliction of Duty*, 215; and George W. Allen, *None So Blind: A Personal Account of the Intelligence Failure in Vietnam* (Chicago, 2001), 184.

46. McNamara, *Argument Without End*, 207; Seymour Topping, *Journey Between Two Chinas* (New York, 1972), 162; Hubert H. Humphrey, *The Education of a Public Man: My Life and Politics* (Garden City, N.Y., 1976), 483n6.

47. Harlech (Washington) to London, February 1, 1965, FO 371/180539, PRO; telcon, Bundy and W. Bundy, February 4, 1965, *FRUS, 1964–1968*, II: 151; Bundy to W. Bundy, February 6, 1965, NSF/CF/VN, Box 13, LBJL; Johnson's comments in memo for the record, February 7, 1965, *FRUS, 1964–1968*, II: 170–171.

48. Bundy to Johnson, February 7, 1965, *FRUS, 1964–1968*, II: 175.

49. Bundy to Johnson, February 7, 1965, ibid., 175–181.

50. Bundy mission paper, undated, ibid., 181–185. Emphasis in original. The drafting information is from Kaiser, *American Tragedy*, 400. McNaughton's contention that "even if [sustained reprisal] fails to turn the tide—as it may—the value of the effort seems to exceed its cost," and that "even if it fails, the policy will be worth it," is simply another version of his infamous "good doctor" analogy. In November 1964 McNaughton endorsed the Working Group's Option C by writing that "even if Option C failed, it would, by demonstrating U.S. willingness to go to the mat, tend to bolster allied confidence in the U.S. as an ally . . . It would demonstrate that the U.S. was a 'good doctor' willing to keep promises, be tough, take risks, get bloodied, and hurt the enemy badly." The good doctor, in other words, would not abandon its patients even when their condition was critical. See Daniel Ellsberg, *Papers on the War* (New York, 1972), 86; Leslie H. Gelb, *The Irony of Vietnam: The System Worked* (Washington, D.C., 1979), 242; Freedman, "Vietnam and the Disillusioned Strategist," 139–142; and Logevall,

Choosing War, 271–272. This analogy was also a favorite of Bundy's. For just one among many examples, recall his opposition to Mansfield's neutralization plan of January 1964: "We may have to move in these painful directions, but we should do so only when there is a much stronger demonstration that our present course cannot work. If we neutralize, it should not be because *we* have quit but because *others* have." Bundy to Johnson, January 6, 1964, *FRUS, 1964–1968,* I: 14–15. Emphasis in original.

51. Meeting notes, February 8, 1965, *FRUS, 1964–1968,* II: 191; memo for the record, February 8, 1965, ibid., 193–196; Bundy to Mansfield, February 9, 1965, ibid., 209–211. On the SIGMA war games, see McMaster, *Dereliction of Duty,* 89–91, 155–158, 162–164, 170–171.

52. Telcon, Bundy and Johnson, February 10, 1965, in Michael R. Beschloss, ed., *Taking Charge: The Johnson White House Tapes, 1963–1964* (New York, 1997), 176; memo of meeting, February 10, 1965, *FRUS, 1964–1968,* II: 215.

53. Meeting notes, February 10, 1965, ibid., 216–217; memo for the record, February 10, 1965, ibid., 222–223; *PP,* III: 321–322.

54. Hughes to Ball, February 8, 1965, *FRUS, 1964–1968,* II: 199–201; Carl Solberg, *Hubert Humphrey: A Biography* (New York, 1984), 271–272; Logevall, *Choosing War,* 346, 356; Hughes interview with the author, March 18, 1999, Chevy Chase, Md.; Humphrey to Johnson, February 17, 1965, *FRUS, 1964–1968,* II: 309–313.

55. Kaiser, *American Tragedy,* 407; Bundy to Johnson, February 19, 1965, *FRUS, 1964–1968,* II: 338.

56. Ball, *Past Has Another Pattern,* 390–392, 504–505n8; Ball to Johnson, February 13, 1965, *FRUS, 1964–1968,* II: 252–261.

57. Following his memo of February 8, Mansfield sent Johnson another antiwar missive on February 10, ibid., 226–227. Bundy's response is dated February 11, 1965, ibid., 237–238. See also Olson, *Mansfield and Vietnam,* 144–145.

58. Albert Eisele, *Almost to the Presidency: A Biography of Two American Politicians* (Blue Earth, Minn., 1972), 258; LeRoy Ashby and Rod Gramer, *Fighting the Odds: The Life of Senator Frank Church* (Pullman, Wash., 1994), 193–194; Dominic Sandbrook, *Eugene McCarthy: The Rise and Fall of Postwar American Liberalism* (New York, 2004), 132–133. Despite the senators' objections, the reprisal policy at first proved to be good politics. In a Gallup poll published on February 16, 67 percent of respondents said they approved of the retaliation for Pleiku and 64 percent said Johnson should "continue present efforts." *Washington Post,* February 16, 1965, A2. Moreover, a poll conducted on behalf of the White House revealed that the president's approval rating had risen by 3 points to 69 percent since the reprisals; that his handling of "the situation in Vietnam" had risen by 19 points to 60 percent; that 83 percent of those polled believed the United States to be "more right" to bomb the DRV now than before the attacks; and that 69 percent answered "yes" to the question, "if the only way to save South Vietnam is to continue our bombing, should we continue?" Gallup polling data, undated, Chase to Bundy, February 16, 1965, NSF/CF/VN, Box 13, LBJL. Perhaps this is why congressional opposition remained, for the time being, confined to private meetings and memos.

59. Bundy to Johnson, February 15, 1965, NSF/MP/McGB, Box 2, LBJL; Bundy to Johnson, February 17, 1965, NSF/Files-McGB/CHRON, Box 6, LBJL.

60. Topping, *Journey Between Two Chinas*, 161; *NYT*, February 8, 1965, 24.

61. *NYT*, February 9, 1965, 4. The *Times* even doubted several aspects of the administration's version of the Pleiku raid, including the source of the NLF's weapons (the newspaper had evidence that they were American-made, stolen from the ARVN) and the true loyalties of the local population. *NYT*, February 8, 1965, 14.

62. White House press briefing, February 8, 1965, NSF/CF/VN, Box 13, LBJL; *Washington Post*, February 18, 1965, A20. See also Douglas Kinnard, *The War Managers* (Hanover, N.H., 1977), 127–128. On Bundy's urgings to Johnson to level with the public, see Bundy to Johnson, June 15, 1964, *FRUS, 1964–1968*, I: 518; Bundy to Goodwin, October 19, 1964, NSF/Files-McGB/CHRON, Box 4, LBJL; Bundy to Moyers, December 27, 1964, NSF/Files-McGB/CHRON, Box 5, LBJL; Bundy to Johnson, February 7, 1965, *FRUS, 1964–1968*, II: 174–181; and telcon, Bundy and Johnson, February 10, 1965, in Beschloss, *Reaching for Glory*, 176.

63. Bundy to Johnson, February 19, 1965, *FRUS, 1964–1968*, II: 330–331; memcon, February 19, 1965, ibid., 332; Bundy to Johnson, March 2, 1965, NSF/CF/VN, Box 14, LBJL.

64. Bundy to Johnson, March 22, 1965, *FRUS, 1964–1968*, II: 469. The tactic seemed to work. "It remains a fact," Bundy wrote Johnson several months later, "that every experienced observer . . . has been astonished by the overall strength and skill of Wilson's defense of our policy in Vietnam and his mastery of his own left wing in the process. The support of the UK has been of real value internationally . . . The only real price we have paid for this support is the price of keeping them reasonably well informed and fending off one ill-advised plan for travel. This is not a very great cost." Bundy to Johnson, June 3, 1965, ibid., 717. See also Sylvia A. Ellis, "Lyndon Johnson, Harold Wilson, and the Vietnam War: A *Not* So Special Relationship?" in *Twentieth-Century Anglo-American Relations*, ed. Jonathan Hollowell (New York, 2001), 180–204; and John P. Young, *The Labour Governments, 1964–1970*, vol. 2, *International Policy* (Manchester, U.K., 2003), 70–82.

65. Ottawa to Washington Embassy, February 8, 1965, RG25, Vol. 10122, File 21–13-VIET-ICSC, Pt. 1.1, NAC; Preston, "Balancing War and Peace," 103–104.

66. "Soviet Government Statement–Pravda," *Current Digest of the Soviet Press*, February 9, 1965, 9–10; *NYT*, February 9, 1965, 12; Gaiduk, *Soviet Union and the Vietnam War*, 29–31; Qiang Zhai, *China and the Vietnam Wars*, 149–150. An intelligence analysis, written exclusively for Bundy, declared that China "is a total puzzle. Unfathomable." The analysis nonetheless concluded, correctly, that "Kosygin's trip to Hanoi was not something Peking desired." Anonymous to Bundy, February 12, 1965, NSF/CF/VN, Box 13, LBJL.

67. Thompson to Rusk, February 23, 1967, NSF/CF/VN, Box 255, Sunflower Folder, LBJL. I am grateful to Ilya Gaiduk for drawing my attention to this document. Meeting notes, February 8, 1965, *FRUS, 1964–1968*, II: 188. The CIA discovered that many Soviet diplomats and officials believed "that the Chinese had inspired the Viet Cong raid in order to embarrass Kosygin and disrupt US-Soviet relations." The CIA also observed, accurately: "The initial Soviet reaction to the

Viet Cong attack at Pleiku the day after Kosygin arrived in Hanoi displayed not only shock and indignation but a clear lack of foreknowledge of this operation." CIA intelligence memo, April 3, 1965, NSF/CF/VN, Box 16, LBJL.

68. Harriman to Bundy, September 8, 1961, Harriman Papers, Box 439, LOC; Bird, *Color of Truth*, 158–165; Cooper to McCone, September 19, 1963, NSF/CF/VN, Box 200, JFKL; Cooper to McCone, December 6, 1963, *FRUS, 1961–1963*, IV: 680–684. See also Harriman's preface in Cooper, *Lost Crusade*, ix–xi.

69. Thomson interview with the author, April 5, 1999, Cambridge, Mass.; Thomson to the author, August 3, 1999; Chester Bowles, *Promises to Keep: My Years in Public Life, 1941–1969* (New York, 1971), 272, 290–291, 293, 296; Bundy to Rusk, December 1, 1965, NSF/Files-McGB/Management File, Box 16, LBJL. And indeed he did. After leaving the administration in 1966, Thomson taught at Harvard, and later at Boston and Tufts universities.

70. Thomson to Bowles, September 2, 1963, Bowles papers, Box 337, Yale.

71. Bird, *Color of Truth*, 346.

72. Thomson to Cooper, February 10, 1965, *FRUS, 1964–1968*, II: 228–229; Cooper and Thomson to Bundy, February 22, 1965, NSF/Files-McGB/CHRON, Box 6, LBJL (emphasis in original).

73. Thomson to Bundy, February 19, 1965, NSF/CF/VN, Box 14, LBJL. Emphasis in original.

74. Cooper to Bundy, March 1, 1965, *FRUS, 1964–1968*, II: 384–388.

75. Bundy to Johnson, February 19, 1965, NSF/MP/McGB, Box 2, LBJL.

76. Lloyd C. Gardner, *Pay Any Price: Lyndon Johnson and the Wars for Vietnam* (Chicago, 1994), 177–178.

77. Chester Cooper, "Fateful Day in Vietnam—10 Years Ago," *Washington Post*, February 11, 1975, A14. Emphasis in original.

78. Meeting notes, February 10, 1965, *FRUS, 1964–1968*, II: 217; McNamara, *Argument Without End*, 209; Halberstam, *Best and the Brightest*, 533.

8. Bundy Ambivalent

1. Bundy to Rusk, March 26, 1965, NSF/CF/VN, Box 14, LBJL.

2. CIA intelligence memo, March 15, 1965, Cline to Bundy, March 16, 1965, and anonymous to Cooper, March 22, 1965, NSF/CF/VN, Box 15, LBJL.

3. Sherman Kent intelligence memo, April 30, 1965, NSF/CF/VN, Box 16, LBJL; CIA monthly report, June 4, 1965, NSF/CF/VN, Box 18, LBJL. On the general state of deterioration in South Vietnam in the spring and early summer of 1965, see George Kahin, *Intervention: How America Became Involved in Vietnam* (New York, 1986), 310–312, 317, 341–346. On the early failings of sustained reprisal, see James Clay Thompson, *Rolling Thunder: Understanding Policy and Program Failure* (Chapel Hill, N.C., 1980), 35–56, 71–82.

4. Lodge paper, March 8, 1965, NSF/CF/VN, Box 14, LBJL. Interestingly, two years later, during his second stint as Ambassador to Saigon, Lodge would largely reverse course and tell Johnson to rely on U.S. military power and place less emphasis on political and soft hawk measures. In fact in 1967 Lodge derided

political reform in Saigon entirely and urged Johnson simply to support the rather undemocratic pairing of Ky and Thieu in the contentious upcoming South Vietnamese elections. James McAllister, " 'A Fiasco of Noble Proportions': The Johnson Administration and the South Vietnamese Elections of 1967," *Pacific Historical Review* 73 (November 2004), 630–632.

5. Telcon, Bundy and Lodge, March 8, 1965, Lodge papers, Pt. V, Reel 19, Vietnam papers, MHS; Bundy to Johnson, March 8, 1965, NSF/CF/VN, Box 14, LBJL.

6. Cooper to Bundy, March 4, 1965, ibid.; Cooper to Bundy, March 10, 1965, *FRUS, 1964–1968*, II: 432–435.

7. Bundy paper, March 24, 1965, NSF/CF/VN, Box 15, LBJL; Melvin Small, *Johnson, Nixon, and the Doves* (New Brunswick, N.J., 1988), 39; Lloyd C. Gardner, *Pay Any Price: Lyndon Johnson and the Wars for Vietnam* (Chicago, 1995), 188–192; Kai Bird, *The Color of Truth: McGeorge Bundy and William Bundy, Bothers in Arms* (New York, 1998), 315.

8. W. Bundy, Vietnam memoir, 22:28, LBJL.

9. Bundy to Johnson, March 20, 1965, NSF/Files-McGB/CHRON, Box 7, LBJL. See also Ronald Steel, *Walter Lippmann and the American Century* (Boston, 1980), 561–565; and Kathleen J. Turner, *Lyndon Johnson's Dual War: Vietnam and the Press* (Ithaca, 1985), 117–118, 124–126, 131–132.

10. Cooper to Bundy, April 1, 1965, NSF/Files-McGB/CHRON, Box 7, LBJL; Bundy to Johnson, March 28, 1965, NSF/CF/VN, Box 15, LBJL. On the Johns Hopkins speech, which Lloyd Gardner has aptly called "the Johnson Doctrine," see Gardner, *Pay Any Price*, 186–200.

11. Thomson to Bundy, March 31, 1965, NSF/CF/VN, Box 15, LBJL; Cooper and Thomson to Bundy, April 3, 1965, and Cooper and Thomson to Bundy, April 21, 1965, NSF/CF/VN, Box 16, LBJL.

12. Bundy to Johnson, April 23, 1965, *FRUS, 1964–1968*, II: 604–605.

13. Cooper to Johnson, May 25, 1965, ibid., 685–688; Bundy to Johnson, July 7, 1965, NSF/Files-McGB/CHRON, Box 10–11, LBJL.

14. Bird, *Color of Truth*, 322; Tom Wells, *The War Within: America's Battle over Vietnam* (Berkeley, 1994), 29. See also Charles DeBenedetti, *An American Ordeal: The Antiwar Movement of the Vietnam Era* (Syracuse, 1990), 106, 108.

15. Bundy quoted in Max Frankel, *The Times of My Life and My Life with The Times* (New York, 1999), 282; Galbraith to Bundy, undated, Bundy to Hoffman, May 29, 1965, and Bundy to Kissinger, April 30, 1965, NSF/Files-McGB/CHRON, Box 8, LBJL; John Kenneth Galbraith, *A Life in Our Times: Memoirs* (Boston, 1981), 479; Walter Isaacson, *Kissinger: A Biography* (New York, 1992), 117–118; Jussi Hanhimaki, *The Flawed Architect: Henry Kissinger and American Foreign Policy* (New York, 2004), 14.

16. Bird, *Color of Truth*, 342; Rhodri Jeffreys-Jones, *Peace Now! American Society and the Ending of the Vietnam War* (New Haven, 1999), 55; Wells, *War Within*, 107.

17. Valenti to Bundy, April 23, 1965, and Cooper to Valenti, April 24, 1965, NSF/CF/VN, Box 16, LBJL; Small, *Johnson, Nixon, and the Doves*, 44–45; Wells, *War Within*, 34–35; Trench (Washington) to London, April 23, 1965, FO 371/180541, PRO.

18. *Time*, May 7, 1965, 24.

19. *Washington Post,* May 15, 1965, A1.
20. Bundy himself later suspected that Johnson's sole purpose was to keep him away from the Washington teach-in. Small, *Johnson, Nixon, and the Doves,* 50; Bird, *Color of Truth,* 320.
21. *HC,* June 15, 1965.
22. CBS News—Special Report, "Vietnam Dialog: Mr. Bundy and the Professors," June 21, 1965, in Louis Menashe and Ronald Radosh, eds., *Teach-ins, U.S.A.: Reports, Opinions, Documents* (New York, 1967), 206; Thomas Powers, *The War at Home: Vietnam and the American People, 1964–1968* (New York, 1973), 67–70. Rumor had it that the palpable animosity between Bundy and Morgenthau dated back to when dean Bundy allegedly blocked Morgenthau's appointment at Harvard. Small, *Johnson, Nixon, and the Doves,* 51.
23. Meg Greenfield, "After the Washington Teach-In," *Reporter,* June 3, 1965, reprinted in *Reporting Vietnam, Part One: American Journalism, 1959–1969* (New York, 1998), 145.
24. *Washington Post,* May 16, 1965, A1; Fred Halstead, *Out Now! A Participant's Account of the American Movement Against the Vietnam War* (New York, 1978), 51; Bird, *Color of Truth,* 323.
25. Telcon, Moyers and Johnson, May 13, 1965, in Michael R. Beschloss, ed., *Reaching for Glory: Lyndon Johnson's Secret White House Tapes, 1964–1965* (New York, 2001), 320–321; telcon, Fortas and Johnson, May 19, 1965, ibid., 332–333; Richard N. Goodwin, *Remembering America: A Voice from the Sixties* (Boston, 1988), 400.
26. Bird, *Color of Truth,* 322–323; Small, *Johnson, Nixon, and the Doves,* 51.
27. For different perspectives on the development of mass protest movements in the 1960s, see Cyril Levitt, *Children of Privilege: Student Revolt in the Sixties* (Toronto, 1984); "Introduction," in Carole Fink, Philipp Gassert, and Detlef Junker, eds., *1968: The World Transformed* (New York, 1998), 1–27; and Jeremi Suri, *Protest and Power: Global Revolution and the Rise of Détente* (Cambridge, Mass., 2003).
28. On Morgenthau and realism, see Peter Gellman, "Hans J. Morgenthau and the legacy of political realism," *Review of International Studies* 14 (October 1988), 247–266; Robert Jervis, "Hans Morgenthau, Realism, and the Scientific Study of International Politics," *Social Research* 61 (Winter 1994), 853–876; and Jack Donnelly, *Realism and International Relations* (New York, 2000), 15–16, 44–50, 160–167, 186–188. Morgenthau's most influential work is Hans J. Morgenthau, *Politics Among Nations: The Struggle for Power and Peace* (New York, 1948). Over the next 30 years, the book would be published in four subsequent editions.
29. "Vietnam Dialog," 198–206; David L. Schalk, *War and the Ivory Tower: Algeria and Vietnam* (New York, 1991), 53–54; Ellen Glaser Rafshoon, "A Realist's Moral Opposition to War: Han J. Morgenthau and Vietnam," *Peace & Change* 26 (January 2001), 55–77; Hans J. Morgenthau, *Vietnam and the United States* (Washington, D.C., 1965), 12. See also idem, *A New Foreign Policy for the United States* (New York, 1969), 111–156.
30. Fredrik Logevall, *Choosing War: The Lost Chance for Peace and the Escalation of War in Vietnam* (Berkeley, 1999), 56.

31. John Lewis Gaddis, *Strategies of Containment: A Critical Appraisal of Postwar American National Security Policy* (New York, 1982), 238–239, 260; Walter L. Hixson, "Containment on the Perimeter: George F. Kennan and Vietnam," *Diplomatic History* 12 (Spring 1988), 149–164; Anders Stephanson, *Kennan and the Art of Foreign Policy* (Cambridge, Mass., 1989), 172–175.

32. George F. Kennan, *American Diplomacy, 1900–1950* (Chicago, 1951), 95.

33. "Vietnam Dialog," 199.

34. Steel, *Walter Lippmann,* 574–575; Bird, *Color of Truth,* 327–328.

35. Telcon, Bundy and Johnson, April 29, 1965, in Beschloss, *Reaching for Glory,* 290–291; Goodwin, *Remembering America,* 406; Robert Dallek, *Flawed Giant: Lyndon Johnson and His Times, 1961–1973* (New York, 1998), 264; Peter Felten, "Yankee, Go Home and Take Me with You: Lyndon Johnson and the Dominican Republic," in *The Foreign Policies of Lyndon Johnson: Beyond Vietnam,* ed. H.W. Brands (College Station, Tex., 1999), 106, 112–113.

36. Stephen G. Rabe, *The Most Dangerous Area in the World: John F. Kennedy Confronts Communist Revolution in Latin America* (Chapel Hill, N.C., 1999), 97–98.

37. Telcon, Fortas and Johnson, May 19, 1965, in Beschloss, *Reaching for Glory,* 332; Eric Thomas Chester, *Rag-Tags, Scum, Riff-Raff, and Commies: The U.S. Intervention in the Dominican Republic, 1965–1966* (New York, 2001), 174.

38. Dean Rusk, *As I Saw It: A Secretary of State's Memoirs* (New York, 1990), 375; Chester, *Rag-Tags,* 153–80, 190–98.

39. Gordon Walker memo for the record, June 30, 1965, FO 371/180542, PRO.

40. Bundy to Johnson, June 24, 1965, NSF/Files-McGB/CHRON, Box 9, LBJL; Bundy to Johnson, April 6, 1965, NSF/Files-McGB/CHRON, Box 7, LBJL; Bundy to Johnson, June 5, 1965, *FRUS, 1964–1968,* II: 725.

41. Bundy to Johnson, March 16, 1965, *FRUS, 1964–1968,* II: 449; Bundy to Johnson, April 1, 1965, ibid., 507.

42. NSAM 328, Bundy to Rusk, McNamara, and McCone, April 6, 1965, ibid., 537–539; Bundy to Johnson, April 27, 1965, NSF/MP/McGB, Box 3, LBJL; Bundy to McNamara, June 18, 1965, NSF/CF/VN, Box 19, LBJL.

43. McNamara to Johnson, July 1, 1965, *FRUS, 1964–1968,* III: 97–104.

44. Bundy to McNamara, June 30, 1965, ibid., 90–91.

45. Ball papers, both undated, ibid., 106–113; Rusk paper, July 1, 1965, ibid., 104–106; W. Bundy paper, July 1, 1965, ibid., 113–115 (emphasis in original).

46. Bundy to Johnson, July 1, 1965, ibid., 117.

47. W. Bundy, Vietnam memoir, 26:25, LBJL. Several recent histories of the war have reached this same conclusion. See, for example, Logevall, *Choosing War;* and David Kaiser, *American Tragedy: Kennedy, Johnson, and the Origins of the Vietnam War* (Cambridge, Mass., 2000). For a contrary view, see Larry Berman, *Planning a Tragedy: The Americanization of the War in Vietnam* (New York, 1982); and Brian VanDeMark, *Into the Quagmire: Lyndon Johnson and the Escalation of the Vietnam War* (New York, 1991).

48. Bundy to Johnson, *FRUS, 1964–1968,* III: 166–167.

49. Cooper and Thomson to Bundy, June 29, 1965, ibid., 73–75; Cooper to Bundy, June 30, 1965, NSF/CF/VN, Box 18, LBJL; Cooper to Bundy, July 21, 1965, *FRUS,*

1964–1968, III: 204–205; Bowman to Bundy and Cooper, July 23, 1965, Cooper to Bundy, July 24, 1965, and Thomson to Bundy, July 24, 1965, NSF/CF/VN, Box 20, LBJL.

50. Bundy to Johnson, July 21, 1965, *FRUS, 1964–1968*, III: 188.

51. Meeting notes, July 21, 1965, ibid., 196; memo for the record, July 21, 1965, ibid., 203. See also Clark Clifford, *Counsel to the President: A Memoir* (New York, 1991), 412.

9. Bundy Resilient

1. Bundy to Johnson, October 20, 1965, NSF/Files-McGB/CHRON, Box 12, LBJL; draft telegram, Bundy to Lodge and Westmoreland, October 26, 1965, *FRUS, 1964–1968*, III: 499.

2. Bundy to Johnson, November 8, 1965, ibid., 533. Bundy repeated these options in the agenda for a meeting a few days later. Bundy to Johnson, November 11, 1965, NSF/Files-McGB/CHRON, Box 12, LBJL.

3. Bundy to Johnson, July 27, 1965, *FRUS, 1964–1968*, III: 259; Bundy to Johnson, September 21, 1965, NSF/CF/VN, Box 22, LBJL.

4. Memo for the record, September 29, 1965, *FRUS, 1964–1968*, III: 420.

5. Bundy to Johnson, "The Week's Developments in Asia," October 22, 1965, NSF/MP/McGB, Box 5, LBJL; Bundy to Johnson, "World News Round-up," October 22, 1965, NSF/Files-McGB/CHRON, Box 12, LBJL.

6. Bundy's handwritten additions to the draft State Department cable to Lodge, September 12, 1965, Bundy to W. Bundy, September 14, 1965, and Bundy to Johnson, August 28, 1965, NSF/CF/VN, Box 22, LBJL; Bundy to Johnson, October 5, 1965, NSF/MP/McGB, Box 5, LBJL; Bundy to Rusk (LBJ Ranch), December 2, 1965, NSF/CF/VN, Box 24, LBJL.

7. Lansdale to Lodge, August 3, 1965, and Bundy to Johnson, August 3, 1965, NSF/MP/McGB, Box 4, LBJL. See also George C. Herring, *LBJ and Vietnam: A Different Kind of War* (Austin, 1994), 67. On Lansdale's second tour of duty in South Vietnam, see James McAllister, "The Lost Revolution: Edward Lansdale and the American Defeat in Vietnam, 1964–1968," *Small Wars and Insurgencies* 14 (Summer 2003), 1–26.

8. See, for example, Bundy to Johnson, August 26, 1965, NSF/CF/VN, Box 22, LBJL; Bundy to Johnson, September 30, 1965, and Bundy to Johnson, November 17, 1965, NSF/MP/McGB, Box 5, LBJL. For Lodge's recommendations, see, respectively, Lodge to State Department, August 26, 1965, *FRUS, 1964–1968*, III: 351–353; Lodge to Johnson, September 30, 1965, ibid., 421–423; and Lodge to Johnson, November 17, 1965, ibid., 569–571.

9. Rusk to Lodge, September 14, 1965, ibid., 388; memo of meeting, September 29, 1965, ibid., 420.

10. Memo for the record, August 3, 1965, ibid., 295; memcon, August 10, 1965, ibid., 324.

11. Lloyd C. Gardner, *Pay Any Price: Lyndon Johnson and the Wars for Vietnam* (Chicago, 1995); Herring, *LBJ and Vietnam*, 66–73; Jeremi Suri, *Protest and Power: Global Rev-*

olution and the Rise of Détente (Cambridge, Mass., 2003), 146–151.Bundy whole-heartedly agreed that reform at home and reform in Vietnam were not mutually exclusive and could even be symbiotic. McGeorge Bundy, "The End of Either/Or," *Foreign Affairs* 45 (January 1967), 200–201.

12. Thomson and Ropa to Johnson, November 12, 1965, NSF/Files-McGB/Daily Regional Staff Reports, Box 19, LBJL; Thomson and Ropa to Bundy, November 10, 1965, NSF/CF/VN, Box 24, LBJL.

13. Cooper paper, September 10, 1965, *FRUS, 1964–1968*, III: 380–383; Bundy and Cooper to Johnson, September 23, 1965, NSF/Files-McGB/Daily Regional Staff Reports, Box 19, LBJL.

14. Bundy to Johnson, October 22, 1965, *FRUS, 1964–1968*, III: 484–485; Cooper to Bundy, November 19, 1965, ibid., 575.

15. On Ia Drang and U.S. strategy, see Andrew F. Krepinevich, Jr., *The Army and Vietnam* (Baltimore, 1986), 164–171; and A. J. Langguth, *Our Vietnam: The War, 1954–1975* (New York, 2000), 395–408.

16. Bundy to Johnson, September 12, 1965, *FRUS, 1964–1968*, III: 383–385; Bundy to Johnson, September 23, 1965, ibid., 414–415.

17. Bundy to Johnson, December 6, 1965, ibid., 607.

18. Cooper to Bundy, "Another Pause," August 5, 1965, ibid., 300–303. Emphasis in original.

19. Cooper to Bundy, "Contact with the NLF," August 5, 1965, ibid., 305–307.

20. Cooper and Thomson to Bundy, August 17, 1965, NSF/CF/VN, Box 22, LBJL; Cooper to Bundy, September 24, 1965, *FRUS, 1964–1968*, III: 416; Komer to Johnson, September 18, 1965, NSF/MP/McGB, Box 4, LBJL.

21. Cooper to Bundy, October 20, 1965, *FRUS, 1964–1968*, III: 468.

22. *Times*, March 12, 1965; Wade-Grey (London) to Saigon Embassy, March 17, 1965, FO 371/180539, PRO; Geyelin, quoted in Stewart (Washington) to London, September 2, 1965, FO 371/180544, PRO. Geyelin reported on his conversation with Bundy to Michael Stewart, the British Foreign Secretary then visiting Washington.

23. Bundy to Johnson, October 4, 1965, NSF/Files-McGB/CHRON, Box 12, LBJL; Bundy to Johnson, September 2, 1965, NSF/MP/McGB, Box 4, LBJL; CBS News transcript, "Viet-Nam: Winning the Peace," *DSB*, September 13, 1965, 431–432, 442; Bundy to Johnson, September 2, 1965, and Lodge to Johnson, August 31, 1965, NSF/CF/VN, Box 22, LBJL (emphasis in original).

24. Bundy to Johnson, August 5, 1965, *FRUS, 1964–1968*, III: 304.

25. Telcon, Bundy and Rusk, October 18, 1965, in editorial note, ibid., 456; draft telegram, Bundy to Lodge, October 26, 1965, ibid., 499; Bundy to Rusk, October 28, 1965, NSF/Files-McGB/CHRON, Box 12, LBJL.

26. Bundy to Johnson, November 8, 1965, *FRUS, 1964–1968*, III: 533.

27. Bundy to Johnson, November 17, 1965, ibid., 571–572; telcon, McNamara and Ball, November 23, 1965, ibid., 579.

28. McNaughton to McNamara, November 9, 1965, and McNaughton to Bundy, November 9, 1965, NSF/CF/VN, Box 24, LBJL. On the McNamara-McNaughton relationship, see Deborah Shapley, *Promise and Power: The Life and Times of Robert*

McNamara (Boston, 1993), 302–303; Lawrence Freedman, "Vietnam and the Disillusioned Strategist," *International Affairs* 72 (January 1996), 134, 138–139; and Paul Hendrickson, *The Living and the Dead: Robert McNamara and Five Lives of a Lost War* (New York, 1996), 313–315. Bundy's opinion of McNaughton was similarly high. In March 1965 he had recommended that Taylor be replaced by his deputy, U. Alexis Johnson, and McNaughton succeed Johnson as Deputy Ambassador. H. R. McMaster, *Dereliction of Duty: Lyndon Johnson, Robert McNamara, the Joint Chiefs of Staff, and the Lies that Led to Vietnam* (New York, 1997), 252.

29. Bundy to Johnson, November 5, 1965, and Bundy to Johnson, November 11, 1965, NSF/Files-McGB/CHRON, Box 12, LBJL.

30. Meeting agenda for July 22, 1965, drafted by Bundy, *FRUS, 1964–1968*, III: 217; Stewart memcon with McNamara, Rusk, and Bundy, October 11, 1965, FO 371/180545, PRO; Bundy to Johnson, December 6, 1965, *FRUS, 1964–1968*, III: 608.

31. Guenter Lewy, *America in Vietnam* (New York, 1978), 389–396; Robert A. Pape, *Bombing to Win: Air Power and Coercion in War* (Ithaca, 1996), 176–195.

32. CIA intelligence memo, October 27, 1965, and Smith to Bundy, October 27, 1965, NSF/CF/VN, Box 23, LBJL.

33. Bundy to Johnson, November 27, 1965, *FRUS, 1964–1968*, III: 582.

34. Ibid., 582–584.

35. Memcon, Bundy and Anatoly Dobrynin, November 24, 1965, NSF/Files-McGB/memcons, Box 18, LBJL; Bundy to Johnson, November 27, 1965, *FRUS, 1964–1968*, III: 583; Bundy to Johnson, December 9, 1965, ibid., 624; Lyndon B. Johnson, *The Vantage Point: Perspectives of the Presidency, 1963–1969* (New York, 1971), 235; Dean Rusk, *As I Saw It: A Secretary of State's Memoirs* (New York, 1990), 464–465.

36. Bundy to Johnson, December 2, 1965, *FRUS, 1964–1968*, III: 594–597; Bundy to Johnson, December 3, 1965, ibid., 597–598; Bundy to Johnson, December 4, 1965, ibid., 599; Bundy to Johnson, December 9, 1965, ibid., 631; NSC staff paper, December 15, 1965, NSF/CF/VN, Box 25, LBJL. Bundy's point that renewed bombing could be justified by Hanoi's refusal to respond to the pause was the argument that eventually convinced Johnson. Johnson, *Vantage Point*, 235.

37. Larry Berman, *Lyndon Johnson's War: The Road to Stalemate in Vietnam* (New York, 1989), 52–53; Wilfried Mausbach, "Auschwitz and Vietnam: West German Protest Against America's War During the 1960s," in *America, the Vietnam War, and the World: Comparative and International Perspectives*, ed. Andreas W. Daum, Lloyd C. Gardner, and Wilfried Mausbach (New York, 2003), 284.

38. Bundy to Johnson, December 6, 1965, *FRUS, 1964–1968*, III: 608; Bundy to Johnson, December 14, 1965, ibid., 639–640; Bundy to Johnson, December 17, 1965, NSF/MP/McGB, Box 5, LBJL; meeting notes, December 17, 1965, *FRUS, 1964–1968*, III: 645.

39. Meeting notes, December 21, 1965, ibid., 678; Bundy to Johnson, December 27, 1965, ibid., 710. The length of the pause would provide a continuing source of conflict between Bundy and Rusk. Telcon, Bundy and Rusk, December 27, 1965, ibid., 714; and Bundy to Johnson, December 27, 1965, ibid., 715.

40. *Globe & Mail* (Toronto), December 31, 1965, 1; meeting notes, January 3, 1966, *FRUS, 1964–1968,* IV: 10–11; Bundy to Johnson, January 7, 1966, Bundy to Johnson, January 10, 1966, and Bundy to Johnson, January 19, 1966, NSF/MP/McGB, Box 6, LBJL.

41. Cooper to Bundy, December 8, 1965, NSF/CF/VN, Box 25, LBJL. See also Chester L. Cooper, *The Lost Crusade: America in Vietnam* (New York, 1970), 292–293.

42. Draft cable for Saigon, Bundy to Johnson, December 24, 1965, NSF/CF/VN, Box 25, LBJL. The civilians in the Pentagon, including McNamara, agreed with Bundy's reasoning and simply overrode or ignored objections from the JCS. Herring, *LBJ and Vietnam,* 41–42.

43. Bundy to Johnson, January 24, 1966, NSF/MP/McGB, Box 6, LBJL; meeting notes, January 28, 1966, *FRUS, 1964–1968,* IV: 174.

44. Helms to Bundy, January 24, 1966, NSF/CF/VN, Box 27, LBJL; CIA intelligence memo, January 24, 1966, and Bundy to Johnson, January 24, 1966, NSF/MP/McGB, Box 6, LBJL; CIA weekly report, January 12, 1966 (received by the NSC staff January 13, 1966), and CIA weekly report, January 26, 1966 (received by the NSC staff January 27, 1966), NSF/CF/VN, Box 26, LBJL.

45. Bundy to Johnson, January 24, 1966, NSF/MP/McGB, Box 6, LBJL; meeting notes, January 27, 1966, *FRUS, 1964–1968,* IV: 167.

46. Meeting notes, January 20, 1966, ibid., 99; memcon, Bundy and Ritchie, January 19, 1966, NSF/Files-McGB/Memcons, Box 18, LBJL.

47. Bundy to Johnson, January 21, 1966, NSF/MP/McGB, Box 6, LBJL; meeting notes, January 26, 1966, *FRUS, 1964–1968,* IV: 154; Bundy to Johnson, January 12, 1966, NSF/MP/McGB, Box 6, LBJL.

48. McNaughton to Bundy, January 20, 1966, NSF/CF/VN, Box 27, LBJL; meeting notes, January 24, 1966, *FRUS, 1964–1968,* IV: 126–128; Bundy to Johnson, January 26, 1966, ibid., 158–159; Cooper to Bundy, January 24, 1966, NSF/CF/VN, Box 26, LBJL; Cooper to Bundy, January 22, 1966, and Cooper to Bundy, January 28, 1966, NSF/CF/VN, Box 27, LBJL.

49. Meeting notes, January 27, 1966, *FRUS, 1964–1968,* IV: 169; meeting notes, January 10, 1966, ibid., 39; Bundy to Johnson, January 22, 1966, ibid., 103–104.

50. Bundy to Johnson, January 11, 1966, Bundy to Johnson, January 20, 1966, and Bundy to Johnson, February 3, 1966, NSF/MP/McGB, Box 6, LBJL; Bundy to Johnson, January 14, 1966, *FRUS, 1964–1968,* IV: 63–64; meeting notes, February 26, 1966, ibid., 263; Bundy to Johnson, January 17, 1966, NSF/MP/McGB, Box 6, LBJL.

51. Bundy to Johnson, January 19, 1966, and Lodge to Johnson, January 19, 1966, NSF/MP/McGB, Box 6, LBJL.

52. Bundy draft speech, January 7, 1966, NSF/MP/McGB, Box 6, LBJL. In the speech, Johnson used Bundy's ideas but not his actual words. Annual Message on the State of the Union, January 12, 1966, *Public Papers of the Presidents: Lyndon B. Johnson, 1966,* Book 1 (Washington, D.C., 1967), 8–9, 11.

53. Bundy to Johnson, January 11, 1966, NSF/MP/McGB, Box 6, LBJL.

54. Press conference transcript, January 31, 1966, NSF/CF/VN, Box 26, LBJL.

55. Cooper, *Lost Crusade*, 296.

56. Bundy to Johnson, December 4, 1965, NSF/MP/McGB, Box 5, LBJL; Kai Bird, *The Chairman: John J. McCloy, The Making of the American Establishment* (New York, 1992), 520, 581–582; Langguth, *Our Vietnam*, 393–394; Volker R. Berghahn, *America and the Intellectual Cold Wars in Europe: Shepard Stone Between Philanthropy, Academy, and Diplomacy* (Princeton, 2001), 239.

57. Telcon, Bundy and Johnson, May 2, 1964, in *Taking Charge: The Johnson White House Tapes, 1963–1964*, ed. Michael R. Beschloss (New York, 1997), 341; Richard N. Goodwin, *Remembering America: A Voice from the Sixties* (Boston, 1988), 258–259; Kai Bird, *The Color of Truth: McGeorge Bundy and William Bundy, Brothers in Arms* (New York, 1998), 325; Robert Dallek, *Flawed Giant: Lyndon Johnson and His Times, 1961–1973* (New York, 1998), 296.

58. For former colleagues, see Glenn T. Seaborg, *Stemming the Tide: Arms Control in the Johnson Years* (Lexington, Mass., 1987), 183; and Robert S. McNamara, *In Retrospect: The Tragedy and Lessons of the Vietnam War* (New York, 1995), 235. For historians, see Doris Kearns, *Lyndon Johnson and the American Dream* (New York, 1976), 320; Nancy Zaroulis and Gerald Sullivan, *Who Spoke Up? American Protest Against the War in Vietnam, 1963–1975* (Garden City, N.Y., 1984), 77–78; Stanley Karnow, *Vietnam: A History*, rev. ed. (New York, 1991), 520; Charles DeBenedetti, *An American Ordeal: The Antiwar Movement of the Vietnam Era* (Syracuse, 1990), 142, 191; Adam Garfinkle, *Telltale Hearts: The Origins and Impact of the Vietnam Antiwar Movement* (New York, 1995), 90; and Tom Wells, *The War Within: America's Battle over Vietnam* (Berkeley, 1994), 71.

59. Wylie (Defense) to Bundy, January 10, 1966, and Kent (CIA) to Bundy, January 20, 1966, NSF/CF/VN, Box 26, LBJL; Thomson and Ropa to Bundy, January 7, 1966, *FRUS, 1964–1968*, IV: 26–32.

60. Bundy to Johnson, January 20, 1966, and Bundy to Johnson, February 21, 1966, NSF/MP/McGB, Box 6, LBJL.

61. *NYT*, November 14, 1965, 1, 45; Bundy to Johnson, January 14, 1966, *FRUS, 1964–1968*, IV: 64; Bundy to Johnson, February 3, 1966, NSF/MP/McGB, Box 6, LBJL.

62. *Meet the Press* transcript, February 20, 1966, NSF/Files-McGB, Box 16, LBJL. For Kennedy's comments, see Arthur M. Schlesinger, Jr., *Robert Kennedy and His Times* (Boston, 1978), 735–739; and Evan Thomas, *Robert Kennedy: His Life* (New York, 2000), 315.

63. Bundy to Johnson, February 11, 1966, NSF/MP/McGB, Box 6, LBJL; Bundy to Kennedy, February 21, and draft cable, Bundy to Lodge and Westmoreland, undated, 1966, NSF/CF/VN, Box 28, LBJL; Rusk to Lodge and Westmoreland, February 21, 1966, *FRUS, 1964–1968*, IV: 239–240.

64. Bundy to Johnson, February 16, 1966, ibid., 231–235; Bundy to Johnson, February 16, 1966, NSF/MP/McGB, Box 6, LBJL.

65. Bird, *Color of Truth*, 346–347; Frank E. Vandiver, *Shadows of Vietnam: Lyndon Johnson's Wars* (College Station, Tex., 1997), 175.

66. Bundy to Johnson, undated, NSF/MP/McGB, Box 5, LBJL.

67. Komer to Johnson, December 1, 1966, *FRUS, 1964–1968*, IV: 883. Emphasis in original.

68. William Conrad Gibbons, *The U.S. Government and the Vietnam War: Executive and Legislative Roles and Relationships,* Pt. IV, *July 1965–January 1968* (Princeton, 1995), 575–576.

Epilogue

1. Theodore H. White interview notes, December 15, 1967, White papers, Box 32, JFKL. I am grateful to Dominic Sandbrook for drawing my attention to this document.

2. George C. Herring, "America and Vietnam: The Unending War," *Foreign Affairs* 70 (Winter 1991–1992), 104.

3. Bundy to Johnson, May 3, 1967, *FRUS, 1964–1968*, V: 370–377; Bundy to Johnson, October 17, 1967, ibid., 882–886; meeting notes in Jones to Johnson, November 2, 1967, ibid., 954–970; Rostow to Johnson, November 3, 1967, ibid., 981; Herbert Y. Schandler, *The Unmaking of a President: Lyndon Johnson and Vietnam* (Princeton, 1977), 64–65, 129; Walter Isaacson and Even Thomas, *The Wise Men: Six Friends and the World They Made* (New York, 1986), 676–681; quotes from Larry Berman, *Lyndon Johnson's War: The Road to Stalemate in Vietnam* (New York, 1989), 97, 99.

4. Meeting notes, November 2, 1967, *FRUS, 1964–1968*, V: 958; McGeorge Bundy, "The End of Either/Or," *Foreign Affairs* 45 (January 1967), 194–201; George C. Herring, *LBJ and Vietnam: A Different Kind of War* (Austin, 1994), 60. See also Bundy to Johnson, November 10, 1967, *FRUS, 1964–1968*, V: 1007.

5. Berman, *Lyndon Johnson's War,* 196; *NYT,* October 13, 1968, 1, 24; *NYT,* May 17, 1970, 8; Kai Bird, *The Color of Truth: McGeorge Bundy and William Bundy, Brothers in Arms* (New York, 1998), 397–398; Harrison E. Salisbury, *Without Fear or Favor: An Uncompromising Look at* The New York Times (New York, 1980), 192–193, 270; Max Frankel, *The Times of My Life and My Life with* The Times (New York, 1999), 337; Russo quoted in *HC,* March 10, 1973; McGeorge Bundy, "The Americans and the World," *Daedalus* 107 (Winter 1978), 292.

6. *HC,* October 14, 1968; McGeorge Bundy, "Shadow and Substance in 1980," in *Presidential Promises and Performance,* ed. McGeorge Bundy and Edmund S. Muskie (New York, 1980), 49; "Lessons Learned: Views from Two Generations," MacNeil/ Lehrer NewsHour, April 30, 1985, www.pbs.org (accessed 9/20/03).

7. Bird, *Color of Truth,* 403. Bundy had not finished his memoir when he died, but his research assistant has endeavored to publish a posthumous, edited version of the manuscript. As of this writing the memoir has not been published.

8. Michael Ignatieff, *Isaiah Berlin: A Life* (London, 1998), 262–266; Volker R. Berghahn, *America and the Intellectual Cold Wars in Europe: Shepard Stone between Philanthropy, Academy, and Diplomacy* (Princeton, 2001), 206, 239. See also Edward H. Berman, *The Ideology of Philanthropy: The Influence of the Carnegie, Ford, and Rockefeller Foundations on American Foreign Policy* (Albany, 1983), 12.

9. Waldemar A. Nielsen, *The Big Foundations* (New York, 1972), 11, 95–97, 355–357; Bird, *Color of Truth*, 378–391; Berghahn, *America and the Intellectual Cold Wars*, 265.

10. Waldemar A. Nielsen, *The Golden Donors: A New Anatomy of the Great Foundations* (New York, 1985), 62.

11. McGeorge Bundy, "The Issue Before the Court: Who Gets Ahead in America?" *Atlantic Monthly*, November 1977, 41–42; idem, "Shadow and Substance," 33–39, 40.

12. *NYT*, May 22, 1979, B8; Bird, *Color of Truth*, 402.

13. McGeorge Bundy, "Foreign Policy: From Innocence to Engagement," in *Paths of American Thought*, ed. Arthur M. Schlesinger, Jr., and Morton White (Boston, 1963), 293.

14. Henry Kissinger, *Diplomacy* (New York, 1994), 500. See also Michael H. Hunt, *Ideology and U.S. Foreign Policy* (New Haven, 1987); Alan Cassels, *Ideology and International Relations in the Modern World* (London, 1998), 207–212; and John Fousek, *To Lead the Free World: American Nationalism and the Cultural Roots of the Cold War* (Chapel Hill, N.C., 2000).

15. Lloyd C. Gardner, "Lost Empires," *Diplomatic History* 13 (Winter 1989), 3. This was a danger prevalent in U.S. foreign policy even before the Cold War. For example, in 1903 William Sumner, the American anti-imperialist, warned of "the danger of having a doctrine lying loose about the house, and one which carries with it big consequences . . . You accede to it now, within the vague limits of what you suppose it to be; therefore you will have to accede to it tomorrow when the same name is made to cover something which you never have heard or thought of. If you allow a political catchword to go on and grow, you will awaken some day to find it standing over you, the arbiter of your destiny, against which you are powerless, as men are powerless against delusions." Jonathan Haslam, *No Virtue Like Necessity: Realist Thought in International Relations since Machiavelli* (New Haven, 2002), 4.

16. See, for example, John Lewis Gaddis, *We Now Know: Rethinking Cold War History* (New York, 1997), 290; and M. E. Sarotte, *Dealing with the Devil: East Germany, Détente, and Ostpolitik, 1969–1973* (Chapel Hill, N.C., 2001), 173.

17. Henry A. Kissinger, *White House Years* (Boston, 1979), 14. The rise and fall of Bundy's conviction reflect the cyclical nature of ideologies. As Frank Ninkovich notes, the "systems of ideas that govern our political sensibilities tend to go through a cycle of creative articulation, preliminary organization, and attainment of power, only to be followed by a period of self-contradiction and perhaps even decay as a result of having to deal with the complexities of power inevitably encountered once enthroned. In a very rough way, the typical careers of ideologies tend to correspond to the patterns of institutional creation and decline . . ." Frank Ninkovich, *Modernity and Power: A History of the Domino Theory in the Twentieth Century* (Chicago, 1994), xvii.

18. Walt W. Rostow, *The Diffusion of Power: An Essay in Recent History* (New York, 1972), 40–49, 264–295, 435–525, 550–563; Rostow's foreword in C. Dale Walton, *The Myth of Inevitable U.S. Defeat in Vietnam* (London, 2002), ix–x; Walt W. Rostow,

The United States and the Regional Organization of Asia and the Pacific, 1965–1985 (Austin, 1986); idem, "The Case for War," *Times Literary Supplement,* June 9, 1995, 3–5; idem, "Vietnam and Asia," *Diplomatic History* 20 (Summer 1996), 467–471. For an excellent critique of Rostow's "buying time" theory, see Robert J. McMahon, "What Difference Did It Make? Assessing the Vietnam War's Impact on Southeast Asia," in *International Perspectives on Vietnam,* ed. Lloyd C. Gardner and Ted Gittinger (College Station, Tex., 2000), 189–203. Intriguingly, Bundy himself thought Rostow had a point. In 1967, for example, he agreed with Joseph Alsop that the anticommunist coup in Indonesia in 1965 would not have happened without the American military presence in Vietnam. "I think more and more the truth of Vietnam is in the nearby countries," he wrote Alsop. "I share the feeling that's where we have done best." Bird, *Color of Truth,* 354. Later, when asked about it directly in 1985, Bundy refused to reject Rostow's thesis and claimed to be an "agnostic," arguing: "I do not think it can be dismissed." "Lessons Learned," MacNeil/Lehrer NewsHour.

19. McGeorge Bundy, "Vietnam, Watergate, and Presidential Powers," *Foreign Affairs* 58 (Winter 1979–80), 406.

20. *HC,* February 6, 1989.

21. The quotations are from, respectively, Maureen Dowd, "Who's Losing Iraq?" *NYT,* August 31, 2003, WK9; and David Ignatius, "A Foreign Policy Out of Focus," *Washington Post,* September 2, 2003, A21. For excellent preliminary overviews of Rice's role, see Nicholas Lemann, "Without a Doubt," *New Yorker,* October 14–21, 2002, 164–179; and David J. Rothkopf, "Inside the Committee that Runs the World," *Foreign Policy,* March/April 2005, 32–34.

22. "Rice to Lead Effort to Speed Iraqi Aid," *Washington Post,* October 7, 2003, A01.

23. On Hadley, see David Ignatius, "Bush's Clark Kent," *Washington Post,* February 11, 2005, A25; and Peter Baker, "Bush Aide Influences Policy from Offstage," *Washington Post,* January 29, 2006, A1, A16.

24. "A Forum on the Role of the National Security Adviser," Woodrow Wilson International Center for Scholars, Washington, D.C., April 12, 2001, in Karl F. Inderfurth and Loch K. Johnson, eds., *Fateful Decisions: Inside the National Security Council* (New York, 2004), 142–143, 146. The former advisers at the discussion were Berger, Brzezinski, McFarlane, Rostow, and Frank Carlucci. Though never technically a national security adviser, Andrew Goodpaster—who served Eisenhower in much the same manner before Bundy institutionalized the role—also participated.

25. *Newsweek,* December 20, 1965, 25.

26. Robert S. McNamara, *In Retrospect: The Tragedy and Lessons of the Vietnam War* (New York, 1995), 95.

27. See, for example, Bird, *Color of Truth,* 403.

Bibliography of Primary Sources

Archival Collections

COLUMBIA UNIVERSITY, ORAL HISTORY RESEARCH OFFICE, BUTLER
LIBRARY, NEW YORK, N.Y.
Oral Histories
  Chester Bowles
  Harvey H. Bundy
  Sigmund Diamond
  W. Averell Harriman
  Roger Hilsman
  Alan G. Kirk

JOHN F. KENNEDY LIBRARY, BOSTON, MASS.
McGeorge Bundy Correspondence
Roger Hilsman Papers
Carl Kaysen Papers
Robert W. Komer Papers
Arthur M. Schlesinger, Jr., Papers
Theodore H. White Papers
National Security File
  Country File
      Germany
      Vietnam
  Regional Security Series: Southeast Asia
  Departments and Agencies: National Security Council File
  Meetings and Memoranda
      Meetings on Vietnam
      National Security Council Meetings
      Special Group (CI) Records
      Staff Memoranda
          Michael V. Forrestal
          Carl Kaysen
          Robert W. Komer
          Walt W. Rostow

Arthur M. Schlesinger, Jr.
Maxwell D. Taylor
Trips and Conferences
Oral Histories
  Chester L. Cooper
  Roger Hilsman
  Carl Kaysen
  Frederick Nolting
  Benjamin H. Read
  Walt W. Rostow
  Dean Rusk
  Bromley K. Smith
  Maxwell D. Taylor
Pre-Presidential Papers
Presidential Office File

LIBRARY OF CONGRESS, MANUSCRIPTS DIVISION, WASHINGTON, D.C.
Felix Frankfurter Papers
W. Averell Harriman Papers
Archibald MacLeish Papers
J. Robert Oppenheimer Papers
U.S. Congress, Senate Oral History Project

LYNDON B. JOHNSON LIBRARY, AUSTIN, TEX.
George Ball Papers
McGeorge Bundy Papers
Bromley K. Smith Papers
William C. Westmoreland Papers
National Security File
  Country File: Vietnam
  Files of McGeorge Bundy
  Files of Chester L. Cooper
  Files of Bromley K. Smith
  Memos to the President: McGeorge Bundy Memos
Oral Histories
  George W. Ball
  William P. Bundy
  Clark Clifford
  Ray S. Cline
  Chester L. Cooper
  U. Alexis Johnson
  William Jorden
  John McCone
  Robert S. McNamara
  Benjamin H. Read
  Dean Rusk

Walt W. Rostow
Bromley K. Smith
William H. Sullivan
Maxwell D. Taylor
James C. Thomson, Jr.
Cyrus Vance
William P. Bundy Vietnam Memoir (unpublished manuscript)

MASSACHUSETTS HISTORICAL SOCIETY, BOSTON, MASS.
Henry Cabot Lodge II Papers

NATIONAL ARCHIVES OF CANADA, OTTAWA
Manuscript Group 30, E 144: Arnold Heeney Papers
Record Group 25: Records of the Department of External Affairs

NATIONAL ARCHIVES AND RECORDS ADMINISTRATION, COLLEGE PARK, MD.
Record Group 59: Records of Dean Rusk

PRINCETON UNIVERSITY, SEELEY G. MUDD LIBRARY, PRINCETON, N.J.
George W. Ball Papers
Council on Foreign Relations Archives
Allen W. Dulles Papers

PUBLIC RECORD OFFICE, KEW, SURREY, UNITED KINGDOM
FO 371: Foreign Office Files
PREM 11: Prime Minister's Office Files

UNIVERSITY OF GEORGIA, RICHARD B. RUSSELL LIBRARY, ATHENS, GA.
Dean Rusk Oral History Collection
  McGeorge Bundy
  William P. Bundy

UNIVERSITY OF MONTANA, K. ROSS TOOLE ARCHIVES, MANSFIELD LIBRARY,
MISSOULA, MON.
Mike Mansfield Papers

YALE UNIVERSITY ARCHIVES, STERLING MEMORIAL LIBRARY,
NEW HAVEN, CONN.
Dean Acheson Papers
Chester Bowles Papers
Walter Lippmann Papers
Henry L. Stimson Papers and Diary

Personal Interviews

Francis M. Bator
Thomas L. Hughes
Nicholas Katzenbach
Carl Kaysen

Robert S. McNamara
Walt W. Rostow
Arthur M. Schlesinger, Jr.
James C. Thomson, Jr.

Published Government Documents

U.S. Department of State, *Foreign Relations of the United States* (Washington, D.C.:
Government Printing Office)
1931
  III: *Japan*
1931–1941
  I: *Japan*
1961–1963
  I: *Vietnam, 1961*
  II: *Vietnam, 1962*
  III: *Vietnam, January–August 1963*
  IV: *Vietnam, August–December 1963*
  V: *Soviet Union*
  VII: *Arms Control and Disarmament*
  VIII: *National Security Policy*
  X: *Cuba, 1961–1962*
  XI: *Cuban Missile Crisis and Aftermath*
  XIV: *Berlin Crisis, 1961–1962*
  XV: *Berlin Crisis, 1962–1963*
  XXIV: *Laos Crisis*
1964–1968
  I: *Vietnam, 1964*
  II: *Vietnam, January–June 1965*
  III: *Vietnam, June–December 1965*
  IV: *Vietnam, 1966*
  V: *Vietnam, 1967*
  VI: *Vietnam, January–August 1968*

*The Pentagon Papers: The Defense Department History of United States Decisionmaking on
  Vietnam,* Senator Gravel edition. Boston: Beacon Press, 1972.
Public Papers of the Presidents of the United States: John F. Kennedy, 1961. Washington,
  D.C.: Government Printing Office, 1962.
Public Papers of the Presidents of the United States: Lyndon B. Johnson, 1966. Washington,
  D.C.: Government Printing Office, 1967.
U.S. Senate. *Organizing for National Security: Inquiry of the Subcommittee on National
  Policy Machinery of the Committee on Government Operations, United States Senate,* 3
  vols. Washington, D.C.: Government Printing Office, 1961.
United States–Vietnam Relations, 1945–1967, 12 vols. Washington, D.C.: Government
  Printing Office, 1971.

Other Published Documents, Letters, and Records

David M. Barrett, ed., *Lyndon B Johnson's Vietnam Papers: A Documentary Collection.* College Station, Tex.: Texas A&M University Press, 1997.

Michael R. Beschloss, ed., *Taking Charge: The Johnson White House Tapes, 1963–1964.* New York: Simon & Schuster, 1997.

Michael R. Beschloss, ed., *Reaching for Glory: Lyndon Johnson's Secret White House Tapes, 1964–1965.* New York: Simon & Schuster, 2001.

James Goodman, ed., *Letters to Kennedy: John Kenneth Galbraith.* Cambridge, Mass.: Harvard University Press, 1998.

Henry M. Jackson, ed., *The National Security Council: Jackson Subcommittee Papers on Policy-Making at the Presidential Level.* New York: Praeger, 1965.

Ernest R. May and Philip D. Zelikow, eds., *The Kennedy Tapes: Inside the White House during the Cuban Missile Crisis.* Cambridge, Mass.: Harvard University Press, 1997.

Louis Menashe and Ronald Radosh, eds., *Teach-Ins: U.S.A.—Reports, Opinions, Documents.* New York: Praeger, 1967.

Sheldon M. Stern, *Averting "The Final Failure": John F. Kennedy and the Secret Cuban Missile Crisis Meetings.* Stanford: Stanford University Press, 2003.

Newspapers and Magazines

The Atlantic Monthly
Chicago Tribune
Daedalus
Department of State Bulletin
Foreign Affairs
Foreign Policy
The Globe & Mail (Toronto)
Harper's
Harvard Crimson
Newsweek
New York Herald Tribune
New York Review of Books
New York Times
New York Times Magazine
The Reporter
San Francisco Chronicle
Saturday Evening Post
School and Society
Time
The Times (London)
Wall Street Journal
Washington Post
Yale Daily News

Index

Lightning Source UK Ltd.
Milton Keynes UK
UKHW011959051022
410007UK00008B/60